Storytellers

Storytellers

Folktales & Legends from the South

EDITED BY JOHN A. BURRISON

The University of Georgia Press   Athens and London

Designed by Sandra Strother Hudson
Set in Berkeley Oldstyle Medium by the Composing Room
of Michigan, Inc.
Printed and bound by Thomson-Shore

The paper in this book meets the guidelines for permanence
and durability of the Committee on Production Guidelines
for Book Longevity of the Council on Library Resources.

Printed in the United States of America
93 92 91 90 89   5 4 3 2 1

Library of Congress Cataloging in Publication Data
Storytellers : folktales and legends from the South / edited
    by John A. Burrison.
        p.   cm.
    Bibliography: p.
    Includes index.
    ISBN 0-8203-1099-9 (alk. paper)
    1. Tales—Southern States. 2. Legends—Southern
States. 3. Storytelling—Southern States. I. Burrison,
John A., date.
GR108.S76 1989
398.2′0975—dc19   88-37143
                                          CIP
British Library Cataloging in Publication Data available

Frontispiece: *Fairview Community, Lee County, Virginia.*
Kenneth Murray.

Contents

Acknowledgments

This book is a showcase for the collecting achievements of my students, who have made my years of teaching at Georgia State University a joyful and stimulating experience. They and their storytelling contacts are the true authors. To be specific, 92 student collectors and 112 traditional narrators are responsible for the 260 tales included here. As it was not possible to devise an equitable formula for sharing amongst them the royalties derived from sales, these proceeds will be used to support the ongoing operation of the Folklore Curriculum in the Department of English (particularly the purchase of supplies and equipment for continued collecting efforts).

I would like to thank my assistant, Susan B. Deaver, whose word-processing skills and involvement in the storytelling revival movement were ideal qualifications for helping to prepare the manuscript. She was there from the beginning of the project, and her enthusiasm and commitment are greatly appreciated. Toward the end, David Remy helped to relieve some of the word-processing pressure, and Sonja Gardner initiated me into the mysteries of the personal computer. The Georgia State University Research Office awarded me a grant to complete the manuscript, and Virginia Spencer Carr, chairman of the Department of English, and Clyde Faulkner, dean of Arts and Sciences, provided support with released time from my teaching responsibilities. The fruits of this collaboration are here for all to read and enjoy.

Introduction

People have always loved a good story. The narrative impulse—the need to tell of or listen to experience and imagination structured into plot—is one of the traits that make us human. For thousands of years stories were narrated strictly orally, the storyteller performing before an audience of family, neighbors, or patrons. As prime sources of entertainment and knowledge, good stories were too precious a commodity to allow to die on the lips of the originators. They were carried on within the community—and beyond—from one generation to the next, undergoing refinement or degeneration when narrated by successive tellers, depending on the intelligence, memory, and creativity of the individual human links that formed the chain of transmission. Stories circulating orally in this way are known to folklorists as traditional prose narratives and include folktales, legends, and myths (stories can also be recited or sung in verse through such forms as the epic and ballad).

Some five thousand years ago a system of pictographs (symbolic representations of words) was devised in Mesopotamia to maintain the administrative record-keeping of a burgeoning urban society, and by 1600 B.C., Near Eastern myths preserved in the memories of priests were being inscribed on clay tablets, the oldest recorded stories in the world.[1] Indeed, a number of early literary classics, including the sacred stories of the Old Testament and the epic poetry of Homer, seem to have begun in just this way—as "ear literature" transformed into "eye literature."[2] Their removal from an immediate, responsive audience and new orientation to the written page led inevitably to changes in style, form, and content, and the oral and written branches of the river of verbal art grew further apart.[3] So long as writing was in the hands of an elite minority these changes did not affect the masses, who still received their lore orally. Then quite suddenly, with the invention of mold-cast movable type in Germany a little more than five centuries ago, the written word became truly accessible. As literacy increased, people became more and more dependent on the print media for their information and entertainment, to be supplemented, in just the past forty years, by the powerful influences of television and computers.

It should come as no surprise, then, that the importance of oral storytelling has declined in the face of these communications advances that require less human involvement and energy. What may be surprising, however, is the degree to which some types of oral narration continue to flourish despite this competition, even in such a technologically developed nation as ours; face-to-face interaction still fills a need unsatisfied by the impersonal media.

Nowhere in the United States is storytelling

1

more vital than in the South, where skill with the spoken word has always been emphasized. Strong traditions of storytelling from such Old World source areas of the southern population as Ulster, West Africa, and southern England, reinforced by the physical isolation of dispersed settlement and a conservative mindset that valued the old ways, certainly contributed to this tendency. The region's fondness for storytelling has inspired many of its most renowned authors, including Joel Chandler Harris, Mark Twain, and William Faulkner;[4] and it is probably no coincidence that two of the country's most active organizations involved in the recent revival of interest in oral narration, the National Association for the Preservation and Perpetuation of Storytelling and the Southern Order of Storytellers, are based in the region (at Jonesboro, Tennessee, and Atlanta, respectively).

In light of the richness of the South's storytelling traditions, it may seem curious that a truly representative publication on the region's folk narratives has never before been undertaken. To be sure, some forty volumes of southern tales have appeared since the pioneering *Uncle Remus, His Songs and His Sayings* was issued more than a century ago, but all share the same limitations: restriction to a particular type of story (predominantly animal tales in the case of Joel Chandler Harris) or to a single locale or racial group (again with Harris, the Afro-American tradition of east-central Georgia). This is not meant to fault such notable collectors as Elsie Clews Parsons, James Mooney, Richard Chase, Vance Randolph, J. Mason Brewer, Leonard Roberts, and Richard Dorson for choosing to focus on particular groups; they knew they could accomplish only so much alone when recording tales "in the field," an incredibly energy-consuming labor. The

time has come, however, for a less fragmented picture of southern storytelling.

The key to assembling a comprehensive regional collection that is more than an anthology of previously published materials is access to a vast repository holding the efforts of many collectors. One such archives was established by me at Georgia State University in 1966. In my first quarter of teaching I assigned a collecting project as a term paper for my undergraduate folklore classes, and the experiment proved so successful that the Georgia Folklore Archives was soon inaugurated to house the growing collection. Space and budgetary restraints unfortunately have precluded public access, but it embodies the only systematic collection effort for the state and is a goldmine of information on southern folk culture. *Storytellers* represents the first major exploitation of this invaluable resource. The archives contain more than a thousand student collecting or documentation projects (written reports that include transcriptions of accompanying tape recordings and supporting illustrations) covering all facets of southern folklife, from oral, musical, and customary lore to material culture. The geographic focus, understandably, is Georgia and surrounding states, with the students often drawing on their families and contacts in home communities as their folklore "informants." Roughly half the projects contain narratives; the strength in this genre can be partly attributed to my early specialization in oral traditions and to a course on the folktale I taught for some years that required a collecting project.

Selection was the most time-consuming task in editing this book. It meant rereading the estimated eight thousand tales in the archives several times while making careful descriptive notes to guide me through the process. My recollections of listening to the narrators on the tapes sometimes proved misleading, for stories that sound good do not always look good on paper. I began to develop a set of consistent criteria for inclusion, having the luxury of a large body of material from which to select. One of these was that the tales should work both as written and oral literature; they should, in other words, be readable in an entertaining way. Another was that they should be well-developed narratives; when several versions of a story were available (as was often the case), priority was given to the least-skimpy example. Geographic balance was also a consideration. While much of the archival material was recorded in Georgia, I decided not to stop at the somewhat artificial boundaries of the state but to include tales from neighboring states so as to develop a narrative picture of the subregion I call the Lower Southeast. Some of Georgia's best storytellers, particularly those in Atlanta, had moved to the state from adjoining states anyway, and to limit the book to native-born Georgians seemed unnecessarily restrictive. I did feel, however, that greater cultural integrity would be maintained by not straying beyond the six states of the Lower Southeast. Within Georgia—the centerpiece of the subregion—I have striven for representation of the various sections, from the coastal and wiregrass areas of south Georgia to the Piedmont of middle and lower north Georgia to the mountains of extreme north Georgia. Because the bulk of the selected material is drawn from this state, it should be understood that all places mentioned in the text are in Georgia unless otherwise indicated.

As selection proceeded it became clear that there was enough good material to fill two volumes. I decided, then, to concentrate for the present book on the older, rural-based narratives that best characterize the region as it once was and that are in the greatest danger of disappearing as the South becomes more like the rest of the country. If this book is well received, a second volume will be assembled that includes more of the same in addition to material reflecting the changes of the New South, such as the ethnic traditions contributing to Atlanta's international flavor and the recently developed legends and jokes of a more mobile and urban society. Together, the two books will present the tremendous diversity in the South's living storytelling traditions.

The organization of *Storytellers* is meant to reinforce this sense of diversity. The first six chapters are credited to the student collectors and arranged in two parts according to their focus: "Storytelling Communities" and "Individual Storytellers." This way, a variety of approaches to presenting folk narratives can be explored, and the social and human dimensions of traditional storytelling highlighted. The individual narrators featured in part 2 represent the three racial groups forming the population base of the region: red, white, and black; traditions besides the prose narratives are included to give a fuller picture of their folklore repertoires (Lee Drake's "Titanic" toast and Lem Griffis's ballads). Each chapter begins with my italicized headnote, which includes updates on the storytellers, followed by the collector's introduction. There is also a third part, "Individual Tales," which is organized by type. This allows for inclusion of the best material that does not work as part of a more unified chapter but which fills gaps to produce a more thorough selection. While I would not deny that personal taste has influenced my choices for inclusion, I have sought to create from the material available in the Georgia Folklore Archives a well-rounded and revealing picture of southern storytelling that strikes a balance between the typical and exceptional. (Most tale titles, incidentally, were invented by me or the collectors as convenient identification "handles"; unlike folksongs and instrumental tunes, stories are normally not given titles by their performers.)

THE STORIES

Contained in this collection is the full spectrum of traditional prose narratives, from most types of folktales to legends and myths. As defined by folklorists, folktales are those stories recognized by the community as fictitious and told primarily for entertainment. Perhaps the most highly sought are the "ordinary" folktales, an unfortunate name for the classics of the field immortalized by the Grimm brothers. Lengthy stories of adventure, they are known to folklorists by the German word *Märchen* ("fairy tale" or "wonder tale") when filled with magic and by the Italian name *novella* ("romantic tale") when more realistic. In either case they typically revolve around an adolescent hero or heroine who may be unpromising at first but soon displays such traits as generosity, helpfulness, cleverness, and receptiveness to learning that allow him or her to succeed in the trials encountered—an excellent role model for the children to whom such stories were normally told. Although they embody the rags-to-riches theme of the American Dream, these tales were not strongly maintained in the New World, and we know them mainly through bedtime storybooks and motion picture adaptations. An oral tradition of Americanized "ordinary" tales from the British Isles does exist in parts of the South, however, particularly in the Uplands where they form a cycle known as the Jack tales after their central character. The examples in the present collection tend to be of the less fantastic sort, with the hero at times behaving like a trickster.

Trickster tales proper form another body of folk narratives found in the South, where they are concentrated in the black population. While often light in tone, they are underlain by the serious theme of an underdog's survival through cunning. They cluster into two main cycles (groups of related stories wherein the same characters recur): the animal tales popularized in literary form by Joel Chandler Harris through his storytelling character Uncle Remus, a goodly portion of which have been shown to have an African background,[5] and the less publicized but no less significant tales of Old Master and his slave John, which represent the black perspective on the plantation experience. The Master and John stories are not restricted in setting, however, to the antebellum period; after emancipation John still had to deal with his white boss, and in "John Meets Lester Maddox" (chapter 8) it appears that he is alive and well in Atlanta. It should be noted that while Brother Rabbit and his human counterpart John are often triumphant, there are tales in which their deceit backfires and the trickster is caught in his own trap.

Jests, also known as jocular tales or jokes,

comprise, along with legends, the largest and most vital body of folk narratives circulating in the United States. We tend to think of jokes as a modern phenomenon, but printed jestbooks (their material sometimes lifted from oral tradition) were enjoyed in sixteenth-century England, and some of the humorous tales being told in the South date from that time or even earlier. One of the older types of jest is the numskull or noodle tale, which attributes absurd ignorance to a particular community, minority group, or individual. Tending to form cycles, such tales clustered in Elizabethan England around the "wise men" of Gotham, but in the South they most often feature the "fool" Irishmen Pat and Mike. Stemming from Anglo-American alarm at the flood of immigrants fleeing the potato famine of the 1840s, these early ethnic jokes display stereotyped Irish speech, including exclamations such as "faithme-Christ," and are enjoyed as much by lowland blacks as upland whites.

Another important type of jest, rooted in the Old World but flourishing in the boasting atmosphere of the American frontier, is the tall tale, which depends for its humor on absurd exaggeration and is most effective when narrated deadpan in the first person. Southern tall tales concentrate on hunting, fishing, and features of the region's environment, from steep mountains to snake-infested swamps. Each community once had its noted yarn spinners, who were pressured by competition into sharpening their skills to maintain their reputations. As Harrison Barrett, Jr., an elderly storyteller of Hiawassee, in the mountains of Towns County, told student collector Michael Moss in spring 1967,

Why, back in them days a feller had t' know what he 'as about if he walked into a timber camp t' work.

At night before goin' t' bed when ever'body was relaxin', if he tol' a story there 'as sure t' be somebody who could "cap" 'im. An' if he couldn't tell another'n t' sorta hold his ground or one t' cap the last one, he'd might as well packed his bags an' moved on the next mornin'; he'd become the laughin'stock o' the camp an' would really have t' leave.

Southerners—many of whom subscribe to the fundamentalist brand of Protestantism—have taken their religion very seriously, yet no other subject has been so well developed in their jokelore, possibly as an escape valve for the pressures of intense belief. The bulk of this humor centers on the preacher, actually a figure of considerable respect and power in his community. The stories, however, emphasize his human failings, not the least of which are hypocrisy and an insatiable appetite; his somewhat harsher treatment in the Afro-American tradition adds womanizing to the list. Similar stories circulated about the clergy in medieval Europe, but the emphasis placed on preacher tales in the Bible Belt is a regional phenomenon. As student collector Roger Kluge discovered in a 1970 interview with the Reverend Oliver Wilbanks, assistant pastor of the Wieuca Road Baptist Church in Atlanta, these jokes may not be so much a malicious attack on ministers as an attempt to demystify them.

I think one of the reasons [for the frequency of preacher jokes in the South] is—and I don't know, it may be in other parts of the country, too—but that is that through the years the preacher has had a unique place in communities. I mean they've set him apart, you see. He's supposedly different from anybody else. Whether it should be or not, they sort of put him on a pedestal in some ways. And it's just a delight when they can tell something that makes him look a little bit ridiculous. . . . And particularly with the colored minister; because the colored minister, more than even the white minister, has been in a unique position. He has been the leader of his people, you see, in the South. They have looked up to him. And, as a result, the idea here is someone on a pedestal who has clay feet.

Whatever the reason for the prevalence of these jokes, some clergymen enjoy telling them as much as laymen, as Preacher Mull illustrates in chapter 1.

So-called dirty jokes—one of the most active bodies of folk narratives being told today—have seldom received the balanced presentation they deserve in published folktale collections. Their omission in earlier compilations constituted misrepresentation of a type of tale important to many traditional storytellers. Through the pioneering efforts of Gershon Legman in the 1960s, however, risqué humor has come to be treated more thoughtfully and honestly by folklorists and their publishers. Ronald Baker's collection *Jokelore: Humorous Folktales from Indiana* (1986) represents a new era of enlightenment in this matter, for dirty jokes are neither left out nor singled out, but presented in a natural proportion to other kinds of jests. So they are in the present collection.

Parents are advised that they may consider language and situations in parts of *Storytellers* (chapters 2, 5, and 9 in particular) unsuitable for their children, but I suspect that most readers will find this material relatively mild and inoffensive. Animal reproduction and wastes were unavoidable on the farms on which many of our storytellers grew up, so these people tended to acquire a natural earthiness akin to the "street smarts" of urban dwellers. Humor, however, is

not always universal, and an appreciation of certain rural jests may require a knowledge of life on the farm. The following tale, for example, hinges on an understanding of the process of churning cream into butter, an activity with which most Southerners would have been acquainted until the spread of commercial dairy products in the 1920s. It was told to me by Bill Evans, a former Georgia State University Department of English colleague, who was an active farmer; he heard it from another north Georgia farmer. It is presented as a paraphrased summary as I noted it following the telling.

She Flunked the Fidelity Test

A Georgia mountaineer was getting suspicious that his pretty young wife was messing around with other men while he was away in the fields during the day, so he devised a test that would prove whether she was being faithful to him. In the morning, when she was shopping in town, he came back to the house and rigged up a stone to a string which he tied to one of the springs under the bed, and below the suspended stone he set a jar of cream. The idea was that if there was any strong activity going on on the bed later on, the stone would get dipped in and coated with the cream.

Well, at the end of the day the farmer came home, and while his wife was fixing supper in the kitchen he checked under the bed to see if the stone was creamy. By God, that jar was full of butter![6]

The above is a fair example of the bawdy jests included in this book, and reflects my personal preference for the subtle over the shockingly explicit. Racial humor is similarly handled here; racial animosity still exists on both sides of the color line in the region (as it does in other sections of the country), and to pretend otherwise would be less than honest. The examples found here, however, are infrequent and far from extreme.

Instructive tales are designed to teach in an entertaining way and have functioned as an important means of conveying a society's ethical and moral codes. Included among such didactic stories are fables, in which animals behaving as humans usually enact the edifying or cautionary lessons, and exempla, which serve to reinforce religious teachings and have been used by the clergy in their sermons. The old fables popularized by the Greek ex-slave Aesop are rare in southern oral tradition, but they have inspired parodies and jests with cynical morals more in keeping with our present age in which dilemmas are plentiful but clear-cut solutions are not. The effectiveness of instructive tales lies not so much in their literal as their allegorical truth, but some exempla have achieved the status of legends when accepted as factual.

Folklorists have been uncertain about where to classify anecdotes, for they typically have the lighthearted tone of jests but call for the same degree of belief as legends. Anecdotes focus on an actual person, who can range from a strictly local character to a national figure. They sometimes form cycles revolving around the individual's supposed character traits (for example, Uncle Tom's stinginess, as seen in the group of brief tales from Madison County in chapter 11). While some anecdotes are likely to have been generated by memorable events, others may have existed formerly as traditional narratives and affixed themselves to the character when recognized as appropriate. Even when the traits are not positive, such tales seem to represent a group's celebration of the unique personalities in its midst.

Unlike folktales, legends are accounts of events believed by the teller and his audience to have actually occurred. Whether or not they are indeed factually based is, of course, of interest to the folklorist, but just as important are the processes by which legends are created and develop as they circulate orally.[7] Certain situations seem ripe for the legend-making process, and the directions legends take are often predictable in the way they are shaped by floating motifs (traditional narrative elements). A group's body of legends is one means of preserving a record of its past, and it may not be possible to distinguish between historical legends and oral history. Supernatural legends, which reinforce ancient superstitions, are more clearly distinguishable to the nonbelieving outsider, who regards them as fictitious.

Many of the creatures inhabiting Old World legendry, such as fairies, vampires, and werewolves, were seldom maintained by immigrants after crossing the Atlantic. American supernatural legends emphasize ghosts or revenants (returners from the dead), in which many of us retain at least a partial belief. If the existence of ghosts has yet to be "scientifically" verified to everyone's satisfaction, the presence of witches—those whose special knowledge purportedly allows them to control the forces of good or evil—is beyond question (one of my former students is a witch). Thus, stories of witchcraft form the second most important body of supernatural legends in this country, particularly in more rural areas. Encounters with the Devil, a very real figure in Judeo-Christian belief, are also narrated. An important clue to the function of such legends is that they nearly always contain human characters who either benefit or suffer from knowing or not knowing how to deal with the supernatural. These are, in other words, a type of subtle instructive tale, pages from a survival manual for a time when supernatural beings were a palpable part of the environment. These older belief tales are being displaced today by a recent kind of legend (validated by the claim that it happened to a "friend of a friend") that projects the no-less-traumatic anxieties blighting our modern urban society, such as contaminated mass-produced consumables and deranged criminals—the horrors lurking in shopping centers, fast-food establishments, local lovers' lanes, and, worst of all, the presumed security of our own homes.[8]

An understanding of the memorate—a first-hand account of a personal experience colored by traditional belief—casts light on how some legends are created. Let's say that Farmer Jones, who grew up in a community where it was accepted that ghosts appear in white to haunt cemeteries, is walking home from the local tavern after a few sociable drinks. With reluctance he must pass a graveyard reputed to be "hainted," and in the process he sees something white and shapeless making for him. Panicked, he runs the rest of the way home, not bothering to open the screen door as he plunges into his house. After being revived by his wife, he declares earnestly that he's just seen a ghost. The subject of this memorate is, in fact, Farmer Smith's cow, which had broken loose and was seen indistinctly in the dim light under the influence of those drinks. Mrs. Jones recounts her husband's adventure to her neighbors, perhaps adding a few embellishments to heighten the drama, and as the story circulates it becomes a full-blown supernatural legend, to be narrated by successive generations. The following two memorates are revealing in the degree to which each narrator

was aware of how her psychological state affected her interpretation of what she saw.

Three White Angels

Recorded in spring 1979 by Pamela Roberts from Hattie Mae Dawson, sixty, a black resident of Atlanta who spent some of her early years at Gibson, Glascock County.

Well, some people is superstitious about boogers [bogies]. But they *are* real. Now, this is about me. When I was about twelve years ol' I was visitin' in the country. An' my gran'mother, she was cookin' dinnah. An' I useta be ba-a-d about singin' the blues an' dancin'. An' every blues song come out I'd learn it. An' every dance come out I'd learn it. An' my gran'mama she had tol' me, she say, "The Devil's goin' gitchoo." She say, "Your mama don' approve of you singin' all these blues an' all like-a that." An' I'd jes' sit an' look at her.

So this particular day, she was patchin' on my uncle's overall. An' she went ta cook, finish cookin' dinnah. I got the needle; I sittin' down there jes' a-sewin'. An' I was singin' that blues 'bout [sings]

My baby gone an' she won't come back no mo',
An' if she knew how well I loved her
She wouldn't ha' left this town at all. . . .

An' somepin' from the north side o' the house: they was three angels! An' they hit, an' when they hit I looked up an' they went over t' the south, to the co'ner of the house, singin' "Come Ye That Love the Lord an' Let Your Joys Be Known." Like to scared me to death!

I jump up an' I ran in there, an' I was so scared I was shakin' like a leaf. An' I was tellin' Mama, "Mama, can you hear? Don't you see 'em?"

She say, "I don' see nothin' an' I don' hear nothin'."

An' I tol' her what they was singin' an' how they look jes' like three white angel birds, come from the north an' went over t' the south singin' that song.

I say, "Lord, if that don' ever come no mo', I will stop dancin' an' stop singin'." An' I stop for a lo-o-ng time. You couldn't git me to sing a blues an' you couldn't git me t' dance![9]

A Devilish State of Mind

Recorded in fall 1967 by Claudia Wells from Mrs. F. F. Whitfield of Forest Park, Clayton County.

Well, it was in 1939, and my husband's father he had a nervous breakdown. It looked like he was losing his mind, and we was just worried with him. Nobody could hardly do anything with him; they spoke of sending him to Milledgeville [the state mental hospital], but I didn't want to send him down there. I said, "Let me take him, and see if I can quiet him down." And I had this word with him; you couldn't do anything to *make* him do anything, you just kind of had to go along with him. All night long I had words with him.

And the next morning just about daylight I was standing out on the back porch, and the mist was a-rolling in off the river, right out there on Bankhead just across the Chattahoochee. Big ol' mist just rolling in across the river, and I just felt like all the weight of the world was on my shoulders. And I said then, "I just don't know what I'll do."

And I just happen to raise up my eyes; a hill come right up from the kitchen door, you know, and on top of this hill is a little ol' pile of logs or something out there in the woods, and I saw something that looked just like the Devil! I looked at it, you know, and I thought, "What in the world?" I could see it was something alive, and I could see his eyes a-shining. He'd nod his head up and down, and I looked at him. I could see this little ol' gray beard down here, you know, those two little ol' sharp horns stickin' up here; and it was scary lookin'! It scared me so bad I didn't know what to do. I think it was because of my nervous condition; it had kind of shocked me. So I stood

there and looked at it, and I thought, "If I don't go and see what it is, I'll always think I'd saw a ghost."

So finally I got brave enough to go up there, and it was a billy goat! He was standing on these logs, lookin' down at me; I could just see his head.[10]

The word *myth* has several meanings; in conversational usage it has come to mean a widely held falsehood. To the folklorist and anthropologist, however, myths are "the narrative charter of [a] religion,"[11] the sacred stories supporting religious beliefs and practices. They have as their main characters deities and demigods; often deal with the creation of the present order through the agency of these divinities; are frequently set in the remote past (as opposed to the more recent past of legends); and of all traditional narratives represent the most serious tone and intense degree of belief. Among preliterate peoples such stories circulated orally, usually the possessions of the priestly class, but the classical and Judeo-Christian myths with which we are familiar were long ago committed to writing and exist in fixed literary renderings. The sacred stories of most Americans, then, are embodied in the Bible; the only groups maintaining active oral mythologies are Native Americans, and even many of these stories have been affected by exposure to Christianity. In the South, folk myths are restricted to the remnants of the Indian population, such as the Cherokees and Creeks (the two largest nations once inhabiting Georgia).

In content alone, aboriginal myths may not be clearly distinguishable from other types of narratives; the same character may display divine powers in one story, human frailties in another, and animal attributes in yet another. The attitudes of the community are thus critical in determining what tales are regarded as sacred. In the following two stories, both narrated to student collector Cynthia Tudor in fall 1972 by Ben Checotah, a twenty-one-year-old Oklahoma-born Creek living in Macon, Georgia, the mythic setting of the first and the historical setting of the second may be apparent to us as outsiders but not necessarily to the teller, nor did he seem to see any discrepancy in the two accounts; both are compatible views of the past.

Creek Origin Myth

I've got one that supposedly is of the Creek tribe, where they first came from. I don't know if y'all have heard about people living in clans before; like the Scottish people have the MacIntosh and MacDougal clans, and all that kind of stuff. Well, we have animal clans and wind clans and things. And how they got these: they say that the Creek tribe—or the Muscogees—come from out of the West, beyond the Mississippi somewhere. And they say that at first when the world was formed, people was living underground; there was a hole in the ground where all the people were.

And they say that when the Creek tribe come up out of this hole, it was all foggy. The whole land was foggy. And they knew that other people were out there with 'em, but they couldn't see because it was so thick. And so a great wind come along and blew this fog away, and so they could see things. And so the first people that were out there and could see, they were called the Wind People or Wind Clan. And then the other people that came out and seen different animals, like a bear or a wolf or eagle, they identified with those animals. The first ones, they seen an animal; they say, "Well, there's a bear. That'll be my family." So that's how they got all these clans.

And I think today a lot of people, especially the younger people, are forgetting these clans. My grandmother says that our family belongs to the Wind Clan.[12]

Creek Origin Legend

There's one that says that . . . well, you have heard of the Aztecs. And you know Central American peoples. This kind of goes with that same origin, you know, like the [Creek] people coming out of the West. It says that they were down there close to that Aztec civilization. They weren't it, but they were close to it, kind of a neighboring tribe.

And so when they heard of the Spanish coming in, they were afraid, and they were wanting to get out of the land. Because when Cortés finally did come in Central America, he started taking over their lands and everything. And so the Muscogee people wanted to get out because they didn't want their lands taken away, and they didn't want to be slaves to these people. So that's why they come over this far to Georgia, you know.

Perhaps the most persistent thematic thread running through this collection and cutting across all categories of tales is the hard times of earlier days and the heroic act of sheer survival. This unromantic view of the past, however fictitiously expressed in these stories, is clearly rooted in historical reality. Adding to the general hardships and vicissitudes of farming—the common experience of the South—were the difficulties of life under slavery and, later, Jim Crow segregation; the struggle and defeat of the Civil War and the disruption of Reconstruction; the destruction of the region's chief cash crop by the cotton-boll weevil; and the desperate years of the Great Depression through which most of our storytellers lived. Collectively, these tales are an affirmation of what had to be endured to arrive at the present state of relative financial security, comfort, and convenience. While many of our older narrators acknowledge a breakdown in social values and community cohesiveness in recent years, few would choose to return to the "bad old days."

Wood Stove, Jackson County, Georgia. Doug Brown.

LANGUAGE AND STYLE

I once asked a linguist friend who was teaching a course on dialects if he believed it possible for anyone to converse informally without being influenced by regional speech patterns. "Yes," he replied, "and I'm the living proof." Reared mainly in Atlanta but belonging to a mobile family that lived in other parts of the country as well as overseas, and embracing the academic world with its rather formal language, he thought himself immune from the colorings of regional dialect. As we parted, he reminded me of an upcoming dinner party: "I'll be seeing you Sarraday night." Quite unconsciously, he had fallen into a southern pronunciation of *Saturday*, quickly disproving his claim of being dialect-free.

In school we are taught to write in something approximating Standard English so that we can communicate effectively with an unseen audience without the benefit of face-to-face interaction. Few of us outside the broadcast media or theater, however, are capable of consistently speaking in Standard English, nor is it necessarily desirable most of the time to do so. Regional differences in vocabulary, grammar, and pronunciation (the latter being what we most often associate with an accent and the most difficult aspect to represent on paper) are what give our speech its character and rootedness and reflect the diverse cultural backgrounds that make up our nation. The expressive power of dialect has not been lost on our finest creative writers, whose use of it in dialogue infuses their work with a sense of place. And nowhere in the United States is dialect a stronger identity-marker (among both insiders and outsiders) than in the South. Even those speakers with more urban up-

bringings or advanced educations are likely to participate in such ubiquitous features of southern vocabulary as the plural pronoun "y'all," "fixing to" for preparing or *about to,* and "carry" for *transport* or *take* (someone).

In addition to regional dialect, there are those relaxed elements of speech such as sentence fragments and the dropping of *d* from *and* or the *g* from -*ing* that many of us tend to lapse into when we are comfortable with our audience. As anyone who has listened for the first time to his voice captured on a tape recording is shocked into realizing, the spontaneous language of speech is seldom that of the thoughtfully composed written word. To illustrate this point as it relates to the transcription of folk narratives, here are two versions—one literary and the other oral—of a well-known traditional jest. The first is taken from Ralph T. Jones's "Silhouettes" column in a 1938 Atlanta *Constitution,* and the second was recorded in spring 1981 by Ethel Henderson from Eva Andrews, a black resident of Conyers, Rockdale County.

Giving Credit Where It's Due (1)

A story going around is about the farmer who took a terribly rundown, soil-fertility-depleted, weed-choked farm and made it bloom like an agricultural Garden of Eden. He was so proud of the result he invited his preacher to a special dinner of celebration. After a grand meal the two walked over the place and the farmer pointed out his flourishing crops, his cattle and hogs and chickens and mules and the general success and prosperity of the place.

"Yes, Brother Smith," said the preacher at last, "you and the Lord certainly have done a fine job."

"Sure have," said the farmer proudly. "And, say, you'd oughter seen the place when the Lord was running it alone."[13]

Giving Credit Where It's Due (2)

Well, they said a man bought a farm, and it was all growed up, you know. He bought it and said that he cleaned the land up and planted and had a good crop and everything. And said after he moved out there he 'cided he'd have his pastor to come out and see how he'd done, you know.

And said he got out there and walked him all over his plantation, and he was just showing. "See what I done done, and how I done cleaned up."

And said the preacher would say, "Yes, the Lord has been good to you"; say, "He sho' has blessed you, ain't He?" And say he just kept a-goin', and he didn't never put the man's name in about how nice things was cleaned up.

And say the man just got tired of it, and say, "Well," say, "you ain't give me a bit of credit." Say, "Everything was 'the Lord'; 'the Lord done it.'" Says, "I wish, goddamn it, you'da seen it when the Lord had it by Hisself!"

Perhaps the most vexing problem encountered in editing this book was how to represent the informal speech exemplified by the second version. Opinions among folklorists are divided on the issue. One extreme is to use a phonetic alphabet, or a scientifically precise system for reproducing vocal sounds. This, of course, would be unworkable for an audience not trained to read it. The other extreme is to transcribe speech as if it were Standard English, at least so far as spelling. This approach is advocated by certain folklorists who feel that representation of nonstandard English only contributes to the negative stereotyping of minority groups such as blacks and mountain whites in the South. While humanistically com-

mendable, this approach does a disservice to oral literature by removing the stamp of the vernacular and the characteristics of the spoken word. Between these extremes lies a range of systems for capturing the flavor of informal speech, including some recent experimental ones that attempt to reproduce the cadences and stresses of the narrator's voice.[14]

The system I have adopted helps readers "hear" the storyteller speak, but it is not so elaborate as to create an obstacle. The tale-texts are presented as modified verbatim transcriptions; that is, they are in the narrators' own words but are edited where necessary to achieve greater clarity and continuity or to minimize redundancy (for example, false starts and the pausing device "uh" are eliminated except where functional in the story). Features of dialect and relaxed speech are retained to enhance the regional and oral qualities of the texts, but it is categorically not my intention to equate these with ignorance or other negative traits. In my experience good storytellers are intelligent people who use language creatively to enliven their narratives. Eye dialect—the countrified spelling of words pronounced no differently from the standard (for example, "wuz" and "sez")—has been avoided, however.

The reader may notice a certain inconsistency in the way some words are represented. There are three reasons for this. The first is that individuals do not speak consistently, or at least do not appear to. According to the linguistic laws we all unconsciously follow, a word may be pronounced in different ways depending on its context in a sentence (i.e., which sounds precede or follow it). Further, everyone has a mental model of "proper" speech toward which he or she may strive in certain circumstances (such as when being tape-recorded), and a tale-text may reflect the internal tension between the informal and formal modes. Note, for example, the variations in pronunciation of the word *brother* by the same storyteller, Lee Drake, in chapter 5, from the classic "Brer" of Uncle Remus to "Bur" or "Buh" to the standard "Brother" (which, in fact, may have been pronounced closer to "Bro'," "Broth'," or "Brothuh"). Second, the different subcultures of the southeastern population (for example, mountain versus piney woods whites) and degrees of influence from mass culture and formal education will naturally affect the way the speech of different narrators is represented. Finally, with general guidelines but no uniform system to follow, each student collector had to work out his or her own approach to transcribing speech, and some were more successful than others. I have verified and corrected the transcriptions against the tapes for accuracy of content, but to recheck nonstandard spelling would have delayed publication of this book by a year or more (and I have yet to see a transcript so perfect that it could not be improved, even after much revision). Presentation of the tale-texts thus represents a compromise, but a reasonable one.

It is difficult to generalize about storytelling style; even within a region there are many different styles of presenting oral narratives.[15] One characteristic of the southeastern tradition that can be pinpointed, however, is the frequent use of "says," "say," or "said," functioning not just to introduce dialogue but also, apparently, as a rhythmic device and reminder that this is a story heard rather than experienced directly by the narrator. The origins of this feature—especially prevalent among upland whites but also found with blacks, though usually omitted from published texts in the past—are uncertain, but one possibility is the Scotch-Irish strain in the upland population. The rhythmic repetition of "says" occurs in Ulster speech today, and further research might trace its existence back to the time of immigration in the eighteenth century.[16]

A stylistic device found in southern storytelling that is of considerable antiquity is the formulaic ending. Associated only with folktales, it is a signal that the story is over. On the surface it may seem to be a claim of veracity, snapping as it often does from third-person narration into a first-person witness statement. But the statement is absurd, a comical reminder that the story is fictitious. In Afro-American tradition it appears most often as "I stepped on a piece of tin, the tin bend, and that's the way my story end" or ". . . I skated on away from there,"[17] while the most common Anglo-southern closing tag is "I couldn't hang around because I had on paper clothes, and I was afraid it might rain or the wind might blow," or something similar.[18] Such ritualized endings are now rarely heard.

STORYTELLING AS PERFORMANCE

When a folk narrative is recorded and then reduced to writing, the resulting text represents a mere shadow of the actual telling. Oral tales are not designed to be read; that some hold up and can be enjoyed under visual scrutiny is thus remarkable, suggesting that oral narrators possess verbal skills akin to those of creative writers. Unlike the static medium of the written page, however, oral storytelling is a dramatic and dynamic performance mode hinging on face-to-face interaction with a live audience.[19] It therefore employs techniques closer to those of acting and public speaking than those of written literature (although not so self-consciously learned).

In oral narration, the verbal message—which is what a transcribed text represents—is supported by both paraverbal and nonverbal communication. The former includes vocal inflections, silences or pauses (sometimes used to create suspense), rhythm and tempo, and the imitation of sounds and characters' voices (for example, dialect in ethnic jokes). The latter includes kinesics, or body language, such as hand gestures, facial expressions, and body movement and posture, as well as proxemics, or the spatial relationships and interaction between teller and audience (for example, eye contact and touching). Mastery of these techniques may be a group's basis for judging excellence in storytelling, but this kind of communication is difficult to reproduce on paper, and to do so accurately could take up more space than the verbal text. As Mark Twain said of his tale "The Golden Arm" (learned from a slave of his uncle) in a letter to Joel Chandler Harris, "Two grand features are lost in print: the weird wailing, the rising & falling cadences of the wind, so easily mimicked with one's mouth; & the impressive pauses & eloquent silences, & subdued utterances, toward the end of the yarn (which chain the attention of the children hand & foot, & they sit with parted lips & breathless, to be wrenched limb from limb with the sudden & appalling 'YOU got it!'). . . . It's a lovely story to tell."[20] As a "jump" tale, "The Golden Arm" also requires the narrator

to spring at the audience at the climax of the story.

An important aspect of storytelling as performance art is what I call the flexibility response— the narrator's ability to react and adjust to a specific audience and set of physical conditions. This includes the selection of stories appropriate to the audience and setting (negative examples might be the telling of bawdy jokes at a formal mixed gathering or scary stories in broad daylight) and the determination of and compensation for an audience's general receptiveness and mood (choosing, for example, not to embroider a tale with nonessential details if the listeners seem restless). A good deal of the storyteller's creativity can be directed toward altering his or her material to suit the situation.

The following jest is a good illustration of this flexibility response. It was recorded in fall 1973 by student James Brandt from Johnny Joe Johnson of Keithsburg, Cherokee County, an upright-bass player and standup comedian with a group of old-time string-band musicians. Recalling that I had invited his band to play for a Southeastern American Studies Association meeting at an Atlanta hotel and knowing that I would be reading Brandt's project, Johnson playfully worked me into the jest, which normally is set in Texas.

Everything's Big in Atlanta

I'd like to tell one on the old professor down there, Mr. John Beerison. Anyway, we hadn't known John long when we went down to Atlanter and met him. An' we 'as on about the fourteenth floor of one o' them hotels there. We'd brought us about a half a gallon of hard apple cider, an' we was sittin' up there indulgin' fairly well on the hard cider.

An' John said, "Excuse me, I've got to go to the bathroom; I'll be back in a few minutes." An' out the door he went. An' he'd touched too much of that apple cider, 'cause the restroom was the third door on the right, an' he took the third door on the left an' fell down the elevator shaft! We all run out there an' looked over, an' he's layin' down in there sayin', "Don't flush it, don't flush it!"[21]

Another example of fluidity in narrative performance is the following tale, recorded on two separate occasions from the same storyteller, Minyard Conner of Dillard, Rabun County. Born in 1900, Mr. Conner had learned many of his narratives from his Irish-born grandfather back in Swain County, North Carolina. He told the first version of "The Witches' Dance" following a tall tale (see "The Unlucky Hunt" in chapter 9) and was still thinking in the first-person mode. The second version, recorded two years later, is more typically narrated in the third person. Note also the more subtle differences in detail between the two texts.

The Witches' Dance (1)

Recorded in fall 1976 by Cindy Axelberd.

Way back in those days when they had witches—you heard of 'em—I started to huntin' one night with my dog and lantern, took off to the woods to see if I could catch a possum. And I 'as goin' up the holler, and they's a ol'-timey log house, hadn't been nobody live in it in a long time. And they's a big ol' rock chimney in it, you know; jest a big ol' one-room log house. Got up thar close ta that log house and it 'as growed up all around thar; thought it 'as a good place ta catch a possum. Seen a little dim light in that ol' log house; thought about runnin' and then think to myself, "Well, somethin' could get me out here,

catch me a-runnin' simpler than they would a-standin'."

And I stood thar and looked and seen the lights flash up and go out. And I eased on up to the porch post and peeped on in through a crack, and seen a whole lotta weemen in thar. Young weemen, old weemen: they's all in thar naked! They's doin' somethin' up at the hearth, up at the front of the fireplace. I looked and in fact seen that they had a great big rock turned up thar—part of the hearth rock—and they put their hand on the back side of it and rubbed around there [makes rubbing motion with hands] and said, "Up and out and over all." I could hear 'em sayin' that, ya know. And with that they'd jes' [quickly slaps palms together] vanish, and gone! And every one of 'em done that; and when the las' one left, the light went out.

Well, I took my lantern and went on in thar, and when I looked around, there wadn't nobody in thar. Went to look at the hearth rock, you know; I got ahold of it and pulled on it and pulled on it, stood it up like they had [makes pulling motion with hands]. I put my hand down thar and it felt greasy, jest as greasy behind thar where they been a-rubbin' their hands; and I thought about what they's a-sayin' and I said, "Up and out and through all"—they said "over all" and I said "through all." Well, "Up and out and through all," and said it three times. I jes' went up the chimney like that [smacks hands together], and I's goin' out through the thicket and briars, a-whizzin' jest like an airplane through the briars an' bushes and everything.

And after awhile I come to a big old castle, and they's all in thar a-dancin'! And I've never seen such dancin' in my life: they's a-swingin' around and around and around. I got in thar and looked, and thar's a pretty girl comin' to me, you know. Lord, how we danced, cut up. And after 'while, sometime little later than midnight, they come to me and said, "Don't use God's name; don't you speak the word of God at all, whatever ya do."

And I says "God" in my head.

And went out thar and [they] said, "Now you got somethin' to ride out yonder at the hitchin' rack." Didn't have no automobiles then, jest horses, things like that to ride. And I went out thar to the hitchin' rack, seen a big white horse hitched up thar, saddle all on it, curried up nice. And right down thar at the end is a bull calf, big red bull, had a saddle on it; an' I sure was wonderin' about that. One of 'em pointed it to me: that's my "horse."

Well, I went right down thar and jumped up on his back, turned him loose from the rack and off an' startin'. We 'as goin' down through a great big field, an' come to a ditch. All jumped right over it and calf jumped with 'em. And on and come to a creek, and the horses'd jump and over they went to the other side. And come to pretty good-size river, and they jumped the river; and when they went across, you know, the bull calf just kinda hung on the bank. I said, "God, what a jump [eyes bulge, then flings out hands and shakes body]!"

Everything just went; and now thar I was, way on that river bank, you know, all by myself in the dark, and didn't know where to go!

The Witches' Dance (2)

Recorded in fall 1978 by Anita Salamon.

There was a little boy, and he took a notion to go possum huntin' way back then—and I have heard the old folks tell this tale. And he got his dog and a lantern, took off. And he was goin' along and he come to an old house, and he seen a dim light in thar and he slipped up close. Had a big fireplace, big chimney, and had one of the hearth rocks turned up; and said it was plumb full of weemen in thar. And said they had that turned up edgeways; said they'd put their hands on that and rub their hand around and around and rub it on their breast and said, "Up and out and over all," and they'd be gone, just vanished. And said he kept on, and the last of them went and they were gone.

And he looked in thar and decided to go in and see what they was doin'. He went in thar and got 'hold of the rock and begin to pull and pull, and pret'-near pulled it up edgeways like they'd had it; and put his hand on the rock and it felt right slimy. And he just rubbed it around, you know, like they did and put it on his chest and he said, "Up and out and through all!" And he said, "Oh, oh," and he [claps hands together and slides one past the other to indicate an upward motion] just went up the chimney, down through the briars, through the bushes. He skinned hisself all over, said, just a-whizzin' along.

And said directly he just shot up to a great big mansion. Said they was all of them in thar dancin'; them weemen were just a-dancin', havin' the awfullest time in the world. Said in he went, and they danced awhile. Said everyone was comin' 'round to him—gettin' on to midnight—said, "Now, you can't say the name of God or you'll be in the dark."

And said he went out thar and the hitchin' rack was all along, you know, and said thar was all big white horses saddled up fine. Said they all got on them big white horses. Said thar was his "horse" thar, and said that was a red bull calf with a saddle on it, and they pointed at that for him.

And said they started all at a gallop, you know, just a-goin' through the country; said they just jumped rivers. Said they jumped a big wide river and said them white horses went across, but the bull calf didn't jump; said he just hung on the bank. And he said, "God, what a jump!" Said [clapping his hands together and sliding them to indicate an upward motion] just in the dark! And he couldn't see, and out in the briars and all!

I used to hear that when I was young. I used to hear a whole lot of these tales.[22]

As can be seen from the above examples, the circumstances of narration can significantly affect a text, a fact not always taken into consideration by folklorists when analyzing variation.[23]

STORYTELLING EVENTS

Most of the stories in this collection were recorded in the artificial setting of a tape-recorded interview, removed from the social and physical stimuli that would normally have triggered their telling. The ideal collecting situation is to be present with the recorder running as a folklore event unfolds in its natural context, but this simply may not be possible for the short-term collector.[24] Some of my students were able to approximate a natural context by inviting an appropriate audience, providing refreshments to encourage a relaxed atmosphere, dimming the lights for scary stories, and so forth. But for the older types of tales dominating this book, the original contexts for their telling may no longer exist, and their documentation then becomes an exercise in historical reconstruction from the tellers' memories. By assembling information on earlier storytelling situations from these oral, as well as published, sources, a picture emerges of the social role of folk narration in the South that should enhance a reading of the tale-texts.

In the past, storytelling as well as singing was practiced at group work activities to relieve the monotony of a tedious chore. James Lamar described such entertainment at corn shuckings in Muscogee County, west-central Georgia, during his boyhood in the 1830s:

The parties would gather about dark, take their places at the corn pile, and, while the work went steadily on, would chat and joke, and chew tobacco, and tell anecdotes. There was one man named Lewis Skinner, who seemed to have an inexhaustible stock of anecdotes. He had a quiet manner. He was dry and deliberate. He never seemed to crack a smile himself, but he kept all

who were in hearing of him in a state of pleased expectancy, knowing that he would be sure to get there; and when he did, there was always a roar of laughter. This would "remind" somebody, and by the time he got through, Skinner would be ready again. And so it went on for an hour or two. Someone would wake up to the fact that, owing to the attention given to the anecdotes, the work of the evening was lagging.[25]

Waiting for grain to be ground was another occasion for storytelling, according to Harden Taliaferro, who included two tall tales by miller Larkin Snow in his account of life in Surry County, northwestern North Carolina, in the 1820s:

Every man has ambition of some kind, and Larkin, though nothing but a humble miller who gloried in his calling, had his share, and a good one too, of ambition. His ambition consisted in being the best miller in the land, and in being *number one* in big storytelling. He had several competitors . . . but he held his own with them all. . . . [The Story of the Eels] he would tell you coolly, while he would occasionally feel of his meal—while the old tub-mill would perform its slow revolutions as though it was paid by the year—to see whether it was ground fine enough to suit him. He would then give you one of his peculiar looks, having just got his hand in [i.e., gotten warmed up], and would tell you the story of the Fast-Running Dog.[26]

In her 1987 collection of tales from southwest Georgia, Mariella Hartsfield documents a very specific storytelling occasion for the residents of that area, the annual family treks by covered wagon to Shell Point, Florida, to buy salt fish to last through the winter, a custom practiced in the late nineteenth and early twentieth centuries. She also describes the more widespread southern context of fall molasses-making.[27]

The blacksmith shop, barbershop, and general store were gathering places for men when they had some idle time. The latter, with its liars', or whittlers', bench out front for warmer weather and potbellied stove inside for winter gatherings, was an important setting for the telling of jests and local-character anecdotes. Caleb Ridley, writing of mountain life in Macon County, North Carolina, in the later nineteenth century, reminisced in a chapter entitled "Spinning Yarns":

The old-time country store, with its high plank front and all sorts of signs on it, is rapidly passing away and will soon take its place alongside of the razor-back hog, home-knit socks and the Populist Party. When I was a boy the sight of a country store made the goose-bumps break out all over me. It was the one advertising center of the neighborhood. It was the place where we met and talked about those who could not come. Looking back across the years to the old-time country store, I recall scene after scene in which the lights and shadows played across faces now hidden from view. I can hear again the clear ring of voices long hushed in eternal silence, and see the flash of eyes now curtained by the darkness of death. . . .

Everybody . . . turned to listen to Gum Dalton, who told of a justice trial he had attended a few days before. One fellow had his neighbor arrested for keeping a vicious dog, which dog he affirmed had bitten him. The neighbor denied the allegation most positively:

"My dog did not bite you."

"Guess I know when I'm dog-bit," said the complainant, "an' yore dog done it."

"What sort o' dog is my dog," queried the defendant, and the reply was:

"Yore dog is a yaller dog."

"I know my dog didn't bite you," said the accused. "In the fust place, my dog ain't no yaller dog; in the

second place, my dog ain't got no teeth; an' in the third place, I ain't got no durn dog in the fust place."

The court ruled accordingly.

Alex Holdbrooks told of two neighbors in one of the backwoods communities of an adjoining county who fell out over a kettle one had borrowed from the other. The owner of the kettle claimed it was cracked when brought back, and the other man ought to pay for it. Rising to his full height of more than six feet, the defendant addressed the court:

"I jist want to say three things, yer honor. In the fust place, the blamed ole kettle was cracked when I borrowed it; in the next place, it wuz whole when I tuk it back; in the third, I never had it nohow."[28]

Unlike certain other folklife activities, storytelling was not rigidly gender restricted, but the jests associated with the general-store setting tended to be oriented to adult males. As recorded by student collector Beverly Hensley in spring 1977, Fanny Tow of Suches, in the mountains of Union County, recalled the "vulga'" jokes told at her father's store. "They'd come and gather 'round the store, jist men, you know; and Dad, he wouldn't let us around when they'd come 'round like 'at. Then they'd start lettin' jokes, an' we'd slip around an' git under the floor an' listen at 'em. We was mean as snakes! They didn't know we was a-listenin' at 'em. Later I'd tell 'em to girlfriends; maybe we'd stay all night an' get to tellin' jokes." Tall tales and practical jokes were also enjoyed in this setting, as student collector Jerry Cook discovered to his chagrin in winter 1969 when he inadvertently became part of a folklore event. "I was advised to locate a man named Coley Coffee, who ran a general store between Jonesboro and Erwin, Tennessee. As I entered the store I asked an old-timer, clad in overalls and sporting an old hat and a pipe, if he knew Coley Coffee. The answer I got was, 'He

Farm Outside Cherokee, North Carolina. Barbara McKenzie.

jist left to go fishin' 'bout a half-hour ago.' As I further probed into the group of people sitting around the potbellied stove, I found that the man I had confronted was Coley Coffee himself!"

A good deal of storytelling occurred at home in the bosom of the family, by the fireside during the winter and on the porch or under a shade tree in warmer weather. Greta Worley Miller of Atlanta, who was reared at Lakemont, in the mountains of Rabun County, supplied this lengthy description of family folklore activities to student collector Lyndell Gliedman in fall 1967:

Used to, we didn't have any movies or anything like that, or any kind of entertainment other than what we made ourselves. And so we'd sit around the fire at night and sing and tell stories and laugh and cut up. We used to have this one story that we always loved to hear Mother tell, and she'd always tell it when us kids'd ask for it.

The Tobacco Thief and the Voices

She said that one time there's this ol' man, and said that he wanted some tobacco. And said that there's this other man across the swamp that just had a big barn full o' tobacco. And so he went across the swamp and he stoled all the tobacco he could get.

So he started back through the swamp and all of a sudden he heard somethin', and it sound like it was goin' [said in a deep, slow voice], "You stoled. You stoled. You stoled!" So the ol' man listened for a while; he stopped dead still and he listened. And it started again. It said, "You stoled. You stoled. You stoled!"

So the ol' man got kinda fed up and he said, "Stole what?"

And it sounded like something said [very fast in a high voice], "Tobacca. Tobacca. Tobacca. Tobacca. To-bacca!" [It's understood that the sounds were actually made by frogs but were misinterpreted by the guilty man.][29]

While we were sitting around that same fire, lotta times we'd tell ghost stories, first one thing and then another. And they'd always turn out right silly. But my daddy used to tell us this one.

The Trestle Ghost

Said that there was this old shabby-lookin' house, and had a river runnin' behind it. And the river was called Tallulah River, incidentally; and the house, I think, still stands. But he said that he used to have to walk across the trestle. And in the mornin's, why, he'd start across the trestle and he could see this headless man; he was always carryin' a lantern. And he said that he would follow it and then he'd get to a certain point and he'd go away.

So a bunch of eager boys one time decided that they were gonna find out what it was. They followed it several times, and every mornin' it'd go across the trestle, and it was still that same man holdin' a lantern. And they'd foller it and it'd go to a certain point and then it'd go away. So they follered it one night up underneath a waterfall that was behind this house. And they said that behind the waterfall was a cave-like affair. And when they went into the cave, they dug out rocks and found this pot of money in there. Now how much truth there was in it I don't know, but that was a tale they told.[30]

Mrs. Miller's sister, Kathryn Worley Lanford, added this recollection during the same recording session:

We had just moved into a new neighborhood, and my oldest sister—her name's Dot—met this boy. And he came to see her, and all the neighbors had gathered around and we were sittin' in there. First we played

music and sang for a while, and then they sorta settled down and told ghost stories. So they told 'em
awhile, and everybody got sleepy and started goin'
home, except my brother-in-law now—'course it was
her boyfriend then.

And after everybody went on to bed, why, he decided he had to go on home. So he went on home—at
least we thought he went home. My daddy kept hearing this noise outside and got up in the middle of the
night—dogs barkin' like everything—and he went
outside on the porch. And he kept hearin' this mur-
murin' sound, and looked over at the chimney corner
and there stood my brother-in-law with a fishing cane
in his hand and he was saying, "Don't ya come near
me, don't ya come near me!" He was so afraid when
they got through tellin' the ghost stories until he
wouldn't go home.

Claire Jackson, an elderly black resident of Atlanta who was reared in Rome, Floyd County, remembered for student collector Deborah Hill in
fall 1971 her childhood mixture of pleasure and
fear when listening to such tales:

Papa told us this ghost story about "The Creeping
Hand." I was sitting there, looking all around, you
know, crying. And my mother said, "You should be
ashamed of yourself, to frighten those children like
that."

So Papa said, "Well, they want to hear it."

I said, "Go on, Papa!" Crying, just crying and looking all around.

So that night we all went to bed. And my sister and
I slept together—she was two years younger than I.
And I was lying there watching the window, a window
right next to us. I just knew that hand was going to
creep in there and get me.

All of a sudden something said, "wap"! And fell
right across my neck. I said, "Oh, he got me!" I was
just lying there waiting to be choked to death, like the
hand had done in the story. And nothing happened,

so I decided I would see what was going on. I started
feeling the hand; it was still on my neck. But it was
my sister! In her sleep, she had thrown her hand out
and it had fallen right across my neck. I just reached
out and pinched her, and she screamed bloody
murder and everybody in the house came running.
And Mama said, "What happened, what happened,
what happened?"

My sister said, "She pinched me, she pinched me,
and I didn't do a thing to her!"

I said, "You did, too. You choked me."

And then Mama got angry with my father: "I told
you to stop telling those children those crazy stories!"

And we just loved them, but they'd scare the living
daylights out of us.

Another aspect of southern storytelling contexts is the degree to which the two races exchanged traditional narratives. In certain
respects the Afro-American repertoire is quite
distinctive, but it does share some material with
the white population and includes tales of clear
European origin. There were certainly opportunities for blacks and whites to swap tales during leisure interludes, both before and after the
Civil War. Joel Chandler Harris's literary framework of the old ex-slave, Uncle Remus, entertaining the little white boy is fictitious, but
similar situations are historically documented,
and Harris himself, by his own account, figured
in an interracial session in summer 1882 at Nor-
cross, then a railway station twenty miles northeast of Atlanta:

The writer was waiting to take the train to Atlanta,
and this train, as it fortunately happened, was delayed. At the station were a number of negroes, who
had been engaged in working on the railroad. It was
night, and, with nothing better to do, they were waiting to see the train go by. Some were sitting in little

groups up and down the platform of the station, and some were perched upon a pile of cross-ties. They seemed to be in great good-humor, and cracked jokes at each other's expense in the midst of boisterous shouts of laughter. The writer sat next to one of the liveliest talkers in the party; and, after listening and laughing awhile, told the "Tar Baby" story by way of a feeler, the excuse being that someone in the crowd mentioned "Ole Molly Har'." The story was told in a low tone, as if to avoid attracting attention, but the comments of the negro, who was a little past middle age, were loud and frequent. "Dar now!" he would exclaim, or, "He's a honey, mon!" or, "Gentermens! Git out de way, an' gin 'im room!"

These comments, and the peals of unrestrained and unrestrainable laughter that accompanied them, drew the attention of the other negroes, and before the climax of the story had been reached, where Brother Rabbit is cruelly thrown into the brier-patch, they had all gathered around and made themselves comfortable. Without waiting to see what the effect of the "Tar Baby" would be, the writer told the story of "Brother Rabbit and the Mosquitoes," and this had the effect of convulsing them. Two or three could hardly wait for the conclusion, so anxious were they to tell stories of their own. The result was that, for almost two hours, a crowd of thirty or more negroes vied with each other to see which could tell the most and the best stories. Some told them poorly, giving only meagre outlines, while others told them passing well; but one or two, if their language and their gestures could have been taken down, would have put Uncle Remus to shame. . . . It was night, and impossible to take notes; but that fact was not to be regretted. The darkness gave greater scope and freedom to the narratives of the negroes, and but for this friendly curtain, it is doubtful if the conditions would have been favorable to story-telling.[31]

Harris, then, was orally returning to his black audience tales he had borrowed and popularized from the telling of blacks on the Turnwold Plantation near Eatonton where he had worked as a teenager; they, in turn, no doubt pleased that a white man would trouble to entertain them, shared with him stories that would find their way into his subsequent publications.

Student collector Carl Van Baker documented a real-life Uncle Remus situation in spring 1967 related by his father, Paul, who was ten and living in Columbus, Muscogee County, at the time of the incident:

Well, this happened around Thanksgiving of 1917. My brother was a student up at Georgia Tech, and he had a friend by the name of Ernest Childs who was also a student at Georgia Tech. They roomed together, and they came home for Thanksgiving vacation.

Anyway, had this old colored man, called him Uncle Ben; he lived on my daddy's place. My daddy had a big lease on some timberland, and old Uncle Ben lived in this cabin. It had a dogtrot—a breezeway between the two rooms. Old Uncle Ben lived there alone. Daddy kept him up, fed him. He didn't work; he was way up in his eighties or nineties, no one knew how old he was. He claimed he had been a slave back before the Civil War. And he was a real white-headed colored man. He only lived in one room of this cabin; the other room was empty. And he kept him a garden in the summer. He raised sweet potatoes, and outside every fall he'd have a big mound of dirt that he'd put his sweet potatoes in and pile them up, and he'd eat them all during the winter.

As I said, no one knew exactly how old he was, but he was very venerable. And we boys used to go around there a lot at nighttime. He had a great big ol' fireplace in the cabin, big ol' clock on the mantle, great big ol' bed. And he cooked in the fireplace. He lived completely in that one room. And he used to tell us ghost stories a lot. We'd go down there and sit with him at night, three or four of us; and he'd tell us about ghosts and about this cabin that he lived in, that someone over in the other room had been murdered years before. And he could hear the ghost come back at night and wail around the house, especially when the wind was high. And he used to keep us really entertained with these stories.

Well, anyway, the man died. Didn't really have undertakers in those days way out in the country like that. So my daddy went out there, and he and some other fellows dressed the man up and put him on a board between two chairs over in the vacant room, put a sheet over him. This happened around Thanksgiving, when the old man died. And, as I said, my brother and his friend were home for vacation. So my daddy asks us if we wouldn't go sit up with him. The old man didn't have any family or any friends, so far as we knew. So we volunteered and said we'd go sit up with the old man. We dug some potatoes out of this mound out there and was baking them in the fireplace. Sitting there and the clock strikes twelve, and we were talking about this old man and Ernest said, "Well, this is about the time for his ghost to start walking."

About that time we heard an awful noise over in the other room; sounded like somebody had taken a plank and put his foot on it and slammed it on the floor. So my brother said, "Uh oh," said, "looks like old Uncle Ben has fallen off the plank." So we took the lamp off the mantle. The wind was kind of blowing through the dogtrot; we went across, and the door of the other room was standing wide open. So my brother held the lamp up real high, and we were peering around in there to see. The sheet was off the old man, but he was still on the board. And about that time we could all feel just like somebody had come up behind us, and there was a definite huff that blew the lamp out. Scared the real dickens out of us, and we ran. Needless to say, we left the old man there by himself the rest of the night!

The days of huddling around a dogtrot-cabin fireplace are coming to a close, but if many of the old rural contexts are disappearing, there are ample settings for traditional storytelling in our urban environment. Jokes are exchanged during breaks from work and at bars, scary stories are told at slumber, or spend-the-night, parties and around Scout campfires, and urban legends circulate in beauty parlors and school cafeterias. As long as there are occasions when people gather and are receptive to hearing a tale well told, the art will live on.

LAY THERE, YOU'VE SLAYED MANY: A TALE-HUNTING ADVENTURE

It is a June weekend in 1967, my first year in Georgia, where I had come, fresh out of graduate school, to teach folklore at Georgia State University. This is a wet summer in the mountains, but they are majestic in any weather, and the rain tends to keep folks at home where I can find them more readily.

Looking for folklore to collect, I am riding with one of my students, Joe Treadway, just below Blairsville, in Union County, when through the misty downpour I glimpse an elderly gentleman seated on the porch of an abandoned general store by the roadside. Waving economically to us as we pass, he has the expectant look of one hoping for visitors to stop and chat. We turn into the next convenient driveway and head back to the store, on the chance that he may have something for us. We are not disappointed.

After only the barest of preliminaries, James Satterfield, seventy-three, is singing and telling tales. The songs are fragments, which include the lament "Only a Miner" and a northwoods lumberjack ballad, curiously out of place in the South. Mr. Satterfield explains that he had worked for many years in the mining and logging camps of north Georgia and North Carolina and that itinerant Yankee lumbermen would bring such lore with them on their southerly migrations. The stories are personal-experience narratives, in which Mr. Satterfield plays the role of peacemaker in the rough-and-tumble frontier environment of the camps, and a couple of the most interesting bawdy jests I have ever heard. We do not record the tales, but one of them sticks in my mind long after our return to Atlanta; its repeated formula, "Lay there, you've slayed many," which the hero addresses to his pistol by way of bragging of his accomplishments to his girlfriend, has the ring of antiquity. This folktale continues to nag at me; I've read it somewhere, but can't find it in the standard reference works.

More than a year later, in October 1968, I'm traveling just south of Blairsville with another student, Ed Prince. It is raining again (although this time just a drizzle), and as we approach the general store we see that James Satterfield is still sitting on the porch. We stop, for I am determined to record "Lay There" with my new battery-powered machine. But it is Sunday, and Mr. Satterfield, feeling religious, is reluctant to tell the tale. So we strike a deal: he'll let us record the story if we help him study for his state driver's examination (it seems that, although Mr. Satterfield has been driving much of his life, he thinks now might be a good time to obtain a license). After we had quizzed Mr. Satterfield from the Department of Public Safety booklet for an hour, we are invited to set up the recorder, and to the accompaniment of cars passing on the highway we preserve the tale for posterity. It is exactly as I recall it from the earlier telling.

Lay There, You've Slayed Many

That 'as a man that 'as a-courtin' a girl. An', she played a trick off on him. He rode an ol' white-face horse that he called Baldy. An' he ca'ied a pistol all time; an' he'd go in, an' she'd be dressed settin' in a parlor at the table, an' he'd pull that pistol out an' th'ow it down an' say, "Lay there, you've slayed many."

An' she decided she'd see if he *was* a brave a man as he let on like he was. He had to go away around—an' it 'as just a li'l ways, it 'as 'bout a quarter across the hill, little ol' rough trailway—an' he had to go about a mile aroun' to git thar. She dressed in men's clothes an' shoes an' took a gun an' hit out across thar to waylay her sweetheart, see if he was brave.

An' he come ridin' along, y' know, whistlin'; an' she walked out in the road in front of his horse an' took hol' the bridle an' tol' him t' get down offa that horse! [Chuckles] He got down. She said, "Now, you kiss that horse's ass!" 'At's what his sweetheart told him. Says, "You kiss that horse's ass."

Said he got behind the horse an' he'd pat the horse on the ass; the horse'd jump up, "Whik!"

He said, "Now, whoa, Baldy. Whoa, Baldy. Now, whoa, Baldy." She made him kiss the horse's ass. Told her man to git on his horse an' ride on. An' he got on 'is horse an' ride on.

An' she jist lit back out across thar, an' was dressed an' a-settin' in a parlor at the table when he come in. He rode up t' the bars an' hitched his horse up, an' walked in an' jerked his pistol out an' th'owed it down on the table, says, "Lay thar, you've slayed many."

    She said, "Now, whoa, Baldy!" [Laughs]

    I guess I better not tell the rest of it.

    [After some encouragement:] Well, he played a trick off on her. Give her gran'mother fifty dollars then ta help 'im get it back on 'er. She tol' him she fix for him ta get it for fifty dollars. "Well," he says, "I'll give it," an' he just give the old lady fifty dollars. She told him what time to come back—he didn' have a date with her [the granddaughter] on that day. An' her gran'mother had fixed it on that time for him ta come in an' go t' bed with her granddaughter.

    So, she told her granddaughter—it 'as in the night, y'know, after bedtime—'at she'd have to get up an' go out. She made out like she had a peter [dildo] in 'er, an' her granddaughter wanted 'er to try it on her. An' she told her she would after she came back, an' said, "I'll be right back in."

    Well, she went out, an' she sent this girl's sweetheart in an' he got in the bed with her. An' he got ta pourin' it to her, an' she'd say, "Stick it in a little deeper, Granny. Stick it in a li'l deeper, Granny." Well, he got all he wanted of it, an' he went on off. An' 'er gran'mother come back an' got in the bed with 'er, an' she didn't know what it 'as her granny doin' that, y' know. 'At's the way he got tricked back on it.

    Well, the next time 'at he come in, on the next Saturday night, he hitched his old Baldy horse up, walked in an' th'owed his gun down, said, "Lay thar, you slay many."

    She says, "Now, whoa, Baldy."

    He says, "Stick it in a li'l deeper, Granny!"

    That's all of it. That's the way he got the trick back on her. I don't know what happened after that. [Laughs][32]

A stimulus to recording this story was the recognition of just how old and rare it is, for after ransacking my folklore library I finally found it, predictably altered in setting and detail, as

"Beranger Longbottom," from a thirteenth-century French manuscript. It is included in a translated collection of *fabliaux,* narrative poems recited (and sometimes written down) largely by a class of medieval entertainers called *jongleurs.*[33] "Beranger Longbottom" is attributed to Garin, but it exists in another manuscript version and was very likely based on a tale already in oral currency.[34] It concerns the lazy son of a lower-class moneylender who is given knighthood and the hand of a nobleman's daughter to pay off a debt. She, however, scorns the young man's base origins, and to redeem himself in his bride's eyes he boasts of valiant deeds, going so far as to fake combat with nonexistent enemies by repeatedly riding off in his shiny new armor and returning with his shield and lance hacked to bits. The wife becomes suspicious and decides to test her husband's valor by donning an old suit of armor and overtaking him in the woods, where she finds him attacking his own shield with his sword. She gives challenge, and the cowardly peasant, taken in by her disguise, immediately consents to do her will, which is to kiss her posterior (this inspires her alias, Beranger Longbottom, when the husband asks the name of the unknown knight). She then takes a shortcut home, changes into more womanly attire, and invites a lover into her bedroom, where she knows her husband will find them on his return. The peasant-who-would-be-knight, furious at this brazen act, prepares to punish her, but she retaliates by threatening to call to her rescue the knight who had just humiliated him in the woods, Lord Beranger Longbottom. He is cowed, and, as in an inverted *Taming of the Shrew,* she holds this power over him henceforth.

    "Beranger Longbottom" is in many respects a typical fabliau of the sort that inspired Chaucer's

Canterbury tales of the Miller and Reeve: bawdy, cynical, hinging on deception and counterdeception. It has cropped up a couple of times in later French literature but to my knowledge has never before been reported in English. How, then, can we explain its appearance in twentieth-century Georgia? My suspicion is that the tale was carried by early French immigrants to Canada, whence it was introduced to the lumber camps of the upper United States, then brought south by the same itinerant loggers who transplanted "The Jam on Gerry's Rock," a fragment of which was known by Mr. Satterfield.

Clearly, "Lay There" is more than "Beranger Longbottom" in translation. Beyond the obvious transformation of European feudal society to a generalized American frontier setting, the class consciousness underlying Garin's fabliau is absent (as indeed it is in the other known medieval version), and the focus instead becomes one of sexual one-upmanship and ultimate male domination. This is certainly understandable within

the *macho* context of the lumber camps; not so understandable is the liberated heroine of the medieval fabliau, for those times were hardly less male dominated. The episode with the grandmother, which provides a conclusion satisfying to the male ego, makes our mountain tale more complex structurally than the fabliau, and it is conceivable that such an ending was original to the French tale and that Garin's version is eccentric in its omission.

Though "Lay There" is of more ancient pedigree than most southern folk narratives, its background offers insights into a little-known migration pattern and adds to our knowledge of storytelling as a major form of entertainment within the occupational subcultures of the region. That the tale has managed to survive for at least seven centuries without the support of the mass media and exists in a culture radically different from the one that spawned it is a testament to the durability and adaptability of oral literature.

Part One

Storytelling Communities

CHAPTER ONE

Four Storytellers of Cedartown, West Georgia

Betsy Ostrander and Kay Long

Spring 1970

Here we have four storytellers living in the same community, all of whom were acquainted with each other. With this common background and network of associations, we might expect them to share a community-based group of stories and anticipate a chapter of variations on the same tales. But such is not the case. Each teller emerges as a distinct personality in terms of her or his narrative repertoire, and with the aid of interviews conducted by the collectors (one of whom, Betsy Ostrander, is the granddaughter and niece of the two women tellers), we come to understand something of the relationships between each narrator's outlook, interests, and experiences and his or her choice of tales. This chapter is a study of contrast rather than cohesiveness, even for mother and daughter.

Of the four, Mrs. Ruth Casey (who died in 1987 following a long illness) had the most striking repertoire. Her specialty was the upbeat instructive tale featuring animal characters, suitable for instilling positive values in the children she reared and taught. Such stories are not common in southern oral tradition; a few (for example, "Turpie and

the Hobyahs") are so rare that they may have been learned from Mrs. Casey's "old books," but if so, she adapted them to her style and taste. She did not mention printed sources when interviewed.

Her daughter, Mrs. Emily Ellis, chose a group of shorter, more realistic, and far more typical jests to share with the collectors although she likes to tell her mother's stories to the children she teaches. It is particularly interesting that while both women told the tale known to folklorists as "The Sexton Carries the Parson," they are quite different versions ("Dividing the Corn" and "Dividing the Walnuts"), evidently derived from different sources.

Reformed-moonshiner-turned-Baptist-minister James Mull (now deceased) also enjoyed telling jokes, but his specialty was the preacher tale, which he used to humanize and add comic relief to his sermons. The four he chose to record concern ill-received preaching and may reflect his own struggles in the early days of his ministry when he was learning to read.

W. R. Jordan (who died in 1976) was, by contrast, more literate, and his love of reading and writing seems to have contributed to his thoughtful oral composition. This is especially true of "The Church Ghost and the Traveler," a remarkably imaginative and dramatic version of a well-known southern legend. To become part of Mr. Jordan's repertoire a story had to have at least a semblance of historical veracity; he might have been disconcerted to learn that "The Faithful Guard Dog," which he believed to be local, is an ancient international folktale distributed from India to Ireland (and the basis for the name of the Welsh village Beddgelert).

Polk County is located in the Appalachian foothills of northwest Georgia. It was settled largely by people of English and Irish descent, many of whom came to this area from the Carolinas in the 1830s.

Many former farmers now work in Cedartown mills, although they still live out on their farms. As the area's main occupations, dairy farming and the poultry industry have replaced cotton farming, which was almost completely destroyed by an invasion of the boll weevil.

Mrs. Casey and her daughter, Mrs. Ellis, live in the area known as Casey Valley, named for their family, which owns most of the valley land. Mr. Jordan lives in the Jackson Chapel area on the Cave Spring road. This area takes its name from the nearby Methodist church of the same name. Mr. Mull lives in the area known as Lake Creek.

Ruth Casey:
"I've told children many a story."

Ruth Hopper Casey was born in Polk County in 1897. Although she was probably our least willing informant, she may have had the most extensive background in oral tradition, coming from a family in which the children learned the old stories from their elders, and seems to have enjoyed passing these stories on to her own children and grandchildren in the same manner she learned them. As a child, Mrs. Emily Ellis, Mrs. Casey's daughter, heard her mother telling many of the stories we collected.

The most striking thing about Mrs. Casey during our two recording sessions was her rehearsal of every story before she would tell it into the tape recorder. Unfortunately, her stories were much more spontaneous during their first telling than when recorded. In striving for perfection of detail and plot, Mrs. Casey became nervous and confused, and much of the charm of her delivery was lost.

While recording, she sat quietly except for sweeping hand gestures at various times. Her manner of delivery for the most part was engaging, for she would convey characterization through her tone and voice mannerisms.

Casey: I was reared in a large family on the farm, an' lived a regular farmgirl's life. I had

Cooking Stew, July 4, Morgan County, Georgia. Doug Brown.

eight brothers an' sisters, an' we never was at a loss for a game to play. They was enough of us to play anything we wanted.

Ostrander: Okay, how did you learn the stories? Were they told to you as a child or did you learn them after you were older?

Casey: Well, some of them I heard when I was a child, an' others my husband has told that he had learned, an' that's the way I learned most of mine.

Ostrander: Okay. Who was the typical person you learned the stories from? Would it be your parents, or someone else?

Casey: I think grandmothers as a rule are good. They usually have time to tell 'em.

Ostrander: What are your favorite stories?

Casey: Well, I like the ones that my grandmother told. She was of Irish descent, an' she would tell stories with Irish flavor that appealed to me more than anything I have heard.

Ostrander: And what kind of stories do you like to tell the best?

Casey: I like happy tales the best.

Long: Why?

Casey: It makes people feel good.

Ostrander: When do you usually tell tales?

Casey: Well, most of the tales I've ever told was while I was relaxin' after lunch.

Ostrander: Who'd you tell 'em to?

Casey: Grandchildren, an' my children, and schoolchildren. I taught school seven years. I've told children many a story.

Ostrander: Do you think telling these stories in front of a tape recorder has changed the way you told them any?

Casey: It has! I just can't think straight, knowin' it's recordin'.

Ostrander: Do you like to tell stories to other people?

Casey: Yes I did, especially when I was younger. Now I forget things, an' that bothers me.

Ostrander: Do you think people tell stories as much as they used to?

Casey: No, I don't think so. They have TV an' radios an' all like that. I don't think that they tell as many stories as they did when I was a child.

Long: Do you think it's bad that they don't?

Casey: Well, from my view, I enjoyed stories more than I did reading.

Ostrander: Do any of these stories have any special meaning for you?

Casey: Well, all of 'em have some good meaning. They teach us to be unselfish, teach us to be neighborly, an' teach us to love one another. They's some good in almost every story that you have.

Ostrander: When you're telling stories do you get involved in them?

Casey: Formerly I lived my stories when I was tellin' 'em, but I'm out of practice so they don't affect me too much.

Long: Was telling these stories in the past more an important part of your life than now?

Casey: Well, one thing, when I was rearin' my children it kept them quiet while I was tryin' to rest.

Billy Bobtail

Once upon a time there 'as a little boy who was known as Billy Bobtail. An' he really didn't have much family, but he lived with one of his uncles, an' he felt like he was not wanted. So early one morning he decided that he'd just go out in the world an' seek his fortune. So he gathered all the clothes he had an' tied them on a stick an' went off down the road, an' he passed under the gate goin' out. Well, ol' cat was sittin' up on the gatepost an' said, "Where you started, Billy Bobtail?"

An' said, "I've started out in the world to seek my fortune."

He said, "Well, may I go with you?"

An' he said, "Well, I don't know what kinda life it'll be; but," he said, "nobody wants me here." So the cat went down an' went along with him.

An' then got a little further, an' the ol' dog was lyin' down the side of the road, an' said, "Billy Bobtail, where you started this mornin'?"

"Well, I'm not wanted here, so I'm goin' out in the world to seek my own fortune."

The dog said, "May I go with you?"

He said, "Why, yes, I guess so."

An ol' rooster was sitting on the fence crowin', an' Billy Bobtail said, "Why you crowin' so early this mornin'?"

He said, "Well, I heard them say they was gonna cook me"; an' said, "I don't care for that."

An' Billy Bobtail said, "Well, get down an' come an' go with us. We've started out in the world to seek our fortune."

"Well, good." So the ol' rooster flew down an' went on.

An' the last one he came to was an ol' donkey on the side of the road, grazing. An' he said, "What are you doin' way off down here grazin'?"

Said, "Well, my master's turned me out to make my own livin'"; said, "I'm too ol' to be any he'p to him."

Billy Bobtail said, "Well, come along; we're all started out in the world to seek our fortune."

"Well, I will just go with you."

An' they walked an' walked an' walked, an' after awhile they saw a big forest of pine trees down there. An' Billy Bobtail said, "Now, fellas, you see that forest there?" Said, "The tale is that they's robbers lives in that forest. Are any of ya afraid?"

An' they said, "No, we'll go along with ya."

An' they went on an' on, an' they all got tired. Billy Bobtail said, "Well, let's stop an' rest awhile." An' so there was some pine straw under the tree, an' he lay down under the tree. An' the donkey lay down beside of him, an' the dog lay down, an' the cat went a little higher up in the tree, an' the rooster went to the very top, an' he said, "Oh, I see a light."

An' Billy Bobtail said, "Where?"

"Just over the way, there."

An' they all wanted to go see about it. So they all went. When they got there the door was fastened, an' the windas were high, an' so the dog got up on the donkey's back an' then the cat got on his back an' the rooster flew up on the cat's head an' looked in the winda. "Oh, there's some robbers in there, an' they have the biggest pile of money. They countin' it."

So he come down an' they talked about it, an' Billy Bobtail said, "If we could frighten them off we'd have enough money to live on." An' so they agreed to how 'ey's gonna do it. Billy Bobtail stood on one side of the steps with a great stick, an' the donkey stood on the other side with his heels turned toward the door, an' the rooster got up on top of the, ah, thing [lintel?], an' the cat an' the dog got on either side of the steps. An' said, "Now, whenever I say go, let's all make all the noise we can."

An' the rooster crowed an' the cat mewed an' the dog barked an' the donkey brayed an' Billy Bobtail hollered. An' it frightened the robbers, so they jumped up an' ran out, didn't git their money. An' as they went out, the rooster pecked one of 'em on the head an' Billy Bobtail hit one with the stick an' the donkey kicked one an' the dog bit one an' the cat scratched 'em.

An' you never heard such tales as those robbers told about all those things that got after them. An' anyhow, they was so frightened they never come back. An' they [Billy Bobtail and the animals] found enough money in this house to buy food for all of 'em. They lived happy ever after.

The Three Foolish Bears

There was once a little squirrel that lived in a holla in the top of a great big oak tree. An' down below him there were three bears that lived in a large holla in the tree. And they were all good friends.

An' one day the squirrel had been hunting nuts an' came back, an' the bears were all sitting out, crying. An' he said, "Well, friend bears, why are you crying?"

They said, "You see that large limb over there?" Said, "If we was in our house an' that blew across the door, we couldn't get out. An' if we was outside an' it blew across, we couldn't git in."

An' the squirrel said, "Oh, you foolish things! Why don't you take it in your mouths an' drag it way off where it won't blow across your door?"

"Well, we never thought about that." An' so they drug it off.

An' the squirrel told 'em, "I'm going away, an' unless I find three people as foolish as I think you are I'll never come back here to live."

An' so he was goin' friskin' along down the road an' he heard a little noise, an' looked over an' there was a ol' turtle tryin' to climb over a high rock with a flat side. An' he said, "Friend turtle, what're you doin'?"

He said, "My cousin, snappin' turtle, is very ill an' I want to go see him, but I can't get over this rock."

Squirrel said, "Well, why don't you just walk around it?"

"Well, I never thought about that."

An' squirrel said, "That's one of 'em!" An' he went on further an' he went across the purtiest little stream of water, stopped an' got 'im a drink. An' hadn't gone very many feet until he came to a rabbit just sittin' lookin' up at the sky. An' he said, "Good mornin', little rabbit. What are you lookin' for?"

Said, "See that little cloud?" Said, "I think it's gonna rain an' I'm so thirsty."

An' the squirrel said, "Why wait 'til that cloud . . . why don't you just go to this little stream back here an' get you a drink?"

"Well, I never thought about that."

An' he said, "Well, that's two of 'em!" An' he skipped an' hopped on down the road an' came to a plum orchard. An' the ground was just covered in red plums, an' there sat a great big ol' bear. He was just lookin' up. He said, "Good mornin', mister bear. What are you lookin' at?"

He said, "I am so hungry"; said, "you see those lovely red plums up there in the top of the tree? I'm waitin' for 'em to fall where I can eat one."

Said, "Why don't you eat some that's on the ground already?"

Bear said, "Well, I never thought about that."

An' so the little squirrel hopped an' skipped an' went back home, an' he an' the bears lived happily ever after.

The Cat, the Monkey, and the Chestnuts

A cat an' a monkey were talkin' one day, an' they were discussin' where to find some food. An' they saw some hunters a-roastin' some chestnuts. An' the monkey thought, "Well, just makes me hungrier an' hungrier," while they were watchin' them roastin' 'em.

An' after the hunters went on, the monkey talked to the cat, an' talked the cat into puttin' some chestnuts in the fire to roast. An' then he begun tellin' the cat what a beautiful hand he had for a foot, that it was just like a person's hand. He could get those chestnuts out without gettin' himself burned hardly at all. An' the foolish cat believed him, an' so he went to goin' in the coals, bringin' out the toasted chestnuts, an' burned himself very much.

An' after, when he got the last one out, he looked aroun' just in time to see the monkey eat the last chestnut he had. An' the monkey said, "Well, it looks to me like that you was getting old enough not to believe everything that people told ya. An' so you have to suffer for your being so silly."

Going to Squeetum's House

This story's about a fox. He an' his wife were sitting around one dreary day, an' he was tired of the house. An' he told his wife, said, "Hand me the bag there behind the door"; said, "I'm goin' out ta see what I can find." An' she handed him the bag an' he went out, an' as he started out the door, there 'as a bumblebee came sailin' by. He caught the bee an' put it in the bag, tied it up an' went on over 'til the first house he came to. He knocked; the lady came to the door, an' he said, "Lady, may I leave my bag here while I go to Squeetum's house to get some pumpkin pie?"

An' she said, "Oh, yes, I suppose you may."

An' he laid it down. An' she was so curious she just couldn't wait 'til he got out of sight, 'til she looked in to see what was in it. An' it was a bee, an' it flew out an' her rooster caught it an' ate it.

So when the fox came back, said, "Where is my bumblebee?"

She said, "Well, I opened the sack a bit an' it got out an' my rooster ate it."

Said, "Well, that's all right; just we'll catch the rooster." So they caught the rooster an' put it in there, tied it up.

An' he went on a piece further an' came to another house, an' he knocked on the door. The lady of the house came an' he said, "May I leave my bag here while I go to Squeetum's house to get some pumpkin pie?"

"Oh yes, yes, you may leave it."

So he put the bag down an' went on down the road. An' she could see something wigglin'; she opened the bag to see what it was, an' the ol' rooster jumped out an' her pig caught it an' killed it, ate it.

An' when the fox came back, he asked her what became of his rooster.

She said, "My pig caught it."

"Well," he said, "that's all right; I'll just take the pig."

An' she told the little boy, said, "Well, go out an' catch the pig." An' he chased, an' chased, an' chased, an' couldn't catch it.

An' fox said, "Well, that's all right. I'd as soon have the little boy." So he put the little boy in the bag an' tied him up an' went on.

He came to another house an' knocked on the door, an' this lady came to the door. An' he asked to leave his bag an' she said yeah, he could leave it. An' the lady of that house was makin' cookies, an' the little boy could smell the cookies. An' he thought about his mama's cookies an' wished he could see his mama, an' he went to cryin'. An' the lady said, "Oh, what are you cryin' about?"

An' he said, "Ol' fox put me in here"; an' said, "I want to go home to my mama."

She said, "Well, we'll fix him." An' she took the little boy out an' filled his pockets full of cookies an' sent him home. An' she called up her ol' houn' dog an' put it in the bag an' tied it up.

An' when the fox came he thought it was the little boy, an' he put it acrost his shoulder an' started home. Went across a hill an' he thought, "Well, I'm tired an' hungry. I guess I 'bout as well eat the little boy here." An' when he opened the bag to eat the little boy, out jumped the huntin' dog an' gobbled the fox up.

Drakesbill

There was a family of ducks that were really prosperous, an' the head of the family was known as Drakesbill. An' he had made lots of money. An' the king of the country where he lived found out he had the money, an' he 'as always borrowin' some from him; an' he borrowed quite a bit of money.

An' so Drakesbill sent word to him that he'd like for him to pay it back, an' he didn't hear from the king. He wrote him; he didn't hear from him. One mornin' he got up an' said, "Well, I'll just go to the king's house an' ask for my money."

An' so he started out just quackin' away, an' he came to a ladder leanin' up against the wall there. An' the ladder said, "Drakesbill, where you started so early this mornin'?"

He said, "I'm goin' over to the king's house to get some money he owes me."

An' the ladder said, "'Ell, I'd like to go to the king's house. May I go along with ya?"

He said, "Yes; fold yourself up very small an' get under my wing." An' the ladder did. An' they went on down the road just [sung] "Quack, quack, quack, I'm goin' to get my money back."

An' met a fox in the road. An' the fox said, "Where you goin' so cheerily today?"

An' he said, "I'm goin' down to the king's house to get some money he owes me."

Fox said, "I've heard about what fat turkeys an' geese he has." Says, "Can I go with you?"

"Oh, yes," he said; "fold yourself up very small an' crawl in my pocket." An' the fox did.

They went on down the road further, an' there's a wasp nest hangin' up on a bush there. An' he was very nice not to touch the wasp nest; an' the wasp nest asked him where he's goin'.

Said, "I'm goin' over to the king's house to get some money he owes me."

Wasp nest said, "May I go with ya?"

An' he said, "Yes, if you'll call your children all in an' fold yourself up very neat an' crawl in the other pocket, ya may go." An' so the wasp nest did. An' he went on singin', "Quack, quack, quack, I'm goin' to get my money back."

He started across a little stream of water an' the little stream said, "Where are you goin' this mornin'? You seem so happy."

He said, "I'm goin' over to the king's house to get some money that he owes me."

An' the little stream said, "I'd like to go to the king's palace. May I go with you?"

He said, "Yes; fold yourself up very small an' get under my other wing." An' the stream did.

An' the ol' drake went on 'til he came to the king's palace an' knocked on the door, an' a man came to the door. Said, "I came to see the king to get some money he owes me."

An' the king said, "Don't let him in." An' so he wouldn't let him in.

So Drakesbill just marched around the king's palace singin', "Quack, quack, quack, I come to get my money back." He sung it louder an' louder an' louder.

An' the king become angry. He said, "Go out an' catch him an' throw him in the poultry yard an' let the geese an' turkeys peck him to death."

So he was caught an' put in the poultry yard, an' they all went to pickin' at him. An' he said to his friend the fox, said, "Friend fox, now's the time for you to he'p me." An' fox came out an' he just snapped off geese heads an' turkey heads. An' Drakesbill went on sayin', "Quack, quack, quack, I've come to get my money back."

An' the king was very much irritated. He said, "Throw him in the well."

An' they caught him an' threw him in the well. An' Drakesbill swam around in the water singin', "Quack, quack, quack, I came to get my money back." An' he thought about the ladder an' he said, "Friend ladder, come out an' stretcht yourself along the wall, stretcht yourself both long an' tall." An' the ladder did. An' he hopped up the ladder an' marched around the palace singin', "Quack, quack, quack, I come to get my money back."

An' the king was *very* irritated. He said, "Build a fire an' burn him, if there's no other way to get rid of him."

They built a fire an' started to throw him on. He said to the little stream of water, "Now's your time to he'p me."

An' the stream came out an' he was so angry with the king, the stream just got larger an' larger 'til it filled the palace. An' the king had to get up on top of his throne. An' everybody was gettin' afraid, an' they went to throwin' things at Drakesbill. He was just swimmin' around in the palace singin', "Quack, quack, quack, I came to get my money back." An' they went to throwin' every object they could get aholt of at him.

An' he said ta this wasp nest, said, "Friend wasp, now's your time to he'p me." So the wasps got out an' stung everybody that was tryin' to drive Drakesbill out, an' they ran off.

An' Drakesbill sat down on the throne to rest; an' the people saw him an' they said, "Oh, what a good king he'd make! May long live King Drakesbill!" An' he lived happy ever after.

The Cow Going Down in the Mud

Back in the early times when the animals were all friends an' they could talk to one another, there was a rabbit an' a bear that were good friends. An' they had been off on a journey an' decided they'd buy this [live] beef an' carry it home. An' as they 'as goin' home with it the beef was stubborn an' hard to drive. An' the rabbit thought up this idea, an' he said, "Mister Bear, the thing for us to do is just go an' git a wagon an' carry this calf home in the wagon, an' then it won't lose all of its weight."

"Well," he said, "that would be a good idea."

An' the rabbit said, "I don't believe I'm quite big enough to pull the wagon down here."

He said, "No, I don't believe you are, either. So, I'll go get it an' you just watch after the calf."

An' so, quick as he got out of sight, well, this rabbit butchered the beef an' carried all of it out an' hid it all but the tail. An' when he heard the

Albert and Skeeter. Roy Ward.

bear coming in with the wagon, he stuck the tail down in the mud an' he went to hollerin', "Run, run; the cow's goin' down in the mud! Run, run; the cow's goin' down in the mud!"

An' bear ran just as hard as he could an' he got there; well, the bear caught aholt of the tail. The rabbit pulled down an' the bear pulled up an' the rabbit pulled down an' the bear pulled up, and directly the bear gave a hard tug an' pulled the tail out of the rabbit's hand.

An' the rabbit said, "Now you've played it; you've pulled his tail off. You can't get it." An' said, "Well," said, "you was such a good friend to go get the wagon"; said, "I'll just give you the tail."

An' so he throwed it in the wagon an' pulled it on home. An' one day the bear was passin' by the rabbit's house an' he heard the rabbit just a-singin', said [sings], "I eat the beef an' the bear eat the tail!"

An' he said, "What did you say?"

An' he said, "I was sayin' [sings], 'I done without an' the bear eat the tail, I did without an' the bear eat the tail.'"

He said, "Well, I'd thought you said somethin' else, an' I know it'd just be terrible for you if you did."

The Untidy Girl

There was once a mother who had a daughter that was not interested in men; they didn't seem to like her an' she didn't care anything about them. An' so the mother begun to try to teach the girl how to catch a man. An' she told her, said, "You have to be very dainty. You have to use good manners an' learn to keep house, an' all these things that will attract a man to you."

An' so the girl had a date with a young man, an' the mother insisted that she have him to come an' eat with them. An' so they served peas that night, an' that girl was so dainty that she cut every pea in half before she'd eat it, an' everything like that. An' she ate so daintily, an' the boy was very well impressed with her an' he thought, "Well, she is a real little lady."

An' when the time came for him to go home, he went out the back to untie his horse to get on it an' ride home, an' he looked in the winder an' she was standin' there at the pot they cooked the peas in just eatin' with the cook-spoon, just shovelin' 'em in! An' he decided she wadn't so dainty after all.

But his mother told him he mustn't give up, an' she told him what to do to find out if she was a good housekeeper. An' [after another visit] he started home, but he came rushin' back in the house an' said, "My horse has the colic!"

"Well," the girl's mother said, "could we get up anything to he'p?"

Said, "What'll cure him is a teaspoonful of dust off of a bed-slat is the only thing that I know of that would cure him."

An' the lady said, "Well, you couldn't find a teaspoonful of dust in this house."

An' the girl said, "Why, Ma, I bet there's a double handful under my bed!" An' [laughs] so she lost that young man.

Dividing the Corn

This is a rather amusing story about two fellas that went out to steal a load of corn, an' they got to thinkin' about how they 'as gonna divide it; they wanted to divide it equally. So as they were goin' along they came by a cemetery, an' they jus' drove up in the cemetery so they'd be out of the road. An' they made two piles of corn an' they counted, "I'll take this one, you take that one, I'll take this one an' you take that one."

An' there's an ol' nigger man comin' through, an' he heard it. An' he listened a little bit, an' then he went tearin' down to where his boss lived an' said, "Boss, Judgement Day's done come!"

"Well, how do you know, Mose?"

"Well, I heard the Devil an' God dividin' up the folks up there in the cemetery."

An' the boss thought about it a minute an' he thought, "Well, I'll go see just what happened." An' he went up there an', sure 'nough, he could hear, "I'll take this one an' you take that one, I'll take this one, you take that one." An' he listened awhile, an' he went over there an' he recognized that they were dividing a load of his corn!

The Cornmeal

There was a ne'er-do-well that lived in a community where there was some people that were well-to-do, an' whenever he knew they were going to have a good meal he'd manage to be present.

An' so there was a wealthy family had a wedding in the family an' he knew they were going to have a big dinner, so he wanted an excuse to go by there. So he loaded him up some cornmeal, put it on his back, an' walked by an' stopped, an' they invited him in to eat. He ate an' ate an' ate an' ate. They were polite an' asked him wouldn't he have something else? He said, "No, I don't think I want anything to eat." Said, "I have a sack of yaller meal over here that's good enough for such as me to eat."

Tying the Cow's Tail to the Bootstrap

One day there 'as a southern farmer milkin' his cow, an' she 'as just switchin' the flies. She'd hit him across the head an' across the eyes, an' he was gettin' worried with her. Didn't know how he 'as gonna stop it.

An' a man came walkin' down the road, said, "Well, I'll tell ya how to stop that cow from switchin' you." Said, "In Holland they just tie the tail to the bootstrap."

So the man tied the ol' cow's tail to his bootstrap an' she [laughs] became frightened an' started runnin'; an' oh, he had a time. Sometimes he was behind her, sometimes he was in front of her, an' sometimes on her hips. When he finally got loose from her, he looked at the ol' cow an' he said, "I'll never try that again. I'm not gonna try anything those furriners do, especially if a Yankee tells me to."

Long: Where did you learn that one?

Casey: Oh, that's just a family tale. See, we're Southerners, so we had about a Yankee in it.

The Last Word

Speaking of people who like to argue, I want to tell you about a couple that were the worst people to argue I've ever seen. One time the man was fixin' to cut a piece of heavy material ta mend the girth to his saddle, an' he got his knife out. An' his wife said, "The scissors'd be better ta cut that with."

He said, "No, a knife'd be better."

She said, "Well, I know the scissors would be better."

He said, "No, a knife."

An' they went on that way for a while an' he became so angry, he picked her up an' threw her in the river! An' when she came up the first time she says, "Scissors!"

He said, "Knife!"

She came up the second time, she said, "Scissors!"

He said, "Knife!"

An' as she went down the third time, he said, "Knife!" And [makes cutting motion with index and middle fingers] she made the sign of the scissors!

Twisted Mouths

This story is about a family that had something wrong with their mouths. The ol' man's upper teeth overlapped his lower teeth, an' his under-lip was under [extends upper lip]. The ol' lady's underlip overlapped her upper lip [extends lower lip and jaw]. An' they had a daughter, Sal, an' her mouth was twisted to the right [twists mouth to the right]. An' they had a son, Bill, whose mouth was twisted over toward the left [twists mouth to the left].

An' one day the power went off, an' they had to light a candle when preparin' for bed. So when the ol' man went to blow the candle out he blew an' he blew an' nothing happened. An' he called his wife, an' they was holdin' it right out in front of her, an' she blew an' blew an' nothing happened. An' the daughter came; she blew an' nothin' happened. An' then the boy came, an' nothing happened.

An' one of the neighbors saw it, an' he come in an' explained to 'em that if the ol' man went to blow it out, he would have to hold the candle be-low his mouth, an' the ol' lady would have to hold the candle above her mouth, an' the girl would hold hers to the right, an' the boy would have to hold it over to the left. An' they were so happy they had learned how to blow out a candle!

Why the Rabbit Has a Short Tail

A long time ago the rabbit had a long tail like the squirrel's, an' he was very vain of it. He an' the squirrel were always showing off their pretty, plumy tails.

The squirrel came through town one day with a big string of fish, an' the rabbit asked him where he caught those fish. He said, "Oh, it's easy"; said, "just go down to the millpond an' hang your tail off the mill dam, an' when the moon gets to the top of those trees the fish will bite."

An' the rabbit thought, well, he'd try it. An' he went down one cold night, sat down on the mill dam an' hung his tail off in the water. An' when the moon got up to the top of the trees, he tried to get up to see if he had any fish an' his tail was frozen hard in the ice. He pulled an' did every way he could, but he couldn't get it out. An' he thought, "Well, daylight's coming, an' if my friends come along an' see me like this, they'll laugh."

An' 'bout that time an ol' owl come flying by. Owl asked him what he was doin' there.

He said, "Well, my tail's stuck in this pond, frozen in here." An' said, "I wish you'd help me get it out."

An' the owl said, "Gladly." So he flew down an' snipped off the rabbit's tail right at the top of the ice an' flew on off. An' so ever since that day rabbits have had short tails.

The Hanging Attic

There are people in this world that manage to say the wrong thing so many times. I'm reminded of a lady that could do that. One of her friends' husband had become despondent an' hanged himself in their attic. An' the neighbors all decided they'd go over an' console the widda, an' they reminded this woman, "Be careful what you talk about. We don't want to make her grieve any worse."

"Well, all right, I'll be careful."

So they went over an' talked aroun' a little bit. An' this ol' lady decided the weather would be a safe subject, an' she said, "Aren't we havin' terrible weather?"

The bereaved woman said, "Yes, there's just so much rain, look like I could never get caught up with my washin'."

She said, "Well, you shouldn't mind that at all"; says; "you have such a nice attic to hang things in."

The Preacher Who Couldn't Read

This is a story that one of my neighbors told me. She knew a man that was called to preach that couldn't read. An' he hired one of his neighbors to go down an' sit under the pulpit, an' as he ran his finger along the Scripture, he [the hired neighbor] read it quietly an' then the preacher would repeat it aloud to the congregation.

So they read a few lines, an' the man under

the pulpit said, "You'll have to move your finger, I can't see to read."

He said [loudly], "You will have to move your finger, I cannot see to read."

He said, "You dern fool, I didn't mean for you to say that."

An' he [the preacher] hollered, "You dern fool, I didn't mean for you to say that." An' that broke up the congregation!

Turpie and the Hobyahs

There was an ol' man an' a ol' lady that lived down at the foot of a hill. An' they had a little dog that was their constant companion. But it got to where that every night after they would go to sleep, the little dog, Turpie, would start out barkin'. He would bark an' bark, an' it worried the ol' man an' he threatened the little dog, "If you don't quit barkin' so much I'm gonna have to git rid of ya." But the next night the little dog would bark an' bark.

An' right over the hill from them there was some Hobyahs, little dwarfish men that slept through the daytime an' got out an' prowled around at night an' stole things to live on. An' the little dog was tryin' to keep them away, which the ol' man did not know.

An' it went on awhile, an' finally the ol' man told the little dog Turpie, "If you do that again, I'm gonna cut your tail off." An' the next mornin' he got up an' cut the little dog's tail off.

An' he barked the next night. "Well," he said, "I'll just cut yer legs off." An' he kep' on 'til he cut all the legs off, an' the little dog barked on. He said, well, he'd just cut his head off.

An' then the next night he just went to sleep an' slept so sound. In fact, he slept so sound that the Hobyahs came over the hill an' put his ol' lady in a sack an' carried her home with them. An' when they got there, they were tired an' sleepy an' they just hung her on the wall.

An' the ol' man woke up an' he called to his wife; couldn't find her anyplace. An' he didn't have any idea which way to go to hunt her, an' he thought about his little dog. So he got out [the pieces] an' put it back together again. An' the little dog sniffed around awhile an' took off acrost this hill, the dog ahead an' the ol' man following.

An' when they came to the home of the Hobyahs, they were all sound asleep. An' the ol' man slipped in the house, lifted his sack off the wall, an' carried his ol' lady home. An' the ol' lady an' the ol' man an' little dog Turpie lived happily ever after.

The Brownies and the Boggarts

Once there was an ol' tailor lived near some woodland with his ol' mother an' two small children. He barely made enough to feed them, an' it worried him. His mother was old an' she wadn't able to he'p him much, an' the boys were just boys, just careless, did not see a thing to do.

An' one day he said, "I wish that I had some brownies livin' with me rather than boggarts."

An' the mother said, "Well, maybe things'll change."

So the boys came in one day from playing an' said, "What's for supper?"

An' the grandmother said, "There's no supper tonight"; said, "we only have a little food, an' it's more important that you have food for breakfast an' just go on to bed."

An' they went to bed. They were hungry, an'

they got to thinkin' about what their father said about wishin' he had some brownies. They knew what a boggart was. A boggart was a person that never wanted to he'p anybody. An' they went to the grandmother an' asked her, said, "Grandmother, where could we find some brownies?"

She said, "The ol' owl could tell."

An' says, "Where's the ol' owl?"

"Oh, he lives in the deep woods."

So that night after they went to bed, Tommy got to thinkin' about it, an' he looked out an' the moon was shinin' so bright. He slipped out the door an' went out in the deep wood. An' he could hear the ol' owl say, "Who, who."

He said, "It's Tommy"; said, "I came to ask you where the brownies lived."

An' the ol' owl said, "Go to the pond, stand on the north side, say 'Show me where a brownie,' turn around three times, look in the pond, an' you'll see where to find the brownies."

Well, he did it, an' it was a clear moonshiny night, an' it was himself! An' he looked at the ol' owl, said, "This is just me."

He said, "So it is, so it is."

An' so he realized what it meant. An' he went back an' waked his brother up an' told him, said, "I found out who the brownies are."

An' he said, "Who?"

Said, "It's us behavin' like we should."

An' so early next mornin' they got up an' went down an' cleaned up that room, folded the ol' man's material an' everything carefully. An' when the ol' man awoke he came down tired, said, "Oh, if I could just learn how to make more money to keep my family goin'." An' he saw all this cleaned up, an' he called up to his mother, said, "Mother, come down"; said, "the brownies have been here!" An' so she came down an' he said, "Well, how could I pay 'em?"

She said, "Just put out a bowl of clear water ever' night. That's all the brownies ask for."

Well, every night the ol' man very carefully put out a bowl of cool water for 'em, an' next mornin', when he'd come down, everything would be in apple-pie order. An' it just heartened him so, he did more work, got more orders, an' he was just makin' a good livin' for the family. An' the boys were very happy.

So he told his ol' mother, said, "Mother, I want to do something for those brownies. How do I go about doin' something for a brownie?"

An' she said, "Oh, I don't know."

He said, "I think I'll just make 'em a suit. What size would I make?"

She said, "Oh, Tommy's about the size I'd think a brownie'd be."

So he measured Tommy carefully an' made him a cute little suit, an' tried it on Tommy an' it fit. An' so he made another'n exactly like it. An' the next night he put out the bowl of water, laid the suits on the chair, an' went on to bed.

An' in the night, the boys came down an' they cleaned up the house an' they came across these little suits. An' they said, "Oh, bless him, he made us a suit." An' so they tried 'em on an' they exactly fit, an' they were just dancin' around. An' he [the father] heard a little noise an' he crept down the stairs an' he could see 'em, but he didn't let them see him. An' he saw how happy they were, an' then he went on back to bed.

An' the next mornin' he told the family, he said, "I had the greatest experience last night; I got to see the brownies." An' said, "Come to think about it, they look about like my own boys."

An' the grandmother said, "Bless ya," said, "they usually look like some of the family."

An' he said, "Well, this I'm thankful for, that the boggarts left our home an' the brownies come to live."

The Lady from Philadelphia

In a small town there was a Peterson family lived. There was the mother an' a grown daughter—almost grown—Elizabeth Ann. Then she had a grown son who'd had one year in college, an' a small boy. An' they were peculiar people.

She decided it was time for Elizabeth Ann to go takin' music lessons. An' she called the furniture people an' they brought a piana, an' the workmen happened to set it down with the keys toward the wall. Well, she worried an' worried how in the world Elizabeth Ann was gonna practice her music. An' so they just raised the winder an' put the piana stool outside on the porch, an' Elizabeth practiced the piana that way.

An' so they were gettin' along fairly well, an' come Christmas time she said, "We've been so blessed. We gonna have the biggest Christmas this time." Told the boy, said, "You go out an' buy a nice tree, a purty tree."

So he went out an' bought a large tree, an' they brought it in. It was too tall for their ceiling, so they just got up an' sawed a hole in the ceiling! An' the tree would not be steady that way, so they put a box under it an' stuck more of the tree up in the loft to steady it. An' they was always doing things like that.

An' so after Christmas was over she said, "Now, the first of the year, we always go out to the shut-ins an' the less fortunate people an' carry them gifts." An' told her big boy, said, "Harness the horse an' put him to the carriage." An' she got up jelly an' jams an' cookies an' things like that an' put in the carriage. Well, they all got in, picked up the lines; horse didn't start. They whistled, they clucked, an' they begged, an' the horse didn't move. So finally she laid the whip on him, an' he still didn't move. She said, "Children, this buggy is just too heavy."

So she got out, set the jelly an' the jams an' the pickles an' the cookies all out on the ground, an' crawled back in; an' the horse still wouldn't move. An' she said, "Well, this lady from Philadelphia always knows the answer." Said, "You go on up there an' ask her what to do about this horse."

So they went up there an' asked her what to do. She said, "Well, I'm sick in bed, but I'll tell you what I'll do. If you'll get my opera glasses, I'll try to look down there an' see if I can see what's wrong." So she looked through her glasses an' said, "You go back an' tell your mama to unhitch the horse from the hitchin' post, an' I think he'll go on." Well, they were so pleased with that.

So after they had made that strenuous day of visitin' around, the next mornin' the ol' lady woke up very tired an' she said, "Well, I'll just get up an' brew me a good cup of coffee; that always picks me up." An' not noticin' what she did, she put salt in it instead of sugar. Well, she couldn't drink that, so she put a little of ever'thing she could think of in there. It didn't take the salty

taste out. She sent the boy over to the druggist an' told him to send her something that would kill the taste of salt. An' he sent her some drugs, an' she put a little of this in, a little of that in, an' it didn't taste any better. Said, "Well, go to the ol' herb woman"; an' said, "she has an herb for almost anything you can think about."

An' they found her in the woods gatherin' up roots an' leaves an' things, an' they told her what their mother said. An' she said, "Well, I'll do my best." So she come in, put a little tansy in it; didn't taste right. An' they put a little peppermint in it; didn't taste right. A little ginger root; in fact, a little of all the things that she'd collected. An' the coffee just didn't taste like coffee.

An' the lady said, "Well, I'll tell you what; go over to the lady from Philadelphia an' ask her what to do." So they went over an' told the lady of Philadelphia what had happened an' all the trouble they'd gone to, an' the coffee still didn't taste like coffee.

She thought a little bit; she said, "I'll tell you what do. You go back to your mother an' tell her just pour that coffee out an' brew her a fresh cup of coffee." An' she did, an' enjoyed her coffee very much!

I don't know whether that's all of it; I think it is.

Emily Ellis:
"I like the real 'ha ha' kind."

Mrs. Ellis, born in 1930 and the daughter of Mrs. Casey, seemed to enjoy telling her tales to us, even though she said the recorder made her nervous. She seemed to relax more as she began to tell her amusing stories and laughed with everyone else at the punch lines. Although she worked with a list of story titles in her hand to help her keep them straight, she knew the stories well from memory and did not have to rehearse them before they were recorded. Mrs. Ellis talked from a sitting position with her hands folded. She kept her body still during the session and showed little animation for the most part.

When we first contacted Mrs. Ellis, she could remember only a few stories, but by the time she had thought about what she knew for a few weeks she was able to remember many more. The people in her family all said that Mrs. Ellis was the best storyteller in their family, both for her good memory of detail and her manner of delivery.

Ellis: I grew up here in Polk County, and my father farmed. We always had enough to eat an' enough clothes to wear, but we weren't wealthy by any means.

Long: Could you tell me how you learned your stories? Did you learn them as a child, or when you were older?

Ellis: Some of these I heard as a child, but most of these are stories that my father-in-law told. An' he is dead now, but he had a wealth of stories an' he was always glad to tell 'em.

Long: Would you say that there was anyone in the community that was known as the storyteller?

Ellis: Well, one person, when I was a child, was a great-uncle of mine, Uncle Sterling Young. He was always a great storyteller and he was known as sorta a local wit.

Long: Do you have any favorite story, and if so why is it your favorite?

Ellis: I guess my favorite is the one where the preacher had the pigeon in the loft; it's my favorite just because I think it's particularly funny. I like the real "ha ha" kind.

Long: When do you usually tell your tales? Is there any special time?

Ellis: I have found that a lot of stories, like the ones that Mother told me, are more children's stories than this sorta thing that you've been recording. I tell my first-graders the same ones Mother told, like "Billy Bobtail" and "Drakesbill," an' all those that were told me as a child. An' some of them you find now in storybooks, but at that time when she told them to us you usually didn't.

Long: Why do you like to tell stories?

Ellis: Just for the reaction that people have. An' if you tell them to people that don't seem to enjoy them, it's not any fun. That takes all the kick out of it.

Long: Do you think people tell stories to each other now as much as they used to?

Ellis: Well, probably not, because they have so many other means of entertainment. In fact, I know I don't tell my own children stories as much as Mother told them to us.

Long: You think this is bad?

Ellis: Yeah, I do to a certain extent. 'Cause a lot of things that children git from television are good, but you lose a lot of warmth and contact with your parents and other members of the family.

Long: Does it make a kind of bond between people who've always heard the same stories?

Ellis: Yeah it does, it does.

Long: Are there any stories that have a special meaning to you?

Ellis: Well, I guess this one you have on tape, "Billy Bobtail," does to me, an' I don't know why this jus' meant home. I guess Mother must have told it to me thousands of times.

Family Reunion. Jack Leigh.

Long: Do you think that a person can learn anything about how to live from these stories, or are they just for entertainment?

Ellis: Oh, sure; this is not original, but I read in a book about Lincoln one time the reason he enjoyed them is that they were so typical of people, and the way people react to different situations. An' in a way that's what makes the low-key story funny. It's because it's so typically human.

Long: How do you feel when you're telling these stories? Do you get personally involved?

Ellis: Yeah, usually; and you find yourself—'specially these short funny ones—you find yourself tellin' it a little bit differently every time. And if you remember the way you told it that was the funniest, then that's the way you tell it.

Long: Do you think that telling stories to your children that were told to you gives you a feeling of continuity?

Ellis: Yeah, I think that. And I think that you have an obligation to tell your children this sort of thing. It's part of their heritage, and they should be allowed ta enjoy them and ta feel part of the family.

The Dove in the Loft

Once this ol' country preacher had heard of using different sorts of props to make his sermons more meaningful, and he decided that he'd put a little boy up in the loft with a dove; and he was gonna preach his sermon about Jesus' baptism. And he told the boy when he got to the place where "lo, the Dove of the Lord descended from the Heavens" to let the dove loose.

Well, he got all warmed up with his sermon, and he said, "And lo, the Dove of the Lord descended from the Heavens"; and nothin' happened. So he said it again [louder voice]: "And lo, the Dove of the Lord descended from the Heavens," and still nothin'. So he repeated it a third time, this time a little louder.

An' the little boy stuck his head down from the loft and said, "Preacher, the cat done et the pigeon; you want me ta throw the cat down?"

Pound Cake

And then there was this lady that had prepared a wedding feast. And her specialty was a pound cake. And she put dozens of eggs and good rich country butter and all sorts of things in it. And just as they got the table spread with the best cloth and all this good food, this poor old man came by and asked for somethin' to eat. And the hospitality of those days demanded that they invite him in.

And he set down to the table, and she noticed that he cut him off a big slice of pound cake and lathered it up with butter and ate it with his vegetables. And then another slice and another slice; and she kept passin' loaf bread and biscuits, and he wouldn't have any. And finally she just got real insistent as the pound cake got thinner and thinner, and he said, "No," said, "you just keep that for your other guests and I'll just eat this ol' yeller [corn] bread."

Uncle Billy Packs His Gun

This was a story that was told about Uncle Billy. Now, Uncle Billy was a preacher. And he was known to be very conscientious and to believe in divine revelations and things of this nature.

And he also believed in predestination, that when your time came to die that you'd just die and there wouldn't be anything you could do about it.

But he was gittin' ready for a trip through some dangerous Indian territory, and he was gittin' his gun all ready. So somebody meaning to kid him a little bit said, "Well, Uncle Billy, they's no use you takin' your gun"; said, "if it's time for you to die," said, "you just goin' to die anyway." Said, "Just accept it and just leave your gun at home."

He said, "Yeah, but you cain't ever tell; it might be some Indian's time to die."

Uncle Billy and the Vision of the Corn

And another one of his neighbors tried to take advantage of this belief of Uncle Billy's [in revelations]. Went up with a empty corn wagon. And he said, "Uncle Billy," said, "the Lord spoke to me last night and told me to come up here and git a load of corn from you."

And Uncle Billy stood there for a minute and he said, "Well," said, "that's strange." Said, "The Lord spoke to me too, and told me that he'd changed his mind and he didn't want you to git it."

Letters in the Sky

And then one time there was this preacher that was supposed to be "called," and he'd been a boy that was fairly young and he'd just been awfully rough. And just overnight he was converted and called to preach.

And the church where he was supposed to be licensed was divided about whether they should license him to preach or not. The older people at the church just couldn't believe in this quick conversion. And some of the younger members thought they oughta go ahead and license him. So they were arguin' it, and one of the younger ones got up and said, "Well now, you just cain't doubt that this boy is called." Said, "He looked up in the sky and said he saw in flamin' letters GPC." And said, "He knew this meant Go Preach Christ." And he talked on about how sincere this boy was an' all this sorta thing.

And when he finally set down this old deacon stood up in the back and he said, "Now, I don't doubt that this boy's been converted"; an' said, "I don't doubt that probably he saw the flamin' letters in the sky. But," he said, "I know this boy real well"; and said, "I think that he's just made a mistake in judgment and didn't understand what God meant for him to do." Said, "I firmly believe, brethren, that this GPC meant Go Pick Cotton." [Laughs]

Courting

Then there was this country boy that had gone down to court one of the neighbor girls. And so he was sittin' out on the porch talkin' to his girlfriend, and he got just a little bit too friendly with her. And her father was lookin' out the winder, and he came out with a shotgun under his arm.

And the boy jumped off the porch and split to run just as fast as he could go, hit the cabbage patch and stirred up an old rabbit. He said, "Git out of the way, rabbit, and let somebody run that knows how!"

The Boy at the Horse Sale

An' then there was this little boy that had a horse at a horse sale. An' the little boy'd been paid a quarter to ride the horse around, make him look good. And one of the prospective buyers sorta sidled up to the boy and said, "Boy," said, "tell me confidentially," said, "hadn't this horse got the splints?"

And the little boy looked at him and he says, "Well, I really don't know, feller, but if it's good for him he's got it an' if it ain't he ain't."

All of These Are Mine

This man went off into a neighborin' community and married. An' he sorta lied about what his possessions were. But anyway, on the way home every time they'd come to a herd of sheep or cattle or anything of that nature he'd stroke his whiskers and say to his new bride, "All of these are mine." And on down the road to the next pretty farm and he'd stroke his whiskers and say, "All of these are mine." And the next field that had good-lookin' hogs he'd stroke those whiskers and say, "All of these are mine."

And finally, at the end of the road they stopped at this old tumbled-down shack. And he said, "This is home."

And she said, "Why, you been lyin' to me all this time."

He said, "No, I haven't." Said, "When I was strokin' my whiskers I said all of these are mine."

And she said, "You're the biggest durn liar I've ever seen," and she went back home!

The Mule and the "Highlife"

Then there was this colored man that had a big load of fence posts on a wagon, an' the ol' mule pulled and pulled and he finally just got to where he couldn't go any further, and he stopped. An' the old man couldn't git him started for nothin'. So this man came along on a horse and he said, "What's the matter?"

And he said, "This ol' mule done stopped." And said, "I cain't git him a-goin' again."

So he said, "Well, I've got a little 'highlife' here in my saddlebag"; said, "let's see what that'll do for him." So he got out the highlife an' put a little bit under the mule's tail. An' the ol' mule stood there for a minute and swished his tail from side to side, laid his ears back, and then he just split to run. And slung posts ever'where, an' tore the wagon up, tore the tongue out; just went over the hill in a great big hurry.

And the ol' nigger just stood there. And after all the dust had settled he said, "Well," said, "Master," said, "I reckon you'd better put a little of that highlife on me; I got ta catch that mule!"

Me All Face

Oh, there 'as an Indian walkin' along with his very few clothes on, an' this white man said to him, said, "Aren't you cold?" Said, "This is mighty bad weather to be walkin' around with no more clothes on than that."

An' the Indian said, "No."

And the man just wouldn't leave him alone;

said, "Well, you just look silly to be goin' along with no more clothes on than that." Said, "You sure you're not cold?"

And the Indian said, "Is your face cold?"

An' he said, "No."

And the Indian said, "Me all face."

The Deacon Meets the Bears

One time this deacon was goin' to church; and they had to walk in those days, had a long way to go. And he set out in the woods just spic and span with his best clothes on. An' when he got to church he was the worst-lookin' feller you've ever seen, just dirty and wet all over, just soakin' soppin' wet, and lost his hat. An' the preacher said, "Deacon, what happened to ya?"

He said, "Well, you know down there where I have to cross the creek on a footlog?" Said, "I just had stepped up on the footlog an' I looked up at the other end, and there was a great big bear." And said, "I looked around behind me an' there was another great big bear." And he said, "I just jumped off in that creek and swam across."

He said, "Well now, that was a foolish thing for you to do." Said, "Why didn't you just call on the Lord?"

He said, "Now listen, Preacher"; said, "the Lord Almighty is just great in a prayer meetin', but he ain't much at a bear meetin'!"

Dividing the Walnuts

One night two tramps were walkin', and they had to pass a cemetery. And they heard voices, so they stopped and listened. And they heard this voice saying, "You take this one an' I'll take that one, you take this one an' I'll take that one." And what they didn't know was that two men had come along earlier and shook a walnut tree, and they were dividin' up the walnuts. And they set there listenin' to "You take this one, I'll take that one."

And they said, "What is that?" And one of them said, "Well, I think it's the Devil an' the Lord dividin' up the people in the cemetery."

And just as they had reached this conclusion one of the men said [loudly], "And I'll take the two on the outside." An' nobody saw the tramps anymore!

The Two Colored Men and the Pig

An' then one time two colored men were goin' down the road in a wagon. And they saw a pig. And they looked around an' they decided it didn't have anybody that belonged to it; it didn't look like it was goin' anywhere particular. So they got it up an' trussed it up right good an' put it in the back of the wagon. And no sooner had they done this than here come the sheriff. So one of 'em said, "Grab him up here an' put your coat on 'im." So they put the coat around the pig and put him up between them on the wagon seat an' tried to look very nonchalant.

An' the sheriff came along beside of 'em and, sure enough, he drew up his horse an' stopped. And he said, "Where you boys goin'?"

They said, "Goin' home."

"What you been doin'?"

"Nothin'."

"Well, what's your names?"

One of them said, well, his name was Robert, and the other one said, "Well, my name's Herbert."

"Well, what's your name there in the middle?"

An' one of them jabbed the ol' pig with his elbow an' the pig said, "Oink."

An' the sheriff said, "Well, that's all right then, go on."

So they went on down the road. And after they left the sheriff stood there for a minute and scratched his head, you know, and he said, "Well, I've seen that Robert somewhere before, I think, and that other feller; but I swear, that durned Oink is the ugliest man I ever saw!"

The Hog That Wore Buttons

An' then there was one about the ol' man that went out to celebrate. An' when he got home he missed the house and wound up out at the pigpen. An' he got all settled down in the hog waller. An' he reached over and put his arm around the old sow an' rubbed his hand up and down her stomach, and he said, "I swear, Maude, I didn't know you had all them buttons on your gown."

The Clever Peddler and the Razor Straps

In this community was a little ol' store, an' the people that hung out there had got the reputation of bein' real smart alecks. They could just git the best an' outwit anybody that happened to come by.

So one day this peddler came by, and he was sellin' razor straps to sharpen straight razors on, and he got in the store an' they asked him what he had. And he said he sure did have some fine razor straps—or strops, I think they call them.

But anyway, the local wit said, "Well, how much are they?"

And the peddler said, "Well, I git a dollar for 'em."

So the wit said, "Why," said, "you can git a razor strap like that anywhere for fifty cents."

And the peddler said, "Well, I'll tell you what"; said, "if you buy one of my straps for a dollar and then you see one like it sell anywhere for fifty cents, I'll give you fifty cents back."

So he bought one an' then turned to his friend—another one of the bright boys—an' said, "Would you like to buy a razor strap?"

An' he said yeah, he'd like to.

Said, "Well, I'll sell it to you for fifty cents."

Well, they all had a big laugh and the peddler joined in laughin' with 'em, and he said, "Well, you really outwitted me, so here's your fifty cents." So all the other men in the store, since the peddler'd been such a good sport, bought straps too; so he made a right good sale.

And on his way out there was a man leanin' against the door-face and he said, "Well," said, "there's just nobody comes in here that these guys don't git the best of."

An' the peddler says, "That's what I had heard, so I was prepared for them." He said, "I always sell these straps for twenty-five cents apiece."

Take My Coat to Town

An' there's this man was goin' down the road so hot and tired and dirty, and this man came by in a real fancy-lookin' buggy an' didn't offer to stop an' give him a lift. So after he had gotten by the man hollered to him real loud, "Hey," said, "friend, would you take my coat to town?"

An' the man drew up his horse and said,

"Why, yeah, I guess I would. But," said, "how are you gonna pick it up?"

He said, "Well, I thought I'd just stay inside of it."

Resaca

And then they's a tale told about how Resaca, Georgia [Gordon County], got its name. These men went by this settlement and picked up a woman in the night, kidnapped her an' crammed her in a sack an' took her along with 'em.

An' when they got to this particular place they went in this cabin an' took her out an' lit the lamp. And when they saw what she looked like, one of them said to the other, "Oh Lord, resaca [re-sack her]!"

How the Drunk Got Out of the Grave

An' then one night, a drunk was goin' through a graveyard. Previously though, this plain ol' sober man was goin' through the same graveyard an' he fell into an open grave. He tried an' tried to git out; he tried to make some little footholes an' get out, an' he couldn't do that. So finally, after wearin' himself out, he thought, "Well, I'll just have ta stay in here 'til mornin', an' maybe help'll come by." So he lay down an' went to sleep.

An' then the drunk came along stumblin' through the cemetery, an' fell in the grave too. An' he was tryin' to git out. An' the first man said, "There's no use in you tryin', you can't get out."

But he did!

The Pig and the Local Politician

Then there's one that's always told on a local politician. He came in one night in the same condition [drunk] and got in the hog waller. An' he was lyin' out there with the old pig, an' he was rollin' around, an' he said, "This sure is a good waller we got out here, us pigs, ain't it?"

He jabbed the ol' pig next to him and the ol' pig said, "Oink, oink."

An' so he slept on awhile. Then he roused up again an' he said, "I declare, this is the nicest, softest, juiciest waller I ever was in. Idn't that the way you feel about it?"

An' the old pig, "Oink, oink."

So he had another comment or two to make, an' the ol' pig didn't say nothin' but just a regular ol' grunt. And he said, "You're not bein' very friendly"; said, "you'll just have ta remember that tomorra when the daylight comes, I'm goin' be Judge Fuller of the Supreme Court and you're goin' to be the same ol' hog."

Eat 'til Ya Bust

Then there was a man in the neighborhood that had a big flock of the poorest goats that anybody had ever seen. Now, all the neighbors would speculate about what he fed 'em an' how bad they looked, an' there wadn't a bit of grazin' in the pasture or anything.

So it just so happened that a neighbor was at this ol' man's house when feedin' time came, so he saw the old man go out to the crib and get about eight or ten [corn] shucks an' throw it over to the pasture to the twenty goats and said, "There, damn ye; eat 'til ya bust!"

The Stingy Man and His Mule

An' this same ol' man had a crippled mule. An' he worked him so hard. An' a neighbor happened by one day when he was workin' and he said, "Doesn't it bother you to work that ol' mule, him crippled up like that?"

An' the old man stood a few minutes an' said, "I'll tell you the way I feel about it, Mr. Ellis"; he said, "I just don't let it worry my mind."

The Well-Trained Mule

An' then there was a mule that was supposed to be so well trained. Man had him down at the trade day tryin' to trade him off, an' he said, "Why, this mule's the best-trained mule"; said, "you don't have ta say anything to him, just one little inclination of what you want him to do and he just does it." Said, "You never have ta speak harshly to him or anything."

But it so happened he didn't sell the mule, an' he had to take him on back home. An' a neighbor happened by one day just in time to see him just beatin' the tar out of the ol' mule. And he hollered up there to him, said, "Neighbor," said, "I thought that mule was well trained."

An' he said, "He is, he is; but," said, "you have ta git his attention first!"

The Shoe Salesman's Bald Head

An' then there was a shoe salesman that was just as bald as he could be; he didn't have a hair anywhere on his head. An' he was kneelin' down at this lady's feet, tryin' on a pair o' shoes—this was in the days when ladies wore long skirts. An' just as he was tryin' to git the shoe on the lady's foot, she looked down an' saw that bald head an' thought it was her knee an' threw her dress over it!

Reverend James H. Mull:
"I've always enjoyed good stories on preachers."

James Hosea ("Hosey") Mull, born in 1902 and in his youth a moonshiner, was a very willing informant. On our first visit with him we didn't record his few stories because we failed to recognize their traditional nature. But we did return to record them the next weekend. Preacher Mull said that he had difficulty in remembering stories for our interview because he usually found a story from his repertoire to fit the situation.

During the recording session he seemed relaxed for the most part, although the machine put him on guard at first. He leaned over facing the microphone, and did not move his hands or body in gestures while speaking, except to spit tobacco juice into a can at his feet.

Mull: I was born in a little log cabin over heah on the Southern Railroad in Floyd County,

Georgia. I lived in Floyd County until I was ten years ol', an' my family—there 'as thirteen of us—moved down here to a farm joinin' where I live now. An' I lived there until 1920. I joined the United States Army an' served for four year, 1920 to 1925. I got discharged an' come home, an' I'm sorry to say I fell in with the wrong bunch an' lived very rough for a coupla years. But then I began to date a little girl that lived out here in the community that I'd knowed all of her life. I begin to feel I wanted to get away from the rough life which I was livin', an' me an' her married. I moved up 'bout a quarter of a mile above Lake Creek an' rented me a farm, started to workin' a crop, started goin' to church.

An' I went back to church, 'pologized to the church for the life in which I'd lived. This happened in 1927. I attended church 'til 1930, an' I felt like the Lord had called me to preach. An' they give me an appointment on the second Sunday in August 1930, an' I been a minister ever since. But it taken me several years. I never did go to school any to 'mount to anything; when I'd entered into the ministry I still hadn't learnt how to read to do any good, an' I had to learn how to read before I could read the Bible an' understand it well enough to teach it. We have a lady here in the community now, ex-schoolteacher, that when the first church, Southside Baptist Church in Cedartown, called me in 1933, I'd go down an' get her to learn me my Scripture lesson through the week so I could read it on Sunday, until I learnt how I could read it myself. I had the privilege of preaching in my county, right around my own door, for thirty-three year. I never been asked to retire; I never been asked to resign from any church. The people in Polk County have been unusually good to me. I'm very grateful for it, both to God an' to man.

Long: Could you tell me how you learned your stories? Did you learn them as a child, when you were older, or after you started to preach?

Mull: I learnt some of 'em when I was a child, but God blessed me with a good memory. I even remember the text of the first sermont I preached, I remember the text of the second sermont I preached, the third sermont I preached, an' the first homecomin' sermont I preached. The fact of the business, when I were a young man in my late thirties, I could read over a passage of Scripture two or three time—a whole chapter of Scripture—then sit down an' tell you ever'thing was in it. I had sort of a photostatic mind. I'm sorry to say that my remembry is not that good now, but I've had other ministers in the association to refer to me as havin' a mind like an elephant. I never forgit anything.

I was brought up by uneducated parents. My father didn't know *A* from *B*, didn't know a one-dollar bill from a five-dollar bill; but he implanted somethin' in my life that has meant so much to me. The people that knowed him the longest an' the best said he would walk five mile to pay you a nickel if he owed ya. He'd also walk five mile to collect one off of ya, if you owed him. An' that's always been my philosophy of life. If a man owed me anything, I wanted him to pay me. If I owed him anything, when it came due I always paid him, or I went an' made arrangements that was satisfactory to him about my obligations.

Long: Was there anyone in the community where you were raised who was known as a good storyteller?

Mull: Fact of the business, I been considered the storyteller ever since I 'as grown in this community.

Long: Well, good. Do you have any one favorite story, and if you do could you tell me why you like it?

Mull: There's so many good stories that I have heard over a period of years; some of 'em was inspirin' to me, an' some of 'em fascinated me, an' some of 'em was just downright funny.

Long: Do you like the stories about preachers?

Mull: Yes, ever since I've been in the ministry I've always got a lotta joy outta stories concernin' ministers, because I knew them better'n I knew anything else an' I guess would understand 'em an' prob'ly get more out of it; I've always enjoyed good stories on preachers.

Long: Is that why you tell stories about preachers?

Mull: Yes, I get a kick out of it. I always did get a lotta enjoyment out of it, tellin' a joke on a preacher an', fact o' the business, anybody that I always felt very close to. I always did like to tease 'em a little bit, to joke 'em a little bit. I felt like that was sort of a indication of good fellowship—close friendship—between ya.

Long: Then you wouldn't say that in a community where people tell a lot of jokes on their preachers that they're being in any way, well, sacrilegious or anything?

Mull: In some respects it is, but generally speakin', no. Most o' the people, a-judgin' other communities from my own, thinks very well of the minister. We do, now. The young minister we've got now, we think well of 'im an' we don't mind teasin' 'im a little bit an' jokin' with 'im a little bit, an' you'll hear some of the persons say some little somethin' or other funny about 'im ever' once in a while; but it's all done in the spirit of love an' friendship, really. The average person that I've knowed in my life, if they didn't like anybody, they didn't say nothin' about 'im, good or bad. They just didn't wanta say anything

about 'im. But gen'lly when you say somebody's always tellin' a joke on somebody or teasin' somebody, it's somebody that gen'lly likes 'im an' feels like they're very close to 'im.

Long: Well, since religion does play such a major part in your life, then telling stories about religion and about preachers, would that tend to reinforce your thinking?

Mull: If it's told with the right motive an' has the right application, I think it would enhance religion.

Long: When do you usually tell these tales, and who do you tell them to? Do you tell them just to your friends, in church, or to other preachers?

Mull: Well, a joke or a story is never enjoyed unless the circumstances is so that that joke or story is appropriate. A good story told in an inappropriate place is dead; it has no life in it. The surroundin' circumstances must be applicable an' suitable for the story in order for it to have life an' have meaning to it. I'm gen'lly used to speakin' to a large group of people in church. The jokes that I tell then is always somethin' that's in the service that reminds me of that joke that makes it appropriate for the occasion. They are certain things that you can work into your message that will put life an' meaning in your message, that bears out an' conveys a thought that will he'p the people understand what you're talking about an' will he'p you put over your point.

Long: Could you tell me why you like to tell tales and stories to other people?

Mull: I reckon if I was to go back an' say where I got that from, would be from my parents. My father an' mother were good ol'-timey people, lively. They jus' loved young people, an' we had a large crowd o' young people at our house visit us very often. An' Mama an' Papa conducted themself in a way where the young people would always come back. They were always funny an' lively an' jokin'ly, an' I guess it jus' rubbed off on me.

Long: Do you think people tell the same kinds of stories as they use to when you learned your stories?

Mull: Well, of course everything is improved in some way or 'nother. We don't use so much of the ol' southern drawl, as some people calls it, an' sometimes it takes something like that to actually bring out what's in a story. We speak in more fluent English now than we did back then, an' maybe some o' the stories sounds better with that type of language than the ol' folk stories did; some of 'em don't.

Long: Are there any stories or tales that have a special meaning to you?

Mull: Yes, things that continually reminds me of things that's happened in my life.

Long: Do you think a person can learn anything about how to live from these stories, or are they just for entertainment?

Mull: Well, part o' the stories, of course, are constructive an' has a deep meaning in 'em that we can benefit from, an' some of 'em's just purely entertainment.

Long: Do you ever feel personally involved with the story that you're telling?

Mull: Well, unless you do feel personally involved, your story's not gonna go over very good. Anything that we can't get in, ourself, we're not apt to be very successful in it. You got to become involved personally if you are to put your story over.

Long: And another question. Why do you think some people tell the ol' stories an' others don't? What is it in some people that make them tell stories?

Mull: They's people that got life in 'em. A person that's lively, they like ta spread some sunshine in people's lives. Now, even our doctors an' our science tells us there's nothin' any better for us than a good laugh ta actually he'p you.

The Long-winded Evangelist

I always did get a kick when I thought of a little boy after a evangelist preacher had run his service fer three weeks. On the closin' night he said, "Ever'one that has attended all the services, stand up."

A large overgrown woman about three pick handles across the hips stood up. He said, "Sister," says, "you attended all the services?"

She says, "I been here ever' night."

He said, "Well, now, you just go ahead an' tell the people how you feel about the services."

She tore a face up an' said, "I'm so full I can't talk!" Sat down.

Her little boy stood beside of her. Preacher said, "Now, son, tell us how you feel about it."

He said, "I'm like Mama; I just about got a belly full of it."

The Windmill Preacher

I used to get a lotta kick outta teasin' the young preachers after I had several years' experience under my belt; an' I was always interested in young preachers. I liked to invite 'em out because I knew they had to have some practice. I'd let 'em preach for myself an' my folks, an' I had a

Rooftop Preacher. Jack Leigh.

joke I used to tell [laughs] on 'em, especially George. I had a lotta respect for George an' I loved 'im very much, an' I liked to tease him.

George was a man that always was religiously inclined. When he was a striplin' of a boy, he had a tendency to want to be a preacher. He said people were so nice to 'em. They'd fix nice meals an' invite 'em out to eat with 'em, an' after they got through with the message in the church, why, people'd come up an' shake hands with 'em an' compliment 'em an' say nice things about 'em; an' he said he just had a hankerin' he wanted to be a preacher.

So finally he felt that he had the call, an' he got him an appointment out to a little country church. So him an' his wife got in the ol' jalopy an' throwed the two children in the back seat an' out they went. An' they approached the church. As he walked in the door, he seen the glass o' water that use ta always sit on the pulpit in every church. He said, "Why, this church is right up to date"; says, "there's that glass o' water."

Sunday school was over, and they turned the service over to him. An' he got up there an' read his Scripture lesson, had prayer, an' tore loose an' preached about ten minutes, turned up the glass an' drank about half of it. Tore loose again for about ten minutes, turned up the glass an' emptied it an' preached about fifteen minutes; dismissed. But nobody didn't come up an' shake hands with him. Nobody didn't compliment him ner ask him to go home with 'em. It sorta got him at the pit of his stomach. But George was a good man; he could take it.

So him an' his wife an' children got in the ol' jalopy an' started back home. He thought surely his wife would say some encouragin' words to him, but as they rode along back home she never even mentioned it. So when they turned in the driveway he turned an' said, "Honey," said, "what'd you think about my sermont this mornin'?"

She says, "George," says, "you are the only windmill ever I seen that run by water."

Discouraging Words

A long time ago, most of us greedy country preachers pastored four churches, an' sometimes some of 'em was a good long ways from home. An' we'd go down an' preach on Sunday, an' rather'n have to come back Sunday night over them rough roads, we'd just spend the night an' come home on Monday mornin'.

After a Sunday night service, started home one Monday mornin' an' I met a little boy in the road an' I picked him up. An' as we was riding along he noticed the Bible layin' 'longside of me. He said, "Is you the man that preached down at the church last night?"

I said, "I tried it."

An' the little feller said, "Well, you couldn't hardly make it, could ya?"

To Eat or Not to Eat

Here's one that was probably more truth than fiction. I used to get a lotta kick about the ol' minister that refused to eat supper. Said if he eat supper that he couldn't preach to do no good. Well, the rest eat supper an' all went on to church.

An' after the service the little boy come aroun'

an' said, "Preacher," said, "you just might as well a eat your supper, hadn't ya?"

The Haunted House

I'll never forgit when I was a young kid at home—an' that's been a long time ago—'bout the only way there was to pass off the time then—there was no TV, no radio—was to go spend bedtime with a neighbor or them come spend bedtime with us. An' the ol' folks sat around an' talked about these ol' ghost stories back yonder, an' I used ta go to bed scared to death to hear them tell about the ol' haunted house.

They couldn't get nobody to stay in that house. Ever'time a person'd go there to spend the night, why, a ha'nt'd run 'em off. So this ol' feller, he decided he'd stay. He wadn't a-scared o' nothin'. So he taken the job, an' built him up a good fire in the fireplace an' had his supper an' got ever'thing ready. Pulled off his coat an' hat; he'd brought his paper along to read an' set down, begin to readin'. The ol' haunt walked around in front of him an' pulled the paper back, said, "Ain' nobody here tonight but you an' I, are they?"

An' the man said, "Naw, an' if you wait 'til I get my hat, there won't be nobody here but you!"

The High Ball

I'm reminded of the ol' Georgia boy that worked his way up into the major leagues; the New York Yankees was carr'in' him along on their list as a pinch hitter, or as we sometime call it, a bench warmer. They were locked horns with the Washington Senators; went into the ninth inning with the score all tied.

The manager called the ol' Georgia boy offa the bench an' told him, "Now, you go over there an' you just lose that ball. Knock it plumb outta the park."

The ol' boy went over to the plate, taken his position, an' ol' Walter Johnson—the ol' speed-ball king—he wound up an' turned that ball a-loose. It said, "Zip!"

Umpire said, "Strike!"

He turned around an' said, "Mister Ump," said, "did you see that ball?"

He said, "No."

Ol' boy said, "I didn't either; but," said, "it sounded a little high."

W. R. Jordan:
"I can amaze you with facts."

William Ralph Jordan, who was born in Cedartown in 1906, was very happy to talk to us when we interviewed him, and he showed no signs of nervousness during the recording session. He was really eager to talk, although we had to collect a lot of local and family history along with the four tales that he told us. As Mr. Jordan himself said, he likes truth better than fiction; and he seemed very intent on qualifying any unlikely elements in his stories by either declaring them to be true or saying they had to have a logical explanation.

Mr. Jordan talked in a very relaxed manner and used many hand movements. He has a pleasant voice and can convey dramatic coloring through his speech. His experience as a writer for his mill paper has given him a very organized, detailed, and literary style of story delivery.

Jordan: I was born within two hundred yards of where I started my life's work in a textile plant. A little later my people, bein' from the country, wanted to go back, an' they did. I had the pleasure and the privilege of living my early years in the same house with my grandfather and grandmother, Whitlowe by name. He was a Baptist minister of the old school; they used to say a hellfire and brimstone man. He was Irish through an' through. I mention him because he had a profound effect on my life. When the time came for me to go to school Mother wanted to come back to town to get me into a good city school, 'cause they were advanced over the country schools at that time. I had to grow up in town against my will. I went to work early in the mills; in those times work was considered such a badge of honor that didn't many boys and girls—boys particularly—finish high school.

I should put in a little bit of my hobbies, which has been centered in the outdoors, exclusively. I've never found any pleasure on the pavements of a city. My love for guns, dogs an' horses is only exceeded by my feeling for my family, my country, and my job. Later I took up

my work in Boy Scouts. I was a Scout when I was a boy. The opportunity came for me to enroll in Scouting with Goodyear down here, which has always sponsored a Scout troop. Finding that the Scouting program fitted in exactly with my hobbies, I spent some wonderful years in that work. I had the pleasure of bein' Scoutmaster for perhaps ten years; served in other capacities for twelve to fifteen years in Scouting. And also, bein' always fond of readin', I've got a real history behind me on readin'. I started writing a column for our mill paper; writing is something that I still dearly love.

I will finish by sayin' that in 1964, with our children all married and gone and the country callin', as it has all my life, we found an opportunity to go back to where we started from an' move back out here with dogs, horses an' animals of all descriptions. At night when I come in from work I stop in the driveway and listen to the owls, look at the stars an' decide what the weather'll be the next day, come in an' go to bed and have a wonderful night's sleep.

Long: I wanted to ask you how you learned your stories. Did you learn them mainly as a child, or have you just learned them all along?

Jordan: I learned them all along. From my earliest recollections. I can remember when I was four years old easily. Mother says I can remember when I was three. And my earliest recollection is about my people talkin' an' tellin' stories. And those things have just seeped into my mind, and they stay there. You were talkin' about fiction an' such as that; I can amaze you with facts.

Long: I think you could. Could you tell me what the typical person you learned the tales from was like?

Jordan: Well, they would be an old farmer, man that really loved the soil; that just enjoyed life. A man with a sense of humor. He wouldn't have to be educated; perhaps he couldn't read and write at all. But he would be the type that liked to go to church. He'd be the type that loved his family. He'd be the type that perhaps would feel just as comfortable in a pair of overalls in the church on Sunday mornin' as I would in a handsome outfit. That's something of the type of man that I've listened to all my life, respected through my younger years as a boy. The type of man that treasures these things. A very patriotic man. You know, patriotism to me is a love of the land. If you love the outdoors, then you're patriotic. A man like my old grandfather that left me so much, the heritage of the love for the things of the outdoors. The old gentleman could sit there an' stroke that long beard an' in a marvelous voice recite passages from the Bible, could talk to his children and his grandchildren. He was always full of love an' thoughtfulness for his fellow man (at the same time keepin' an Irish temper under control). It's hard to describe a person that can hand these things down to you. It seems like that they are such a strong individual, strong-minded. Yet, as I said, they might not have any education whatsoever. My old grandfather, he never went past the fourth grade in a country school. But then he had a tremendous education in life, a deep understandin'.

Long: Do you have any favorite type of story that you would rather tell?

Jordan: I tend to love stories of fact rather than fiction, although the old adventure stories always interested me very much. But in later years, especially, it's history that I really love. The history of our country, the history of our area in particular. And I've tried to get interested in history a way back to the days of Alexander, but [laughs] it didn't catch on too well.

Long: Who do you usually tell these stories to?

Jordan: The people I work with and I'm out with. Now, occasionally I'll speak to a civic club or a brotherhood or somethin' like that. I get called on occasionally to tell some of my stories at different gatherin's. Anytime I'm in a group—men or mixed or whatnot—an' we get started talkin', why, I immediately try to take over and wear my welcome out!

Long: Why do you like to tell stories to other people?

Jordan: I like to influence people. Especially in that which is clean and good. And especially the history of our area, of our people. You know it has been said that "he who forgets the past will have no future worth remembering." Now, you can change that around to make it fit several different ways. If you don't know where you started from, you don't know where you're goin'. And you won't know when you get there. And also you can use history as a yardstick to measure your progress.

Long: Do people tell the same kind of stories they used to like when you were young and sitting around the fire?

Jordan: No, that's one thing that bothers me. That has become a lost art.

Long: Why?

Jordan: We've talked about that in our circles, why it has disappeared. Today they too many other attractions. That [storytelling] came about in a time when people had to turn to each other for entertainment and company. There wasn't anything to distract them from each other, you might say. When you're isolated way back out in the country with no possibility of getting to town to movies or any kind of entertainment, an' that goes on for months an' months, well, they gonna develop some kind of entertainment within their own family circles. And now there's so much outside entertainment for people to have a part in. Well, that has taken the place of our family fireside, and actually it has hurt. You know, family ties an' bonds of friendship were formed there that lasted through the years. And it was such a place as that where parents were able to influence and guide their own children.

Long: Do you ever feel personally involved with the stories that you're telling?

Jordan: Yes, strange as it may seem, it really affects me. I spoke awhile ago about writing a column for our mill paper for so long, and I have set down and wrote out some hilarious silly thing and laughed 'til I cried while I was writing, an' then wonder why the heck I'd laugh at my own works. And I have sat down an' wrote stories an', I declare, tears would be in my eyes. I've always lived everything I've read, told, or wrote. It just affects me inside very much.

Long: One final question here. Why do you think some people tell the old stories and others don't, even though they may have all learned them when they were young children? Why do some keep on telling them to their children and other people just quit?

Jordan: Well, I haven't tried to analyze that very much, and I'm glad you asked that question. We can think about that and talk about it for a minute. As I said awhile ago, I like to influence people. At my age maybe you can say I'm an old fogy, but actually I wish people lived today more like they did back then; an' I'm not livin' in the past, believe me. I wrote a story one time about the old past an' I wound up sayin', "Well, I'm not livin' in the past. I sleep under an electric blanket [laughs] and enjoy all modern comforts, but I do wish I had a floor furnace that would give out with a puff of hickory smoke once in a

while." We have lost much in family associations. I wish our young people could know somethin' about the life that we lived together; a great togetherness, a clan sorta like I was brought up in. It was wonderful. If we went two or three month without seein' all our people we didn't know what to think. The front doors was always open, an' gosh, if you went into any of my mother's sisters' an' brothers' an' cousins' houses in the middle of the night, some old man would raise up in the bed over in the corner an' say, "Empty bed out in the other room; go in there and crawl in it."

Long: So you think these stories that were told helped to bring people together?

Jordan: Definitely. Perhaps you can see some results from that today. Because I'm sitting here an' telling you the things that are so plain in my mind that happened nearly sixty years ago. And, see, I'm sixty-four and I can remember when I was four years old. Well, I have strong links with my past, an' if you have a strong link with your past an' there's a pleasant association filled with love, you gonna have a strong link with the future an' with your Maker.

The Church Ghost and the Traveler

In the days of my childhood, for recreation and pleasure, people turned to themselves and their families, and, isolated far back in the country—distances being gauged in the amount of time it takes to travel by a two-horse wagon—it limited them to where they could go; and for that matter there was no organized activities anyhow for recreation. It all added up to the family comin' together around the fireside—a larger fireplace than this—with that roarin' fire at night. The old grandfather sitting there by the lamp reading his Bible. The daughter and her husband, children, and guests, including our family. And immediately after the supper hour, everything put away, there'd be a big circle aroun' that large fire, in that large old country room. And talk would go back to ghost stories, to the tales of olden times. Be swapped back and forth with the people. And the children listening intently. I delighted in those times. I can still see my grandfather with that heavy beard sitting there under the lamp. He leaned a little bit to one side where he could read his Bible more easily. And it all comes back to my mind right now so plainly. An' I'd like to tell one of the stories that was told. After a little bit when this talk would go on, my grandfather would lay that Bible down, lean back in his chair and stroke that beard, and he said, "Well, I'll tell one." And I've heard him tell it more than once, but it would always be new an' would always give me a shiver.

The story about a young traveler back before the Civil War, ridin' a horse down a narrow, red, rutted country road late in the afternoon of a stormy spring day. Heavy black clouds rollin', showers and heavy rain comin' in gusts. Thunder, lightnin': a very dreary time. If you could see such a scene nowadays—the countryside and the forest—as this old road presented at such a time, even that would give ya an eerie feelin'.

But this tale he would tell: the traveler, lookin' for a place to spend the night. And, in those days, a traveler on the roadside was never turned away when night fell when he came to some house. That was the common practice; all travelers were invited in and made welcome for the

night. And this man, under these very uncomfortable conditions, lookin' for a place to stay and not findin' it, he finally came down a red hillside into a little flat. And over in the right, under some trees, stood a church house, and the doors were open as they usually was with churches at that time. The rain had picked up considerably; it was rainin' very hard. It was almost dark; he just made out the picture of this church sitting there.

He rode up into the churchyard, got off his horse, and stepped just inside the church door, up the low stoop. He was standin' there inside the door holdin' his horse's reins, with the thought that he would wait there a few minutes until the rains let up and he would move on. But the rain kept gittin' harder and harder, and before he realized it, it was pitch dark. And the lightnin' begin to play even more fiercely.

He happen to be lookin' toward the pulpit in one real bright flash of lightnin'. An' in that flash of light, standin' behind the pulpit, he saw a figure there that made his blood run cold. A woman stood there in a long white gown, her black hair in two braids down across her breasts. Her face looked like perhaps it was molded out of dough. Her black eyes was wide, staring and dead-looking. Standin' there with her hands on the pulpit, without moving. He caught that much in that one short space of a flash of lightnin'. It so shook him, so stunned him that he couldn't take his eyes away from that face. And in the darkness that followed that flash, he stood there hardly breathin'.

Another flash followed in a few minutes, and the woman had turned away from that to one side but was lookin' towards him. He became even more immovable; he was absolutely frozen

Letcher County, Kentucky, 1980. Tom Rankin.

in his tracks. He kept busy watchin'. He tried to turn his head from it. He wanted to leave, but he just couldn't make himself go; his will power was completely lost. And each flash of lightnin' would show that the woman had made another move. She had stepped around the pulpit, had started up the aisle directly towards him. And as she came nearer an' nearer, each flash of lightnin' showed her a few feet closer an' a few feet closer. Each flash of lightnin' revealin' that deadly, deadly, doughy look an' those huge black eyes, outlinin' that face just like what we used to call a dough face, actually made out of dough [a home-made mask worn by Christmas revelers known as fantastics or serenaders]. And he noticed that the gown looked molded, soiled-like, yet it wadn't dirty as if it'd been drug in the dirt. And each step braingin' her closer to him. And just as he thought that she would touch him, as she approached she raised her hand like this [gestures].

And as he reached the point of absolute state of shock, perhaps dying from fear, someone stepped up in the door beside him from the outside, a man with a lantern in his hand. An' another man followed behind him. And this feller with the lantern walked over in front of him to this awful ghostly figure, took her by the arm, and they started out. The other feller was talking to this traveler and explained what had happened. This young woman, a young wife and mother, had lost her baby a few weeks previously—died at birth. It was buried in the churchyard right up behind the church there. The mother was in a state of shock, deranged mentally and suffering intently. She would slip away from the house when she had the chance and come back to this church house where they'd had the funeral for her baby and where it

was buried. And it so happened that at this particular time when the traveler came by, she was there. And instead of seein' a ghost, he actually saw this young wife and mother that was in such a state.

Fiddler's Hollow

This may sound odd, but I take it to be a true ghost story, because it's been repeated so often for the truth. Nearby here is an area called Fiddler's Holler, which is really a small cove. And the people who live there tell this story. It's supposedly the way that it got its name. And I can't say this for fact, but they is an eerie, spooky feelin' about the place; especially if one is a little bit superstitious he'll have the chills run up an' down his back when he's in there, at night anyhow.

But I was told the way Fiddler's Holler got its name. At the far end of this place—an' it's about two or three miles long—at a certain spot, preferably at midnight on a partly cloudy, warm-like night with the wind out of the south, you can hear music, the wild strains of a violin playin' old Gypsy airs of the long ago, mixed in with the dancin' tunes of the mountaineers. It's somethin' to really stir your imagination, and the people swear by it.

The Goose and the Grave

This ghost story dates back somewhere into another century long gone by. And it turned out to be an absolutely true ghost story. It is told that on an old road runnin' by a country churchyard—which incidentally is one of the most eerie places that you'll find in the South—a man was walkin' along through the darkness of the night on his way home. An', passin' the graveyard, he was filled with fear and superstition an' feelin' a little uneasy, as [laugh] people would be.

And lookin' up across the graveyard as he passed it, he saw somethin' white flashin' up like this [gestures with hand in an up-and-down motion]. It would show up just above the ground an' then drop back, up above the ground and then drop back. He stopped, because he couldn't very well move himself; he froze for the moment. But he kept watchin' that white thing, whatever it was, and it would keep showin' up. It would come above the ground a little bit, an' then drop back out of sight. He went on when he got his feet movin'; he left there right rapidly.

But he found an explanation for it the next day. There had been a grave dug that day, before this happened that night, up there in the old graveyard. And during the afternoon or aroun' sundown a large white goose had wandered into this grave, and it was tryin' to get out. And it had been close enough to the road to give him a good view of this goose when it would almost fly out of the open grave an' then drop back. And the sight that he saw there was this white goose had got trapped in that open grave, and was enough to start a real ghost story. But actually had a logical endin'.

The Faithful Guard Dog

This, to me, could have been true. It's a story about a dog. It's been handed down from some-where in the many, many years ago. A man whose wife died was left alone with a small child. He was a hunter and trapper, part-time farmer; made his livin' like that. He had a large dog that was supposed to been crossed with a wolf and some domestic-type dog. And it was a very brutal-lookin' thing. People who lived in the neighborhood—and the neighborhood at that time was several miles wide; he was a long ways from the nearest house—who knew the dog, and knew him and his little son, they were always warnin' him about that dog. They was afraid that dog was gonna turn on that child, or even turn on him; or perhaps kill one of the neighbors. But he held on to that dog. He thought so much of it, an' had a lot of confidence in it. The dog was absolutely devoted to this four-year-old boy. And the man had to be gone from home occasionally, sometimes overnight or all day; he'd be runnin' the trap lines or workin' in the field and such as that. So he left that dog with this boy as a guard.

And it so happened that one afternoon late when he came in, he pushed the door open an' there was blood all over the floor. His little boy was on the bed; there was blood on him. He looked around for his dog, and there was blood on that dog. He jumped to conclusions; he couldn't think of anything except that the dog had turned on his little boy, had done what he'd been warned that it would do. He went wild over it with grief and anger. He grabbed up his ax an' split this dog's head open. He killed that dog right there in the house. When he turned to his little son, then the boy woke up. He wadn't hurt.

He got to lookin' around to see what had happened. And, pushed back behind the door an' out of sight in a dark recess, he found the body of a wolf. This wolf had got into the house, and his wolf dog had killed it to protect his son. He, in turn, overcome with shock and grief an' not bein' able to think straight, had grabbed up his ax and killed the dog that saved his son.

That's told for true; possibly it is. There's so many things happened back in those days that, well, they's so foreign to us today that we would think that they wouldn't be so. But they's things that to us are unbelievable now that are actually real and did happen back then.

CHAPTER TWO

A Joke Session by Deer Hunters in Middle Georgia

Nan Gilmer Long

Fall 1967

This chapter approaches a storytelling session in its natural context. What began as an appointment for a more formal interview fortunately turned into a relaxed exchange, as deer-hunting friends of the initial subject dropped by his home to visit. All the stories recorded are presented here, and in their original sequence, so the reader can see the interaction of the three participants and the way one narrative leads into the next as the session takes on a life of its own. Conversational interludes were not recorded; however, these might have provided clues as to what triggered the topics of some tales.

The jests are the sort typical of a gathering of hunters: tall tales and masculine-oriented bawdy humor for the most part. A number have hunting or fishing settings, and the rural background of the tellers is reflected in the farm settings of many. Of the three participants, Joel Crane died in 1986; his brother-in-law and son-in-law live in the Jackson area of Butts County.

Indian Springs, Georgia, is in Butts County, about fifty miles southeast of Atlanta. Joel Crane,

sixty-two, is the assistant superintendent of Indian Springs State Park, the oldest state park in the United States. "Mr. Joel" has lived in Butts County all his life, completing only five years of formal education. His father caught him skipping school and threatened to make him plow the fields if he didn't return; Mr. Joel decided to plow the fields.

Mr. Joel is a long-time friend of my husband, Mac, and felt more at ease telling the jokes to him; this is the reason his name is on the transcript. Another explanation that must be made is the reference to "Pep" or "Pep'ton." What is now known as East Jackson was once known as Pepperton because of the location of Pepperton Textile Mills (replaced by Avondale Mills in 1962).

The day we had agreed to record was the first day of deer season, and Mr. Joel's home was soon filled with men. They were fascinated with my task, however, and eager to help. Woodrow Wilson Turner stole the show; he is Mr. Joel's forty-four-year-old brother-in-law. He was also raised in Butts County but is now a construction foreman in Macon. His formal schooling ended after the seventh grade. Chuck Fitzgerald, about thirty, is Mr. Joel's son-in-law and a truck driver. He contributed the tall tale about the "tarnado." Mr. Joel and Woodrow told most of the jokes and let the other thirteen listen—and laugh!

A Monkey Hunt

Joel Crane

Mac, did I ever tell you about findin' the ol' monkey up in the holla tree?

Mac Long: I don't think so.

Crane: I started out huntin' one mornin' out there below Pep'ton cemetery, at that ol' holla willow tree down there. I'd caught a lotta possums, squirrels out of it. It 'as a foggy mornin', the sun peepin' through o'er the horizon over there a little bit. I climbed up in there an' looked down in the holla. There 'as the prettiest little hairy-faced monkey down 'ere I ever saw.

I eased back down the tree an' got my shotgun, tied it across my back, go back up in the tree, an' got ever'thing ready, an' I 'as gonna shoot that little ol' monkey. I looked in at 'im again, an' I says, "Naw, he's too pretty to shoot." I cut me a forked stick an' I 'as gonna catch this little monkey, capture 'im alive. I jugged down in this tree, an' y'know what I saw in the tree?

Long: What?

Crane: Saw m'self down 'ere in some water! Hadn't had a shave in 'bout a week. The water sloshed all up in m' face. I jes' come on down, said to myself, "You monkey, you; go on home."

A Powerful Tornado

Chuck Fitzgerald

Bunch of us 'as settin' around one night talkin' 'bout tarnados, an' dis ol' man said the worse un he ever seen was out in Bloomfield, south o' Macon. Said he 'as settin' there watchin' one night, an' the wind got up an' the tarnado started t' gettin' worse—rougher an' rougher—an' said he looked out across there, an' said damn tub flyin' in the air out across there. An' said, "You know, that tub was movin' s' fast that lightnin' struck at it three times an' never did hit it!"

A Chilly Corpse?

Woodrow Turner

This ol' fella he was goin' bird huntin'. He got out in the graveyard, an' had a open grave dug. Covey of quail flew up an' he shot, an' it kicked him over in the grave an' knocked him cold.

This night, though, a drunk man was comin' through there—he was really loaded. He heard somebody hollerin' [drawn out], "It's cold down here. It's cold down here."

That ol' drunk man he got on his knees an' looked over in 'ere an' he says, "Hell, well no wonder; you done kicked all the dirt off of you!"

Is It Out?

Woodrow Turner

This ol' drunk, he was standin' on the corner an' had his arms a-wrapped around the lightpost. He was jes' hangin' up there, y'know, jes' drunk as a cock-robin. Ol' officer come by.

He says, "Hey, officer," he says, "is my 'goober' hangin' out?"

He looked at him an' he says, "Naw, your goober ain't hangin' out."

He says, "Well, by God, it oughta be, 'cause I'm a-peein'!"

An Ill Wind
Joel Crane

Y'all talk about bein' in hard luck; y'all don't know what hard luck is. Back durin' the 'pression me an' my wife we got stranded out in the desert, got outta food an' water; had jes' a little bit of meal left. An' I tol' her, "We jes' got to have some bread."

Said, "Well, we ain't got no water to make it up with."

I said, "Honey," I said, "sit down an' pee in that meal an' make it up, an' cook that bread anyhow."

You know, we in such hard luck that she got down an' she went to pee an' she farted, an' she blowed all our meal away!

Bitter Luck
Woodrow Turner

You talkin' 'bout hard luck? Hell, that ain't no hard luck atall. Well, me an' my wife had two kids; drought done got my corn, boll weevils done got my cotton, an' we didn't have [but] jes' a few cold biscuits in the house. An' I had me a beehive out there.

I tol' my wife, I said, "Well, I'll go out there an' rob that beehive, an' we can have some honey an' bread for breakfast." Kids were about to starve to death. I went out there to rob that beehive, an' ol' honeybee done took up with a tumbleturd' [dung beetle] and honey tasted like shit!

Fishy Fog
Joel Crane

You know 'bout the best luck I ever had fishin'? Early one real foggy mornin' I got up an' went down to the lake. Got down 'ere an' I set down on a log an' I fished an' I fished an' I fished, an' just had a whole string of nice catfish. After 'while the fog moved on northward a little, an' I seen I was three hundred yards from the lake!

Yellow Chalk
Joel Crane

Way back yonder, about 1912, 1913, I 'as goin' to school down here at Cedar Rock. Had this old maid fer a teacher, Miss Lois Biles. I wanted to be excused one day, an' I kept poppin' m' fingers and holding up my hand. She wouldn't let me go, an' d'rectly she come back there and got me an' take me up 'ere to the blackboard an' drawed a circle, put a dot in the middle of it an' told me to put my nose on it an' stand there 'til she tol' me t' move.

Well, I stood there all right enough; I even stood there 'til my kidneys moved! I jes' laid that little two inches over in that chalk trough an' it jes' run out an' down to the other end of the chalk trough. She called me o'er there an' tol' me to go on back an' sit down an' behave myself.

Big Sandy, Benton County, Tennessee, 1983. Tom Rankin.

A Precocious Gambler
Woodrow Turner

Back in about 1939, when I was goin' to school, there was this little ol' freckle-face boy in the schoolroom wid us 'at jes' bet all the time; an' they couldn't stop him from bettin'. So his ol' man he called the teacher up, see if she could help him stop him. An' she tol' him, "All right," said she'd see if she couldn't fix him up that evenin'.

So that evenin' that little ol' boy had to stay in; an' he bet the teacher, told her, "Teacher," said, "I'll jes' bet you five dollars that you've got red hairs around your tail." So she showed him, an' little ol' boy he lost his bet an' paid his five dollars, started on home.

Teacher she got on the telephone an' called the ol' man an' said, "Well," said, "I think we got your son broke up from bettin'." Said, "He just lost his first bet"; said, "I don't believe he'll bet no more."

Said, "What did ya bet?"

Said, "Well, he bet me five dollars I had red hairs around my tail, an'," said, "I showed him I didn't."

Said, "Why, that little son-of-a-bitch!" Said, "He bet me twenty-five dollars he's gonna see the teacher's tail 'fo' dark!"

In the Dark
Joel Crane

These two little ol' niggers goin' down the road here got talkin' 'bout which one's the blackest. One of 'em tol' the other one, says, "You ain't black, nigger." Says, "I so black that I cain't even make a shadow at night when I walk."

Say, "Aw, nigger," say, "you ain't black atall." Say, "I so black 'at I went to the hospital last week to have my hemorrhoids cut out"; said, "you know, they couldn't find my hemorrhoids." Said, "They had to get some flour and sprinkle all over my ass, make me fart t' find my hemorrhoids."

Knew It Tasted Funny
Woodrow Turner

This here ol' farmer, y'know, he lived out dere in the country, an' had a pumpkin patch out there. This ol' travelin' salesman come through there one day, an' his bowels had to move; an' he hadn't never been used to goin' out in the woods. He jes' went out dere t' one o' these fine pumpkins, y'know, an' he cut the top out of it an' he set down on it an' had his bowel movement an' he put the top back on it.

'Bout two weeks later, he's comin' through there an' he say, "You know," he says, "it's a damn shame to ruin that man's fine pumpkin like that." Says, "I'm gonna stop there an' pay 'im fer it." He went up 'ere an' he rung the doorbell, an' he says, "That yo' pumpkin patch down 'ere?"

He say, "Yeah."

He said, "Well, I wanna pay you for a pumpkin." Said, "I 'as comin' through here two weeks ago"; said, "my bowels had to move, an'," said, "I ruint that pumpkin." Said, "I had to use it."

That ol' farmer, he didn' say a damn word. He went o'er dere to that ol'-timey telephone an' he rung it, an' said, "Hello, Zeke?" He said, "This is Zip." Said, "That *was* shit in that pumpkin!"

Not So Dear

Joel Crane

This ol' deer hunter out of Atlanta come out here in the country the other day, an' asked this farmer if he could go out there an' hunt a little while. He tol' 'im, "Yeah, go ahead." So he went on down there an' d'rectly the town man shot down there, an' come back up t' the house.

Farmer says, "Well, did ya get 'im?"

Says, "Yeah," says, "I got somepin"; says, "dunno what it is."

Says, "Well, what it look like?"

Says, "Well, it's hairy, an' got the hardest head an' the stinkinest ass o' anything I ever saw or smelt in my life."

Said, "Lawd o' mercy," says, "you done shot my wife!"

What a Deal

Woodrow Turner

Way back yonder, they had these ol'-timey slop jars, y'know, to set under your bed. This ol' Lipton Tea salesman, he was kinda harelipped. He goin' around tryin' to sell 'em; he'd come up to a woman, say [imitating harelipped speech], "Lady, would you like to buy a pack of Lipton Tea? With every pack of Lipton Tea you buy, you get absolutely free one slop jar without any extree cost or charge."

She said, "Well, yeah," says, "I sure would." Said, "What if I was to buy two packs of Lipton Tea?"

"Lady, if you was to buy two packs of Lipton Tea you would get absolutely free, without no extree charge, two slop jars."

Said, "What if I was to buy three packs of Lipton Tea?"

"Lady, if you was to buy three packs of Lipton Tea, you would, without no extree charge or cost, get three slop jars."

She said, "Well, that sounds too good to be true." Said, "What if I was to buy a couple o' cases of Lipton Tea?"

He said, "Lady, I don't know Mr. Lipton personally, but I do believe if you bought three cases, without no extree cost or charge he would absolutely build you one shithouse."

An Unprofitable Year

Woodrow Turner

Way back yonder when I was farmin', had a real hard year, y'know. I had cotton an' corn an' peaches; drought done got my corn, boll weevils done eat up all my cotton, but I had a pretty good peach crop. So I was goin' 'round sellin' my peaches, an' I knocked at this woman's door. She come to the door an' cracked the door, an' I said, "Lady, would you like to buy some peaches?"

She opened the door a little further an' opened her bathrobe an' stuck them pretty legs out there, an' she said, "Well, fella, I haven't got any money"; said, "I sure would like to have some o' them peaches, though." Said, "Tell you what I'll do. I'll trade you a little 'doo-lolly' for 'em."

I started jes' cryin', jes' busted out cryin' all over. She said, "Well, whatcha cryin' about?"

I said, "Goddamn!" Said, "Drought's done got my corn, boll weevils done got my cotton, an' here I am fixin' to get frigged out o' my peaches!"

Too Old for Bugaloo

Joel Crane

Mac, you remember ol' man Hilley, used to drive that gray horse, peddle milk an' butter up 'ere at Pep?

Mac Long: No, I don't think so.

Crane: Anyway, he's my uncle, an' he peddled milk an' butter all the time, an' he had fresh peanuts when they come in. He stopped at this lady's house; she got her milk an' butter, an' he said, "Wouldn't you like to have some peanuts today?"

"Yessir, I would, but I ain't got no money." An' at that time they issued a coupon book up there at Pep'ton; you spent it at Pep'ton store an' nowhere else. We called it "bugaloo." She tol' him, said, "I haven't got any more money, Mr. Hilley; but," said, "I'd give you some boogaloo for some peanuts."

He said, "Come up here, mule! Click-click-click [calling mule]. I'm too old a man fer that kinda foolishness!"

CHAPTER THREE

Two West Tennessee Family Legends across Three Generations

Nancy Phillips

Spring 1969

The examination of continuity and change in a tradition as it is passed from generation to generation would seem to be at the heart of folklore research, but few such studies have been done, perhaps because the opportunity to document more than two generations of tradition-bearers within a family seldom presents itself. In this chapter we have a rare exception. The student collector discovered that her husband's family had maintained two experience-generated legends for three and four generations in the male line and that representatives of three generations were still available from whom to record them. We might speculate that the closer the teller is to the events narrated, the more specific details would be included; this supposition is confirmed here. Yet the grandfather's version of the second tale is disjointed in comparison with his son's, possibly because of his age and deteriorating health.

This chapter opens a window onto generational folklore variation and offers revelations about the legend-making process. "The Ghost Story" began as a memorate with the grandfather but was suffi-ciently gripping to capture the imagination of two successive generations for whom it has become ensconced as a supernatural legend. The son and grandson apparently converted the original narrator's contemplated but not consummated shooting of the ghost into more dramatic action. What was it the grandfather and his friend actually saw? We shall never know for certain. The episodic "Civil War Story" is clearly based on historical fact, again sufficiently dramatic and emblematic of those trying times to be carried on by the grandfather (who died in 1970) from his father's narration and maintained by the next two generations. Nor is it likely that either legend will stop there. The collector and her husband have two sons, and it would be surprising if they could not provide their own versions, representing yet another generation of family folklore.

Finger, a quiet, rural community in southwest Tennessee, has lost population steadily since World War II, when the young men discovered the world beyond it. At the peak of its history,

Finger had five or six hundred steady inhabitants. The one-street town had a train depot, a blacksmith shop, two service stations, a garage, a post office, a bank, two dry-goods stores, two grocery stores, and a cotton gin.

Today, the little town has a population of about one hundred people, most of them at least sixty years of age. Although the depot still stands, the trains that pass through on the switch track have not stopped there for many years. Many of the stores are still there, but only a few are in business. Three tiny grocery stores are open, and two service stations (each with one pump) sell gas and oil, but nothing else. There is a bank, but its main function is the cashing of welfare checks. There is an absence of young people and children in the town. Among the old people much of the lore they learned from their parents and grandparents lives even today.

Informants for these stories are three generations of the Phillips family: William Thomas Phillips of Finger; his son, Jesse Thomas Phillips of Marietta, Georgia; and his son, Robert Thomas Phillips of Decatur, Georgia.

William, who is eighty, completed four grades of school in Milledgeville, Tennessee. For fifty-one years he lived in Leapwood, Tennessee, on a one-hundred-acre farm, cultivating it and driving a school bus. "Pop" now lives in Finger, which is about fifteen miles north of Leapwood.

Jesse received a high school education in McNairy County, Tennessee. He worked as a mechanic and a mail carrier before he left Tennessee at twenty-six. As an installer for Western Electric Company in 1938, he traveled over much of the South before settling in Atlanta. From 1960 to 1963, he was the Georgia representative of the Communications Workers of America to the AFL-CIO. Now, at fifty-six, he is an associate en-

gineer in Western Electric's Engineering Division.

Robert ("Tommy") Phillips, my husband and a graduate student at Georgia State University, was born in Meridian, Mississippi, but has lived in Atlanta for twenty-one of his twenty-three years. An accountant, he works for Canners for Coca-Cola Bottlers in Atlanta. Robert spent many summers on his grandfather's Tennessee farm learning stories, legends and history.

The family stories collected for this project have been passed down from father to son since as long ago as the Civil War. William Phillips delivered his narratives with a great deal of detail and many more direct quotations than his son or grandson did. He did not seem to have a very specific chronological organization for the Civil War story. Evidently, he was less self-conscious than his son and grandson about the recording of his stories, as his tone was more conversational and he did not omit choice bits of profanity.

Jesse Phillips had the stories well organized in his mind and told them with no hesitation. His quotations were less numerous, shorter, and cleaned up for presentation. He did not mind admitting that his grandfather had been a Yankee soldier, as his father did.

Robert Phillips had the stories condensed to capsule length. He did not know the place-names or the names of the characters, nor did he include any quotations. He did, however, interpret the actions by explaining how the actor must have felt in the situation.

The most outstanding discrepancy in the three versions of the ghost story is the insistence of the participant that he did not shoot and the insistence of the son and grandson that he did shoot, once or twice. William is the only one of the three who put any religious significance to the occurrence. As far as the Civil War story is concerned, the greatest inconsistency is one of length. The version collected from Robert left out almost half the action described by the other two informants.

The Ghost Story
William T. Phillips
(FIRST GENERATION)

I never will forget that. Me and my buddy run together, Elgin Johnson. And we dressed just alike, and I played the fiddle and he picked a mandolin. An' he come by one evenin' and said, "Let's go over to Mr. Hardin's and play some music."

An' I said, "Oh, I can't go, I done turned my horse out in the pasture."

An' he said, "That's no excuse"; said, "old Danus'll hold us both."

I said, "Well, all right." So I went and got my fiddle and he had his mandolin. An' I got up in the saddle with him. We rode, then, one man with his right foot in the stirrup and the other'n left foot and both stayed in the saddle together, ye see.

I tol' him that there 'as a old man so mean one time, Sol Thomas, they claimed if you called for him just any shape you called for 'im, why, he'd come. So he says, "I don't believe it."

So we went on up to the corner of the graveyard, and he stopped his horse and called for Sol Thomas to come with his body as long as a rail and head on him like a bulldog with his tail querled over his back. An' we set there a minute or two and he said, "Hell, he ain't a-comin'; let's go."

An' I said, "Well, you got the reins."

So we went on up to Mr. Hardin's and we played music 'til 'bout eleven. An' I'd forgot all about it. And we had to come through a little lane to the graveyard like we went in. An' we got up there, why, I seen somethin' comin' down from this old man's grave, but I wouldn't say nothin'. I just waited to see what he'd say. So when it got up in front of his horse, about, I guess, five or six steps, he said, "Look a-yonder; hell, what is that?"

An' I said, "I don't know what that is." An' it came right on up beside of us and we turned the curve, why, it just turned with us. And we got up there in the graveyard; why, I just retched around and got the reins and pulled the horse back and stopped. An' I says, "I'm gonna shoot that thing."

An' he said, "No you won't, neither"; said, "George Sealey'll shoot us. We got to pass his house." An' his old dog was barkin'. Said, "He'd shoot us just as shore as the world if you shoot that ol' pistol."

Well, we started on and we went down the hill from the graveyard, and we had to cross a stream of water, just a small stream. And the horse just splattered the water and went on across. An' I 'as a-watching; 'twas right 'side o' the horse, and it just jumped the water, looked like. And when he got across, why, I just retched around and got the reins and stopped him again. An' I said, "I'm a-gonna shoot that thing."

An' he said, "You're not t' shoot it neither"; said, "George Sealey'd shoot us just shore as you do." An' his old dog came down the hill barkin' at us. An' he said, "Let's get away from here."

So I never shot at it. We went off and left it; well, it follered us part of the way to the corner of the garden. I don't know what it was and never knowed since, but I reckon it was the Al-mighty showin' him what He could do. I've al-ways been ashamed of it.

Robert Phillips: What did it look like?

William: Well, it 'as just like he called for. It looked like a dog, only its body was as long as a rail and its tail was querled over its back and it had a head on it like a bulldog, just like he called for it. It's the truth, Tommy, if I ever told it!

Robert: Whew! Man, I tell you!

Jesse T. Phillips
(SECOND GENERATION)

Well, my dad and his buddy had been to a dance one night and they were comin' through this graveyard. An' the story had been told that when you came through the graveyard you could hol-ler and call an old man that [had] lived in the neighborhood and had died a few years before and ask for him to appear in whatever form you wanted him to appear in, and that he did. So, they stopped in the graveyard that night and his buddy said, "Let's call for this old man to come with a body long as a fence rail, a head on him like a bulldog and tail curled over his back."

They stood there on their horse—they were riding double on a horse—and they stood there and waited for a while. An' they decided they wadn't going to see anything, an' they started ridin' on. An' my father looked down at the side of the horse and there was somethin' trottin' along beside of the horse. An' he didn't say any-thing for a few minutes; and he said, "Elgin," he says, "you see what I see?"

He said, "Yeah, I been watching it five minutes."

An' he says, "Stop and let me down and I'll see

what it is." An' when they stopped, it stopped and set down like a dog, but he said it wadn't as long as a fence rail.

So Elgin said, "You better not get down. If you do, I'll run off and leave ye." An' he wouldn't let him get down and examine it. So they rode on and it started trottin' along beside of 'em.

An' my father had an old pistol in his pocket, and he tol' Elgin to hold his mare and says, "I'll see what that thing is." So he shot point-blank right straight down at it and it never even moved. So they rode down to the branch and crossed the branch and it trotted right along be-side of 'em. And this dog commenced running out a-barkin' off up ahead of 'em. An' they stopped again, and when they stopped that time it trotted off, trotted off through the woods like a normal dog would have done. But he said he didn't have any idea what it was. But everybody that always tried to pull that stunt always seen somethin'; wadn't ever no explanation of what it was.

Robert T. Phillips
(THIRD GENERATION)

Well, this happened to my grandfather; and, well, he lives right now in Finger, Tennessee. An' at the time this happened he was living in Mil-ledgeville, Tennessee, which is right on the banks of the Tennessee River. An' the way my fa-ther told it to me was that my grandfather and a friend of his were goin' to a square dance one night. And they were on horseback and they were going down this deserted road, and they were gonna take a shortcut through this ceme-tery. An' this particular cemetery was said to be haunted by an old fellow who [had] lived down the road from the cemetery. And I don't know how he died, but the story goes that if you go there to the cemetery at night and shout and call the man's name he will appear in any form that you ask him to appear as.

Well, my grandfather and his friend were going off down the road and they cut through the cemetery. An' my grandfather's friend suggested they stop there and call for this fellow. An' it seemed like a good idea at the time, and so the guy that was with him—with my grandfather— shouted out for him and he asked him to appear as some kind of animal with a body as long as a fence rail and a head like a bulldog and his tail flopped over his back. An' my grandfather is supposed to have waited there with him, and they waited for a little while.

So nothing happened, and so they decided to go on to the dance. And they were riding down the road and my grandfather looked down. An' there was this dog, or something that appeared to be a dog, following along beside the guy's horse who was riding in front of him; and he didn't say anything. An' they rode for a few minutes, and then my grandfather asked the fellow if he saw it and the guy told him yeah, he'd been watching it for a good long while, and they had a discussion over what it was.

An' they decided to stop and see what, you know, what it would do. So when they stopped, the animal stopped itself. An' they rode on for a little piece further and stopped again, and it also stopped. So they decided to find out what it was. An' my grandfather always carried a pistol with him—and he's a good shot with a rifle even now; he's eighty years old and he can outshoot me with a rifle, so it was obvious that he could hit what he was aimin' at. An' my grandfather told

him he was going to shoot it and see what happened. And, well, he pulled out his pistol and cut down on it, and the thing didn't even move. And he shot it again, I think he did, I think he shot twice; but anyway, when he did shoot, nothing happened.

An' then my grandfather told him he was gonna get down and see what it was. An' the guy told him if he got down he would run off and leave him. An' so they decided to ride on to the dance just to see if the thing would follow them. Well, they rode on 'til they approached a house. And there was a dog at this house, an' it started barking at 'em. And the closer they got to the house the further behind the animal that was with them got. An' they said it looked just like what the guy called for the fellow to be. An' so you can make what you want to out of it.

The Civil War Story
William T. Phillips
(FIRST GENERATION)

I'll not tell what side he 'as on, now. That'll not do . . . set so well. [A reference to his father's having joined the Union army.]

Well, he got captured, 'course. They [Confederate troops] captured him, him and a man by the name of Brad Polk—he 'as a humpbacked man. They stripped all his clothes off—I mean his uniform—and put on him some old clothes, throwed 'im across a old mule, no saddle ner no blanket. An' they'd go from one, transfer from one place to another, you know. An' so he'd have to ride that old mule. And they tied his legs under the mule's belly, keep him from getting off; just like a saddle girth, you know. An', 'course it just wore 'im out, nearly. An' it went on fer several days and they . . . uh, I guess I want to leave that off; but no, I'll go ahead and tell it, too.

They rode up to a place one day and . . . but, before that, they had him and Polk tied to a stump close to a corn pile in the edge of a old field. And a neighbor, a friend of his that 'as on the other side and had helped to capture 'im, why, he come to 'im and told him one morning, says, "They're gonna kill you in the mornin' at the sound of the bugle."

He said, "Well, I figgered they's doin' something"; says, "they're digging a hole out yonder."

An' he said, "They're digging a hole to bury both of you." Says, "I'm sorry, Bill, but," says, "it's just one of those things." An' that was Philip Odom. An' he asked Philip to untie 'im and let him walk around a little. And he says, "I can't do that," says, "it's agin the rules."

Went on, and the old captain at the little table writing—they had a folding table, you know, they carried along with 'em. So he [Odom] said, "Now, I can't let you up."

He said, "Well, go ask him again."

An' said he [the captain] looked up over his specs, he said, "Well, yes, if you don't let 'im get away"; but says, "you better not let him get away."

There's a corn pile piled up where they had been feeding the horses. An' he said, "I just want to walk around this corn pile." He 'as barefooted; and he walked around the corn pile three, four times getting his legs limbered up, and he'd get a little further from the corn pile every time.

An' Philip Odom said, "Now Bill, I see what you're gonna do. I don't wanna kill you." He said to him, "Come back now, you're fur enough." An' he said that he looked straight at him, and he

didn't have his gun up like he 'as gonna shoot him, and he kicked his gun out of his hand. An' when he done that he broke to run right down through a old field where they 'as feedin' the horses.

An' he said he guessed there were fifty shots fired at 'im or maybe more; he had no idea. But he said them that was down in the edge of the woods feedin' the horses 'as gettin' behind trees [laughter]. They never teched 'im. An' he said he run and he run and he run 'til he give out. And he run down a big gulley, an' he seen a sinkhole in that gulley like a fox den or somethin' or other and he run into that. An' it 'as sandy, an' said he run in so deep he like to have not got out. Seemed like he could hear the horses' feet runnin' over the ground, you know; come to find out it 'as his heart beatin', he 'as scared so bad! An' so he stayed in there 'til he knowed it was night and he come out, looked at the stars to see which-a-way to go; but he didn't know which-a-way to go, he said, hardly either. But he rambled around and finally got with his regiment an' got away that-a-way.

But they hung 'im over there at Old Harrican the other side of Milledgeville, and he said he went around and around and around and around. And when they let him down, why, he couldn't talk. An' he got up on his hands and knees and they asked him where his regiment was, and he said he told 'em the truth and they didn't believe it. An' he said one of 'em said, "Make him talk or kill 'im." An' one of 'em hit 'im between the shoulders with the butt of the gun, and so he said he made up a lie and told 'em and they believed that.

Well, they came on down across the middle of the creek down there; and they 'as gonna kill old man Pitts. There wadn't no bridge there and he said the water was pretty deep, run up on his side. An' said he thought he'd holler and let old man Pitts wake up where he could run off. An' he did, and said the old captain said if he hollered ary another time, said, "Shoot 'im." He said he never hollered any more. Well, they came on up there then to Gran Smith's old place. An', 'course, you don't know where it is, but I do; and they got his daddy out and he fought 'em to the very last, but they killed 'im. They had a time that day. Well, he got away and got back to his regiment, finally.

Well, while he 'as at the corn pile he said there 'as two of the prettiest girls he nearly ever seen come there lookin' at him and Brad Polk. And said it came a rain that night, and Brad Polk was so hump-shouldered an' the mud got so soft it dug out a hole and it'd splash, you know, when he'd go back. They had their arms tied together an' he said that when one would raise, the other'n have to raise up. So he said he never did know what became of Polk, he reckoned they killed him. But them girls came there.

An' so he said they stopped at a woman's house; he said he didn't know where, who the woman was. An' he said there 'as a old lady settin' up in the corner and two cats in the other corner. An' they stopped and lit their pipes; and the regiment went on, an' they got a mile or two ahead. Why, them girls come to the door and commenced lookin' at one another and laughing. An' he said, "You ladies look like you've seen me before."

Says, "I think we have." Said, "We seen you tied at the corn pile at a certain place." Says, "I thought they 'as gonna kill you."

An' he said that made him mad. And he looked around at that old lady and said, "You got any cats and dogs in here that you don't want burnt?"

She said, "Lord-a-mercy, you ain't gonna burn my house?"

Said he just retched and got the fire shovel and run it in the fireplace and got a big shovel of coals, and just strowed it all over the beds. An' they waited there until it went to blazin'. An' said they got on their horses and started on to catch the regiment.

An' when they got I forget how fur, he said the old captain sent some of them back to see what that smoke was doin'. An' they met 'em, asked 'em what they 'as doin' back there. An' he said, "Well, I ain't gonna tell you a lie"; said, "I set the house afire. There's two girls that made fun of me when I 'as captured." An' said, "I just got mad and set the old lady's house afire."

An' said he [the captain] dropped his head down and he was settin' at his little table and he said, "Well, I don't know as I give a goddamn"; says, "I'm gonna burn the whole place up in the morning, anyhow."

Now, that's the way they done back in the time of the Civil War; they called it a Civil War and it 'as the worst one there ever has been. Burned houses, and killed folks, and robbed and take your horses away from you.

Robert Phillips: Have you got any idea how come it was that he got captured?

William: Ah, he'd told, Tommy, but I forgot, it's been so long. He told me all about it. But he was on Crawley's Ridge. He 'as a cavalry man, you know. He rode on horses; they all went together then, most of 'em did, and he was on Crawley's Ridge with 'em when the war ended in Shiloh.

Willie Schaffer and Bill Pipin, Hilton, Virginia. Kenneth Murray.

Jesse T. Phillips
(SECOND GENERATION)

Well, my grandfather was captured twice. He was raised in west Tennessee and he went to middle Tennessee to enlist with the federal forces at Pulaski, Tennessee, in Giles County. I never did understand why he went so far to enlist, because most of his career was around the community where he was raised.

But he was captured one time by the Confederates and they were taking him to the Confederate company to question him, and they was trying to get him to tell where his company was, where they were camped. And he told 'em right, right off the bat, where they were, but they didn't believe it. So, he made up a lie and told 'em. So they tied him on a little mule—no bridle, no saddle, no nothing—tied his legs under its stomach and turned him loose. So, he rambled around there—that mule wandered and wandered— until he finally found somebody that would take him loose and get 'im off it. An' he finally got back to his company.

An' later on he was captured again there close by his boyhood community, and they were carrying him to be what we call today interrogated, I guess. And they rode across a creek that had . . . in those days they didn't have bridges much, they had to what they call ford 'em. So they rode down in this branch; and he had heard the captain talking about an old fellow that lived on that road and they were gonna take him out and kill 'im, because they thought he was a spy. So when they rode down in that branch, my grandfather hollered right loud, yelled hoping this old feller—which was a friend of his—would hear him. And he did hear him and went out the back

door and ran. So they asked him why did he holler? He said that cold water ran in his boots when they went across that branch, and it 'as cold. So they stopped at this house and this feller's wife, the old lady, was there and they questioned her and tried to get her to tell 'em where he was. But he'd run off, and they didn't do nothing at that particular time.

They carried him on to what is now known as the community of Old Harrican close to the Tennessee River, and they was trying to get him to tell where his company was again, and he told 'em. But they strung him up and hung 'im to a big red-oak tree, just pulled him up on it; and finally they let him down, and carried him on to the camp. They were gonna shoot 'im. An' they tied him and another old feller out in the open on their backs, stretched 'em out like Indians, tied their hands and feet stretched out. An' it was cold and they was about to freeze. My grandfather always said that if he had to die he'd rather freeze to death than anything else, because after you got so cold you didn't feel anything, you're perfectly numb and you'd go to sleep and it was an easy death, from the experience he had at that time.

So while they were layin' there they had wallered out a hole, just the imprint of 'em in the mud and the slush; tried to, you know, get the circulation goin'. They was a lady and two daughters visited the camp and they were showing them around, and they walked up and was looking at these two old men and they were laughing about them tied down there in the mud. An' on during the day, he said he was tied right close by a little bush and there was a little bird kept flying across the field and lightin' in that little bush and would tweeter and look down on them and fly right across the field, and in that field they had the horses tied out. An' he'd made up his mind, if he could get loose he was goin' to run and run in the direction that little bird was flying. An' he said all day it just made little trips, little trips back and forth, back and forth.

An' this Confederate soldier knew my grandfather; they'd been raised together, but they's on opposite sides. And he came out and asked him how he's feeling one day, that day. And they were out there digging their graves, two graves. An' he said he was about froze, and since they had been friends all their life would he go ask the captain could he let him up and let him walk and get some circulation. He told him yeah, if he would promise him he wouldn't run.

And he said, "Yeah, I'll promise you that."

So he went and asked the captain and the captain said, "Yeah, let him up; but," said, "if he starts to run, shoot him."

So they went off out in a open spot and he commenced walkin', and this boy set down against a tree; he had his gun leaned on his shoulder and they were talking, and he said every circle he'd make he would get a little closer to him. Said he walked until he thought he was limbered up enough to run, and he came by this boy and he said he kicked his gun stock, said he kicked it hard as he could, way out from him. Said he broke and run, and he run right through the horses and 'cross the field. An' he said it was almost sundown at that time. Said he went into the woods; said they had already started firing into the horses—he had the horses between him and them. An' he run into the woods, and said he run until he was about give out.

Said he come to a creek, and he got in the water and run up this creek so they couldn't track

him. An' he said he found a hole and he crawled back under this creek bank. He said he like to crawled too deep, because he lay there and lay there. He said he kept hearing something like the horses running on the ground above him and he thought it was dark; but said he come to find out it wasn't the horses, it was his heart beating in that hole. He started trying to get out; said the sand commenced caving in around him and said he got stuck in that hole, and he wiggled and twisted 'til finally he made one last effort to get out and said he slipped loose, and he got out. So he wandered for a few days and hid out 'til he could get back to his company.

Said the only thing he could remember ever doing that he regretted was later on they was on the move and it was cold and they passed this big white home. He and one of the other soldiers stopped to warm awhile and get 'em some fire and light their pipes. An' said there was a lady in there and two daughters. Said he asked her if she was down at the corn pile a short time before that at the camp. Said yeah, they were down there. He said, "You remember these two old guys that 'as tied down in the mud?"

They laughed and said, "Yeah, wonder what happened to 'em?"

He said he didn't know what happened to one of 'em, but he knew what happened to him; he got away. Then he said he reached over at the corner of the fireplace and picked up a shovel, and told 'em if they had any cats and dogs or anything they didn't want burned, they better get 'em out. Then he said, "I strowed fire all over the house and we run, jumped on the horses and took off." Said, "We looked back and," said, "we couldn't see nothing but black smoke a-billowin' up."

An' the captain asked them what they had

done. Said he told him. He said, "Well, you shouldn't have done it," he said, "but I don't much blame you."

Robert T. Phillips
(THIRD GENERATION)

Well, my great-grandfather was a veterinarian in the Union army and he lived in Milledgeville, Tennessee, which is in McNairy County. But, anyway, at the time of the war he went to east Tennessee and I forget the name of the town that he went to join the Union army at, but it's in east Tennessee. An' about a year after he joined the army in 1861 or '62, he wound up back in McNairy County with the Union army. An' he had been raised, I think, with his cousin; for some reason or other they were raised both in the same household, and his cousin was in the Rebel army. An' I don't know what the circumstances were that my great-grandfather was captured by the Confederate army, but anyway he was, and as a matter of fact it was the same outfit that his cousin was in. An' it seems as though the commander of the Confederate unit there wanted to know where my great-grandfather's unit was and, naturally, under those circumstances he decided it would be best to tell 'im the truth, so he did.

But the fellow didn't believe him, and they told him if he didn't tell 'em the truth they were gonna hang him. Well, they hung him; but they cut him down before he'd died. An' they started questioning him again, and he told 'em a lie and they believed him.

Well, they put him on horseback and tied him to the horse and started out in the direction of where he had told 'em that the unit was. They crossed a creek and was headed for one of his friends' house; they were going to take him also. So when they crossed the creek my great-grandfather let out a yell, and the officer in charge came back to find out what was wrong with him. An' he told him that the water ran in his boot and it was cold, so he screamed. Well, actually the fellow that they were going after heard him, and he ran out the back door of his house and got away. An' later on—I don't know if this was before or after—they went to investigate where my great-grandfather said his unit was; but they finally decided that they were gonna shoot 'im.

So they staked him out spread-eagle on the ground and told him they were gonna shoot him the next morning. An' so my great-grandfather's cousin came to see and talk to 'im, and then went to the Confederate commander and asked him to let him up off the ground and let him walk around a little bit before they shot him the next morning. An' they agreed, provided that he guarded him himself.

An' so they cut him up and let him walk around a little bit and, uh, let's see, I think he was walking around a corn pile. Well, this particular place where they had him was where the residents in that part of the county used to bring their corn to be sold, and they called it the corn pile. An' he was walking around this tree or corn pile or something, and my great-grandfather's cousin was guarding him. An' he was setting down, had his rifle propped on his shoulder with the butt of it between his legs.

An' as my great-grandfather would walk around in a circle, he kept getting in a wider and wider circle. An' his cousin, it didn't take him long to figure out what he was doing, and told him if he got one foot further out he'd shoot him. An' so he stepped back toward him, and walked around him—his cousin—one time and then next time around he kicked his rifle out of his hands and broke to run, down between where they had their horses tied. An' my grandfather who told me the story said that his father told him that they must have shot at 'im a hundred times, but it's no telling how many times they actually shot because a man in that state has a tendency to exaggerate. But, anyway, he did get away. An' I think it took him several days to get linked up back with his unit. An' that's about all there is to it.

Part Two

Individual Storytellers

CHAPTER FOUR

Lloyd Arneach: Cherokee Indian Myths and Legends

Edwina Roland

Spring 1970

Having apparently migrated from Ohio, the Cherokee Indians became the mountaineers of the southeastern states until their displacement by white settlers through treaty cessions and the infamous Trail of Tears, in 1838–39, on which most of the remaining Cherokee nation was forcibly removed to Oklahoma. A small group of fugitives was allowed by the federal government to stay in western North Carolina; this became the Eastern Band of Cherokees.

Concentrated on the Qualla Boundary of Swain County, North Carolina, in the Great Smoky Mountains, these Cherokees have established a cultural center and tourist attraction composed of the Oconaluftee Indian Village, an outdoor museum; Qualla Arts and Crafts Mutual; and the Museum of the Cherokee Indian, which publishes the Journal of Cherokee Studies. *Intermarriage and trade with whites, Christianization, public schooling, and the general impact of modern American life have eroded much of their native heritage, but some, like our young storyteller, struggle to maintain their identity and to inform outsiders about their culture.*

Toward the end of the last century many pre-Christian origin myths, legends, and wonder tales were told to anthropologist James Mooney by surviving storytellers in Oklahoma and North Carolina. In 1900 these were published as Myths of the Cherokee *by the Bureau of American Ethnology, a branch of the Smithsonian Institution. Although elders still remember some of these old stories, Mooney's book has been an invaluable resource to those Cherokee who, like Lloyd Arneach, wish to preserve their storytelling tradition. Arneach learned a number of tales in this chapter from oral tellings later reinforced by print. He tells them in his own style, smoothly merging elements read with elements heard.*

A librarian friend in my home town of Kennesaw, Georgia (just north of Atlanta), had heard about Lloyd Arneach—his folk tales and Indian background—from several of the neighborhood children. She referred me to him as a fellow folklore enthusiast. Mr. Arneach, who is twenty-six years old, was more than happy to share his heritage of Cherokee myths and legends.

Lloyd Arneach was born on the Cherokee Indian Boundary at Cherokee, North Carolina, where he spent the first twenty years of his life. For the first grade he went to a Cherokee school, with the same teacher his mother had. He then transferred to a non-Indian public school to which he rode fourteen miles on the school bus.

After graduating from a public high school, he went to Guilford College, a small, four-year Quaker college at Guilford, North Carolina, and majored in mathematics. But after two years he became restless and left so that he could earn a living. He became a heavy-equipment operator on a construction crew, but quit after deciding that "this is kind of hard work, and you don't have time to do anything or feel like doing anything when you finish at the end of the day." So he entered the United States Air Force and became an aircraft electrician "through the courtesy of Uncle Sam."

Lloyd Arneach now works as a computer programmer and enjoys living in the Atlanta area. His hobbies include karate and reading, and he lectures on Cherokee culture to Scout groups and civic organizations. The stories he tells here were learned in his youth from elders on the Cherokee Boundary, particularly his uncle, George Owl.

How the Earth Was Formed

The Cherokee have many legends of how things were created or how they came to be. This one is about how the Earth was formed.

Long ago, before the beginning of time, there were only animals, and they lived above the Earth in the sky. Now, the Earth at that time did not exist, but it was just a large body of water. And the animals were multiplying and they were beginning to get very crowded. So they decided they'd go down and see if they could find a place to live. So they sent down the water beetle. And the water beetle went down to the Earth, and he couldn't find any land on top of the water. So he dove underneath the water and came up with a bit of mud and left it floating on top of the water. And he went back up into the sky with the other animals.

Now, this mud began to grow 'til it became larger and larger, until it finally became an island. And then the island spread and became larger still. The animals were getting impatient to find out if they could go down and live on the mud yet, if it was dry. So they sent down the great buzzard to check. And he flew over the water, searching for the land—because the beetle wasn't very good on telling people where to go or giving directions of any kind. The buzzard flew all over looking for this, and when he came to the island he finally discovered that it was still wet, and he kept looking for a dry spot. Well, when he got to the Cherokee country he was very tired and his wings began to flap, and when they came together they formed valleys and when the wings went up they formed mountains. The animals saw this and they were afraid that the whole earth was going to be nothing but mountains, so they called the buzzard back. Well, he went back up into the sky, but to this day the Cherokee country is full of mountains.

They were still looking for a large amount of dry land and they hadn't found anything, so they waited and they waited. And finally they decided,

"Well, we can't wait any longer; we've got to send down another messenger and have him stay if he can." So they sent down the possum. And the possum swam around 'til he came to the island, and he left his tracks in the mud here and there. He discovered that the land was really quite dry in some places, but near the water it was very muddy. So he sent the word back and said, "We can live if we stay in the center of the island." And the animals came down. But to this day, as a result of this, the Cherokees call the possum "the messenger," because he sent the word back that the land was ready to be lived on.

The Animals Obtain Fire

The animals discovered after living on the land that at different times of the seasons they became very cold. So they wanted something to keep them warm. Fire was unheard of at this time. And the thunder gods looked down on them and they decided that they'd help. So they sent lightning down to a hollow sycamore tree and struck it. This lightning set fire in the tree and it started burning. Well, the animals could see that the sycamore tree was on an island off of the piece of land that they lived on, and they wanted to get the fire so they could keep warm. So they had a council meeting and among them they asked for volunteers to go over and get the fire.

Well, the black racer [snake] was one of the first to volunteer. So he swam across the water and reached the island and went up through the grass, and when he came to the stump he went in a little hole down at the bottom. And the fire was not very big yet; but when he went in, he slipped and fell. And he rolled through the coals, and he kept running around inside and trying to

find the hole and get back out again before he was burned to death. He finally found the hole, and he swam back to the island. But he'd been in there so long that he's burned completely black all over. And to this day, he runs loops and circles back on his track as if he is trying to escape from a fire or hot coals.

They had another council meeting and asked for another volunteer. This time the great black-snake volunteered. He swam across, and instead of going in the hole at the bottom, he climbed the outside of the tree as a blacksnake does nowadays and looked down inside. But as he looked inside he lost his grip on the tree and fell inside the hollow stump again. And he had to go out through the hole which the black racer had found. And he too was scorched and burned black. And he came back.

After this, no other snakes would go across, so they asked for a volunteer from the birds. And the screech owl volunteered. By this time the fire was building up higher and higher. So he flew over to the island and perched on the side of the stump and looked down. And a gust of hot air came up and burned his eyes, and ashes were deposited all over his coat of feathers. And to this day, his eyes are red and his coat still looks like somebody had thrown ashes over it. So he came back.

And they sent two more over. The horned owl went over and the barn owl went over. And together they flew above the fire this time, and they looked down, and again the wind came up and blew ashes up to their eyes. And to this day, they have white circles around their eyes where the ashes stuck and they couldn't rub them off.

Well, the crow decided that he'd go over next and see if he could get the fire for them. Well, he flew over and he pushed on the stump, but the stump had been burned so badly that it broke and gave away under him, and he fell into the fire and was nearly burned before he could get away. But, to this day, he is charred black all over. So, after he came back, none of the other birds would go over.

So they asked for a volunteer from the insects. And the black widow [spider] volunteered. And she went across the water and on the island, and she wove a little silken net to carry the coal in. She put the basket on her back, dropped the coal in it and hurried across. But, by this time, she was tired from going across the water and then coming back with a heavy load. And so she slowed down on the way back. And the coal began to burn through this silken net, and eventually burned through and burned her back. But she made it back with the coals, so the animals had fire. But, to this day, the black widow carries the marks of those burns on her back.

How the Mink Got His Dark Coat

Among the animals, the mink was known as a notorious thief. He stole all the time; he could never be trusted in any dealings in which he gave his word, because he always went back on his word—his word meant nothing. And they couldn't leave anything out that they possessed, because he would steal it. And if he couldn't use it, he'd destroy it.

So the animals decided that they'd teach him a lesson. They caught the mink and built a large fire and threw him in the middle of it. And the fire was burning up very high and the mink was squirming around the fire, and every time he would jump out they'd throw him back in. They finally decided he'd been punished enough, so

they let him out of the fire. But they discovered that his coat had been burned black and he smelled like roasted flesh. And to this day, the mink's coat is dark, and when he's excited or angry he gives off a smell very similar to roasted flesh.

The Possum's Tail

Long ago, the possum had a very bushy tail, and he was very proud of it. The other animals didn't mind so much, but he always bragged about it wherever he went. "Look at my long, bushy tail. See how fine the fur is."

Well, the rabbit was a very mischievous fellow, and he decided that he'd do something about this. He was just tired of the possum bragging about this all the time. So they had a big dance coming up and the rabbit went over; he was in charge of inviting everybody to the dance. He went around to see the different animals, and when he came to the possum's house he asked him if he would come to the dance.

The possum said, "Why, yes I'll come, but only if I have the best seat in the house."

The rabbit said, "Why?"

"So everybody can see my long, bushy tail. I want everybody to be sure and see this."

The rabbit said, "All right, we'll get you the best seat in the house, and I'll even send someone over tomorrow morning to groom and clean your hair for you."

The possum said, "Well, fine; in that case, I'll come up."

So the rabbit went on his way and he stopped by the cricket's house. Now, among the Cherokees, the cricket is known as an expert barber. Well, the rabbit told the cricket to go

Cherokee Indian Child, Banner Elk, North Carolina. Kenneth Murray.

over and fix up the possum for the coming dance the next morning. But he also told him what else he wanted him to do, in addition to that. So the next morning the cricket showed up at the possum's house and said, "I'm here to get you ready for the dance tonight. I want to comb and wash your tail for you."

The possum said, "Fine."

And the possum sat down and the cricket went to work. He had a long red ribbon which he started wrapping around the possum's tail after he'd washed it. But what he was also doing was cutting the hair at the very roots so the possum wouldn't know, and then wrapping the ribbon around the hair so it wouldn't fall out. And when he'd completed the job he told the possum, "Now, don't unwrap the ribbon until you get to the dance tonight." So the possum left the ribbon on all day.

When he went to the dance that night, sure enough, the best seat in the house had been selected for him. So he sat down. Everyone was dancing and singing, and when it came the possum's turn to dance he stood up, pulled the ribbon off of his tail, and then he started dancing around the circle, saying, "Look what a beautiful tail I have." And everybody laughed and carried on. And he decided, "Well, I'll do it again." So he ran around the circle and said, "See how fine the fur is." And everybody was laughing and carrying on. And he said, "Well, I'll go again." He was very proud of his tail and he said, "See, I have the best-looking tail in the world." And at this, everybody laughed out loud, right in his face. And he couldn't understand what they were laughing at.

So he suddenly realized that they were all laughing at him. And so he turned around to see if there was somebody behind him or if someone had put something on his back. And he discovered that his tail was bare as a lizard's tail. At this he became so ashamed that he rolled over and grinned. And to this day, when he's surprised or frightened, he rolls over on his back and grins.

The Bear's Tail

The bear also had a bushy tail, but it wasn't as long nor as handsome as the possum's tail used to be. One day, the bear was walking along the river when he came on the fox. And the fox was carrying a large string of fish in his hand which he had just stolen from an otter that had been fishing on down the creek.

The bear asked him how he caught all the fish. And since it was wintertime the fox told him, "Well, I went out, cut a hole in the ice, and stuck my tail through it. And it started stinging, but this just means that the fish are biting. So I sat there and the more it hurt the longer I sat, 'cause I knew I was catching more fish. And finally I decided I had enough fish. I stood up and I had all these fish hanging onto my tail. So all you have to do is go down there, cut a hole and sit there until, you know, it really starts stinging. And then pull your tail up with your fish."

The bear, well, he wasn't really the brightest of any of the animals, and the fox was pretty sharp. And he thought he'd teach the bear a thing or two about getting his own meal. So the bear decided, well, he'd go down and try it. So he went down to the river, cut a hole in the ice and sat down. Sure enough, in a little while his tail started burning and stinging and he decided, "Well, that's just one or two fish. I want a whole bunch, like the fox had. I'll catch even more than the fox got."

So he sat there awhile longer and he kept burning and stinging some more and he thought, "Well, that seems like as many as the fox had. I think I'll stay just a little bit longer, and make sure I've got more than he has." So he sat there a little while longer, and it kept burning and stinging and it got so bad that he didn't think he could stand it any longer. So he thought, "Well, I think I'll get my fish and go home. I've got enough."

So he started to stand up, and he couldn't. And he realized that the ice had frozen around his tail. And so he tugged and shoved and pushed and tried to stand up. And finally he gave one last great heave, and he broke free. But when he broke free he realized that he had left his tail in the ice. And to this day, the bear carries nothing but a very short stub of what's left of that beautiful tail of his.

Why the Deer's Teeth Are Blunt

The rabbit and the deer had a race one day to see who would win the honor of being able to wear horns for the rest of their life. And due to the deer's long legs, he beat the rabbit a great distance. And the rabbit was mad about this, but he didn't tell the deer. So the deer won the honor to wear horns, and the rabbit didn't win anything.

So he planned to get back at the deer, and the way he planned to do this was very unique. He strung a vine across a trail, and before he hung it up between the two trees he cut it almost in half with his teeth. Then he hung it up between the two trees and went back down the trail a bit. Then he would run up and jump at the vine, and then go back, and come running up and jump at

the vine again. 'Til finally the deer came along and asked him what he was doing. The rabbit said, "I'm so strong I can cut that vine through with one bite and one jump."

And the deer said, "Well, I don't believe you. You're not that strong."

And the rabbit said, "All right, I'll show you." So he backed up the trail a bit, went running down and jumped up at the vine and bit it. And he hit it right where he'd gnawed through halfway, and he cut it in two.

So when he dropped back down to the ground again, the deer said, "Well, I can do that, too."

The rabbit said, "All right, prove it."

The deer said, "Well, give me a vine."

So the rabbit went out and found a larger vine than the one he had used, and he didn't cut this one nearly in two. And he put it in the middle of the trail, and the deer came running up and jumped. Of course, the vine only caught in his mouth and threw him back. And he was stunned a little bit at this, because he had seen how easily the rabbit had done it and he was certainly bigger and stronger than a rabbit, any day.

So he went back down the trail a bit and he came running up and jumped at the vine again, and the same thing happened. Well, he kept running and jumping at the vine 'til he was starting to bleed from several wounds when he'd hit the ground. And he was tired and aching.

The rabbit finally came up to him and said, "Let me see your teeth." Now, the deer had teeth like a wolf. And the rabbit said, "That's the reason. Your teeth aren't filed down enough; they're not sharp." And he said, "Look at this. See what I can do." And he picked up a black locust twig that he had peeled with his teeth before the deer had come along and he showed it to him. And he said, "See how I can do that; and you can do that too, if your teeth were sharp. So, sit down. Let me sharpen up your teeth for you."

And the deer sat down, and the rabbit got up a very rough stone and started grinding the deer's teeth down. Well, he kept grinding and grinding, and finally he ground them almost down to the gums. And the deer started complaining and said, "It's hurting."

And the rabbit said, "Well, it hurts a little bit, but you have to get used to that if you want real sharp teeth."

So the deer said, "All right, I'll sit a little longer."

And the rabbit kept grinding some more, and he ground them almost all the way down to the gums. And he finally stopped and said, "All right, they're ground down enough."

And the deer jumped up and ran at the vine again. And, of course, it didn't do anything but just throw him back on his back again. And he was laying there on the ground, quite stunned and tired and aching.

The rabbit was bounding off in the bushes, but before he did he turned and said, "Now you got your blunt teeth also. From now on you'll only be able to eat twigs and grass," and left.

The First People

The first people to come and live with the animals were a brother and sister, and there were no other people. Until, one day, the brother hit the sister with a fish. And seven days later she had a baby. And in seven more days she had another baby. And seven days after that she had another baby. Well, they were worried that the world would not hold all of them if they kept multiplying at a rate like this. And so the brother consulted with the gods, and they decreed that from now on the woman would only be able to bear one child a year.

Origin of the Races

The Cherokee believe there's a person who lives above them that controls what they do and what is going to happen. And they say that in the beginning, before men and women had ever come to Earth, that this great power was sitting there—now that the Earth had been formed, had been brought up by the water beetle and had grown with all the animals—to put somebody down to help control the animal population. And he decided he'd make a man.

So he got some clay and made a figure of what he thought a man should look like, and put it in the oven. Well, he'd never made a man before, so he didn't know how long to keep it in the oven. And when he went to get it out, it had been overdone. Actually, burned black. So the man decided, "Well, let's see. I don't want to waste him; I'll put him down here somewhere." So he put the man down in Africa.

And he thought, "Well, I left it in too long that time; I'll make it a little shorter time." So he made another figure, and he put it in the oven again. And this time he took it out too soon. And he said, "Well now, I don't want to waste this man either. I've gone to all this effort to cook him, and make the figures, so I think I'll put him down there somewhere." So he dropped this man down in Europe.

And he thought, "Well, I'll try it again." So he

made another figure. And this time he put him in the oven and he split the difference of the time he took it out too soon and the time he took it out too late. And he took it out when this time was up, and the figure was just right. He said, "That's what I was looking for." And this figure he put down in America.

The Milky Way

A long time ago, some people who lived in the south owned a corn mill. They would grind corn every day and leave it overnight, put more corn in in the morning. Well, one night they discovered that some of their corn was missing when they got up.

So, this happened several mornings in a row. And they decided they'd wait and see who was doing this, who was stealing their cornmeal. So they knelt behind their hut there and sat and watched. And, sure enough, along about midnight a great big dog came down and started eating the cornmeal.

Well, they had some long hickory sticks in their hands, and they jumped out and started beating them. The dog was so surprised that he jumped up and started running into the north. And, as he ran, cornmeal trailed out of his mouth. And this trail is known as the Milky Way today; and the Cherokee know this as where the dog ran.

The Rattlesnake Clan

The Cherokee never kill a rattlesnake. And the reason for this is an old legend.

Long ago, when man could still speak with the animals, a hunter had been away for many days to find food for his family. And the wife was at home. And one day she noticed a rattlesnake was crawling across her yard. So she took a stick out and killed it. And the Rattlesnake Clan spread the word, because then they were going to go back and kill the wife.

And on the way they met the husband returning home from his trip. So the chief of the Rattlesnake Clan told the hunter what had happened. And he pleaded with him, "Don't kill my wife. Let me talk with her. First let me go and talk with her."

And he said, "All right, but if she doesn't agree to your terms or to what we say then we'll kill her. And we'll come and kill both of you."

And the hunter paled at this, because he realized if he didn't convince his wife, they were going to kill him. And he knew how stubborn women can be sometimes. So he went to his wife and he told her, "You killed the wife of the chief of the Rattlesnake Clan, and they're coming to kill you. What will save your life is if you agree never again to kill a rattlesnake. And all your descendants must agree never to kill a rattlesnake. Ever. But if you don't agree to this, they're going to come and kill us both."

And the woman hemmed and hawed and fussed with him quite a bit; but she finally agreed with him, because she really didn't have any other choice. And the hunter went back and told the chief of the Rattlesnake Clan.

And he said, "All right, we'll leave you alone. But if you ever kill any of our people again, we will come and kill all of your mates."

And so, to this day, the Cherokees do not kill the rattlesnake, regardless of what happens.

The Little People

What the Cherokees call the Little People are similar to Ireland's leprechauns; and there are stories of Little People throughout the different nationalities of the Earth.

The Cherokees' Little People were good people. The old people of the tribe, when I was a child, would occasionally leave bowls of milk at their back doorstep. In the morning the milk would be gone. Now, I would assume that this would mean that some wild animal had come down and drank the milk.

In the Smoky Mountains there is a phenomenon that is called a bald. Now, this is a mountaintop where no trees or large shrubbery grows, only grass and weeds. The old people of the Cherokees say that this is where the Little People camped for a night and danced. The Little People don't exist anymore to the younger generation, mainly because the younger generation don't believe in the tales and the legends of the old people. But it's been said that at night, when a hunter is coming back from a hunt, that occasionally drums can be heard and singing and dancing. And when the man gets to where the dancing or the sound seems to be coming from, nothing is there. And yet, when he passes on, it comes from behind him. Now this is the Little People. The adults could not see them, but young people could. And, occasionally, children who were lost in the woods were brought home. When asked who brought them home, they would say, "The Little People brought me."

Until recently, I considered this a legend, as did many people. But around Franklin, North Carolina, small caves were found. The caves were definitely manmade. Artifacts were found in them that would fit a child's hand. And yet they were definitely fashioned by skilled craftsmen. And these caves were found to be hundreds of years old. The caves were so small that an adult had to get down on all fours to navigate them, and even then some of the caves were too small, which indicates people of a very small stature. This gives some doubt in my mind as to whether this is really a legend, or is it a story based on fact?

CHAPTER FIVE

Lee Drake: Afro-American Tales

Judith J. Nelson

Spring 1968

A relatively young man, Lee Drake rivals the finest southern storytellers ever discovered. His repertoire covers a broad range of story types, from animal and Old Master and John tales to supernatural legends, local-character anecdotes, and fool-Irishmen jests. While reading this sampling—the product of two relatively brief recording sessions—a reader gets the impression that the narrator was just getting warmed up and that the collector has only scratched the surface of Drake's repertoire. Unfortunately, he dropped out of sight before follow-up collecting could be accomplished, but we are thankful for what we have.

How did Drake come to be a master storyteller? Biographical information is far from complete, but it appears that as a child he put enough value on the tales of his elderly Alabama mentor, R. C. Flowers, to retain them as the core of his repertoire. Clues about his personality given by the collector in her introduction—use of the tales both to maintain his internal fantasy world and solidify relationships with his associates at work (constructive application of artistic skills to overcome shyness)—add to the picture. Clearly, these stories

play a central role in Lee Drake's life, and he does not take them lightly. Neither should we.

Thernover Lee Drake was born in Alexander City, Alabama, in 1928 and lived there until 1956, when, after serving in the Korean War, he moved to Atlanta. He drove a taxi for a while and did odd jobs such as manual labor and house-painting. Finally he came to work for the United States government at the Communicable Disease Center (now the Centers for Disease Control) as a stagehand in the motion picture–TV section.

It was at the C.D.C. that my husband, Craig, first met Lee and developed a friendship with him. Craig enjoyed listening to Lee's colorful stories during leisure moments at work. I had often heard Craig talk about Lee and his reputation at the C.D.C. as a real "spinner of tales."

Craig brought Lee home from work one afternoon for an hour and we managed to tape about twenty minutes of animal and ghost stories. Since, as it turned out, Lee's wife doesn't care for his stories or "jokes," as she calls them, it did not seem possible for us all to get together in a social setting. Craig then decided to tape what he could of Lee at work. As it turned out, this was for the best. He and Craig had already established a relationship, so Lee was freer and more open than he would have been had I been present (especially since some of the tales are off-color). Thus it is primarily through Craig's effort that these stories were collected.

Lee learned the majority of these tales as a child from an old man in Alexander City named R. C. Flowers. He says that Mr. Flowers would tell them to a group of children sitting around a big shade tree. Lee says that he seldom gets the opportunity to just sit around and tell stories anymore but that he does find that almost any everyday occurrence will bring a story to his mind.

It isn't strange that Lee should stand out at the C.D.C., where a tale-teller is viewed with a bit of amusement and a raised eyebrow here and there. At work among his fellow crew members, he is affectionately known as "the Colonel," but for what specific reason, if any, I am not sure. Except perhaps that Lee claims to be the master of a thousand skills, and there seems to be nothing in which he doesn't profess some skill, from photographing the birth of a mosquito to riding an occasional sea horse. As George Shields, a fellow worker and friend of Lee's, once said to several other crew members, "Guess what, boys? I've actually found something that the Colonel can't do." Asked what this could possibly be, George replied, "Skate! The Colonel can't skate!" However, Lee claimed that if given a week he could skate as well as the next man.

Lee is a strange fellow. He tends to have moments during which he is totally preoccupied with his own fantasies and daydreams. This only adds to his mystique among his fellow workers, who are apt to accuse him of being a dreamer. Although they enjoy his stories, they don't really appreciate them and often tease him about them. Lee is more of a loner than his comrades and tends to be shy, restrained, and more reflective; he is seldom seen with the others at coffee break. Though not a great gesticulator, he is a joy to listen to when he tells these stories, not only because they are fun and entertaining but because it's so evident that he enjoys the telling of them. Lee lives in a nice house in a middle-class Negro neighborhood and has a wife named Pearl who is a nurse. He also has two dogs, a cat named Light Foot, and no children.

Though one can give facts about his life and his relationships with others, the really nice thing about Lee is that although he's been delightfully open in the telling of these tales, he still remains in many ways a mystery.

Observations on Rabbit Cunning

It's like if you're rabbit-huntin', you notice a rabbit, wherever you jump him at—if you want to be the smartest hunter and wanta kill the morest rabbit, if you got a pack of dogs with you—you stay near the place where you jump him, because the dogs goin' to take him on off somewhere. And he goin' make a big circle and he comin' right back where he jus' left or where you jumped him, 'cause he run off to throw the dogs off the track. Then another thing: you watch him, you'll notice he'll try to wash his feet, wash the rabbit scent off so the dogs can't track him. You'll notice when he set down, he'll lick his feet real fast and jump up and he'll make a circle—

run around and around right fast—right on that same place and then he'll take off again. That's true.

Brother Rabbit Steals the Lard

They told me, I'd heard about, er, uh, it was the animals: the rabbit, the fox, and the possum, and maybe a few more. They was workin' hard, y'know, one day, and they had a big can of lard; that was for all of 'em to eat when they got off at lunchtime. The animal that they was workin' for had that lard to feed 'em on at lunchtime. Brother Rabbit, he was smart; he knowed this other animal had the lard, see. And this other animal was king over them, anyway, and he could do 'em like he wanted to.

So they work along awhile and Brother Rabbit say, "Oh, I believe I hear somethin'." He says, "I got to go see what my wife wants." He take off down across the hill and he'd eat some of the lard.

Say, "What is it?"

Say, "She had a baby."

Say, "What'd you name him, Brother Rabbit?"

He say, "Top Off." That mean he jus' took the top off the lard! So 'ey worked a li'l while longer. He say, "Listen, I believe I hear somethin'."

"Well, you better go back and see what it is, Bur Rabbit." He take off down the hill again. Come back. Say, "What happen, Brother Rabbit?"

Say, "She had another baby."

Say, "What ya name that one?"

"Half Gone."

So when he went back down there the last time, he eat all the lard up. Come back up there, he was jus' as full as he could be.

Say, "What happened that time, Brother Rabbit?"

"Aw," say, "she had another baby. I hope she don't have another one."

Say, "What you name that one, Brother Rabbit?"

Say, "All Gone."

Anyway, Brother Rabbit worked on all right then 'til lunchtime. This other animal went down to git the lard, bring up to feed 'em. It was all gone. Says, "Lawd." Say, "Somebody, some of you animals eat all this lard up, and I don't know which one it was; but I'm goin' to find out."

Brother Rabbit say, "I can tell you how to find out the buck that done it."

Say, "How, Brother Rabbit?"

Says, "You see that big flat rock out there?" Says, "Put us all on that, stretch us all out on that big flat rock. The one eat that lard," say, "it'll melt out of him 'cause the sun's so hot."

So they put 'em all out there on the big flat rock: the possum, the rabbit, and the squirrel, and so forth and on. They put Brer Rabbit next to Brother Possum; you know the possum, he's fat anyway. He jus' eased up and drug Brer Possum over in his place, because Brer Possum he's hard to wake up and surly anyway. Drug him over to his place. Then he went to sleep.

After 'while, Brer Rabbit woke up right quicklike. "Oh," just dancin' around; "I told you, you'd find out the buck that done it! See that old Brer Possum, he's the buck that done it!"

So they had to kill the possum on account of it was Brer Rabbit so smart.

Brother Fox and Brother Rabbit at the Well

'Bout the fox and the rabbit. The rabbit he wanted some water, and he went by this old well, you know, that they have buckets on—bucket on one side and bucket on the other side—on a whirl, y'know. So Brother Rabbit wanted some water so bad, he hopped in the bucket and down to the bottom he go. Hit down there, and Brother Rabbit couldn't git out from down there. He got all the water he wanted, but he couldn't git out.

Brother Fox come by, and he was hungry; he wanted to eat Bur Rabbit. He say, "Hey, Bur Rabbit! Is you down there?"

Brer Rabbit say, "Yeah, I'm down here, Brer Fox."

He says, "How did you git down there?"

He says, "All you have to do is jump in that other bucket up there." See, Brother Rabbit knowed Brother Fox was heavier than he was; seed he'd come right to the bottom and he'd go up. So he hopped in this bucket at the bottom of the well. Say, "Jus' hop in the bucket up there and you'll come right down, safe and sound."

So Brother Fox hopped in the bucket; he knowed when he git down in there he'd eat Brother Rabbit up. He hopped in the bucket and down he go. And when they passed one another—Brother Rabbit was comin' up and Brother Fox was goin' down—he told Brother Fox, when he hopped off of the edge of the well up there, say, "Take care of your clothes, Bro' Fox, 'cause Brer Rabbit is gone!"

Brother Rabbit and Brother Fox at the Sawdust Pile

You know how they have sawdust piles in the country or, well, anywhere they have a sawmill or either a planer mill. And the foxes usually den in those places. They have their little ones and so forth, you know, in those places.

And the dogs had been runnin' this fox all night, and he was tired. And so he jumped in a rabbit's trail and put the dogs in behind the rabbit. Sorta detoured 'em, y'know. And he went up on the top of the sawdust pile and sit down. And the rabbit he was jus' runnin'. Dogs right in behind him; gittin' purty close to him, tryin' to catch him. Look like every round he makes, Brother Fox sittin' up there, he say, "Bear 'round, Brother Rabbit, bear 'round!" When he'd start comin' up to exchange with him, see. Brother Rabbit would bear 'round again, goin' around; make another round.

Brother Rabbit gittin' tired, y'know. He wanted to go up there and sit down an' rest and let Brother Fox run some. He started up the sawdust pile; Brother Fox say, "Bear 'round, Brother Rabbit, bear 'round." Bur Rabbit bear on around again, y'know.

Well, a'ter awhile, they was jus' about to ketch Brother Rabbit: old dog jus' snappin' at his tail as he come around that time. So Brother Fox say, "Bear 'round, Brother Rabbit, bear 'round!"

Brother Rabbit say, "I'll be damned if I'm goin' to bear 'round this time; damned if I ain't comin' straight through this time!"

Brother Rabbit and Brother Fox Meet Man

They was a rabbit and a fox a-walkin' through the woods one day, and they was jus' a-skippin' and a-hoppin' along, both side to side together. So they passed two little kids playin' in the sand bed. Brother Fox asked Brother Rabbit, says, "What is that, Brother Rabbit? What's them two things sittin' over there?"

So Brer Rabbit told Brother Fox, say, "Oh, hell, that's a goddamn 'gonna-be.'"

And they went on down through the woods a little further, y'know. Happened to run across a real old man, so old he was walkin' bent over wit' a walkin' stick. And Brother Fox asked Brother Rabbit again, says, "Hey, Brother Rabbit," says, "What's dat right there?"

He says, "Shoot, that's a 'has-been.'"

So they went on down through the woods a little further, and they had to go through a briar patch. Just as they went to step out of that briar patch, there's a young man standin' out there wit' a double-barreled shotgun. And so, Brother Fox asked Brother Rabbit again, say, "What's that yonder, Brer Rabbit?"

'Bout that time this young man hauled off and shot wit' dat shotgun, and hit Brother Rabbit, y'know. Brother Rabbit said, "That, that, that's a 'still-is.'" Say, "He lightnin' an' thunderin' and stuck splinters all in my asshole!"

Brother Crow and Brother Buzzard Up North

Both the crow and the buzzard, they 'cided they would take a trip up North. An', y'know, the buzzard he don't eat somethin' 'lessen it's dead, and a crow'll eat anything. So they got up North, and they both lit in a big ol' dead tree—which a buzzard lights in all the time. And they stayed up there long time; a week or two.

And the crow he was jus' full and happy 'cause he eat some of anything that hit the ground; the crow would eat it. The buzzard wouldn't eat nothin' 'lessen it died. Plenty snow and ice on the ground, and the buzzard couldn't git nothin'. If anything died or froze to death the people would take it and bury it, 'cause they was in town where they was, or near a town. So this ol' crow jump in a tree and jump back down on the ground and git him somethin' to eat and sang, "Caw, caw, caw." Say, "Hey, Brother Buzzard, why don't you sing?"

So Brother Buzzard say, "Hell, it ain't my time to sing yet." Brother Buzzard was gittin' hungry. Last on two or three days like that. Brother Buzzard sittin' up in that tree waitin' on somethin' to die, and wouldn't nothin' die. 'Bout to starve to death. Brother Buzzard was gittin' poor [thin].

So, way late on that third day in that last week, Brother Buzzard say, "It's my time to sing, Mister Crow; it's my time to sing, this mornin'." He stretched his wings out.

The crow looked at him. He say, "What you gonna sing, Brother Buzzard?"

Brother Buzzard sailed off, he said [singing],

"I'm going back South
Where they don't bury the dead!"

Brother Buzzard and the Lazy Mule

Here's a tale about an ol' mule. He didn't like to work, y'know, especially when it got hot in the summertime. So, people had a little ol' pasture they kept him in down below the barn, and lot of trees around it. So, lot of buzzards around that place. And old mule, he was too lazy to work. He went out there and pretend he was sick, so the man wouldn't plow him. He stretched out in the sun, tail all stretched out, eyes walled up to the

Brer Rabbit, Eatonton, Georgia. Barbara McKenzie.

sun. Y'know when the sun hit in a mule's eye it turn glassy lookin', kinda like he's out cold, sho' 'nough; but he actually don't be.

So this old mule was layin' out there, and this old buzzard sittin' up in the tree, y'know, he'd turn his head to one side and he'd look down out of one eye. And then he raise it up, turn it to the other side and look out the other eye, lookin' down at the ol' mule, hopin' he's dead. An' this old crow was over there in the corn patch, jumpin' up and down on a limb, hollerin', "Try 'im, try 'im, Brother Buzzard; try 'im, try 'im!"

Brother Buzzard looked down at him out of the one eye again; then he turned his head on the other side and looked back down at him again. So ol' crow told Brother Buzzard again, say, "Try 'im, Brother Buzzard, try 'im!"

Y'know, when a buzzard starts to eatin' a dead mule or cow one, he start at the back end, under the tail. So old Brother Buzzard walked around to the front of him and looked at his eyes—after he flew down from where he was—and he turned around and walked back to his tail and look at him. Brother Crow still tell 'im, "Try 'im, Brother Buzzard, try 'im!" He walked back to his eyes and look at him; the ol' mule wouldn't even bat his eye. Come back to the tail end again and he look up under there and he drawed way back. Brother Crow told 'im, say, "Try 'im, try 'im, Brother Buzzard!"

Directly he soused it to him [struck or plunged into him]. When he soused it to him under the tail, say that old mule jumped up, clamped his tail down on Brother Buzzard's neck, and started runnin' down through the woods with Brother Buzzard. Say the crow told him, "Hold 'im, Brother Buzzard, hold 'im!" Say, "Hold 'im, Brother Buzzard, hold 'im!"

Brother Buzzard say, "How in the hell can I hold this son-of-a-bitch when ain't neither one of my feet touchin' the ground?"

Why the Woodpecker Has No Song

Willy the woodpecker: why he have to go around and peck hard wood for a livin'. You never hear the peckerwood sing a song, 'cause he doesn't have a song. So I'm goin' tell you why he don't have a song to sing. Only song you hear is his bill hittin' a hard dead tree, and that's his song.

When God got through makin' all the birds and so forth, he had 'em all sittin' around in the room. And he was goin' give 'em a song to sing; and he was givin' out songs, might say, like you'd go 'round handin' out books in a classroom. So he gave the mockin'bird a song, and he gave the redbird a song, and he gave the jaybird a song, and so forth. And so he hadn't got to Willy Woodpecker, y'know. Old woodpecker sittin' over in the corner, he says [fast], "God-a-mighty, God-a-mighty, what shall I do?"

He say, "Jus' sit there and wait 'til I git to you. I'll give you a song to sing." God started givin' out songs again.

Old woodpecker hollered out again, "God-a-mighty, God-a-mighty, what shall I do?"

He say, "Okay, I done told you I'll give you a song in minute; you jus' wait 'til I git to you and I'll give you a song to sing." God went back to givin' out songs.

He bleated out again, "God-a-mighty, God-a-mighty, what shall I do?"

God told him, said, "Hell," says, "you can't wait 'til I give you a song to sing?" Say, "You jus' go out here and peck hard wood for your livin' and don't come back." And so that's why he pecks hard wood for a livin' today.

The Parrot and the Maid

This tale's about a parrot. You know, the sayin' is—I don't know it myself—if a woman pull up her dress and turn her butt to the parrot and he see all that hair in that split, it'll kill him, he'll die.

This parrot belonged to a couple, was real rich people, and they had a maid workin' for 'em. And they wouldn't let the maid eat none of the food they had at home. She had to go home and fix her somepin' after she worked there all day. And so, after she cooked her biscuits for the family, she would hide her a panful and put 'em in the chair, put the cushion over 'em there. So this parrot, he would tell everything. He says, "I'm goin' tell on you. I'm gonna tell on you."

So she say, "Shut up!"

"I'm gonna tell on you. I'm gonna tell on you."

So, when the people came in, she had the biscuits; she didn't get a chance to move 'em out the chair. They came in early. She usually take her biscuits home and eat 'em, see. And so the lady what had the maid hired, she went and started to sit down in the chair, talkin' to the girl. Called, "Mary?" Says somethin' another to Mary.

Anyway, this parrot say, "Look out there! Look out there! Hot biscuits burn your ass! Hot biscuits burn your ass!"

She says, "God damn!" Say, "I'm goin' to git rid of you tomorrow, you little son-of-a-bitch, you!" That's what the maid told the parrot.

So, people ready to leave the next day. She say, "Mary, why you put the biscuits in the chair?"

Says, "I thought maybe they'd cool faster." And that was all of that.

So the next day this ol' parrot was there. The maid came; she says, "I told you I was goin' to git rid of you today." And so she pulled up her dress and turned her butt up to the parrot. And the parrot say, "Oh, Lawd have mercy! Turn it the other way! I can't stand it!"

She say, "I told you! You ever goin' to tell anything else on me?"

"No, I'm not goin' to tell anything else on you. Please don't kill me!" So she let the parrot alone that time.

The Parrot Goes to Church

It's the same parrot. This is a devilish parrot, you know. So anyway, this same old parrot and this lady what had the maid hired, her husband was shavin', and the parrot was lookin' in the mirror at him while he was shavin'. Say he told him, "Look out there, God damn you! You goin' to cut yourself!"

This man says, "All right; if you don't shut up," says, "I'm goin' to wring your neck."

Says, "Look out there; God damn it, you goin' to cut yourself!"

He says, "I told you, if you don' hush your mouth I'm goin' to pull all the feathers out the top of your head."

The old man would carry the parrot to church with him every Sunday, y'know. And set him way over in the amen corner or either set him in the pulpit. And so he lived-off again. "Look there, you goin' to cut yourself."

"I told you, damn it, I was goin' to pull all the feathers out your head." So he grabbed him, pulled all the feathers out of his head, and th'owed him back in his cage. So that made that parrot bald-headed. And told him, "Git back in there, you hen-fuckin' son-of-a-bitch, you!" That's what he told the parrot. He was mad wit' him, y'know.

So he took him to church that day—that same parrot—took him to the church. Old parrot settin' . . . he put him way off over there in the corner by hisself, 'cause he was ashamed of him, see. And they went to havin' service, prayer meetin', and devotional and everything. And so, the preacher got up preachin'. And things got kindly quiet. Here come in two old bald-headed men, way late. Old parrot looked up and seen 'em. Men lookin' all way 'round for a seat. Church was full; they couldn't find a seat. Even the ushers couldn't find 'em no seat. Lookin' all way 'round. So that parrot flopped his wings, say, "Hey, you two!" So the men wouldn't pay the parrot no attention. "I say hey, you two!" Say, "You two hen-fuckin' son-of-a-bitches, come on over here where I'm at!"

The Devil and the Lord Dividing Souls

Here's a story about two slaves. Long years ago, they worked for the old master, and the old master never would give 'em enough to eat. And so, why, so they didn't git enough to eat, they would steal stuff and take home, and they would cook it at night after they git home. They would do all their stealing at night after they done gone home.

And so one day they had a lot of potatoes, and they knowed people didn't fool around the graveyards at night. And so they took these potatoes and carried 'em in the graveyard. Both of 'em had a sack apiece, and had two great big uns they laid down at the gate 'cause they was so tired when they got there with those big bags of potatoes apiece. And they went on inside. They was goin' to divide the potatoes up. Neither one of them could count, and the way they had to do to divide anything they had, they always say, "You take this one and I'll take that one."

So here come up another slave; he stayed at this other master's house. He'd go off at night, but he'd come back and spend the night 'cause he had to tote the old [crippled] master everywhere he went. He came by this graveyard that night and he heard this, "You take this one and I'll take that one. You take this one and I'll take that one." He stopped; thought that might have been a ghost or somethin'. And he stopped still and listened, see was it his heart beatin'. He helt his heart right tight, see was it his heart beatin'; and it wasn't his heart beatin'. Still he heard this sound: "You take this one and I'll take that one. You take this one and I'll take that one." So old John 'cided he'd run on up to the house and tell Boss about this God down there dividin' up souls!

So he went on up to the house. "Hey, Boss! Hey, Bossman!"

"Yes, John; what is it, John, what is it?"

He said, "God and the Devil down here dividin' up souls at the graveyard!"

He said, "Aw no, John, ain't no such thing!"

"Yes it is, yes it is. You don't tell me, 'cause I heard 'em!"

He says, "Okay, take me down there and let's see God and the Devil dividin' 'em up. I want to hear it, too."

So John picks him up and take him on down there. Sit him down 'side the gate. And so, sho' 'nough, he heard this noise. "You take this one and I take that one. You take this one and I'll take that one." Sound went on for a long time.

Old Boss reach over and touch John: "You, you was right, John. You was right! You was right!"

Later on they got through dividin' up what they had in there. They had two real large potatoes they left at the gate; they was so tired, they just dropped them at the gate. One say, "Oh, you forgot somepin'."

He says, "What is it?"

"You know. You remember dem two we drop at the gate, don't ya?"

So John cut out! See, he didn't take time to pick up Old Master that time. So when John got to the house, Old Master was already in there, done slammed the door in his face!

John and Old Miss in the Barn

Here's a ol' tale, kinda slavery-time tale 'bout John and the old miss. And they give John a mule named Betsy, and John almost raised the mule up. He was crazy about Betsy, y'know. And, uh, husband stayed out of town travelin', you might say like a travelin' salesman; he stayed gone all the time. So she wouldn't cut out on him, she'd let John take up where her husband lef' off, when her husband leave, y'know.

And so, it'd get better and better to John, y'know. Every time John have intercourse with her, he'd jus' fall out hollerin'. He jus' couldn't help but holler. And you could hear him all outside the house, he'd be hollerin' so loud. So she told John there one day, say, "John," says, "I'm not goin' to love you anymore."

He say, "Why, Ol' Miss, why, why?"

Say she tol' him, "'Cause you holler." Say, "You holler so loud you goin' to disturb the neighbors,

and the neighbors goin' find out that I'm lovin' you."

He say, "Naw, Ma'am, I'm not goin' holler; I'm not goin' holler anymore."

And she say, "No, I'm not goin' do it anymore, John, 'cause you holler."

So John got up a stiff there, y'know. She looked down and seen the stiff. She say, "John, you promise me you ain't gonna holler?"

John say, "No, Ma'am, I'm not gonna holler, I'm not gonna holler."

She say, "Well, I'm goin' tell you what. I'm goin' to make a deal wit' you, John." Say, "If you holler," say, "I'm goin' to take ol' Betsy back and sell her. And if you don't holler, I'll give you some more."

John: "No, Ma'am, I'm not gonna holler, I'm not gonna holler."

So she 'cided she goin' give John some up there in the barn on the hay. And so they started with the intercourse, and John every now and then he say [short gasps, then], "Oooh, oooh," every now and then, y'know. It gettin' better and better to John.

Say, "John, you know you tol' me you wadn't gonna holler?"

"No, no [gasp], I'm, I'm not gonna holler now, I'm not gonna holler." So every now and then it would git a little better and a little better. John: "Oh!"

She say, "John, you better not holler."

"I ain't gonna holler, I'm not goin' holler."

So way on down the road, she say, "You know what I told you about Betsy, John?"

He say, "No, I'm not gonna holler."

In a few minutes it got good to John. He come. The point come now. John say, "Lawd; farewell, Betsy, farewell, I can't help it! Oh, *Lawd have mercy!*"

John Learns a New Language

This is a tale about John. He always lived up North, and he got tired of northern states and 'cided he would come South. So John came South and stopped at a white fellow's house and asked him 'bout a job. White fellow told him, "I don't know"; says, "I can hire you, but I can't pay you as much as they do in the northern states. But, anyway, we'll make out." So he say, "What is your name?"

He say, "My name is John." Anyway, they got acquainted with one another. And so at night, see, in those days they didn't have gas like we have now and lights, so forth. They made a fire with pine wood in the fireplaces.

Anyway, they was sittin' at this fireplace at night and talkin' over different things; the differences between the South and the North. So this fellow, since he was goin' to hire John, he asked him, says, "What is that sittin' over there in the corner?" Which it was a cat.

John says, "That's a cat."

And he says [thinking he'd have some fun with the newcomer], "No, John." Says, "That's not a cat," says, "that's a bald-eye eagle."

John say, "Okay, that's bald-eye eagle."

And he looked down at John's feet, say, "What's that you got down there, John?" Pointed at John's feet.

John say, "That's my shoes."

He say, "No, John." Say, "That's your creepers." So he looked at his clothes; he pointed, say, "What's that, John?"

John says, "That's my clothes."

He says, "No, John, that's your creeders." So one word to another, and he took John to the door, asked him, say, "What's that out there, John?" Which was a barn, y'know.

John say, "That's the barn."

He say, "No, John, that's not a barn." He say, "That's High Top Mountain." And this fellow had ate and got sleepy and 'cided he'd go to bed.

So, woke up the next morning; John got up first since the man had hired him, and he was goin' to make a fire so they could git warm and have breakfast, y'know. Anyway, John got up and he was foolin' around there and the cat came up, which the man called bald-eye eagle. Come up and he hauled off and hit John with his paw. And John had this fire already lit, and he stuck the fire to the cat, y'know. Cat run out of the house, run up there in the barn, got up in the hay and stuff and set the barn afire. So John couldn't catch the cat and couldn't put the barn out. He run back to the door and he called the boss. "Hey, Boss!"

Say, "Yes, John."

Says, "Git up and put on your creepin' creeders." Say, "Bald-eye eagle done set High Top Mountain afire!"

Say, "Hey, what you say, John?" See, he done forgot he told John that jive there during the night. So he still didn't understand.

So John say, "You better git up and put on your damn shoes and clothes." Says, "That cat done set the barn on fire, and you better hurry up and make it snappy!"

The Foolish Bride

This boy was goin' to see his girl, and he had promised to marry this girl. So he 'cided he would have dinner with the girl before he married her. That's back a long time ago. Instead of goin' to town and buyin' syrup [molasses] like they do these days, they made it, and they kept it in barrels. And when they wanted syrup on the table, they'd take a container out and turn the keg up over it and let the syrup come out; and it would come out slowly, y'know, until it filled the container up, and then they'd take it back to the kitchen.

So they had dinner fixed—mother, father, and everybody—for this guest. And this boy, they called him in and they got to the table and the mother says, "Oh, Sister, we forgot something. We don't have any syrup on the table." Says, "Sister, will you go draw some syrup?"

Sister say, "Yes, Mother, I'll go draw some syrup." So she went out there to draw the syrup, and she turned the keg up over the container and let the syrup start runnin' in. And she put her hand to her jaw, and she was thinkin'. She says, "Lawd, I'm tryin' to think what Brother's oldest son is named." And she set there and thought.

And so she stayed so long, her mother say, "Lemme go see what's wrong with Daughter." Say, "She's stayin' too long." So she goes out. She say, "Daughter, what are you doin'?"

Daughter say, "Mother, I'm just tryin' to think what Brother's oldest son is named." So Mother, she started helpin' think, too! She stays a long time.

So Father, he say, "Let me go see what's wrong with Mother and Daughter." So he goes out. "What are you all doin'?" he says.

"We . . . Sister's jus' tryin' to think what Brother's oldest son is named, and I was jus' here tryin' to help her think."

So this boy he still sit there, he sit there. He 'cided he would go out and see what all of 'em was doin'. So he went out there and looked. Syrup done run all out on the groun'! And he says, "Hey, what are you all doin'?"

Mother say, "Daughter was jus' tryin' to think what Brother's oldest son is named, and I started tryin' to helpin' her think."

And Father say, "Well, I tried to help them think what Brother's oldest son is named."

The fellow that was goin' to marry the daughter say, "Damn!" Says, "I'm goin'. I don't want no dinner." He say, "Now, if I find three more fools like y'all, I'll marry your daughter. Unless that, I won't." And he left.

So he went on down the road. He got down the road, he saw a lady goin' 'round and 'round the house with an empty wheelbarrow, 'round and 'round the house. So he stood and watched the lady. He say, "Lady, what you doin'?"

She says, "I jus' washed off my back porch, son, and," says, "it ain't no sunshine around there"; says, "I'm tryin' to roll some of this sunshine around there to dry the back porch."

He say, "I'll be damned!"

He went on up the road a little further and man had a pretty, nice brick house, pretty lawn with fine grass on it. And the man had a rope th'owed across the housetop and he was jus' swingin' down on that rope for all he's worth. Jus' sweatin' up everything. Boy asked him, "Hey, mister," say, "what are you doin'?"

He say, "Son, I'm goin' tell you somethin'." Say, "I got some old oxen 'round behind the house there." And say, "They so poor, I'm tryin' to pull 'em over on the grass."

He say, "Mister, take the rope off and drive the oxes around." And say, "They'll come on around."

He told him, "I hadn't thought of that." He took the rope and drove 'em on around, and they went to eatin'.

He say, "Damn, look like I'm goin' to have to marry that gal anyway." He say, "I'm goin' to leave the road; I'm goin' down through these woods."

So he went down through the woods, turn off the road so he wouldn't meet nary another fool. He got thirsty and wanted some water. He say, "Well, there's an old spring down here; I'm goin' to stop at this spring and get me some water." Got to the spring. Happened to look up: man had a hog by its back legs jus' pushin' him, y'know. Juggin' him like he's tryin' to push a wheelbarrow or somethin'. Says, "Hey, mister, what are you doin'?"

He say, "I got a hog here and he's so poor, he won't even root." He says, "I'm tryin' to make him root."

He say, "Mister," say, "put him down; he'll go out there and go to rootin'." So he put the hog down and he went on out there and jus' started to rootin' and eatin' up everything, sticks and all.

He says, "I'll be damn. I guess I'll go back and marry her." He turned around and went on back. And he married the girl.

So he told her, "Honey," says, "here's ten dollars"; and say, "I want you to keep this for Mister Hard Times, hear?"

She say, "Okay, Honey."

And he says, "I got a big old ham of meat in there." Says, "That's to go on these cabbage greens during the summer." He says, "Okay?" That means the cabbage greens they was goin' to raise, y'know.

So they went on, made it up 'til the summer, y'know. They had nice greens and everything, plenty to eat. Then things got kind of hard, and he wanted some of that ham meat that he had told her to go in the greens. So he asked her, says, "Honey," say, "you say you don't have anything to eat." Say, "How 'bout some of that ham meat I told you we goin' to put in them greens this summer?"

She say, "Honey," says, "when those cabbage first come up," says, "I cut it [the ham] up in little thin slices and put a thin slice on every head."

So that made him mad. He says, "I shouldn't a married this fool at the start with." He say, "Where my ten dollars?"

She say, "Next day after we got married," say, "Mister Hard Times come by here and I give it to him."

So he quit her, and that's the end of that story.

The Suitor and the Bear

One time there was a boy. He had a nice girlfriend. He enjoyed her all right; quite a, y'know, good deal. And he would go and see his girl. But he was afraid, y'know, to be out at night, see. And, nine times out of ten, every time he would go see this girl he would overstay hisself, and it'd be night when he leave, y'know.

So he went to see his girl one time and he stayed real late, and it was a real dark night. He happened to look up and it was dark outside, so he goes to this girl's father and asked him could he spend the night.

This girl's father say, "No, you can't spend the night here." Say, "Fact about it, I don't have any place for you to sleep." So he says, "Why you want to spend the night?"

He say, "'Cause I'm afraid to go home."

He says, "Son, it's nothin' out there'll bother you, but *bears*." And he say, "If you do everything the bear do, they won't bother you."

So the young fellow took the old man at his word. He 'cided he'd leave. He left slowly; he was undecided about goin', y'know. So he went on across the hill, down through the woods; it was real dark. Finally, he come out of the woods, y'know, into a nice fair place, goin' up a hill befo' he get to some mo' woods. But still he wadn't home, see.

And he finally looks up and he right up in a bear's face! So he thought about what the old man had told him. The bear shook his head. The boy shook his head. So the bear got down on the ground on his all-fours, started pawin' up dirt. He did the same thing. He stood back up. The old bear, see, pulled up his tail and started doing his business, y'know. So the little old fellow he says, "Oh, I'm sorry, Brother Bear, but, I, I, I did that when I first saw you!"

The Boy and the White Dog

Now, this is a true story. This fellow he was kindly young too; about, I guess, twelve or fifteen years old. And kindly similar of the story about this bear and this other little fellow. And he liked to go out a lot at night, and he went off. And he believed in a lot of h'unted [haunted] places, y'know. And he had to come through woods the same as this other young fellow did, that run up on this bear that time. And he was afraid of dead people. So he had to come by a house that a lady had died in durin' the wintertime, and weeds had growed all up around it. Didn't nobody else live there, 'cause it was an old lady and I guess she was the last of the family. So this fellow come through the trail, a little old narrow trail, y'know.

And a white dog was at this house, and he run across the path into the weeds. So this boy took a little runnin' start and run on up the hill there. And finally he saw two stones. He picked up the two stones, y'know, and he went on down; had to go 'cross a creek. He waded across the creek on the rocks. And he didn't see the dog no more. He thought that was that lady he saw. Anyway, he went on across the open field and he still didn't see a thing, but he still had his two stones in his hand.

Finally, he come on into another patch of woods. This little dog got in the road in the front of him again. Goin' up the hill, and he was 'fraid to throw the two rocks because it was dark and he couldn't find no more; he afraid he goin' to miss. So he went on further and further. Further he got the 'fraider he got. So 'fraid, sometimes he feel like he could hear somethin', but it wadn't nothin' but his heart beatin'! But sound like he hear somethin' walkin' in steps.

So then he had open road, y'know; got just about home. And his father had a fence 'round his yard, a picket fence. But the gate was closed. His trail runnin' right into the road, and he had to go 'cross the highway into the gate.

After he got there, there this dog was standin' right there at the gate! Standin' up with his head high, lookin'. The dog wouldn't say nothin'; and he'd holler, "Boo! Git away from there, sir!" Dog still wouldn't move, just lookin' at him. So finally he thought about he still had those two stones. He drawed back and th'owed one of those stones, and he hit the dog. The dog fell on the road; went to kickin', turnin' 'round an' 'round. That's how he got by.

He run to the gate and opened the gate. And when he got to the door, he didn't have time to tell his father and mother he was comin' in or to open the door. He hit the screen and went through the screen door, knocked the inside door open and fell in, just fell up in the house. And he was 'dead' there for a while. When he woke up they was pourin' water on him. And that's true. But I won't call the name of who that feller was.

Rosa Campbell, Her Mother, and Friends, Monticello, Georgia. Barbara McKenzie.

The Flash of Heat

See, he was ridin' down this road on his horse one night and it was real dark; and he believed in haunts, y'know. So he always heard that a ha'nt would, er, uh, if you ever tried to fight it, it would right away and slap you, y'know. So he was ridin' down the road on this horse one night and all a sudden a warm flash of heat came across in the front of him. Say he knowed that was a ha'nt. So after then, he was just settin' there 'fraid to death on this horse.

He ride a little piece. And another warm part of heat went by him. He says, "Lawd, this haint goin' to git me afore I git home." So a'rec'ly he saw somethin'. It was right beside of him, and say it look jus' like a man with no head on! Finally he hauled off and slapped the man with no head on, and it turned out to be a pine bush! That's right!

How to Stall a Ha'nt

Older people believes in ha'nts and so forth. Long time ago, they said, when they be walkin' at night, if they thought it was a haunted trail they was on they would carry whiskey along. If a ha'nt would get after 'em, they would pour it in the tracks, y'know. So, he would stop and drink, and finally [they'd] get home, y'know.

When Bozo Comes

One time it was an old haunted house. They couldn't git nobody to stay in it at night. People would move there, and they would hear such a racket at night they would leave the next day.

And so people got to talkin' about it—couldn't git nobody to stay in the house—and they wanted to let somebody stay in it free or either pay somebody to stay in it. This old fellow says, "I'll stay in the house. All I want you to do is just to pay me."

They says, "All right," say, "we'll pay you for stayin' in the house, if you'll just stay in it one night."

So this fellow he got his ax and his shotgun and gathered him up some food, such as bacon meat and so forth, and carried it on out there 'fore night. And before night, he got him some wood and so forth up. Built him a fire to keep warm and cook his food too, 'cause he had to cook it on the fireplace. Night come; he sittin' up there, ready for the haints if they came like all these other people that lived there said, y'know. So he got hungry. He had his good fire and hot coals there, and he got his skillet out the bag over there and set it on the fire and started fryin' him some bacon.

So while he was fryin' the bacon, here come in a great big ol' somethin': look like a cat, bigger than any ordinary cat you ever saw. He stood right up in the corner beside his shotgun, jus' rared up on his back feet and stood up. So he asked the old fellow, says, "Is you goin' to be here when Bozo come?"

Fellow looked over there at him in the corner, he say, "Yeah, I'm goin' to be here when Bozo come." Kept on fryin' his meat.

Later on another one came in. He was larger than that one. Stood up in another corner. He asked him the same thing: "Is you goin' be here when Bozo come?"

Old man got to gittin' afraid, then. "Yes, I'm goin' to be here when Bozo come!" Kept on stirrin' his meat, turnin' his meat over, so forth.

Little while longer, *another* one came in. He stood up in the next corner. He asked the same question, but he was a little larger than the other two. "You goin' be here when Bozo come?"

Looked around at him; "Yes, I'm goin' be here when Bozo come."

Well, about a hour or two later, another one came; that was the fourth one. He stood up in the fourth corner, and he was larger than the other three put together! Asked him—he sounded a little louder, "You goin' to be here when Bozo come?"

Man looked up, say, "Yes, I'm goin' to be here when Bozo come." Kept on fryin' his meat, turnin' and stirrin' his meat, y'know, to keep from burnin'.

Said later on, about three or four hours later, here come in one big as all of 'em in the house. He didn't say a word when he first come in. Said he reached in the fryer of hot grease and got that meat out—hot as it was—and just swallowed all of it at one time. Then he reached down and got the fryer and turned it up and drank that hot grease out the fryin' pan, and reached behind hisself and got his tail and heist his tail up and wiped his behind with that fryin' pan and [louder and faster] th'owed it back there in the floor and looked back at him again and say, "Is you goin' to be here when Bozo come!?"

So he says, "No; if you ain't Bozo, naw, I won't be here when Bozo come!" And he left!

A Hoodoo's Work?

I was goin' to school and workin' durin' the summer months at the hospital. And I actually seed . . . I don't know what it was, but it would move; it was kindly round like a chestnut, and it had stickers on it like a chestnut, when they operated on him and took it out. I don't know what that thing was. But the doctors kep' it and they put it in alcohol and they still got it, I think. And I don't know, they don't know what it was and what it is. That's real and I saw it, 'cause I was workin' in a hospital. And the doctor would mash on it like that and it would—like you mash a worm—and it would raise back up, but it was round.

Old Doctor and Young Doctor

Once upon a time, it was two doctors: young doctor and a old doctor. Young doctor he was studyin' doctorin', and the old doctor he'd been at it for years, y'know. So this young doctor got this old doctor to teach him, so fur as he had money to pay. It was in the olden days, long time ago. People had horses and buggies and so forth; that was they best way to get around, travelin'. So this old doctor would teach this young doctor how to judge his cases and so forth. And so, as he was teachin' him, he'd take him out on different calls with him. And he [the young doctor] say, "Doctor, what does that patient have?"

"Well, you see all of those cans piled up out there in the backyard?"

This young doctor say, "Yeah."

He say, "Well, that's how I judge my cases. I put on a diary, so and so many canned foods; that reduces those cans, so I call it the can fever. So that's one of the ways to judge your cases."

And so this old doctor taught this young doctor for years and years and years. Got down 'til this young doctor didn't have no more money.

This old doctor ready to git rid of him. Say, "Well, you graduate next week, but it's one more thing I got to learn you before you graduate."

The young doctor says, "Doc, I don't have any money." He says, "I can't pay you, I don't have anything to pay you with."

He say, "Well, I'll teach you for that black horse and buggy you got." And he say, "That's the last thing you'll need to know." And so this young doctor, he loved this black horse and buggy. He 'cided he'd give up the black horse and buggy jus' to learn; he done went that fur. So he gave up the black horse and buggy.

And went on; this old doctor, he didn't see him in a long time. So the old doctor got sick. And they called this young doctor to come wait on him. This young doctor came over to wait on him. He waited on him and waited on him. He give 'im somethin' to do him good a day or two, and then he give 'im somethin' to give him a backset. Until he got all the old doctor's money back that he done paid him. So he [the old doctor] told him, say, "Well, Doc, I don't have any more money."

He [the young doctor] say, "Well, I tell you what it takes to git you well. It takes that black horse and buggy. It take my black horse and buggy back." So he 'cided to give him the black horse and buggy 'cause he wanted to git well. So he gi' 'im that black horse and buggy. This young doctor give him somethin' to git him well, and didn't have to come back an' see him anymore.

Well, weeks later, this old doctor and young doctor met up downtown. They was talkin', goin' on, glad to see one another, y'know. So this old doctor say, "Hey, Doc." Asked the young doctor, "Say, what was my trouble here awhile back when I was sick?"

He say, "Well, Doc, I tell you." Say, "You had the black horse fever." So that was the end of that.

Shorty, Slim, and the Judge

Two gals down on the creek fishin', a short gal and a tall gal. And while they was fishin', one of 'em broke wind, y'know. After this one broke wind, this other one laughed, "Hee, hee."

Say, "What's the matter?"

She say, "I can beat ya, I can beat ya doin' it." She say, "You had a little short one"; say, "I can make a long one."

She say, "Naw." From one word to another, these gals got to fightin'. So while they was fightin', the game warden come up and locked 'em both up 'bout fightin'. Locked 'em up; and then, quite naturally, they had to have trial before they could git out.

So when trial day come up, carried 'em before the judge, both of 'em. So judge made a statement before court come into session. Said if they did like he wanted—he said do—they would go free; unlessen they did, each one be charged a twenty-five dollar fine. So they called court in session, and first one they called up there was this slim, tall girl, y'know. He say, "Okay," says, "now court's in session." And says, "I'm goin' give you your fine up here if you don't act like I tell you." Say, "You goin' to have to pay a twenty-five dollar fine or either spend twenty-five days in jail."

So she says, "Okay, Judge, your Honor."

So he say, "Now I count," says, "I want you to fart, hear?"

Slim say, "Yes sir, Judge, your Honor."

So Judge 'cided he would count. "One, two, three, four."

Old Slim said, "Boot, boot, boot, boot."

He say, "Your case dismissed." Called Shorty up there. He goin' mess Shorty up now, 'cause he didn't git nothin' outta Slim; he meant to git fifty dollars outta that case. He got little Shorty up there. He say, "Okay, Shorty," says, "now, I want you to do like I tell you." Says, "As I count, I want you to poot."

Shorty say, "Okay, Judge, your Honor."

So old judge say, "One, two, three, *and a half.*"

Shorty says, "Boot, boot, boot, poooo."

So he say, "Case dismissed." He didn't git a thing out of that!

Roosevelt and the Law

One time, old fellow lived over in Alabama. He used to make home brew, y'know. His name was Roosevelt. It was against the law, in a dry county too, to have any kind of alcoholic drinks to make anybody intoxicated, and they would lock you up and charge you a big fine if they caught you doin' it. So this fellow he made home brew anyway, whether it was against the law or not.

So one day there, he was makin' him some home brew. You had to stir it, y'know, before you put it up, so he told me. Old Roosevelt, he was jus' sittin' there stirrin' this home brew. He stirrin' and stirrin', jus' kept stirrin'. Didn't think nobody was close around. The boys always come by and pick at him, y'know, that bought they home brew from him. So anyway, this time it wadn't a boy, it was the sheriff! He walked in the house; Roosevelt had left the door open and the sheriff walked on in. Roosevelt ain't even looked up; still stirrin' his home brew. So the sheriff

asked, "Hey, what are you doin', Roosevelt, makin' home brew?"

So Roosevelt say, "Hell, yeah. Y'know I ain't makin' no damn wine."

So he say, "What you goin' to do with that home brew, Roosevelt? You gonna sell it?"

He say, "Hell, yeah, I'm goin' to sell it; I ain't gonna give it away." So on down later, Roosevelt 'cided he'd better look up; that voice sound kinda familiar to him. He happened to look up, and looked up in the sheriff's face. "Oh, oh, oh!" He say, "You Mr. Harris, you the law! You the law! Uh!" Says, "Uh, uh, Mr. Harris, uh, uh, uh, you, you, you gonna take me to jail?"

He say, "I ain't gonna take you to church, Roosevelt."

Say, "Uh, uh, uh, uh, Mr. Harris," says, "uh, uh, uh, is, is, is you, you, you gonna, you gonna, is you gonna make me pay a fine?"

He says, "I ain't gonna let you out free, Roosevelt."

Say, "Uh, uh, uh, Mr. Harris," says, "if, if, if I don't pay this fine," says, "is you gonna, you gonna take me to the chain gang?"

He says, "I ain't gonna take you to heaven, Roosevelt!"

On the Cooling Board

I ain't gonna call no names 'cause, ah, this is true. And this guy got quite a few rich people around, you know. But now, this is a true tale on this undertaker guy. Anyway, he loved to get bodies, especially when people had a wreck, especially these wild teenagers get out there like they is now. Shoot, he was glad of that! He likeded that because he knowed he was goin' to git some business.

One day they're goin' to school. This old boy he was a Tuck; that was his last name, Tuck. His father and mother buy him a brand-new car every year. And so, he liked to go off and have him a drink of beer or somepin', and fool around and git to talkin' to the boys. And he'd run late, and he'd drive his car wide open jes' about all the time, jes' about as fast as it would go.

Anyway, on the way to school this mornin', runnin' about as fast as his car would run, he had a wreck and turned over. Well, it didn't kill him; it just knocked him unconscious. Anyway, somebody pretty close around called the undertaker to come pick him up and take him to the hospital. This undertaker man picked him up; on the way to the hospital, he looked back at him and he say, "Aw, shoot, he dead. I might as well take him on to the undertaker." So he took him on to the undertaker; put him on the coolin' board and spread the white sheet over him.

That guy was layin' up there on the coolin' board; and this undertaker man was foolin' around back in there, fiddlin' with his black box, needle, and so forth, gettin' ready to give him the blackout. So while he was fumblin' around in the back room, this guy what he brought in in the ambulance he raised up and looked around; he come to, see. Looked around and saw all these castets in there and he said, last thing he could remember he was on the way to school. Look around, saw all these castets; he started slidin' off o' the table after he saw all those castets. And so this old guy came back. Says, "Hey," says, "wait a minute, wait a minute."

By that time, say he started running then. This guy reach and grabbed the rubber hammer, an' started behind him. Say, "Hey, wait a minute, wait a minute," say, "you death-dodgin' son-of-a-bitch! You wait a minute, wait a minute!" So

the guy was runnin' so fast; he was afraid, the one had the sheet over him. And so he [the undertaker] say, "If you ain't comin' back, you death-dodgin' son-of-a-bitch, I wish you'd leave my sheet!" And so this boy dropped the sheet and kept goin'.

Little Boy Who Cussed

They couldn't keep this little boy from cussin', y'know. So this fellow came by, he says, "I can break him up from cussin'." That's what the man told the little boy's mother.

She says, "No," says, "all these years and we hadn't broke him; we don't believe you can break him from cussin'." But say, "I tell you what we'll do. I'll give you five dollars if you break him from cussin'."

So the fellow say, "Wait 'til the night and I'll break him up." Quite naturally, the mother and the father and all of 'em wanted to see him break him up from cussin', 'cause he a young kid, it'll grow up in him.

This fellow goes to town to the undertaker to git a castet. While this little boy asleep—he sleep sound, you know—put him in this castet and took him out to the graveyard and set him up on a table out there in the castet in the graveyard.

This boy slept all night. Mama and Daddy and the preacher and everybody settin' around tryin' to watch when the boy wake up, see if he'll cuss, 'cause he usually cuss every mornin' when he wake up, y'know. So they was hidin' behind tombstones to keep the little boy from seein', seein' what he gonna say, before they paid this man off fo' breakin' him up from cussin'.

So the sun rose this morning; little boy always wake up about sunrise. Sun rose, little boy woke up and raised up and looked all 'round. He saw he was in the castet. He thought he'd done died and they'd buried him and he was jus' raisin' from the dead. So the little boy jumped out of the castet down on the ground and say, "Hey," say, "Gabriel blowed the trumpet and I'm the first son-of-a-bitch rose!"

Teacher and the Bad Boy

Once there was a teacher, she 'as giving class—arithmetic—to different kids in school. She had some good children; then she had one little bad boy, kep' up some devil all the time, you know. So she called the class up to the stage that morning. She had 'em puttin' numbers on the board.

"Mary," says, "just think up you a number and go put it on the board." So Mary thought up her a number; she went and put twelve on the board. She said, "Now, Mary, if you turn that 'round backwards," say, "what would that be?"

She say, "Twenty-one."

She say, "That's right. Go sit down." She called John up to the board. She say, "John," says, "put you a number up there." John wrote him a number up there. Thirteen. Says, "What's that? Thirteen?"

He says, "Yes Ma'am, that's thirteen."

She says, "You turn it around backwards, what will it be?"

John says, "Be thirty-one."

So she come on 'round to this little bad boy. So he went to the board. She says, "Put your number on the board, son."

He says, "Yes Ma'am." He went up there and put two numbers up there—straight, straight marks—eleven.

Say, "What is that number you got up there?"

Say, "It's eleven." He says, "Now you fuck with that!"

Jew Girl, White Girl, and Colored Girl

One time there was three girls: there's a white girl, a Jew girl, and a colored girl. They always git together and have little talks together to themselves, y'know, and ask one another a lot of different questions about their husbands and so forth. So one day they got deep in a conversation 'bout what make each other hot. And so this white girl she finally ask this Jew girl, say, "Hey," says, "what can your husband do to make you hot?" White girl say, "Mine come in and kiss me every day and that makes me hot." So she say, "What makes you hot?"

Jew girl say, "Well, my husband have to come in," say, "he have to hug me and squeeze me and pet me. And that makes me hot."

So asked the colored girl, say, "What makes you hot?"

And she say, "Hell, my husband come in on Friday and don't give me none of that damn check; that's what makes me hot!"

Jew, White Man, and Colored Man

One time there was three mans: a Jew, a white man, and a colored man. And God told their bossman, 'spec' they'd go to heaven if each one of 'em had a dollar apiece. And so the bossman decided he would give this dollar to 'em and let 'em go to heaven.

Next day they got this dollar apiece, and they started on to heaven. First thing, the white man went on to heaven. He went up there and knocked on the door. Says, "Hey, my Lord Jesus," says, "how much is it to go to heaven?"

Say, "One dollar."

So he paid this dollar and went on to heaven.

So a few minutes later here comes this Jew steppin' in there. Says [in clipped accent], "Hey, my Lord." Says, "How much is it to go to heaven?"

My Lord told him, "It's one dollar."

He says, "I don't have but ninety-eight cents."

So God says, "Well, give me your ninety-eight cents and come on to heaven." So he shut the door.

Well, this Negro, he had done stopped and bought him a brand new suit. He got dead sharp, cool; as sharp as a tack, cool as a cucumber. He had a quarter left. He stopped by the liquor house and got him a quarter-shot of liquor. Got about high. And so later on, 'bout the shank of the evening, this Negro staggered up and knocked on the door: bop, bop, bop, bop! Say, "Whatcha say there, J. C.?" Say, "How much is it to go to heaven?"

My Lord told him, say, "One dollar."

He say, "Well, can I pay you Saturday?"

He say, "Naw, go on back down yonder to hell." So he messed up; he had to go to hell!

The Irishman and the Overcoat

This is a story on a li'l old I'shman. He worked hard every day; he was a carpenter, do carpenter work. He had a great big overcoat he wore in the summer, in the winter; had a big, full linin' in it. An' it didn't make no difference how hot; if it got a hundred and ten degrees Fahrenheit, he would have that coat on. And so one of the guys that

was workin' with him on the job there one day says, "Hey," says, "why do you wear that big, heavy coat all the time?"

Say he told him, "Fee-fee-fetter-me-Christ! What keep the cold out, 'll keep the hot out." And he just kep' nailin'!

The Sneezing Irishman

Story 'bout an I'shman. He believed in witch doctors and so forth and what people tell him, signs and so forth. So he had a cold, and he went to this old witch doctor. And while he was there he hauled off and sneezed. "Hut-choo!"

So this witch doctor told him, say, "Well, you don't have long to live." Says, "You gonna die." Say, "You don't have but three more times to sneeze like that and you goin' die."

So this I'shman say, "Fetcher-me-Christ! Me got to go to the mill and git me some corn ground so me can have some meal." So he gits on his horse with a big sack of corn. He believed in this witch doctor so strong, y'know, he thought it was still true. And on the way up the road, he had to sneeze; but he tried to hold off long as he could. He just—"Hee, hee . . ."—tryin' to keep from sneezin', because he was tryin' to stay here long as he could, y'know.

He got up the road a little further and he tried to hold off again. Finally, he had to sneeze, anyway. So he come out, "Hut-choo!" Says, "Lawd have mercy! Fetcher-me-Christ! Me don't have me but two more times."

So he rode on up the road a little further and he tried to hold off again. So finally he just had to sneeze that second time. "Hut-choo!" He says, "Fetcher-me-Christ! Fetcher-me-Christ! Me no have but one more time and that'll be it!"

So he went on up the road. He tried to keep from it—he gagged [heavy breathing], tryin' to keep from sneezin'. Way after 'while, he just *had* to sneeze. He haul off and sneeze again. "Hut-choo!" And he jus' fell off his horse, corn and all, down on the ground. He jus' give up dead! He believed in the witch doctor so bad, give up dead. Fell over, and so the corn sack busted and the corn jus' spread out all on the ground there. The horse was there lookin' at him down on the ground.

And so a great big old sow with a lot of pigs came up there and they started eatin' the corn, jus' eatin' all his corn up. He layin' there, believin' that he was dead. Wouldn't even git up and move the corn or nothin'. He glanced up with one eye at the old sow. He says, "Fetcher-me-Christ, if me wadn't dead me git up and kill you, you son-of-a-bitch!"

The Titanic

You know the eighth of May
Was a hell of a day!
When the Titanic struck the big iceberg.

Up jumped Shine from two decks below.
He said, "Captain, Captain, the water's
All over that boiler room floor."

Captain looked at him, told him, say,
"Go back down there, Shine, and pack your sacks";
Say, "I got ninety-nine pumps on here to keep this
    water back."

Shine started back down the stairs kinda slow,
But that water was risin' too fast.
He got down about the second or third floor,
Run back upstairs; he didn't have time to talk to the
    captain.

He jumped overboard and begin to swim;
There was thousands of millionaires
Standin' up there lookin' at him.

So the captain told Shine, say,
"Come back here, Shine, and save poor me";
He say, "I'll make you rich as any Shine can be."

Shine told the captain, says,
"Captain, Captain, your word might be so,
But they's people got money on that other shore."

You know Shine could swim, Shine could float,
He could outswim any motorboat.
'Bout that time the Titanic was goin' down fast.

Here captain's daughter jumped up on the deck,
She had her titties in her hand
And her drawers up around her neck.

She say, "Come back, Shine, and save poor me."
She say, "I give you all this white ass that you see."

Shine say, "You hate my color, an' you despise my
    race."
Say, "Jump overboard, bitch,
And give these sharks a chase, like me!"

So when the news reached the seaport town
That the Titanic was sinkin' down,
Guess where Shine was?
He was over there on Auburn Avenue drinking
    liquor.

And guess where he was
When the news reached the seaport town
That the Titanic had sunk?
He was over on Edgewood, dead drunk!

Now if you want to know who proposed this toast,
Tell 'em it was ol' Lee, who's been from coast to
    coast.

CHAPTER SIX

Lem Griffis: Okefenokee Swamp Yarns

Kay L. Cothran

Fall 1966

Lem Griffis, who died in 1968, was Georgia's best-known traditional storyteller. His fame is linked to his job as guide to the fishermen and hunters who visited his camp on the edge of the Okefenokee, for he would entertain them with jests that they would take back to their homes elsewhere in Georgia, Florida, and even farther afield. He was also an important influence on the local storytellers of the swamp rim, among whom he has achieved legendary status.

Griffis specialized in the whopper, a hyperbolic description with minimal plot, and the more fully developed tall tales, but he also told puns and other kinds of humorous narratives. Many of his jests were exercises in illogic. While not formally schooled, he was literate. Much of his material he learned orally from locals, but he also wrote down tales told by customers and mined such popular publications as Captain Billy's Whiz Bang, *a humor magazine dating to the 1920s. He contributed to, as well as borrowed from, the print media, writing a weekly column called "Tall Tales" for the Clinch County newspaper and publishing a booklet of his humor.*

Kay Cothran Craigie was one of my first stu-dents. Continued research led to her 1972 doctoral dissertation at the University of Pennsylvania, "Such Stuff as Dreams: A Folkloristic Sociology of Fantasy in the Okefenokee Swamp Rim, Georgia." Her article "Talking Trash in the Okefenokee Swamp Rim, Georgia," originally published in the Journal of American Folklore, *was reprinted in* Jan H. Brunvand, ed., Readings in American Folklore *(New York: W. W. Norton Co., 1979), pp. 215–35.*

Lem Griffis country is extreme southeastern Georgia. His fishing camp, motel, and restaurant are located in the southern area of the Okefenokee Swamp in Clinch County by the Suwannee River, a greenish brown yet beautiful stream. The surrounding countryside is absolutely flat and largely deserted. The forests are owned by paper and turpentine companies, and most side roads are logging roads scraped through the sandy dirt. Spanish moss swings from the hardwood trees, outnumbered by the pines, and the ground is densely covered with palmettos.

The Griffis camp is about fifteen miles north

of Fargo, and hunters and fishermen come from all parts of Georgia and Florida to stay there. Griffis says his camp was the first one established in the state and was begun in the second decade of this century.

Lem Griffis is a browned, stringy man who does not look seventy years old. He and his wife had four children and raised five others. He is *the* local character and entertainer. His jokes are printed in the (Homerville) *Clinch County News*, and he has several newspaper articles which have been written about him. He once printed a booklet of his sayings, but only one copy remains with him. As a yarn spinner he is all grins and jokes, but as a singer he is rather serious, as though his songs were very important and no joking matter. Griffis's singing style is straightfaced, detached, unemotional, and oriented more toward the words than the tunes. His memory is fantastic, since he can produce several jokes on the spot for almost any subject one mentions.

Griffis wears the mantle of comedian comfortably. When I first came in I asked, "Are you Lem Griffis?"

He replied, "Yes, but I cain't he'p it."

As I was setting up the tape recorder, he continued. "I come from a family of long livers. One relative had one two feet long, an' when he died they had t' beat it with a stick t' kill it." While I was having dinner at the restaurant in his camp, he came over to the table to return thanks for us.

"Lord, make us able
To eat all the food on the table;
And if there's any more in the pot,
Please bring it while it's hot."

He then added, "I never did like food; it spoils my appetite."

Taking me through his swamp museum, he showed me various stuffed snakes, birds, and bear heads, as well as skeletons and fossils. He said, "I'll show you my mousetrap," and hauled out a monstrous bear trap. The museum also contained old tools, toys, and other artifacts which had been in his family for years. He showed me his father's rifle—his grandfather's before that—and said, "We've had it since it was a pistol." He brought out his mother's wool carders and a bedspread she had made by rolling up cut strips of worn-out clothing and weaving them together with homespun wool thread. He told me, "We had t' get every last thing we had off this spot of land. We didn't have no money, but we had no use for it. You couldn't eat it, drink it, nor wear it, so it wasn't a bit of good to us." On a shelf were several ingenious wooden toys and puzzles he had made for his grandchildren, including a dancing "limber-jack" doll, movable jointed snake, and climbing monkey on a stick.

When Griffis learned that I went to school, he said that he could read my mind with figures, adding that he had "studied figures on the beach." He proceeded to confound me with a series of number tricks. What struck me was the situation itself: a sly, unschooled country person hilariously getting the better of an educated city slicker. Griffis never went to school, but he claims he taught himself to write with his finger in the sand. After my visit, I understood fully what Stephen Collins Foster State Park superintendent L. H. Day meant when he said, "That Lem, he's a doozy."

Griffis is extremely easy to work with in a session, although setting one up can be tricky. He tries to beg off, but with scarcely a pause for encouragement, he spouts jokes and anecdotes. Later, he will not tell anything for all one's coaxing. These sessions were held in the small general store in Lem Griffis's fishing camp. The listeners included the collector's parents, Mr. and Mrs. J. L. Cothran, and several deer hunters who wandered in and out.

Lem Griffis: This sign over here, this is one I put up a few days ago: "Make America beautiful, get a shave and haircut, keep it that way, walk backwards, put something pretty on the junkyard. If you don't see what you want, you have come to the right place." You recorded all that?

Kay Cothran: Yeah.

Griffis: Well, I didn't know it. I'd oughta been tellin' you somethin' interestin'.

Good Fishing

I carried a lady a-fishin' not long ago, y'know, an' she caught so many fish she couldn' put 'em in one pile.

Cothran: Is that a fact?

Griffis: Yeah. I stopped at the root of a big cypress tree, an' she went t' catchin' fish, an' she jus' caught 'em an' caught 'em an' caught 'em 'til the tree jus' fell over; nothin' there t' hold it up, all the fish was in it. Ha!

Cothran: Is that right?

Griffis: I was fishin' fer bass down there a few days ago, an' I cast my plug over side of a big log, an' a bass struck at m' plug, an' missed it, an' swallowed that log.

Fella hooked a big un down there, an' the fish pulled an' pulled, an' he jus' gritted his teeth an' helt t' the pole. An' the fish pulled 'im in an' dashed with 'im, an' pulled 'im so fast, skiddin'

on top o' the water, 'til 'is britches got s' hot they caught afire, an' he had t' turn 'is pole loose an' go t' fightin' fire.

Remarkable Kinfolk

Cothran: What was that you were tellin' me about this relative of yours who's so tall?

Griffis: That was one o' m' uncles; he growed so tall he had t' climb a ladder t' shave 'isself.

Cothran: Hoo-ee.

Griffis: One o' m' uncles, he was so short an' chunky, 'til ever' time he'd fall down he'd fall right back up agin.

Oh, you talk about ancestors, but I had a bunch of 'em. An' I have a bunch of in-laws—an' out-laws—now. Me an' m' wife, we live in a 'leven-room house, but when all m' in-laws an' out-laws git here they fill it up.

Cothran: You say you've traced your family back a good way? Why don't you tell me some more about 'em?

Griffis: Well, I traced 'em all the way back, placed my family tree all the way back t' where they lived in it. [Chuckles] I know some of my ancestors hung by the neck, an' I expec' some of 'em hung by the tails.

Healthy Country

Cothran: Well, you got any more?

Griffis: We live in the healthies' place out there is, I guess, in the worl'. We haven't had but two deaths in the last ten years. That was a doctor an' an undertaker, an' they both starved t' death. We had t' kill a man t' start a graveyard!

Dispensable Doctors

Doctor come out here one time, plunderin' aroun'; fell in the well an' got drowned. We did not have no mercy for 'im, because he should of been a-tendin' to the sick an' leavin' the well alone.

Cothran: Ohhhh me, now.

Griffis: I never did have t' go t' but three doctors. I went t' one many years ago, an' he give me so many pills, I still got ball-bearin' knee-joints. Few years later I went to 'nother one; he give me s' much medicine I was sick for two months after I got well. Then m' wife, she would have me t' go see one o' them psychiatris' doctors, one o' them kind thet'll help you t' go crazy?

Cothran: Yeah?

Griffis: I went in 'is office, I said, "Doc, I'm in tur'ble bad fix, I ain't slep' a wink in over two weeks. Every night when I lay down on my bed an' close my eyes t' go t' sleep, hippopotamusses, rhinoceros, gorillas, lions, tigers, baboons, monkeys jus' go t' marchin' right from under my bed."

He looked at me kinda cross-eyed, an' he says, "Well, I'll admit you're in a *bad* fix, but I cain't see nobody noway, only by appointment. You'll have t' come back tomorra."

But I didn' go back. Week later I met up wi' that doctor; he ast me why I didn' go back. I tol' 'im I didn' need t' go back, I went t' see another feller.

He says, "The other feller a doctor?"

I said, "No, he was a carpenter. He cut the legs off my bed, an' now I sleep perfec'."

An Uppity Blackfish

There 'as a colored feller down hyer one day, standin' on the banks o' the river a-fishin', an' he hooked one o' them large blackfish—we call 'em Johnson bass now.

Cothran: How come you call 'em that?

Griffis: Well, 'cause they're black [allusion to President Lyndon Johnson's support of racial integration].

Cothran: I see.

Griffis: And the fish was s' heavy he couldn' pull it out with 'is pole, so he 'as just a-walkin' backwards up the bank, draggin' 'im out. Ground went slick an' 'is feet slip from under 'im; he fell in the river, turned 'is pole loose, an' the fish went swimmin', draggin' the pole off. An' this colored feller he crawled up on the bank, spit the water out of his mouth, an' looked back at 'is pole a-bein' drug off by that fish. He said, "Now, what I wanta know am dis: is dis nigger fishin' or am dat fish niggerin'?"

Swamp 'Gators

Cothran: What about some of the animals in the swamp, Lem; what-all have you got out there?

Griffis: Well, we got many different kinds of animals hyer. I just motored 'long by an alligator a few days ago up here 'at was so long he was sweatin' in the face an' had frost on 'is tail.

Cothran: Hoo-ee.

Griffis: An' I have t' tell the lady-folks t' don't be afraid 'em alligators, because they're just man-eaters.

Cothran: That's comforting; I'm glad to know about that. What about snakes?

Cannibal Snakes

Griffis: Oh yeah, we have a good many snakes hyer. Y'know, snakes they're tur'ble 'bout fightin' each other. Now, when they run together t' fight, they always fight until death, and when one kills the other he always do swaller 'im; 'e never fails, always eats 'im.

I saw two of 'em run together for a fight, an' they caught each other by the tail an' went t' swall'in', an' they swallad an' they swallad 'til there wasn't anything but two heads there, an' gave one more swalla, an' 'twas no snake atall!

The Snakebit Walking Cane

We have some o' the most deadly poison snakes here 'an most anyplace in the world, I reckon. Uncle Paul, he come down to see us one time. An' he walked with a walkin' cane; went t' carry one after he was ninety-six. An' he was walkin' aroun' through the woods out here; one o' them poisonous snakes struck at 'is leg an' hit that walkin' cane. He walked little ways fu'ther, noticed that walkin' cane begin t' get heavy, an' he looked at it an' it 'as all swollen up. He couldn' carry it but a little ways fu'ther, before it got s' big an' heavy he jus' *had* t' leave it.

He thought lots of 'is walkin' cane, so nex' mornin' 'e went down t' see about it. By that time it 'as swollen up 'til it was just an enormous-size log. He notified feller t' have a sawmill t' come git that log an' saw it inta lumber. But by that time it 'as swollen so large it couldn' be moved; so 'e moved 'is sawmill to it, an' 'e sawed enough crossties outta that swollen-up walkin' cane t' build ten miles of railroad. After 'e got 'is railroad built there come up a awful heavy rain, washed all the poison outta them crossties; so he gathered 'em up an' sold 'em for toothpicks!

Cothran: What's the biggest snake y' ever saw?

Griffis: Ohh, 'bout as big [in diameter] as a gallon jug: cottonmouth. They git bigger.

Extraordinary Hens and Hogs

"Uncle Buddy" Griffis (Lem's brother): Lem, I think I'll go feed the chickens an' hogs now.

Griffis: Okay. He's a-goin' t' feed my hens; y'know, got hens out there 'at lay eggs so large it don't take but five of 'em t' make a dozen.

Cothran: Is that so?

Griffis: An' my hogs out there, I feed them fish, y'know, fatten 'em on fish; an' I killed one not long ago 'as fat on fish an' fried the grease out of 'im; got nine gallons o' cod-liver oil.

People they butcher a lot o' catfish out there, an' them catfish is tur'ble bad t' swalla the hook. So they jus' cut the catfish head off, throw 'em out there hooks an' all; an' my hogs they just eat fish heads, fish hooks, an' all as they come to it. An' one o' my hogs got so full o' fish hooks I had t' sell 'im for junk.

Cothran: Scrap metal, huh?

Griffis: They couldn' cut 'im up; they had t' melt 'im.

Nothing Spooky

Cothran: Did you ever hear anything about there bein' anythin' spooky or haunty out there in the swamp? Ghosts or anything?

Griffis: Ohh, no.

Cothran: Ain't no such thing?

Griffis: I been here too long, y'know. I been here seventy years, five months, an' one day, right here in these jungles of this Ok'fenokee Swamp, an' I think I should be acquainted with all 'ese here creatures down hyer. And I never could b'lieve in nothin' spooky. You hear plenty o' spooky noises out yonder, 'specially at night, but if you'll trace 'em down you always find that it's either some kind of bird or an animal a-makin' 'em. So, I never could b'lieve too much in what the people call spooks, y'know, such as ha'nts an' things like that. I never could b'lieve in none o' that, because I never have been able t' find none of 'em. Anything I seen an' didn' know what it was, I was always mighty inquis'tive t' find out what that thing was.

Unusual Birds

'Course we have queer kinda birds hyer, different kinda birds f'm like they have at other places. We have twilldo birds hyer; they fly backwards. They don't care where they're goin', they jus' wanta see where they been. An' then we have flippo birds, too: they're different. They fly with their back down an' their breast up all the time, an' it's impossible t' kill one o' them birds an' git 'im because he falls upwards.

Odd Insects

See that honey a-sittin' up there on the shelf?
Cothran: Yeah.
Griffis: Well, I crossed my bees with lightnin' bugs so they could see how t' work at night, an' they make a double crop o' honey every year.

Good Hunting Dogs

Cothran: What about dogs? D'you have any huntin' dogs?
Griffis: Ohh, yeah, I got some tur'ble good deer dogs. I useta coon hunt a lot, but I don't have any coon dogs now. I useta have a good un, he 'as often treein' five an' six coons up one tree; but I went to 'im one day where 'e's treed up a large, tall tree wi' long branches on it. I looked up that tree an' it was jus' coons, coons, all over that tree. I started at top t' shootin' 'em out. When I got down t' the bottom, my pile o' coons was higher than the tree, an' the last un I shot had t' fall ninety foot straight up t' be on top.

An' I have a deer dog now, he is so good after deer 'til I have t' peg up one side of 'is nose t' keep 'im [from] runnin' two deer at the same time.

I lost one o' m' good deer dogs. He 'as a tur'ble fast-runnin' dog; he was a black dog with a white ring aroun' 'is tail. An' he was a-chasin' a deer jus' as fast as 'e could. But he 'as deathly afraid of a snake, an' that deer jumped over a snake. An' when that dog got t' that snake he was a-runnin' so fast, an' stopped so quick, 'til that white ring from 'is tail slid up around 'is neck, an' choked my poor dog t' death.

Another Odd Insect

Cothran: What about bugs?
Griffis: Well, y'know, naturally I been with s' many them bug-ologists, carryin' 'em out t' catch all kinda insects, 'til I know pretty much about all the bugs an' insects we have hyer. Feller tried t' fool me on a bug one time; he taken a beetle, the head of a grasshopper, and the wings of a butterfly, an' 'e put the head o' that grasshopper on 'at beetle, an' then glued the butterfly's wings on. An' he brought me that bug, wantin' t' know could I name 'im. An' I asked 'im did 'e make a hummin' noise when 'e's flyin'?

Green River, Okefenokee Swamp. Jack Leigh.

He says, "Yes, 'e sure did."

I says, "Well, he's a hum-bug."

Jokes on Outsiders

These people comin' out here, s' many of 'em are fishin'. I tell 'em all kinda things. There's some fellers up here not long ago, four of 'em in a car, an' they rented a boat from me an' wanted t' go fishin'. They asked me how the fishin' was; I told 'em it wasn't good, that there's s' much water, 'til it was jus' like fishin' right out in the middle o' the Pacific Ocean.

One of 'em kinda strutched 'is eyes; don't think 'e'd ever been here before. Says, "My goodness, what will we do if the boat was t' sink?"

An' I told 'im, I said, "Go to the bottom, build up a fire, send up smoke signals, an' I'll go after ya."

One day I sat here in front o' this little store, an' station wagon drove up loaded down with people in the biggest kind of a hurry. The feller he slid the wheels an' stopped, the driver did, stuck 'is head out the winder an' said, "Hey, d' you have worms?"

I said, "Yes, why? Are you a doctor?"

You pull all kinda jokes on people comin' all day. A lot of 'em expectin' t' get here an' find people, y'know, that they cain't even converse with. They git down here an' listen at me go on for a while; they begin t' wonder then where in the worl' did such a guy as that ever originate at?

Cothran: Have you lived around here all your life?

Griffis: Not yet.

Cothran: Ohhhh. That's one on me!

Griffis: I was born hyer, in a log cabin I helped my father t' build.

Cothran (after pause): Now wai-i-t a minute! *That's* a *good* trick.

Growing Up in the Swamp

Griffis: I was raised away out hyer in 'ese backwoods an' in 'ese swamps, an' was nineteen years ol' 'fore I ever put on a pair o' shoes, an' m' feet was so rough an' tough 'til I wore the inside o' my shoes out first.

I must o' been a tur'ble mean boy whenever I was very small, because my mother spanked me so much, I can still go t' a fortune teller an' have her palm read.

Cothran: When did y' start goin' around through the swamp?

Griffis: When I was about ten years old, got t' goin' aroun', me an' other youngsters, just us by ourselves. 'Ere's plenty o' room in 'ere, y'know. The Okefenokee Swamp is so large, 'ere's two rivers flows out of it; it's almost a worl' within itself. One o' them rivers flows east an' the other one flows west. One flows out on the east side, the Saint Mary's, an' goes t' the Atlantic Ocean; an' the Suwannee, which flows right by my camp here, flows out on the west side, an' goes t' the Gulf o' Mexico. This is the same river right hyer that Stephen Collins Foster made famous when 'e wrote the song "Swanee River."

Cothran: How did you learn to tell 'em like you tell 'em? Just sorta come naturally?

Griffis: I guess it jus' came natural, livin' away off down here; part o' the time nothin' else t' do but study up tall yarns.

Cothran: What does your wife think about your storytellin'?

Griffis: Oh, she's gettin' used to it after thirty-seven years.

To Live Alone

I'm all-time a-writin' poems; I made one up here
not long ago. The fishin' was good, an' I'd been
up ten times that night, f'm the time I lay down
up a-'til then; an' I was layin' there on the bed
afraid t' go t' sleep, 'fraid the doorbell'd ring
again. An' while I 'as layin' there, made up this
poem, an' it goes like this:

If I could only find a place
Where I could hide from the human race,
I think it really would be grand
To live in such a peaceful land.
And my life I'd gladly give
For a place like that to live.
Where there'd be no woman to raise a fuss,
And no man, the hateful cuss,
But just a place to live alone
With all my troubles past and gone.
I often have a very good notion
That I will search the Pacific Ocean,
And try to find a very small isle
And rest in peace for a little while.
It's always been my greatest wish
To not do anything but loaf and fish.
Then maybe I could land a whale,
Head first by the tail.

Hitler's Dream

I wrote Hitler a dream durin' the Secont Worl'
War an' had it printed in the paper for the Sixth
War Bond Drive, an' other newspapers an' maga-
zines picked up that thing, an' it was even
printed in the *Stars an' Stripes*.
　Cothran: Do you remember how that went?
　Griffis: Oh yeah, I remember it. Ever' word
of it.

There's a story now current,
Though strange it may seem,
Of that great man Hitler
And his wonderful dream.

Bein' tired of the Allies
He lay down in bed,
An' among the other things,
He dreamed he was dead.

And in a fine coffin
Was lying in state
With a guard of those Russians,
The cause of his fate.

He wasn't long dead
Until he found to his cost,
That his soul like his soldiers
Had surely been lost.

On leaving the Earth
To heaven he went straight,
And arriving up there
Gave a knock at the gate.

But Saint Peter looked out
An' a voice loud and clear
Says, "G'wan, Hitler,
We don't want you hyer."

"Well," says Hitler,
"That is very uncivil.
I suppose after this
I must go to the Devil."

So he turned on his heel,
An' off he did go
At the top of his speed
To regions below.

When he got there
He was filled with dismay.
While waiting outside
He heard Old Nick say

To his imps, "Look here, boys,
I give you a warning.
I'm expecting Hitler
Down here in the morning.

"But don't let him in
For the man's quite a fear [?].
He's a dangerous man,
And we don't want him here.

"If oncet he gets in
There'll be no end of quarrels.
In fact, I'm afraid
He'd corrupt our good morals."

"Oh Satan, my dear friend,"
Hitler then cried.
"Excuse me for listening
While waiting outside.

"If you do not admit me,
Where can I go?"
"Indeed," said the Devil,
"I'll be damned if I know."

That ain't all of it.

"Oh, do let me in
For I'm weary and cold,"
Said Hitler most anxious
To enter Nick's fold.

"Let me sit in a corner
No matter how hot."
"No," said the Devil,
"Most certainly not.

"We do not admit people
For riches of pelf.
Here's sulphur and matches;
Make a hell for yourself."

Then kicked Hitler out
And vanished in smoke.

And just at that time
Mister Adolf awoke.

He jumped out of bed
In a shivering sweat.
He said, "Well, that dream
I will never forget.

"I won't go to heaven,
I know very well;
But it's really too bad
To be kicked out of hell."

Another Joke on Outsiders

Cothran: What-all kinda jokes have you played on people that've come down here?

Griffis: Well, I useta be a lots worser'n I am now. There's some fellers down here from Texas one time, an' 'ey're a-tellin' about what big things they had in Texas. So one night, I slipped a turtle—oh, he'd a weighed about four or five pounds—under the cover, an' that feller went t' bed, an' found that thing in the bed, an' jumped out. He hollered, wanted t' know what that thing was. I told 'im that was just a common-size Georgia bedbug. Did 'e have anything in Texas that'd beat that?

Monster Winds

Cothran: Does the weather ever get kinda bad down here?

Griffis: Oh yeah. We have some monster winds down hyer. Bad winds. Y'know, we had a storm several years ago 't blowed the washpot wrong side out, blowed it through the front yard s' fast lightnin' struck at it three times an' missed; twisted the [well] cover s' crooked we had t' draw water with a corkscrew; scattered the days of the week 'til Sunday come up late on Wednesday evenin'.

Years ago I 'as drivin' m' car down the road, an' I had a blowout. That 'as the days when y' had t' pump up your own tire. I patched m' tire an' then found out I didn't have the pump along with me; an' I 'as a-waitin' aside the road, in hope someone would come by with a pump an' I could pump up m' tire an' keep goin'. An' while I was a-waitin' there come up one o' them hard-blowin' winds, an' I turned that valve stem the way the wind was comin' from; blowed forty pound o' air in that tire b'fore I could put m' thumb over the hole. Now, I put it back on the wheel, an' drove it fer sixty thousan' miles; an' the tire all wore off, an' left the roll o' wind around the wheel!

Cold Weather

Cothran: Ever get cold down here?

Griffis: Cold? Got s' cold this last winter my hens didn't lay nothin' but snowballs.

Cothran: Hoo!

Griffis: One ol' hen set on 'er nest full o' them snowball eggs an' hatched out a covey of ice-cream biddies.

Hot Weather

Cothran: Well, if it gets that cold, how hot does it get?

Griffis: Oh, these here old tree stumps, you can see 'em a-crawlin' up in a shade. Yeah, got s' hot this last summer my hens laid hard-boiled eggs.

Rich Soil

Did you look at m' beans? See some o' them butter beans a-growin' up, springin' up?

Cothran: Yeah. [Griffis grows bean pods as long as your hand and half as wide.]

Griffis: I grew 'em like that hyer. People go out there an' look at the vines of 'em, them butter beans growin'; I mean 'ere's tur'ble rich soil hyer. I grow 'most ever'thing here but watermelons; I have a time a-growing watermelons. The vines grow so fast they wear the melons out draggin' 'em.

I hitched two vines one time so they couldn't run t' wear the melons out, an' one perduced two melons, an' the other'n perduced one. An' when them two melons got ripe on that vine, I loaded 'em in a two-horse wagon an' started t' town. Before I'd got there one o' them melons rolled outta the wagon an' busted, an' both mules drownded in watermelon juice an' I floated fer six hours on one o' the seeds. An' the one that made the one watermelon, whenever it got ripe, I cut it open, eat the watermelon out o' the rind; an' then I used one half the rind fer a swimmin' pool, an' the other half fer a fishpond.

More 'Gators

Cothran: What about alligators?

Griffis: We have plenty of 'em. Y'know, they come in real convenient here t' keep people from gettin' drowned. If one falls overboard, an alligator always swallers 'im 'fore they have time t' drown.

You were speakin' about people gettin' lost hyer; y'know, there's *very*, very few people gets lost, because the bear and alligators chase 'em out o' that swamp 'fore they git in there far enought t' git lost.

Big Bear

Cothran: Yeah; y'got bears in there?

Griffis: Oh, we have plenty of 'em. There been one walkin' aroun' my camp hyer; I don't know how much the bear weighs, but 'is track weighs eleven pound after the sand's brushed off.

Cothran: That's a right sizey bear!

Deer Hunter's Logic

Griffis: [Man] down here one time, y'know, wantin' me t' carry 'im a-deer huntin'. I ca'ied 'im out there an' put 'im on the stand; I say, "You stay hyer, now, an' I'll go aroun' back over hyer an' run a deer by you."

He said, "All right."

S' I went over there with the dogs an' run a deer right back by where I left 'im. An' he didn' shoot; an' I come back over there t' see what 'e was a-doin'. He was jus' standin' up there sightin' down 'is gun [sights along fly swatter].

I walked up there an' told 'im, I says, "You can take y' gun down. Deer's gone." He jus' kep' sightin' right on. Finally I told 'im agin, I says, "Why don'che take your gun down? The deer is done an' gone."

He says, "I know. But this worl's round. An' if that deer don't slow down he'll be back in five minutes."

After I had that stroke in the foot I won't git t' kill n' more deer, y'know; because I'd always run alongside of 'em an' feel o' the ribs, an' if 'ey wadn't fat I wouldn' shoot 'em.

The Blind Child

That was wrote by a Griffin girl here on the Okefenokee Swamp years ago. It was wrote because her mother died, and she had a small sister that was blind and helpless, an' her father married again, an' then she wrote this song.

Cothran: Yeah; now when was it that you learned this song?

Griffis: I learned it in nineteen an' fourteen.

Cothran: And what was it you were sayin' about the background of these old-timey songs?

Griffis: Well, I always said that they had a regional background an' was wrote about somethin' that really happened. All the old-timey songs did.

An' this song, hit's a long song, but I think I still remember every word of it.

They tell me, Father, that tonight
You wed another bride,
That you will clasp her in your arms
Where my dear mother died.

They say her name is Mary, too,
The name my mother bore,
But Father, is she kind and true
Like the one you loved before?

And is her step so soft and light,
Her voice so meek and mild;
And Father, do you think she'll love
Your blind and helpless child?

Please, Father, do not bid me come
To meet your newly wed bride,
For I could not meet her in the room
Where my dear mother died.

The Blind Child

Variations

Her picture's hanging on the wall,
Her books are laying near,
And there's the harp her fingers touched,
And there's her vacant chair.

The chair where by her side I knelt
To say my evening prayer.

Please, Father, do not bid me come,
For I could not meet her there.

Now, when I've cried myself to sleep,
As now I ofttimes do,
Then softly to my chamber creep
My new mama and you.

Then bid her gently press a kiss
Upon my throbbing brow,
Just as my own dear mother would.
Why, Papa, you're weeping now.

They laid her in her earthen bed,
And wreathed a marble fair,
And on it graved those simple words,
"There will be no blind ones there."

The New England Shore

An' then I know another song, that I learned from my grandmother, an' she died in nineteen hundred an' eleven. So you know it is a old un. An' I think I know all of it yet. The title of it is "The New England Shore."

At the foot of those mountings
Where the fountings does flow,
No amusement intended,
Where the pleasant winds blow.
There I spied a fair damsel,
She's the girl I adore,
And it's you I will marry
On this New England shore.

So that her old parents
Came this for to hear.
They said they would part her
From her darling so dear.
They gathered an army
Of twenty or more,
To fight this young soldier
On the New England shore.

He drew out his broadsword
And he waved it around,
'Til seven out of twenty

Lay dead on the ground.
Three more he wounded,
And he wounded quite sore.
He gained this fair lady
On the New England shore.

She wrote her love a letter,
And she wrote it quite sad.
No amusement intended,
To make his heart glad.
She cries, "Come back, my dear Dewill,
It is you I adore,
And it's you I will marry
On this New England shore."

The ships on the ocean
Shall sail without sail,
The smallest of fishes
Shall change into whale;
The rocks shall melt, love,
To fill the ocean, you see,
If ever I prove false
To the girl that loves me.

Cothran: That was fine! Yeah, I like that a lot.
Griffis: Well, them songs, them is *old*, old, old. Never been put in print, I don't suppose. You know, back then you learned a song, what we call, from mouth t' ear. Might jus' hearin' it sung. Well, it seemed like I always did have, I don' know, jus' a mighty good remembrance. I could hear a song sung two or three times an' remember every word of it all the way through.

The Butcher Boy

Well, I know another one, but I declare. My great-grandparents brought it from across the

The New England Shore

At the   foot   of   those   mount - ings _____   Where the

fount - ings   does   flow,   No   a -   muse - ment   in -

ten - ded,   Where the   pleas - ant   winds   blow.   There   I

spied   a ____ fair   dam - sel,   She's   the   girl   I   a -

dore,   And   it's   you   I   will ____   mar - ry

On   this   New ____   Eng - land ____   shore. ____

Variations

The Butcher Boy

In Lon-don Ci-ty, where _ I did dwell, The butch-er boy I loved _ so well. He's court-ed me ____ my heart a-way, An' a-long with me ____ he ____ will not stay.

ocean, when they came over hyer. An' I think I still remember that song, all of it. But I know, my grandmother useta sing it years an' years ago.

In London City where I did dwell,
The butcher boy I loved so well.
He's courted me my heart away,
An' along with me he will not stay.

He goes downtown an' he sets 'isself down,
He takes a stranger upon his knee.
He tells to them things he won't tell me,
An' don't you know that it's grief to see.

He courts them shy, I can tell you why,
Because they have more gold than I.
But gold will melt and silver will fly,
But conscious love can never die.

It was late one night when her father came home,
Inquiring where his daughter had gone.
She's gone away her life to destroy;
She's hung herself for the butcher boy.

He ran upstairs and the door he broke,
And found her hanging on a rope.
He taken his knife and he cut her down,
And in her bosom this note was found.

"I love you Johnny, I love you well.
I love you better than tongue can tell.
I love my father an' mother too,
But I don't love them like I do you.

"I wish an' I wish, but it's all in vain,
I wish I was made [a maid?] over again.

Variations

But wishes is all that will ever be,
'Til coffee grows on a white-oak tree.

"Go dig my grave, go dig it deep,
Place a marble stone to my head and feet,
And upon my breast a lonesome dove,
To show to the world that I died for love."

Naomi Wise

I know another one I learned back in the 'teens. There was a girl murdered back up here in Georgia; her name was Naomi Wise. Well, you know, they was a song wrote about that. An' then

Naomi Wise

sung 8ᵛᵃ lower

① Now come all you young peo-ple and lis-ten while I tell A-

② bout a maid they call Na-o-mi Wise. Her face was fair and hand-some, she was

loved by ev-ery-one. In Ran-dolph Coun-ty now her bo-dy lies.

I know another one, "The Sailor Boy"; an' that's about all o' them ol'-timers—them five—that I can think of, right now. That I learned *away* back yonder, over a half a century ago.

Now come all you young people and listen while I tell
About a maid they call Naomi Wise.
Her face was fair and handsome; she was loved by everyone.
In Randolph County now her body lies.

They say she had a lover; young Lewis was his name.
Each evening he would take her for a ride.
She learned to love and trust him, and she believed his word.
He told her she was soon to be his bride.

One summer night he met her and took her for a ride,
She thought that she was going to be wed.
They came to old Deep River, and so the story goes,
"You've met your doom," these words the villain said.

She begged him just to spare her; the villain only laughed.
They say that he was heartless to the core.
And in the stream he threw her, below the old mill dam,
And sweet Naomi's smiles was seen no more.

Next day they found her body a-floating down the stream,
An' all the folks for miles around did cry.
Young Lewis left the country; they brought him back again,
But could not prove that he caused her to die.

Variations

They say that on his deathbed young Lewis did confess.
He said that he had killed Naomi Wise.
So now we know her spirit still lingers 'round the place
To save young ones from some villain's lies.

Now young girls all take warning, an' listen while I tell,
You must take care before it is too late.
Don't listen to these stories some villain's tongue may tell,
Or you'll be sure to meet Naomi's fate.

The following three secondhand Lem Griffis tales illustrate his reputation and influence as a storyteller in Georgia.

Good Fishing

Recorded in fall 1967 by Lynda Carriveau from her father, John Merritt, of Warwick, Worth County.

You orta go see Lem Griffis if you want to hear some stories. He can rightly tell some whoppers! Well, I useta go fishin' a lot. I lived down in Clinch County, and went to Lem Griffis's fish camp on the Suwannee River. Asked Lem how the fish was bitin'. He told me they was doin' purty good, 'cause he'd jest went the day before by an old stump out dere in the river; said he caught 'em so fast that he wore a hole in the water, pullin' 'em out!

The Snakebit Walking Cane

Recorded in spring 1970 by Joan Kidd from Mrs. John Robertson of Atlanta, who heard Griffis tell it years earlier while she was on a tour of the Okefenokee.

When I went to the Okefenokee Swamp, I had a guide that carried us up the river to the dam, and he was telling my grandsons a story of the swamps. He told of a grandfather visiting him who had to walk with a cane. And he cautioned him about the large snakes in the swamp, but he went anyway; and a large snake struck at him, but he pushed him back with his walking cane.

The snake bit the stick, and it started swelling, and it grew so large they had to call in a sawmill to saw up the walking stick. And they made crossties and built a railroad line. But soon it started raining; the crossties shrank so much they had to pick them up and sell 'em for toothpicks!

Smart Hunting Dogs
and a Trained Catfish

Recorded in spring 1973 by Thomas Nerney from Moultrie Warren Bateman, fifty-five, of Atlanta, who was reared in Peach County and has hunted all over Georgia. A good storyteller in his own right, Bateman appends a Lem Griffis tale to a group of other yarns.

You know what that thing is over there? Do the words Victor, Oneida, Newhouse mean anything to you? They're all steel traps. When I was a young boy I trapped at places like Ichiki Creek, Mule Creek, so forth. Even back then—oh, thirty-five, forty years ago—Saint Louis was still a fur trading center; p'haps, still does some. But we shipped the hides to Saint Louis. To S. C. Taylor Fur Company, I remember, in Saint Louis.

One fellow, he didn't have to use the steel traps much. He had a dog. And you know, most of the hides you case. You skin 'em like a glove. An open hide is a racoon that's stretched almost square and open. Most of the hides—otter, mink, mushkrat, fox—are cased. That way the furriers can use them the way they want to, and that's the way they want them. The beaver hide is stretched almost round, round as a silver dollar; you can steam or hook and tie it with rawhide and stretch him in that frame, in a round frame.

But this guy had a wonderful dog, and one day he walked out on the back porch of this little shack he had with one of his stretching boards where you stretch these case hides. Well, the dog looked up and lit out for the swamps, and came back with a mink; and that was a mink-stretching frame.

So the next day he was out there with some mushkrat-stretching boards, and the dog came out and saw him and ran and took off to the swamp again, and came back with a mushkrat. Then he caught on to that; so he walked out with a fox stretching board and the dog took off, and came back with a pretty red fox with a white tip on his tail: prime hide. And that just went on, so he didn't have to put out these steel traps anymore.

Well, one day he lost the dog. His wife walked out on the porch with an ironing board, and his dog took off and he never came back!

That dog was almost as good as a bird dog I heard about. I heard one fellow say that his dog, one time, smelled a bird just as he was jumping over a barbed-wire fence. He said the dog caught the scent of the covey just as he was jumping that fence, balanced himself on the fence, and pointed in a perfect point. Another guy said that his dog was so good, so sturdy on point, that he lost him one day; and walking through those woods a year or so later he found the skeleton of his dog. Knew it was his dog 'cause the collar was still there. And he says he was walking around there in front of the dog and flushed a covey of birds! He thought that was holding 'em pretty good.

'Bout the best dog I ever heard about was . . . once I was walking down in the swamps with a friend. And this friend had a pretty good bird dog. This was, I think, on Deep Creek, in that sandy country of Crawford County where some of the sand from south Georgia runs up in kind of a finger in middle Georgia. And it had gopher holes in there. Now, we're not talking 'bout your little hairy gopher. We're talking about your gopher turtle, tortoise. Burrows under the sand sometimes with a fox or two and a rattlesnake or two, and so forth. I've trapped those gophers. Claim they got nine different kinds of meat in 'em. I'll tell you how to trap those sometime. But, anyway, that ain't part of this story.

Ah, this bird dog pointed there and a bird got up. Man killed him. Another bird got up and the man killed him. And five birds got up—that was back in the days when your shotgun could legally hold five shells—and the man killed five birds right there standing in his tracks. And he reloaded. And then another bird got up, and four more birds got up 'til he'd shot all those shells. And he thought that was a little remarkable, standing there in his tracks and killing ten quail single. And so he reloaded, and another bird got up and one at a time four more birds got up. He killed fifteen birds standing right there, and he couldn't figure out why those quail were acting so peculiar. So he walked up a little closer, and there was his bird dog standing with his foot in a gopher hole—the covey had run in there 'cause it was so cold that morning—and he was letting 'em out, one at a time!

But that was almost as smart as ol' Lem Griffis's catfish. Lem Griffis was a character who lived down on Okefenokee Swamp. And he said it got so dry down there one time that he taught one of those big cats—catfish—how to walk. And one of my buddies wanted to know what happened to 'im. He said, well, he and the catfish were walking 'crost a bridge one time and the catfish fell off and drowned!

Part Three

Individual Tales

CHAPTER SEVEN

"Ordinary" Folktales

Jack the Rogue

Recorded in winter 1967 by James Philip Johnson from a Mrs. Jones, about seventy-five years old, a black resident of rural Aiken County, South Carolina.

Dere was a man, so dey tol' me—a lady used to tell us all dem thing—dere was a man once, him an' his wife raised seven head of boys. And she graduate 'em—way back dere, I don' know when—say she finish 'em, see, such as a finish was, I guess. But anyhow, when she got 'em all a little learnin', say she said, "Now boys, now I done finish y'all." I don' remember but one name, an' dat was Jack; dat was de las' one she talk wit'. But all de rest she axed 'em, "Now, what do you wanna be?"

One say, "I wanna be a preacher."

She axed another one, "What do you wanna be?"

Say, "I wanna be a doctor."

"Well, what do you wanna be?" She was callin' dey names but I don' remember deir names.

An' say, "I wanna be a schoolteacher."

Say, "Well, dat's fine." Now I'm cuttin' de story short. Say, "Well now, Jack . . ." He always wears his hat pulled over one eye an' sorta look at ya when you ain't lookin' at him. Dey always call

him "ol' Jack," 'cause he act different from all de rest of de boys. She say, "Well, Jack, what do you wanna be?"

He say, "Well, Mama, you asked me an' I'm gonna tell ya. I'm gonna be a rogue."

Say, "Ay, we done all we could to raise you an' all de rest wanna be somethin', an' you wanna be a rogue?"

He say, "Yes Ma'am, I wanna be a rogue."

So she grab de fire iron [poker] an' struck 'im in de face, see, an' cut him up dere. Say, "If you wanna be a rogue, don' ya foot my door no more."

So he lef'. An' he went off an' he met with a expert rogue, see, had done trained, had his saploma [diploma]. An' so he tol' him what he wanted ta be. Well, he was one, so he learned under him, see? An' say he stayed off about six or seven years.

An' she thought somebody had done killed him, 'cause he was gone so long. All de res' was jus' what dey wanted to be; but dey had so much chil'ren an' so much up an' down dey couldn' he'p deir parents much, but dey done de bes' dey could.

So, Jack he was off somewhere an' he had it so bad dat, say he say, "I'm goin' home now, see if my parents are livin' or dead," see. So Jack brought his buddy wid 'im. An' he come in; he wouldn' tell her who he was an' wouldn' take off his hat, 'cause she woulda seen de scar. An' say he said, "Lady," he say, "has you got any boys?"

She say, "Yeah, I got six; I had seven, but I don' know where de other one." Say, "He wanted to be a rogue, an' I didn' want the idea of my chil' stealin', so I driv him off, an' I guess somebody done killed him." See, she was talkin' to him and she didn't know it.

Say, "You reckon?"

Say she say, "Yeah, 'cause I haven' seen him in seven years."

So, afta 'while he push his hat up an' say, "Do you know dis scar?"

Say she look, say, "Ohh, looka my chil'! Dis is my chil'! Well, son, what is you now? What you is?"

He say, "I'm jus' what I tol' ya I wanna be"; say, "I'm a rogue."

Tol' her husband, "Well, listen dat."

He say, "Mama, I can do anything you want done, an' I jus' come back here to see how y'all doin'. 'Cause I'm jus' what I wanna be, an' I don' hide what I'm doin'. I got my saploma."

Dis other one say, "Yes he is, he train under me."

So, dat time dere was a li'l boy comin' 'long wit' a tray o' mutton on his head, goin' to town. An' he [Jack] seen it an' say, "Now Mama, would you like to have some mutton for dinner?"

She say, "Yeah, you gonna go to de station?"

An' he say, "I'll get ya some." So he run 'cross de creek. When he seen de boy goin' to de creek, he run 'cross de creek an' took off one o' his slippers an' put it down in de road. See? Den he went away an' hide.

So, de boy got dere wit' his mutton an' he saw dat slipper, so he put his tray down. Say, "I be-lieve I'll look aroun' back on de other side; I might find de other foot of dis slipper, an' I'll have de pair o' slipper." He put de tray down wit' de mutton an' dat slipper, an' he went to hunt de other one. Time he went back over to hunt de other one, he [Jack] jus' run dere an' put on de slipper an' took up de tray of mutton an' went home, see, to his mother. Well, when de boy come back, he ain' seen nothin', don't y'see; come back huntin' de tray.

So, dey tol' de white man what was on de place dat Jack was here. So den he come down an' he say, "Jack, what kind o' trade you got?"

Say he told him, "I'm a profess'l rogue."

He say, "An' you come back here?"

An' he say, "Yeah, I just come back to see my mother an' father." He say, "But I can do anything you want done," he tol' de white man what de place belonged to.

He say, "Well, I know plenty thing I can tell you to do you can't do."

He say, "Name 'em."

He say, "Well, I got ten head o' horses in my lot up dere"; an' he say, "I want you to get all dem horses an' mules," he say, "out my lot an' don't let nobody see 'em. If you don' let nobody see 'em, you have 'em down here to your daddy house by tomorrow," he say, "an' I'll give you two thousand dollars." 'Cause he jus' know he's gonna kill him, y'know.

Jack tol' him that was easy done; "Let me go an' look over your place," see. Jack went up dere an' look, an' he seen where de lot was an' all. So he come on back to de lodge.

So, dat evenin', he went to the station an' bought enough rope to make ten halters. An' so Jack come back an' made dem halters, him an' his buddy, an' throw 'em down. Then Jack went

Seed Houses and the Potato House. Roy Ward.

to de station later an' bought three half-gallons of liquor of different kind, see? An' den dey mixed it, an' he an' his friend took dat liquor an' went behin' de hill from dis white man lot. An' dey put it down, see. An' dis white man, dey say he had all his han's out dere wit' a big fire dat night in de lot lookin' for de rogue, see, an' had gun.

So Jack put on his rogue suit, what he wear: jus' raggedy, y'know? An' de han's was over here to de lot. Jack ran way 'roun' an' come up whistlin' like dis, y'know, bold; an' dey heared him whistlin'. An' he come runnin' up, said, "Boys, what is y'all doin'?"

Say, "We lookin' for rogues to come here an' take Mister So-an'-so mules an' things out yonder, an' he payin' us to mind."

Say, "Yeah?" Say, "Well, dis fire feels so good an' I ain' got on much clothes. You mind if I stay here wit' y'all?"

So dey say, "Yeah, you'd be company."

So Jack sat dere awhile, tellin' tales. After 'while Jack say, "You know, I wish I had somethin' to drink. We could enjoy stayin' out here tonight."

Say dey say, "Yeah, but we can't lef' heah." Say, "De bossman wouldn' want us to lef' an' de rogue might come up."

He say, "Well, if y'all chip in an' give me a li'l money, I'll go to de station an' get some." He already had it, see? So, he wen' on back whistlin', where dey wouldn' think he was nothin', y'know. Went on back an' went 'roun' to his buddy an' got a gallon o' dis mixed liquor.

Brought it back den, lef' his buddy wit' the halters. "I'll drink de 'poison' off"; say he just say, "glug, glug, glug," y'know, and didn't drink none. An' dey all drunk. An' he's settin' by de big fire.

Say he jus' so smart, he puttin' wood on de fire; dat's to make 'em drunk, y'know. An' say after 'while, say dey commenced to start talkin' a li'l bit.

Directly he say, "Let's get a li'l bit more an' dat'll las' us 'til day." He went 'roun' an' stayed a good while for dem to think he was gone back to de station. Then got another gallon an' went back; he's fixin' to make dem drunk. Directly, all of dem really gone; dey went to sleep. So he call, an' dey couldn' answer 'cause dey was drunk an' 'sleep; see, de fire had made dem sleepy.

So den he went 'roun' to his buddy, an' his buddy come an' got dem halters an' come up dere an' open de lot gate an' put 'em on dem hosses an' mule an' led every one down to his daddy house an' put 'em in his lot. Den he went in de house an' went to bed. Bofe of 'em.

Nex' mornin', say here come de white man on de frost, y'know, comin' to see where his hosses; an' seen 'em all in his [Jack's] daddy lot. "Well, Jack, I had people min'in' my lot wid gun, an' how did you get up dere?"

Say, "Well, I jus' got 'em; you see dere an' dey ain't hurt."

So he said, "Well, Jack done get me; I'm gonna write him de check." So he wrote him de check for the two thousand. An' he said, "Well, I got somethin' else I want ya to do. I know I'm gonna kill you now."

He say, "Name it."

He say, "My wife got a gold ring on her finger"; an' he say, "I want you to get dat ring widout hurtin' my wife an' widout me knowin' it. You have dat ring here in de mornin' an' I'll give you two more thousand, 'cause I know I'm gonna kill you now."

Well, dey say dey stayed up on the highway,

an' directly, jus' before sundown come, a hearse pass. Dey jus' buried someone, you understand. Dey [Jack and his rogue friend] dug up dis dead man an' dey toted him to de white man house. So, Jack an' his buddy, one tote de ladder an' one tote de dead person, an' say he put de ladder 'side de house like dis an' den his buddy went up de ladder an' hold de dead man to de window, y'know, where you could see his face. Den he peck on de house.

Well, dat woke de white man an' his wife; an' say when he look he coul' see dat. Say, "Dere's dat rogue now." So he shot through dere, hit de dead man. Dey jus' throwed de dead man down, an' his buddy took de ladder an' run, see? So dis white man put on his shoes an' all, an' got his lantern an' his pistol an' went out to 'zamine de man he killed.

Jack was right under de house to de back step, see, an' time the white man went out an' went around de house to see where dis dead man was, Jack jus' run up de step, an' run upstairs an' tol' the wife, "Say, Darlin'," say, "I kill him, so now you give me de ring; de ring belongs to me now, 'cause I killed him for you."

"You sure you killed him?"

He say, "Oh yes, I killed him." Dat was Jack talkin' to de man wife; man out dere lookin' at de dead man. So den Jack run down an' run back under de house wid de ring.

When de white man came back in de house an' locked de door an' ran upstairs, his wife ask, "Well, Darlin', after you killed him, why did you come up here an' insis' on me givin' you de ring?"

He say, "I ain' asked you for no ring; I ain' been back in dis house!"

Say, "Yes you did, you come to de bed an' insis' on de ring an' I took it off an' give it to you." Dat was Jack [laughs]. So dat man couldn' hardly sleep.

Well, den Jack come on back an' run under de house an' went back wid de dead man, an' he took him on his shoulder an' carried him on back to de cemetery; his buddy done moved de ladder, see. So dey buried de man back an' went on back to his daddy house, an' went on t' bed.

Next mornin', here come de white man again. He said, "Jack, I thought I was gonna kill you las' night. You got dat ring?"

He say, "Yessir, here it is."

"An' didn' hurt my wife?"

He say, "No."

"Well, how did you get it?"

He say, "I didn' took it, she give it to me." See, he ax her for it, but she thought dat was her husband. He say, "I tol' you I could do anything you wanted done."

He say, "Well, listen, dat's de last thing I want you to do; here's another check." See, dat was four thousand right dere. He say, "Now listen: by tomorrow dis time, I don' want you to be no-where on my place."

He say, "Well, thank you, Cap'n." He say, "Dese my las' days anyhow." So he say, "Mama, you hit me, an' didn' want me to be a rogue. De other boys, dey ain' gonna give you nothin', but now here two thousand for you an' two thousand for Daddy. Y'all is old an' you won't have to work."

An' him an' his buddy went on about deir business.

Cunning Jack

Recorded in spring 1967 by Bill Dorsey from Forest Wade, a man in his fifties, of Cumming, Forsyth County.

This is a story that used to be told to me by my grandfather, the late Charlie Bannister. His people, his ancestors, come from England. When I was a boy he used to tell me this story 'bout this Cunnin' Jack.

There was this Cunnin' Jack an' he had a brother, an' his brother was a well-to-do man. Owned a big estate, had race horses, one thing an' another: a well-to-do man. But this Cunnin' Jack he was a ne'er-do-well kind o' feller that didn't care whether he had anything or not, an' jus' lived from han' to mouth an' get drunk an' have a big time is all he cared anything about. So he was always pullin' one kind of trick or another on people an' especially on his brother, tryin' to figure out some way to get somethin' for nothin'. An' by him bein' so cunnin' an' smart—pullin' his tricks—gave him a nickname, "Cunnin' Jack."

So this wealthy brother that he had that he was always tryin' to get somethin' out of, he [Jack] went over to see him one day. An' him an' his wife were out horseback ridin' an' away from home. They had this cook they called Granny Beck, an' so he went in an' she had prepared dinner an' cooked a big pot o' chicken dumplin's. An' so ol' Cunnin' Jack he hit upon a scheme, an' so he killed Granny Beck. Set her down at the table, put her out a plate o' dumplin's, stuck a big dumplin' in her mouth, left her settin' at the table. An' so he left.

An' so whenever his brother an' his wife come back in the house, why, they found Granny Beck settin' at the table. An' his wife exclaimed, says, "Lord-a-mercy," says, "poor ol' Granny Beck," says, "set down to eat dinner an' she got choked on a dumplin'!" So they carried her an' buried her.

An' so the next mornin' when they got up ol'

Granny Beck was settin' at the door! So it scared 'em all to death, nearly, an' so they didn't know what was the cause o' her comin' back. So this feller decided to go ask his brother 'bout it; he always had solutions for all these problems. So he went over an' ask his brother, "Do you have any idea why Granny Beck come back?"

"Well," he says, "I'll tell ya"; said, "she ain't satisfied." Says, "You give a big feast an' have plenty to eat an' drink for about three days. Why," says, "she won't come back an' bother you anymore."

So he done that. Had a big feast. Cunnin' Jack he got plenty to eat and drink; had a big time there for 'bout three or four days.

So this went on from one thing to another, an' finally the people over the country they got it in for Cunnin' Jack; they decided country'd be better off without 'im. So they decided to do away with 'im. So, bunch o' men they went an' caught him an' put him in this sheet an' sewed him up, an' they took him to the river bridge, out about middle-ways of the bridge. An' so they's 'bout to throw him over the rail into the river, an' one of the men says, "I wouldn't do that." Said, "The people never would forgive us." Said, "He got so many enemies over the country here," said, "if they'd find out that we th'owed him in the river an' drownded him an' they never got to see 'im drown," said, "they never would forgive us." Said, "I'll tell you what let's do. Let's jus' everybody here scatter out an' go all over the countryside an' tell the people we got Cunnin' Jack captured, an' we got him now ready to throw off the river bridge an' drown him." Said, "Everybody'll come in an' see him drown." So they set the sack down an' they went one way an' another.

So ol' Cunnin' Jack he's there in the sack sewed up, settin' there by hisself, an' here come along an ol' man drivin' a big drove o' sheep. An' so when he got up to Cunnin' Jack he seen this sack settin' there, an' he said, "What's here?"

So Cunnin' Jack he spoke up an' he says, "Ah, this is Cunnin' Jack."

He says, "What they got you in there for?"

"Ah," he says, "they goin' drown me."

He says, "What they goin' to drown you for?"

"Ah," he said, "nothin' much; they jus' want me to say somethin'—a few words—an' I won't do it," he says. "Now they goin' to drown me 'cause I won't say it."

Ol' man says, "What they want you ta say?"

"Ah," says, "nothin' much. They want me to say I'll be the Lordship of London, an' I ain't goin' say it."

Ol' man says, "Well, I'd do it 'fore I'd be drownded."

Jack says, "Well, if you want to save my life," said, "jus' let me outta here an' you get in here. When they come back," said, "jus' tell 'em then you'd be the Lordship of London." An' he said, "That's all there is to it, an' they'll let you go."

"Well," he says, "I'll do it to save yer life." So he let him out.

Jack he tied him up in the sack, an' he jus' drove the sheep on an' went on 'cross the river with the sheep, an' left the ol' man settin' there.

An' [in a] little bit here come the people from all the countryside around gathered in to see Cunnin' Jack drown. So they's a couple men picked up the sack. The ol' man hollered out, "I'll be the Lordship of London!"

One of 'em said, "We'll give you the Lordship of London, damn you!" An' off he went, kasout!

Well, the people they broke up, an' one party went one way an' one another. An' so one of the parties, in a little bit, came across a feller over there in the village an' he was sellin' sheep. One of 'em hollered out, says, "Looka there"; said, "that's Cunnin' Jack!" So they run up to him, says, "Jack, we thought we drownded you awhile ago."

He said, "Well, you did." Said, "Didn't you notice after you th'owed me in all them little blubbers comin' up?"

He said, "Yeah, we noticed that."

"Well," he said, "they all turned to sheep, an' I'm over here a-sellin' em!"

Jack and the Revenuers

Recorded in spring 1973 by Lamar Blaylock from Mrs. Jimmy Blaylock of Dalton, Whitfield County. Mrs. Blaylock read from a written text based on the telling of her husband, who was unavailable for the recording session.

This is a story about Jack. Now, in this story I call him Uncle Jack or Jack Blaylock. Truth is, though, everybody claimed Jack for their own relative because he was so famous; but nobody really knows his name.

Now, ol' Jack was like everybody else and made his livin' as a moonshiner. And, like everybody else, he was always in trouble with the law. But ol' Jack was pretty smart and always talked his way out of it. So the ol' sheriff decided to git some help, and he called up some city-boy revenuers because he figured they could outsmart ol' Jack.

So one day ol' Jack was walkin' down the road, and these two revenuers walked up to him an' says, "You're under arrest."

And ol' Jack says, "What for?"

They says, "For operating a still."

But ol' Jack says, "I don't see a still." And it

was the truth, because the city fellas had made the mistake of arrestin' ol' Jack before he got to his still.

But ol' Jack was in a sportin' mood, and he says, "I'll make a deal with you. I'll do two dangerous things that you think up if you'll do them too. I'll go first, and if I don't live you've got no problem. If I live you have to do them. If we both live I'll show you my still."

Well, the city boys thought they had ol' Jack this time, so they said okay. The first city boy says, "I want you to swing on the vine at Water Moccasin Lake and drop in. If you can get out alive then I'll do it."

So ol' Jack swung out there and dropped in with all those water moccasins. When they got close, ol' Jack started catchin' 'em and tying 'em into a big rope which he threw up to a tree limb and pulled himself out.

Well, the revenuers couldn't believe it, but it was time for the first one to drop in. Ol' Jack didn't trust him, so he climbed up in the tree and when the revenuer swung out over the lake Jack cut the rope, the revenuer fell in, and nobody ever saw him again.

Now, the second revenuer decided he better give Jack a hard chore, so he tells him, "I want you to go down into hell and bring back a beautiful girl with the mark of Scratch on her."

So ol' Jack went down into hell and he met ol' Scratch himself. And Jack says to Scratch, "I know you got me down here right now, but if you'll send me back to Dalton with a beautiful girl with your mark on her, I'll send you a lawman. I mean, I'm so bad you're gonna get me someday anyway, but this might be your only chance to get this lawman." So ol' Scratch agreed, and sent Jack back to get the lawman.

Now, Jack knew it wasn't going to be easy to git this revenuer to go down to hell, so ol' Jack says, "I brought back this pretty girl here, but ol' Scratch has one down there for you that is the most beautiful girl in the world."

Well, the revenuer couldn't turn that down, so he goes down there and nobody ever hears from him again. In town the ol' sheriff got to feelin' pretty bad about those two revenuers, so he says he'll never bother ol' Jack again because he can't afford to lose no more men.

Whistling Jimmy

Recorded in spring 1969 by Rick Smith and Ann Adams from Comer Vandiver of Helen, White County. The collectors note that "the first part of this story was either not recorded or accidentally erased. As we remember, it was only a preface to the story: there were three brothers, one of which was Whistling Jimmy, whose father had died and left them a farm."

. . . Of course, they didn't divide the farm up, but they decided they'd go in the cattle business together. So they had a big herd of cattle, and one old poor cow in this herd. And that's all they decided that they'd give ol' Whistling Jimmy, that poor cow; and then they'd make him go down and herd the cattle, see. And everybody'd come along he'd say, "All these cows are mine but old poor cow, an' I wouldn't have her." And everybody that came along he'd just tell that story.

So these two brothers decided, well now, they's tired of that, him going and telling people that all those cattle was his but that poor old cow and wouldn't have her. So they decided then that they's gonna kill that cow. So they went down and killed the cow. And so he [Whistling Jimmy]

went and skinned her and put the hide in a sack
and run off to sell its hide.

So he traveled all day long, and that night he
came to a farmhouse out in the country, a long
way from anywhere. And it was dark; and he was
a stranger, too. So he knew there was something
going on there in the house; they was preparing
for a wedding. So he decided he'd see if he
couldn't get a room to stay. So he went and took
his old cowhide and stretched it up some way,
barrel it up some way to where he could make it
walk. And he led this cow to the front of the
house and knocked on the door and asked 'em if
he could spend the night. Said he was a stranger
in that part of the country and he was a long
ways to where anybody else lived, and he'd like
to spend the night.

And they said, "Well, yes"; said, "be glad to
give you a bed." And said, "What is this you got
here?"

Says, "This is my animal." Said, "Always keep
my animal in the same room I stay in."

So they said, "Bring it on in." So they brought
the animal in and put him in the room where he
was. And then he took and tied a string to it, ya
know, where he could pull it an' it'd make a
funny noise, and laid the string under the door
and out into the living room where everybody
was talking and everything. Sorta gettin' ahead of
my story. First he heard them preparing for this
wedding, ya see; and they had the ham and
they's putting it in the first shelf of the cupboard,
and the pie in the second shelf, and the cake in
the third shelf of the cupboard. So he got all that
information. And he stretched his string off to
where he was gonna put it down by the side of
his chair where he was setting, and got to talking
and he'd reach down and a-pull it and it'd make
a funny noise.

And one of 'em said, "What was that?"

"That was my animal."

He says, "What kinda animal is that?"

"Oh, he's an animal that knows everything.
There's nothing he doesn't know." And he
reached and give him another pull.

He says, "What's he making that noise for?"

He says, "Well," says, "he wanted some of that
there ham on the first shelf of the cupboard."

So they went and got him the ham and
brought it back and he went in there, slipped off
the pillowcase and put it in the pillowcase. Went
back and sat down. Reached down and give it another pull.

Says, "Now what'd he say?"

Said, "He wanted some of that pie in the second shelf of the cupboard."

So they went and got the pie for him. And he
put that in the pillowcase. And he went back and
sat down. In a little bit he pulled the string and it
made another noise.

Said, "What'd he say now?"

Said, "He wanted some of that cake on the
third shelf of the cupboard."

Said, "Well, how in the world does he know
that?"

Said, "Well, this animal knows everything.
There's nothing he doesn't know." He says, "Well,
now I believe I'll just go in."

And the old man says, "What'll you take for
him?"

Says, "I'll take five hundred dollars. He's an
animal well worth the money. He's an animal
that knows everything. Anything ya wanna know,
just ask him and he'll tell ya."

He says, well, he believe he'll just buy him. So
he got him up the money and he give it to him.

And he says, "Well, I believe I'm gonna go to
bed now. And in the morning I'll get up and
show y'all the rudiments of how this animal
functions and how to make him talk fer ya."

Back Roads. Jack Leigh.

So they all retired, and he went in the room and got his pillowcase—his ham and his pie and his cake—and his five hundred dollars, and made it out.

And he went back home, and he was setting in the room counting all this money. And these two brothers passed by the window and saw him in there with all that money and him counting it.

Says, "Where in the world did ya get that money?"

He says, "I sold my cowhide."

Says, "What'd ya get?"

He says, "I got five hundred dollars."

Says, "My!"

He says, "Why," he says, "it'd pay you fellows to kill all your cattle and just skin 'em and go off and sell their hides."

So they went to killing cattle, and they killed all day long and skinned; and they got a wagon-load, all they could haul. So they went on the road to sell the hides. They traveled and they traveled, and the hides begin to spoil, and never could find anybody to buy 'em; so they just lost all the hides. Killed all the cattle and lost all the hides.

So they went back home and told Whistlin' Jimmy they's gonna kill him; that he'd caused them to kill all their cattle and they lost the hides and couldn't get nothing for 'em.

So he says, "All right."

So they jus' gonna drown him. They put him in a sack and took him down to the creek to a big deep hole, and they set him down there. And while he's settin' there in the sack that's tied, they went off to hunt rocks to tie to it, ya know, so when they throwed him in, why, he'd sink.

So he was in there whistling up a big tune, and here come this guy along the road with a flock of sheep. And the fellow says, "Hey, what ya doing there?"

Says, "I'm a-learning how to whistle." Said, "Wouldn't you like to know how to whistle well?"

He says, "Yes, I would."

He says, "Well, get down and untie this sack"; says, "I can fix ya right up."

So he untied the sack, and he got out and this fellow got in. And he tied him up. So he crawled on the horse and drove the sheep away; rode off with the sheep.

So the boys came back with the rock and tied the sack and throwed the old man in. And that was the last of him.

So in the next day or two, here he come back, along with this big flock of sheep. And the boys said, "Jimmy, where in the world you get all those sheep?"

Said, "Well, you know where you sent me." He says, "All they deal in down there is sheep and hogs." Says, "I thought I'd bring back a flock of sheep, see how we come out on that."

These two brothers decided that they would like to try some hogs. Whistlin' Jimmy says, "All there is is sheep and hogs," and says, "they's plenty of hogs and you can get 'em." Then he says, "You jes' get in these sacks and I'll send you down there."

So he got 'em in the sacks and he tied up the sacks and throwed them in and sunk 'em, and that was the last of the other two fellows.

So Whistlin' Jimmy ended up with the farm and everythang that was left.

The Wayward Boy

This is a conflation of two tellings recorded in spring 1977 by Fralil Manker and in spring 1981 by Carla Jones from James W. Ellison of Atlanta. Mr. Ellison was born in 1913 in Jackson, Madison

County, Tennessee, where he heard this story from his mother, Fanny, at about age seven. She, in turn, learned it from her grandmother, a former slave.

When I was a boy, my mother would tell us stories on a cold winter day. We didn' have no radio, neither television. So we'd sit around the fireside, especially when it was snowin', an' she'd tell us these stories.

She said, once upon a time there was a boy, said he was goin' out to see the world and make things better. He live with his mother there alone, and so he tol' his mother he was goin' out to see some parts of the world.

Just before he left, he put two bottles of milk up on the shelf, an' say, "Now look, Mama, you watch these bottles, and when one turn green, I'm safe. When one turn red, I'm in trouble; turn my dogs out."

He had seven dogs; always carried the dogs everywhere he went, but this time he left his dogs at home with her. An' so she was there patchin', an' ironin', an' cleanin' up, and the dogs was barkin' an' raisin' sand. But she didn' pay any 'tention to 'em.

So he wandered an' wandered, days after days, an' days after days. One night it went to rainin', stormin'. He looked way 'cross the forest an' saw a little dim light. It was rainin', so he made it to that light. An' when he got to that light it was a little ol' wayward house there. He knocked on the door, an' a lady come with long fingernails and eyes sparklin' like fire. An' she asked him, "What are you lookin' for?"

An' he told her, "I'm a long way from home an' I'm los'. An' I would like to spend the night here."

Ever'body went to her house, she killed 'em. An' so she told him, "Come on in."

An' he went on in. He 'as wet, an' he set down by the fire and he looked over in the corner an' he saw a girl—the old lady's daughter—over there. An' he fell in love with her, first sight. But he knowed he was in the wrong place. So he writ on a paper, "Would you marry me?"

The ol' lady went upstairs to fix his bed where she always put men in there to kill 'em the next mornin'. The girl read the note, but she didn' have time to write back. So she bowed her head at him [answering yes], and put the paper in her mouth and chewed it up. Ol' lady's comin' on down the stairs and say, "Yo' bed's ready."

So he went on to bed. The girl, see, she didn' sleep that night 'cause she know her mother's goin' to kill him. She always killed 'em, cut their heads off. Had a ol' dug well she throwed 'em in, in the back there. She kept all the men.

Meanwhile—my mother said—these dogs were raisin' sand at home, barkin', howlin'. But the boy's mother didn' pay that bottle of milk no 'tention. One of the bottles had turned red and the top had jumped off; he was in trouble! He told her, say, "When this bottle turn red, turn my dogs out." So she didn' pay no 'tention. And my mama . . . we'd set there lookin', you know, just scared; didn't have no electric lights, had lamp lights way back then. We'd set and look at her, and she'd be tellin', and we'd be cryin', you know, just worried.

The old lady got up early in the mornin' to sharpen her ax and knife out behind the house. Told her daughter, "I'm gonna butcher some fresh meat."

So the girl run upstairs and told the boy, said, "Get up outta this bed and run for your life! My mother's gonna kill ya. She kill everybody come here." He jumped up with his clothes in his hand, runnin'. She went on back down where her mother, and her mother had that knife just glitterin', just sharp as could be. She told her mother, say, "You ought to sharpen it a little more." She tryin' to get him away from her, you know.

Old lady went back and sharpened it, see saw, see saw, see saw, sharpenin' that knife. So the girl went upstairs and balled up the cover in the bed, just like the boy was still layin' in there. The old lady sharpened on that ax another thirty minutes; that give the boy time to go through the woods, runnin'. And so after she [the girl] got him off, she thought he had got away from her mother.

The old lady went upstairs with that ax, that double-bit ax, sharp! The cover was balled up; she drawed back and *hit* down in the bed—to kill him, you know. An' he didn't move. She looked there in that bed an' he wadn' there. An' she said, "Oh, I'm gonna git him."

So she went out, an' got down on her all-fours just like a dog, smellin' all the way 'roun' the house. She caught his scent, an' she went to runnin'. An' this is what my mother say she said [rapidly]: "I leap forty miles, I jump four miles. I leap forty miles, I jump four miles. I roll over, an' I roll over. I leap forty miles, I jump four miles. I leap forty miles, I jump four miles."

An' say she was runnin', and he run an' run, run all that morning 'til about ten o'clock. That boy looked back through the woods and he seen her comin', had that ax in her hand, just runnin' wild, crazy.

Them dogs at home were just tearing up; had done dug a hole out from under the fence. Mother wasn't paying no attention, you know.

The old lady got near to him, 'bout maybe two or three blocks, an' he say, "Well, she gonna catch me." So he climbed up a great big sycamore tree.

She passed by him. "I leap forty miles, I jump four miles. I leap forty miles, I jump four miles. I leap forty miles, I jump four miles." She run on by an' lost his track. An' she went back an' caught that scent, and she looked up in the tree and she saw him. Eyes were just like *fire*! Said, "You might as well come on down, I'm gonna getcha anyhow." She got that ax, that double-bit ax, and went to cuttin' on that tree. An' this the way my mama say the ax went: "Bam; bam-ba-lam-ba-lon. Bam, bam, bam, bam-ba-lam-ba-lon. Bam, bam, bam-ba-lam-ba-lon." Great big tree. Say she cut there so long until she begin to blow [breathe hard].

The dogs was all out at home, done got outta the pen. An' he seen the tree begin to reel an' rock. He say, "Ol' lady, would you let me say fifteen words?"

She looked up at him and say, "Say your fifteen words while I rest."

He looked back toward home, and begin to call those dogs [sings]: "Rusteye, Chesteye, Pale and Juneye, Hogwell and Sounder." My mother had a good voice then.

Ol' lady say, "That sound good to me. Say that over."

So he throwed his head back and, "Rusteye, Chesteye, Pale and Juneye, Hogwell and Sounder."

After awhile she went to cuttin' again; the tree went to leanin', fixin' to fall. Bam; bam-ba-lam-ba-lon. Bam, bam, bam.

He look way up through the woods an' he seen them dogs a-comin'. An' *she* saw 'em comin'. She looked into those dogs' eyes, comin' to her; an' she told him, "Come on down! Come on down! I ain't gonna bother you!"

'Bout that time all seven of them dogs had run up to the tree; great big dogs. He said, "I know you ain't gonna bother me. Git 'er, boys!" Them dogs run in and tore her all to pieces. Tore her up!

He got down out of that tree, got them dogs, went on back to the old lady's house—this is the story my mother told—an' married that girl. She and him got on Rusteye and Chesteye and started on back home. He made her a good livin', and they lived happy together. And last time I seen 'em, they doin' the Cincinnati Walk 'round the lake!

Nippy and the Giants

Written in winter 1967 by Gwen Hedden, a student at Towns County High School, Hiawassee; collected by Michael Moss. The writer notes, "I got this from Mrs. J. Y. Denton of Hiawassee."

Long ago there lived a family of giants. This family of giants had two daughters and a servant named Nippy. As these giants were people-eaters, they kept Nippy very busy hunting their food and often scolded Nippy when they were short of food.

One night after a scolding, Nippy stole the pet steers belonging to the giants and took them across the river on the bridge and turned the swinging bridge loose. The daddy giant discovered what Nippy had done and yelled across to him, "Hey, Nippy, you coming back this way?"

"Yeah," answered Nippy.

Well, after a few days Nippy decided to go home. He slipped into the house and hid under the bed and was going to stay hidden under the bed until he knew how mad the giants were with him. But in a short while Nippy began feeling happy about being home. So he decided to sing to himself, "Yankee doodle bow-wow, Yankee doodle bow-wow." Nippy had forgotten about the magic music box that would sing or play any song that anyone was even thinking about, and so all at once the music box started playing, "Yankee doodle bow-wow."

Daddy giant woke up when the music box started playing and singing. He thought mama giant was singing, so he called out to mama, "Old Lady, you sure are happy tonight."

Mama answered, "It ain't me."

So daddy knew that Nippy had returned, and started looking for him. Nippy heard them and ran to the window and jumped out, taking the music box with him. Daddy giant didn't get even near him until he got to the bridge. Nippy turned the bridge loose just in time, and the giant hollered, "Nippy, ye ever coming this way again?"

"Yeah," answers Nippy.

In a few weeks Nippy decided to go home again. In an hour or so the giants all knew Nippy was home and decided to let him stay, fatten him up, and eat him.

But one night when Nippy couldn't sleep he overhears the giants talking about his being almost fat enough to eat. Nippy lived upstairs with the two daughters and noticed they were wearing a lot of jewelry. Also on this day he'd seen how nice and fat he was and had noticed how they were looking at him. So Nippy decided that he'd better talk the girls into changing beds with him, and he asked to borrow the jewelry.

Late that night daddy giant decided that now was the time for killing Nippy. So he crept upstairs to Nippy's bed and felt to find any jewelry, but feeling none knew he had the right bed. So chop-chop!

Nippy woke when he heard the noise and with a "Bow-wow" jumped out the window, ran to the bridge, and turned it loose just in time to escape from the giant. The giant yelled, "You've stole my oxen, my magic music box, and made me kill my daughters! Are ye ever coming back this way anymore?"

"Yeah," answers Nippy.

In a few months Nippy returns home again. The giants caught him right away and put him in a room to fatten. They got him nice and fat. So one day mama giant was to have Nippy ready to eat when daddy giant returned from town. Mama fixed the dough to make dumplings with Nippy.

Nippy had been moved from his upstairs room and chained up in the kitchen where he would be near the stove. Nippy knew mama was preparing the dough for his face, so he pretended to watch with interest to see how it was done. When it looked as if mama was almost ready to cook it, Nippy asked mama to turn him loose and let him put her face in it and she could feel of it and see if it was all right, and then he would know how he would look. The mama giant agreed. Well, Nippy put the dough on mama's face and chopped her head off and put it in the pot.

When daddy giant came home he smelled something burning and hollered, "Hey, Old Woman! Your meat's burning!" About this time he saw Nippy. Nippy started running for the bridge and the giant was right behind him this time. But Nippy jumped on the bridge and turned it loose. And the giant hollered, "Ye stole my oxen, my music box, made me kill my daughters, and you killed my wife. Are ye *ever* coming back this way anymore?"

"No," says Nippy.

Bluebeard

Recorded in spring 1969 by David Turner from his aunt, Ruby Ellis, eighty-one, of College Park, Fulton County.

Oncet upon a time there was an old man named Bluebeard. And he lived near a family that had three daughters. And he married the oldest daughter and carried her home. And so, had a little red house that he had a key to, and he didn't want anyone to go in it. So he kissed his wife goodbye and put a red rose in her hair.

And she said, "I just wonder what's in that little house, and I'm goin' open it and see." So she opened it, and it was so hot in there it withered her rose.

And so when he came back he says, "You been in that little red house."

She says, "No I haven't."

He says, "Oh yes you have. I'm goin' put you in there." So he carried her in there and hung her up by the hair of the head.

And he went and told her mother, he said, "Well, your daughter died"; and said, "I just buried her." And said, "I've come back to marry another one."

So he married the second daughter. And he went to leave, and he kissed her goodbye and put a rose in her hair and said, "Whatever you do, don't you go in that little red house."

So she said, "Well, I'm gonna open it and see what's in there." So she opened it, and her sister was in there hangin' up by the hair of her head. And it withered her rose.

And so when he came home he says, "You been in that little red house."

She said, "No I haven't."

He said, "Oh yes you have. Come on, I'm goin' to put you in there."

So he went back to the same parents and told 'em, says, "I wanta marry your other daughter."

And they didn't want her to marry, and they says, "Somethin' funny's happened to these other two."

And she says, "Oh, but I wanta marry him. I'll find out what's wrong."

So they went on and married. And next morning he kissed her goodbye and he gave her the rose.

"Oh, it's so pretty," says, "I'm goin' take it out and put it in some water." So she takened it out and put it in some water. And so she opened the door to the little red house. So when she opened the door, why, her sisters 'as hangin' up in there by the hair of the head. So she went on back, picked up the rose and put it back in 'er hair.

When he came home he says, "Oh, you hadn't been in there."

And she says, "Well, I wanta send a box to my mother." And says, "Now, if you open this box, I'll be a-peepin' atcha!"

She put her oldest sister in the box, that'd been in there the longest, and sent her. And so he put it down and he said, "Hit's awfully heavy. I'd like to know what's in it."

So when he put it down she [the youngest daughter] said, "I'm a-peeping atcha!"

He said, "Well, bless her heart. She can see me, so I won't open it."

So the next day she said, "I wanta send another box to my mother."

He told her, "All right."

And so she put the other sister in and sent her. And he said, "I just got to look in this."

And so he put 'er down to look in it but she says, "I'm a-peeping atcha!"

So he said, "Well, I won't look in it." And so he carried that sister home.

And while he 'as gone she got ready and went home herself. And the father and mother had all three of their daughters back again.

The Golden Ball

Recorded in spring 1968 by Faye McCollum from her mother, Fannie Maude Folds Wright, fifty, of Hogansville, Troup County.

One time 'ey's a little girl, an' she was out in the yard playin' with her golden ball 'at her daddy had bought her. An' he told her if she dropped it into the well 'at he would whip her. An' so one day she was out playin' with it an' dropped it, an' it went down into the well, an' she sat down an' begin to cry.

An' a little toad-frog hopped up to her an' said, "Little girl, why are you cryin'?"

She said, "I was playin' wi' my golden ball, an' Daddy tol' me if I dropped it into the well 'at he would whoop me."

An' the little toad-frog said, "Well, I will go down in 'ere and get it for you."

She said, "Oh, please do; oh, please do!"

And the little frog said, "But first you've got to promise me one thing. You've got to promise to carry me home with you, let me eat in the plate with you, an' let me sleep wi' you, an' do everything you do."

She said, "I promise, just anythang; just go get my golden ball."

So the little toad-frog went hoppity, hoppity, hop down into the well and got the little golden ball an' brought it back up there. So the little girl started to run home 'en. The little toad-frog said,

"Wait, wait, you forgot your promise. You promised to let me go home wi' you, eat in the plate wi' you an' sleep wi' you."

So the little toad-frog hopped all the way home to the little girl's house. So that night she sat down to the table to eat her supper, an' the little toad-frog went hoppy, hoppy, hoppy up to the chair. Said, "Little girl, I can't hop up into the chair, will you please help me up?"

So the little girl got real mad an' she jumped up and went to the bed. An' so, when she got in there, the little toad-frog went hop, hop, hop an' got to the bed. Said, "Little girl, little girl, will you *please* help me up on the bed? I cannot get up by myself."

So it made the little girl very angry, and she picked it up and threw it against the wall and slung its brains out!

That's all.

An Immigrant's Adventures

Recorded in winter 1967 by Carl Van Baker from Cliff Landcaster, fifty-six, of Cumming, Forsyth County.

I'll tell you one that I heard back when I was about six or seven years old, and I never will forget it. There was an old nigger man lived in the settlement where we lived, and he was a gray-headed nigger and had gray whiskers. His wife died, an' they were the only nigger family there was lived in that settlement; everybody loved 'em. They were just regular old slavery niggers. After his wife died, why, he used to sit on the front porch of his little ol' three-room house when the weather was pretty. And all of us children, we'd like to go out there and talk to him,

'cause he was always telling us some kind of funny tale or joke or something. And we called him Uncle Joe. This particular one that I never will forget, he told.

He said he was raised in the old country across the water, and said all his folks died and left him an orphan. And said there was a rich ol' man over there taken him to raise. Said he was kind of a mean ol' man. An' sometimes he'd kill hogs. Why, he killed some hogs up there; he's gonna let the meat lay out that night an' cool good 'fore he salted it down, packed it down. Said they had to have somebody to watch that meat on account of different kinds of wild varmints, wolves and things. They'd come up thar and tote that meat off and eat it.

So they put it on him to watch the meat. Said the old man told him, "I'm gonna tell ya," said, "you let anything bother this meat tonight," says, "I'm jest gonna have your head cut off in the morning."

He already scared anyhow, scared to stay out there, but anyhow he knowed he had to. So he stayed out there. Said he got so sleepy along in the morning that he jest had to take him a nap, and he dropped off asleep. And, sure enough, while he was asleep some kind of wild varmint come up there and got part of that meat.

The ol' man got up the next morning; part of the meat was gone. Said he jumped on him, told him, "I told you what I was going to do; now you let some of that meat get gone." Said, "I'm just gonna take you over here and cut your head off."

And then his wife begged him not to. No, said the ol' man was going to cut it off. Finally his wife convinced him and begged him not to cut his head off.

Said, "Well, I won't cut your head off; I jest lay you up in a barrel." Said he had a sixty-gallon barrel there. He put him in it and nailed up both ends of it; and the only way he had to get air was through a bung hole there on the side, which all barrels have. They loaded him up, carried him over there on top of that mountain and set him down. Told him, "I'm going to roll you down this mountain, now." Says, "I don't know what's gonna happen to ya, don't care."

Sure enough, he give him a roll. Said down that mountain he went, just a-bouncing from rock to rock. Finally, said the ol' barrel come to a stop down there. He didn't know what was gonna happen. Said that night the wild varmints come around smelling, squallin' around that barrel. Said one of 'em was up there rubbing around on it, and said his tail slipped through that bung hole. And said when it did he jest grabbed it wi' both hands an' held on to it. Said whatever it was taken off, dragging him and the barrel. They got to running, and the ol' barrel was bouncing around there and hit a big rock and busted all to pieces. He turned his tail loose and on he went.

Said there he was, out with nowheres to go, and didn't know what to do. He decided he'd go up there where the ships come into port and see if he could get a way out of that old country; he wanted to get out from over there. Went up to a ship, spoke to the captain, told him he wanted to come across to the United States; didn't have no money. Said this man told him, "Well, you'll work your way across. I'll carry ya." Said he told him he would be glad to work for his way a-comin' across. Which he did. Says that's how come him being in the United States. Worked his way from the old country across there on a big boat.

They landed up here in New York. He didn't know nobody, didn't have no people or nothing, but knowed he had to do something to make a living. So he got out there and hunted around looking for a job. Said he found him a job in a big factory up there where they made rubber boots. Man told him he'd give him a job; said he went to work.

Said he was working up there—this was a tall building; anyhow, he was up on the fourteenth floor working one day. Said he give a fire alarm; the building was on fire. He run to the window and looked out; smoke was coming out all the windows below, and said he jest didn't know what he was going to do fourteen stories up there.

He studied; finally, he come up with the idea he'd jest start putting on rubber boots. He kept putting on rubber boots 'til his head hit the ceiling of the room; he stooped over and kept putting on some more boots. Finally got on all the boots he could possibly get out with. Said he eased up there to the window and he just jumped out that window, fourteen stories high. Said he bounced fourteen days and nights up there; said if it hadn't of been for a professional baseball pitcher to pitch him biscuits, said he'd starved to death bouncing!

CHAPTER EIGHT

Animal and Human Tricksters

The Tar Baby

Recorded in fall 1967 by Rosa Jean Tomlinson from Mary Minter, sixty-nine, a black resident of Atlanta who was reared near Jonesboro, Clayton County.

Well, once there was a rabbit bothering around and eating up a man's cabbages. So the man kept on, he could never catch him. He'd always try, try, and try. So he thought of a plan; he fixed a tar baby. Took some tar and turpentine and made a little doll, and sit him out in the middle of the road to catch this rabbit.

The rabbit went to the little tar baby and says, "Hey, what a pretty little girl. What's yo' name?" And the tar baby didn't say nothin'. So he said, "What's your name, I ast you?" And he [the tar baby] didn't say nothin'. Say, "You think you too cute to talk?" Say, "Tell me your name, or I'm going to slap you." So he slapped, and the hand stuck, you know, to the tar baby.

Say, "Turn me a-loose; turn me a-loose, I said, or I'm going to slap you! I got another big ol' hand over here; I'm gonna slap you with it." And he slapped him; that hand stuck.

He said, "Turn me a-loose, turn me a-loose! I've got two hind feet back here; I'm going to kick the stuffings out of you!" So he kicked him, and them two feet stuck.

And so he said, "Turn me loose, turn me loose! I got a big old head; I'm gonna butt your brains out!" The baby didn't say anything, so he butted him and his head stuck.

So a fox came by. The fox and the rabbit didn't get along so well nohow, so the fox was really glad to see him all there with the tar baby. It just tickled the fox, and he laid down and rolled, he just laughed, thinking of what to do with the rabbit. He was gonna get him, you know, gonna get away with him. So he says, "I'm gonna pull you a-loose, and I'm gonna drown you."

Rabbit says, "Please drown me, just drown me; do anything but throw me in the briar patch."

And the fox said, "It ain't no water around here. I'm gonna hang you up in a tree."

"Well, hang me up in a tree, hang me in a tree; just do anything except throw me in the briar patch."

And so he says, "Well, I'm gonna cut your ears off."

"Cut 'em off, feet, everything, cut everything off; just don't throw me in the briar patch."

And so the fox didn't have nothing to work with nohow, so he says, "Well, I'm just gonna throw you in the briar patch." So he slung him over in the briar patch.

And the rabbit jumped up and run around and says, "Thank ya, thank ya, thank ya, for I was bred and borned in the briar patch, I was bred and borned in the briar patch!"

153

So the fox he watched, looked and looked; that rabbit sittin' there cross-legged with a chaw of tobacco in his mouth. And the fox was so sick; the rabbit, he just sittin' back laughing, "Ha, ha, ha, ha, he, he, he, he!"

So that was the last of that.

Brother Rabbit, Brother Lion, and the Cow

Recorded in spring 1969 by Susan Yandle from Christine Whitehead, fifty-two, a black resident of Macon, Bibb County.

I remember this one was told about a cow, and de lion, and de rabbit; you know, he always have been the smartest. And so Brer Rabbit and Brother Lion, I think they went in together that time. So they were goin' have beef; you know, the rabbit and Brer Lion, either one, didn't have beef much for dinner, so that what they were goin' have for dinner. And so they killed a cow. And so Brother Lion told Brer Rabbit, said, "I've got to go off a piece; and if you don't mind," say, "you be dressin' him while I'm gone, be cleanin' him."

And so he cleant the cow, and so when he cleant the cow Brer Rabbit took the whole cow and carried it to his house and hid it. And then he come back and left the tail, you know, stickin' outta the ground.

And so when he [lion] came back Brer Rabbit was pullin' on the tail. And so Brother Lion said, "Brother Rabbit," said, "what's the matter?"

He said, "Well, the cow has stuck in the ground"; and say, "I've been pullin' on this tail tryin' to get it a-loose."

So Brother Lion he's strong, you know; he went there and he pulled the tail up and he said, "Humph, that's all we got left of the cow, just the tail." Said, "The other done sunk in the ground."

So they took it, halvin' the tail, you know. That's what poor Brother Lion had, you know, and Brother Rabbit had the whole cow!

And so, Brother Lion took and went to Brother Rabbit's house that evenin'. He wanted to borrow some pepper to go on his part of the tail; that's all he had, the tail. So when he got there, Brer Rabbit was sittin' in the corner; he didn't even see Brer Lion comin'. [Sings:]

"Brother Rabbit eat the cow
And Brother Lion eat the tail.
Brother Rabbit eat the cow
And Brother Lion eat the tail."

He said it all, and Brother Lion heard Brother Rabbit. So Brother Lion took Brother Rabbit, you know. And he took him up and he said, "What must I do with you now?" Said, "I believe I'll cut your ears off."

He said, "If you cut my ears off," say, "that'll suit me just right." Say, "I just want you to do dat." Say, "Please cut my ears off."

Said, "Naw," say, "I believe I set you afire."

Said, "Please set me afire." Say, "I been wantin' to be burned up a long time ago."

And so the lion said, "Well, I know what I'm goin' do; I'm goin' throw you over into the briar patch." And he throwed him over into the briar patch.

Brother Rabbit went off laughin'. Say, "I'm glad you throwed me over there, 'cause that's my home. That's where I was bred and bo'n."

And he went around the house and stepped on a pin
And that's the way my story ends.

Rabbit and Fox at the Well

Recorded in fall 1967 by Rosa Jean Tomlinson from Mary Minter, sixty-nine, a black resident of Atlanta who was reared near Jonesboro, Clayton County.

One other time, the rabbit got away with the fox. The fox told the rabbit, says, "Bre' Rabbit, let's go to fishing."

And the rabbit said, "Aw naw, I don't care nothin' about fishin'; you just go 'head."

"Come on and go."

"Naw, you go ahead, I don't like fish."

And so the fox went on an' fished, and fished; he caught a nice bunch of fish.

The rabbit he had in mind he was gonna eat the fish anyhow that the fox caught. So the rabbit he got on the road where the fox had to go on back home, you know, and looked over in the bushes and found a shoe, and laid it in the road where the fox had to come along.

So the fox come along with his fish; seed that shoe laying there. Says, "Oh, there's a good shoe. That really is nice," says, "but just that one; I won't need it, I'll leave it alone."

So he went on with his fish and the rabbit laid there a little bit. He got up, picked up the same shoe and run way around and laid it in front of him again.

And the fox come along and said, "Oh Lord, there's another shoe! I wish I'd picked that first one up. I'm goin' back and get it." So he set his fish down by the side of this shoe, and went back to hunt for the other shoe, you know. And he went back and hunted, hunted, hunted, and he couldn't find it. The rabbit he done took his fish and gone [laughs].

When he got back he couldn't find his fish, but he could smell 'em as he run along. He just running along looking for the rabbit. The rabbit had went on and jumped on a well with two buckets, see; when you get in one bucket, it goes down and bring the other one up. So the rabbit he went on, jumped in the bucket and went down; 'at brought the other bucket up. So he's down there and eat the fish up.

And the fox he just come back a-lookin', and 'rec'ly he jumped up on the well. "Brother Rabbit! You said you didn't love fish; you done got my fish and gone down there and eatin' 'em up."

The rabbit said, "Yes, do you want some of 'em?"

He said, "Yes."

"Well, get in the other bucket and come down." So he got in the other bucket and went down.

As they were passing, the rabbit said, "That the way the world goes: some goes up and some goes down." So he just went on off and left the fox down in the well.

Brother Rabbit Steals the Butter

Recorded in fall 1967 by Carla Cox and Kay Conlee from Nolia Rucker of Jefferson, Jackson County.

Once upon a time, Broth' Beah, Broth' Coon, Broth' Fox, Broth' Rabbit, they was goin' have a log rollin', an' dey had prepa'd deir dinnah: dey had a huge jah o' buttah. An' dey gone on an' dey cut trees, dey cut trees. An' ol' Broth' Rabbit, he claimed he had a sick wife; he done seen de jah o' buttah! He go up an' he cut a little while: Hah, hah, hah. "Listen, Broth' Beah, Ah heered mah ol' lady callin' me. Ah got t' run see about 'er." Dickety, dickety, dickety. He run to the house, see about 'er. Ever' time he run t' the house, he'd eat a cake o' buttah.

He come back, he'd cut a li'l bitty more: Hah, hah, hah. "Listen, Broth' Coon, Ah heahs mah ol' lady callin' me; Ah got t' go." Dickety, dickety, dickety. He run t' de house an' see about de old lady, an' eat a cake o' buttah.

When noontime come, ev'body went t' dinner. Broth' Bear opened de jar an' his buttah were all gone, an' dere was a pearl-handle knife in de jar. He began t' ask, "Broth' Coon, i' dis yoah pearl-handle knife in mah buttah jar?"

"Naw suh, Broth' Bear."

"Broth' Fox, dis yoah pearl-handle knife in mah buttah jar?"

"Naw suh, naw suh, Broth' Bear, hit ain't mine."

"Broth' Rabbit, dis yoah pearl-handle knife?"

"Naw suh."

"We'll see who eat de buttah." Dey build a huge log hill, roll logs togethah, made a huge bresh heap, set it afire. "Ever'body dat didn' eat de buttah, jump ovah de fire." Ev'body jumped ovah de fire but Broth' Rabbit; he said he was sick. Broth' Bear said, "Ef ya don' jump, we'll th'ow ya."

Broth' Rabbit raised up, he jumped ovah de fire. When Broth' Rabbit jumped ovah de fire an' he hit, he was so full o' buttah he busted, an' dey grabbed him an' th'owed him in de fire an' cooked him; had *him* fo' dinnah! An' dat was de end o' de rabbit. [Laughs]

Old Master and John

Recorded in spring 1981 by Carla Jones from James W. Ellison of Atlanta, who heard it as a boy from his mother, Fanny, back in Jackson, Madison County, Tennessee.

It's often said, they always had a black man, John; they called him John, mostly. The old boss and boss's wife were settin' there one night an' he 'as tellin' her what confidence he had in John: John wouldn't do nothin' wrong.

She says, "Awww, 'John, John.' I bet you a thousand dollars John is not as perfect as you say he is."

He says, "I bet you a thousand dollars he is."

They put up [the money].

Say, "How we going to do?"

Say, "We tell him we gonna leave town for six weeks, and we'll leave, but not go far."

She say, "Since you got so much confidence in 'im, I'm going to show you."

So they made the trip up and told John, "We're going to Phillymeyork, Phillymeclain, an' want you take care of this house." Had a lot of niggers on the farm there, so to speak; big plantation. "An' carry us to the depot an' put us off, an' we catch the next train." So John carried 'em on down there an' put 'em off at the depot.

John went straight back home, saddled up one of the biggest, finest stallions that Old Master had, and put one o' them big hats on top his head they used to wear back yonder, an' went 'cross through that plantation. [Calling loudly:] "Hey, mens! Come on over to Ol' Master's house. Ol' Master's gone to Phillymeclain, and I got a key to ever'thin'." [Laughs]

They got together; Mirandy and all them cooks. His wife was name Mirandy. Say, "Mandy goin' cook cakes all night, tonight; we gonna have a ball in the front room." [Laughs]

Them scoun' [scoundrels] got their fiddles that night and went in there. Weren't used to no

house like that back then. Got in Ol' Master's
front room there. [Sings:]

Dee, de yoop, de de yoop, de de yoop, de de yoop,
De de yoop, de de yoop, de de de.
De de yoop, de de yoop, de de yoop, dee.

You sing Sally and I'll sing Sue,
Go up the river and bar-be-que.

Dee, de de, de de, de de, de de, dee.

Baby don't like no button-up shoes,
Just crazy 'bout those gaiters,
All she wants is a bottle of snuff,
An' a great big Irish potato.

Dee, de de yoop, de de yoop, de de yoop, dee de.

Whooo, they's havin' a time then!

Ol' Master come up in the back kitchen there
with ol' flop-down hat on, you know—raggedy.
Went then [knock, knock, knock, knock].
"Would y'all, would you please give me a piece of
bread, please, Ma'am; I ain't had no bread in
three o' four days."

Mirandy says—she talkin' t' ol' boss—"I'll go
back in here an' ask what the boss say. . . . John,"
says, "there's a tramp out there that wants us to
give 'im piece of bread. He ain't had nothin' in
three o' four . . ."
Say, "Tell 'im we'll give him some bread after we
play the next set; if anything's left, we'll give him
somepin'." [Sings:]

Dee, de de yoop, de de yoop, de de yoop, de de yoop,
De de yoop, de de yoop, de de yoop, de de yoop,
De de yoop, de de yoop, de de yoop, he-e-ey ho!
De de yoop, de de yoop, de de yoop, de de yoop,
* wooooooo!*

Women got a quick eye, you know. She went
back there an' Ol' Master cut 'is eye from under

there, an' she looked at him. She went back to
John. Said, "John," say, "that may be a tramp,"
says, "but that man got eyes just like Ol' Master."

"Oh no he ain't! Ol' Master gone to Phillymeclain, I got a key to ever'thin'. 'Joy it, boys,
'joy!"

Ol' John went an' pull that hat up off of Ol'
Master's head. "God, I didn't know it!" Ol' Master
right at him! [Makes a bolting motion to show
John running.] John went up the chimley,
jumped out of that chimley, hit the woods, went
straight to the [river] bottom, straight on down
the swamp an' got in a cave.

[John] had a little ol' boy named Johnny.
Johnny so crazy; you know how little ol' black
boys crazy about their daddies, an' he so crazy
about John. Well, John went off an' stayed an'
stayed; boy stopped eating, wouldn't eat. Little
boy Johnny wouldn't eat 'cause John wasn't
there. 'Bout to run ol' boss an' his wife crazy
'cause that boy wouldn't eat.

So the little boy—he 'as 'bout fifteen or sixteen years old—he fixed up a big shoebox of
ever'thin'. Johnny got on one of them horses,
went on wa-a-ay down in the river bottom. John
way back in the cave back in there; 'bout three o'
four days ain't ate nothin'. Little Johnny got
down there; had a little holler he an' John holler
'round the house when they 'way from one another. [Sings:]

"Hey-ay lay-day, ladle, day-dle,
Day-dle, day-dle, day-dle, day."

John, he knew it: "That's Johnny!

Hey-ay, ladle lay,
Ladle, ladle, ladle, ladle ladle lay."

John come out of the swamp. Boy hollered again,
an' John said,

"Ooooo-oooo-ooo, ooo-ooo-ooo-oo,
Oh-hooo, ooo-ooo-ooo-ooo."

Little ol' boy went up there an' they hugged one another. Johnny an' John, hugged one another. An' that satisfied little Johnny, an' that satisfied him.

Little Johnny come on back home, an' Ol' Master watch Johnny. Little Johnny, he didn't have his box. Ol' Master put Johnny in his [Johnny's] little room an' locked him up. An' he [Master] got him a box an', in 'bout two, three days, he went down there. He got down there, an' he say,

"Aay-ay day,
Lay, day, day day-dle day."

John say, "Uh oh, wrong voice." [Laughs]
He hollered down there all day:

"Hey day-dle, ladle ladle ladle,
Ladle, ladle lay."

"Uh uh," John say, "uh uh; that ain't it, that's t' wrong one. That ain't the one."

So Master kept the boy in there, kep' him 'bout three o' four more days. Then little Johnny got him another box. [Sings softly:]

"Hey-ay lay,
Ladle, ladle ladle lay."

[John answers, singing softly:]

"Hmmmm, mmmm, mmmm,
Mmm, mmmm, mmm, mmmmm."

So the boy went on to him. John was hongry. When he come out of the cave, Ol' Master throwed the gun on him. Said, "Come on, John; I ain't gonna kill you. Come on out. Let's go home." Said, "You made me lose a thousand dollars, on you."

John said, "Ol' Master . . . if you . . . let me . . . go home . . . an' don't kill me . . ."

He say, "I lost a thousand dollars to my wife, I lost a thousand dollars."

He said, "Listen, if you let me go home an' don't kill me," said, "I can fool your wife's nightgown off an' get you back your thousand dollars."

He says, "You can?"

He say, "Yeah! I can do it!"
[Tape stopped and picked back up in the middle of the next sentence.]

He say [to his wife], "Shuck, you ain't done nothin'. John say he can fool your ol' nightgown off of you."

She say, "He can?" She said, "I bet a thousand dollars he can't do it."

He said, "All right, that's a bet."

John come on home an' tol' Ol' Master, say, "Now, listen: 'bout dusk-dark, me an' you gonna start runnin' around the house. At dark, see, she will be gettin' ready to go to bed."

He's runnin' 'round the house, him an' John playin', runnin' around the house. "Brrrraugh." They's just runnin' an' playin'.

John ran in the house. See, there weren't no lamps lit, didn't have no lights. Just had the fireplace, and the fire was out. John say [assuming Master's voice in a whisper], "Ol' Lady, Ol' Lady, give me your gown." Say, "I'm gonna scare ol' John to death." She stripped off right there.

John went on out there, said, "Ol' Master, here it is."

Ol' Master came in an' tol' his wife, say, "Looka here. Get in the bed! Here come John with your gown." [Laughs] So Master win that thousand dollars back. He glad to get his thousand dollars.

Ed Hendrick's Hog. Al Clayton.

Ol' Master went back down there, tol' another white man, say, "Ol' John can tell fortunes."

Say, "That nigger can't tell no fortunes."

Say, "Yes he can tell fortunes, too."

Say, "I bet you a thousand dollars he can't tell no fortunes."

Master said, "I bet you a thousand dollars he can tell." John couldn't a bit more tell no fortunes than I can.

Say, "All right. We'll see. We gonna give him 'til tomorrow at twelve o'clock. I'm gonna do something an' if he can tell what it is, he can tell fortunes." So that man went out that night an' take his dog out an' caught a gre-a-at big black-legged coon, an' put him under a pot.

Give John a cob pipe with "R. J." tobacco [presumably to aid contemplation] an' a deck of cards, an' he gonna have to tell what's under that pot by twelve o'clock that day. An' John, he didn't know nothing 'bout what's under that pot. He know Master would kill 'im then. He kicked 'round that pot all day.

Ten minutes 'til twelve, Ol' Master said—John know he gonna kill 'im—"John," say, "time just 'bout up. You gotta tell what's under that pot."

John went on, says, "Ol' Master, I'm gonna tell you the truth." An' crying, tears in his eyes, says, "Ol' Master, the ol' coon run a long time but you caught him at last." [Laughs] He talkin' about hisself!

My mother said, "'Bout that time, I left." That's the old story she used to tell us back then. Oh Lord, my mother was something else.

John and the Airplane

Recorded in spring 1972 by LeAnn Hulsey from Pauline Gay, a black resident of Atlanta.

Once upon a time, in slavery, there was a man named Jim. And he had a servant name John. And everything that Jim wanted done, he would tell John to do it. And John would always do what his master told him to. He was very patient about that. So John, he was kinda the master's right-hand man. And everything he wanted done that the others didn't do right, John would see to it bein' done right, because he was his right-hand man.

So, one day Old Mahster told John, said, "John, I been had ya wid me fo' a long time, hadn't I?"

"Yes suh, Boss."

Says, "I'm gonna make it a little bit easier on ya." Say, "You been doin' everything I told you to do, and you do it well."

Say, "Yes suh, Boss!"

Say, "I was just thinkin'"; say, "I believe I'll buy me an airplane."

Say, "Boss, whatcha gonna do with an airplane?"

Says, "I'm gonna fly it way up in the air."

Say, "Way up in the air?"

Say, "Yes, I am." Say, "You know somepin'?"

"No, suh."

Say, "I'm goin' take you wid me."

Say, "You goin' take *me* wid ya, Boss?" Say, "When I get dat high, Boss, I wanna be on my way to heaven!" [Laughs]

Says, "Well, John, we goin' take you wid us."

So John begin to think it over, and he begin to wonder. He said, "Boss, I was just thinkin'." Say, "I'm your right-hand man, ain't I?"

"Yeah, John, you is."

"Now, you goin' take me wid you way up in the air, you say."

"Yes, I am."

"I was just thinkin'. I do everything you tell me to do, don't I?"

"Yes you do, John."

"Now, s'posin' we get way up in the air and the airplane break down?"

Says, "Oh well," say, "I 'as thinkin' about that, too."

Say, "Now, if it breaks down, you gonna tell me to get out there and fix it, ain't ya, Boss?"

Say, "Yes I was, John, that's the gen'l idea."

"No thank ya, Boss, I don't think I wanna go wid ya."

And that ends the story of John and his boss.

The Prayer John Gets Paid By

Recorded in spring 1972 by LeAnn Hulsey from Pauline Gay, a black resident of Atlanta.

Once upon a time there was a rich man. He had a servant. His servant's name was John. John worked for him all the time. Whatsoever he paid John, John would be pleased. John knew that his boss was going to treat him right.

So he [the rich man] had a wife name Jenny. He always took care of his business and he never told Jenny anything considerin' financially what went on. So, as years went on, the rich man he got more richer every day. Nobody could understand why he spend but yet he was rich.

One day his health begin to fail him and he got sick. And he call his wife in. He says, "I want to talk to ya, Jenny."

She say, "What is it?"

He say, "I'm sick. I'm gettin' along in age. John has been with me for a number of years. He have worked. I have paid him because I was a Christian. I live by one prayer."

She said, "What is your prayer? You never told me in case, uh, somethin' happen down through the line in life. I would like to know that prayer so I could pray it."

He said, "Well, this is the prayer I always prayed, and I live by it, and I want you to keep it down through the generations."

She said, "Well, I'll do my very best in sight o' God to keep the prayer and your commandment."

He said, "The prayer I'm gonna teach you, Jenny, is the Lord's Prayer that I live by, I pay my servants by; and they always was pleased."

She said, "Well, tell me what the prayer is."

He said, "When you pray, you say,
'Our Father which art in heaven,
'If ya owe John ten dollars, don't pay him but seven.
'Thy Kingdom come. Let thy will be done.
'If he don't take that, Jenny, don't give him none.'
And that's how I stayed rich and lived by this prayer and kept God's commandment."

And that end the story of the rich man, Jenny, and John.

Too Many "Ups"

Recorded in spring 1972 by LeAnn Hulsey from Pauline Gay, a black resident of Atlanta.

I'm gonna tell you a story considerin' the farmer and his boss. In the year when slavery broke [ended], John didn't know what to do about the family situation. He got together and he talked it over with his wife. He was a farmer for his boss. Yet this didn't bring any income in to John and he felt like this would not be a good situation to raise his family on, since he was gonna have to be on his own and not get stuff from his boss. So he talked it over with his wife and he decided, "Well, slavery is broke now. I got to be on my own. I'll try to find something somewhere that my family might survive."

His boss came up to him one morning. He said, "John, I'm ready and it's time now for us to get started with our crop."

John was standin' there lookin' at him, and he was thinkin' all the time. John said, "Well, Boss," say, "let me tell you somethin'. Slavery time is over now, and I cannot make any crops anymore."

He said, "Why, John?" Said, "Didn't you have food when you were working for me?"

He say, "Yes suh, Boss," said, "but you see, hit's not like it used to be. Where I used to get my groceries from your table, I got to provide that now on my own."

He said, "Well, farmin' is a good situation, and you can be able to survive off o' that."

He say, "I was thinkin' and talkin' it over with my wife, just thinkin' about farmin'. It's just a little too many 'ups' in it."

Say, "What's that, John?"

"Well, when you get a farm you've got to start off *up*."

Say, "How is that?"

Say, "When you lay down at night, arise the next morning, you got to get *up*. Then you got to go out to the barn, you got to feed *up*. After you feed the mule up, you got to take him out and water him *up*. Then after you water the mule up, you got to hook him *up*. Then after you hook him up, you go out into the farm, you got to plow the ground *up*. Then after you plow the ground up, Boss, I was just thinkin' all the way down the line, you got to plant it *up*. After you plant this ground up, then you got to gather it *up* when it make. And you gettin' on down through the year at this time. It's beginning to come down to a close. Well, when the end of the year come, after you gather your crop up, then I got to come *up* to you, Boss. When I come to you, you'll say, 'Well, John, I was just goin' over my book. You didn't clear anything this time.' I'll begin to scratch my head and I will be wondering. Say, 'Why not, Boss?' Say, 'I'm sorry, but you et it *up*!'"

So this ends the situation of the farmer and his boss.

John Meets Lester Maddox

Recorded in spring 1972 by Cheryl Ann Reid from J. Smith, in his late sixties, a black resident of Atlanta.

Just after [Martin] Luther King [Jr.] got killed, there 'as this old colored boy, John; he 'as broke, didn't have nothin' to eat. He knowed where Lester Maddox hung out, so he 'cided he'd get out on the street an' cuss Luther King out; he knowed that's what he'd [Maddox] like. So, he got out there talkin' to another colored boy. Say, "I guess y'all know ol' Luther King is dead an' in hell now, an' I'm glad of it! He oughta *done* been dead! He runnin' aroun' here—white folks and colored folks been gettin' along here all these years—and here he done started up somethin'."

Well, after 'while, Maddox comes along, an' he heard it. He stopped right quick. Say, "Hey, boy! Come here a minute."

Boy just kept talkin': "Luther King oughta *done* been dead! I coulda killed him myself, dirty rascal!"

"Come here a minute."

"You call me, Boss?"

"Yeah, come here a minute. Didn't I hear you say you didn't like Luther King?"

"No sir, I never did like that bastard."

"Go over there and get in that Cadillac of mine; I'll be out d'rec'ly."

So the boy went an' got in the Cadillac. Maddox had just got him a cup o' coffee. He come back, say, "Come on, boy, I'm gonna carry you home. I likes you." Got him over there, fix 'im nice dinner: steak, chicken, pork chop, everything. Went an' got all sorts o' liquor, just give it to the nigger.

He was drinking. "Damn ol' Luther King, he oughta *done* been dead."

"Here, boy! Try some o' this."

"Yes suh, Bossman. Yeah, Luther King, he oughta been dead an' in hell years ago."

Ol' Maddox, he thought all the niggers liked King; wondered how come this nigger didn't like King. Say, "John?"

"Yes sir, Bossman."

"How come you didn't like King?"

"I just didn't like him!"

"Everybody else like him; how come you didn't like him?"

"The reason I didn't like Luther King, you really wanta know?"

"Yeah, why?"

"'Cause one thing: every time I got ready to kick your damn ass, he hollered, 'Non-violence'!"

Bobtail Outwits the Devil

Recorded in spring 1967 by Marion Brasington and Edward Prince from Roy Cook of Ball Ground, Cherokee County.

The Devil and the farmer went in farmin' together—it was on the fifty-fifty base [that is, each would contribute equally to land rental and the cost of fertilizer and seed]—and that was Bobtail and the Devil. So Bobtail he made a deal one of 'em would take what's on top o' the ground and the other what's under the ground. Well, the Devil told him that's all right. So Bobtail said, "Now," says, "I'll take what's on top of the ground and you take what's under the ground." He told him he would.

And so he [Bobtail] planted. That year he planted beans and corn and sich as that. Well, that fall wound up, and so Bobtail he got what they'd raised and the Devil he didn't have nothin'.

Well, so the Devil told Bobtail that they would change it next year. Said, "I'll take on top of the ground and you take under the ground." Told him that'd be all right. So they went ahead and planted sweet potatoes and Irish potatoes and all sich as that [that is, root crops]. So they wound up that fall and the Devil he still didn't have nothin'!

And so that's how Bobtail beat the Devil.

Wooden Nutmegs

Recorded in spring 1971 by Joel Rucker from H. W. Kinman, seventy-seven, of Atlanta, who was reared near Calhoun, Gordon County.

Years ago it was said by southern people that when the Yankees came south they came south to criticize. Well, the Yankees no longer criticize the South as much as they once did, because the Yankee has learned that the South has so much that the North doesn't have. We have the southern way that secretly the Yankee wishes that he had.

But right after the Civil War there was a group of Yankees came south just to take a general look around. And they went to a small town, and in their rambling around there they came up on a little plant—it seemed to be a woodworking plant—and they walked inside. There was just one man in there; he had a peg leg. They got to talking with him, asked him did he own that woodworking plant. He said yes. And they said they supposed that he was an ex-Confederate soldier; he said yes he was, he had lost his leg on the battlefield and so now he was running this place of business.

Those Yankees said, "Well, that's fine that you have your own business; in the North, most of the Union ex-soldiers, being so enterprising and aggressive, are doing well either working for someone else or had a business of their own. Because those Union ex-soldiers, they were smart fellows, yeah. We northern people are smart." He said, "Oh, by the way, what do you manufacture here?"

He said, "Nutmegs."

"You mean you make wooden nutmegs?"

He said, "Yes."

Well, they started laughing about it; said, "Well, do you sell any of them?"

He said, "Oh yes, I sell all of them that I can make." Said, "Business is built up to where it's beginning to look like I'm going to have to put on someone else to help me here."

Well, that was real funny to those Yankees. He said, "Well now, you are really enterprising also." Said, "Don't these people around here get mighty mad with you about it?"

He said, "Oh no, I don't sell my product to these local people"; said, "they wouldn't stand for it, they're too smart for anything like that. I wouldn't last any length of time if I start pawning any such deal off on these local people."

They said, "Well, where do you sell them?"

He said, "I ship them up North, sell them to the Yankees."

Said, "Well, don't you get a lot of gripes and complaints?"

He said, "Oh yes, I do; but," said, "when I get a complaint that those nutmegs doesn't seem to have any flavor, I just write back and tell them to use more of them!"

Rock Soup

Recorded in spring 1968 by James R. Hunter, Jr., from his father, Dick Hunter, of Marietta, Cobb County.

This man traveled around the country and come to this ol' widow's house, and she was a real tightwad—she just an old miser-type person—and she wouldn't give anyone anything. An' so he'd walked on off down the road a little ways and he's crossing this little stream and he picked up a little smooth pebble there; and he had this idea.

So he went back up there an' he says, "Will you let me borry a pot of water to make some rock soup with?"

And she says, "Rock soup?" Says, "What in the world is rock soup?"

He says, "Well, I'll make some for us and then you can decide whether you like it or not."

So she got him a pot full of water and he put it on the fire. He dropped in this little rock and he's stirrin' it, and he says, "Say, have you got any old meat layin' around here, any beef layin' around? It'd add a lot of flavor to it."

So she says, "Yeah, I got a little piece of meat."

So she got some meat out, and he chopped that up and dropped it into the boilin' water and was stirrin' it. And he says, "Have you got any potatoes?" He says, "Now, potatoes add an awful lot to this rock soup."

So she says, "Yeah, I got a few potatoes here."

So she got out some potatoes, and he peeled 'em an' cut 'em up and dropped 'em in the soup. He stirred around there and he says, "Hey, have you got an onion?" He says, "Now, an onion adds an awful lot of flavor to this soup."

So she got out an onion, and he diced up the onion and dropped it in there and was cookin' it and everything, and he says, "Do you happen to have any tomatoes?" He says, "Now, tomatoes really add an awful lot of flavor to this soup."

And so she got a couple of tomatoes, and he cut them up and dropped them in the soup and cooked. And he says, "Can I borrow a little salt and pepper?" So he got some salt and pepper an' poured it in there, and he cooked this soup up.

And boy, after they got through, she said that was the best soup she had ever had in her life. And she says, "May I keep this rock?"

He says, "Well, you can keep that rock." He says, "That's the way you make rock soup!"

Now, I don't remember where I heard it [laughs], but I believe it was my grandmother telling me long years ago.

CHAPTER NINE

Jests

NUMSKULLS

The Irishmen and the Mosquitoes

Recorded in spring 1974 by Louellen Wright from Tom Quinton, forty-three, of Talking Rock, Pickens County.

Along the middle of the nineteenth century, you know, there was a potato famine in Arland [Ireland], and thousands and thousands of Arshmen came to help build the railroads and work over here. And there was two young Arshmen who come over from Arland, and they had wandered around seekin' their fortune, and they got down in the Appalachians, you know. They came into Pickens County, and they's walkin' the railroad.

It was gettin' dark, and they went to ask this man and woman if they could spend the night; well, there were no hotel accommodations anywhere around. And they told 'em they'd be glad to share what they had, you know. So they went in, and they ate with 'em, and they went to bed early because you had to burn kerosene, you know, if you's gonna keep a light late. People were kind of thrifty, you know, and didn't like to use too much kerosene.

So they, 'course, didn't have screens on their windows. They went to bed, and they was mosquitoes. The mosquitoes kept bitin' them, you

know, and oh, they just slap, and they couldn't go to sleep. They's just a-gettin' stung. The mosquitoes comin' in at the window, you know. So finally, one of 'em he drifted off to sleep, and the other one he kept slappin' at the mosquitoes, you know.

After a while, he reached over and rolled him out of the bed. He said, "You just might as well get up from there." Said, "Them dang things has done got lanterns and come a-lookin' for us." And it was lightnin' bugs that had flown in at the window! [Laughs]

He thought sure that the mosquitoes had got lanterns and had come lookin' for 'em.

Pat and Mike and the Hanging Job

Written in winter 1967 by Helen Phillips, a student at Towns County High School, Hiawassee; collected by Michael Moss. The writer notes, "This story was told to me by my daddy, Kit Phillips, and it was told to him by his grandfather."

Pat and Mike, two Irishmen, came to America to find jobs. They weren't doing very good, so they separated.

Mike killed a man and he was going to be

hanged. The law then was to put the noose around the person's neck, tie his hands and feet, and leave him for an hour to pray.

While Mike was waiting for the sheriff to come back, Pat came by. He asked Mike how he was doing.

Mike replied, "I'm doing just fine. I've got a good job with good pay. All I have to do is stand here with this rope around my neck and my hands and feet tied. When the man comes back and asks me if I'm ready, I say yes and they let me down and pay me."

"Well," said Pat, "I'm not doing so good. I haven't even found a job yet."

Mike said, "I'm getting kinda tired of this job. You can have it if you want it."

"Okay," replied Pat as he climbed up and untied Mike. Mike put the rope around Pat's neck and tied his hands and feet.

Pat was taller than Mike, and back then they measured the rope to where the person's feet would be two inches off the ground. When the sheriff came back he asked Pat if he was ready. Pat said he was, and the sheriff pulled the trigger to the trap door.

Pat fell through and landed on his feet. He looked up at Mike and said, "It might be a good job with good pay, but I'll be darned if somebody don't break his fool neck doing that!"

The Looking Glass

Recorded in spring 1970 by Nancy Lee from Mrs. Casto (Elizabeth) Wallace, fifty-nine, of Sparta, Tennessee.

Back in the slavery days, there was a white family that owned slaves; and, you know, they [the slaves] didn't have any mirrors. They didn't know how they looked. And this white woman, she got her mirror broken. And she gave this nigger man a piece of it—oh, somethin' like, say, the size of your hand. And he looked in thar and, of course, he saw himself. But he didn't know it was hisself he saw. He'd always been told that he looked like his father—was just the very image of his father—and he thought that was his father he was seein'.

Well, he took that mirror on down to the barn, and he put it under a barrel that was down thar. And every mornin' when he'd go to the barn to work, why, he'd get out that mirror and he would just take to it, and he'd cry and go on.

And his wife, she was out in the yard and she heard him one day. She slipped down to the barn and heard all this commotion a-goin' on, you know. She saw him after he got through and got ready to leave stickin' this under the barrel.

So when he wasn't thar, she went back down to the barn and she looked under that barrel, and thar was the mirror. She never had seen a mirror either, you know; never had seen herself. So she picked it up and she looked at herself. She says, "Huh! So this is the old hussy he's taken on over, is it? Well," says, "I'll end this!" And she just broke that mirror all to pieces!

The Cross-eyed Mule

Recorded in spring 1978 by Joy Breedlove from Randy Picklesimer, twenty-one, an Atlanta college student reared at Culbertson, North Carolina.

Some friend of mine told me this. There were these two guys out on the farm, and they had this ol' mule. And they were plowin' with him one day, and they noticed that he wasn't walkin' down the rows straight. And they looked at him, and they noticed that his eyes had crossed. So they said, "Aw, we have to call a veterinarian, find out what's wrong with him"; said, "we can't stand this." It's the only mule they had.

So they called the vet, and he come over and looked at the mule and says, "Oh yes," says, "I know how to cure this." He says, "Go get me 'bout a twelve-foot-long piece of lead pipe, about one inch in diameter."

Guys going, "My God, what's he goin' do with that?" So they go get the pipe.

Veterinarian says, "Okay, you two go around front, now, and tell me when his eyes uncross." So the veterinarian takes the piece of pipe and sticks it up the mule's rear end, where there's about six feet of it in and six feet of it out [chuckles], and he says, "Okay, y'all tell me when his eyes uncross." Takes a deep breath and blows into the pipe and forces the mule to start swellin' up.

Guy goes, "Nah, not yet." Takes another deep breath and blows into the pipe, and they go, "Yeah, that did it!" And, sure enough, his eyes had uncrossed.

Veterinarian pulls the pipe out and says, "See there, that's all there is to it. That'll be five dollars." They pay him, he goes on home, they plow, everything's fine.

Well, about two months later, they're plowin'; they notice the mule walkin' crooked again. They say, "Whoa," walk around front, and his eyes have re-crossed. One of 'em says, "Well, I guess I better call that vet."

And the other one says, "Nah, they ain't no use in that." Says, "I ain't payin' him five dollars for somepin' I can do myself." Says, "Go get that pipe." So the other fellow goes an' gets the pipe.

[Collector's note: tape ran out here and I unknowingly missed part of the story. The guy stuck the pipe in and told the other one to watch, started blowing in the pipe like the vet had done, and the mule] starts swellin' up. He says, "Are they uncrossed yet?"

And the guy around front says, "Nah, not yet."

Fella 'round back takes another deep breath, blows in the pipe, says, "They uncrossed yet?"

And the guy says, "Nah, not yet."

Fella 'round back says, "Phew"; says, "man, I'm out of breath. Whyn't you come around here and blow on the pipe awhile an' I'll tell you when his eyes uncross."

So the guy around back walks up to the front and the guy around front walks up to the back. He looks up at that pipe stickin' outta that mule's rear end, and he scratches his head an' thinks a minute. He jerks the pipe out, turns it around and sticks the *other* end in the mule, takes a deep breath an' starts to blow in it.

An' the guy around front's going, "Aaah! Wait a minute"; says, "what in the world are you doin'? You crazy?"

Guy around back looks at him and says, "Well, you don't expect me to blow in the same end you did, do ya?"

An Unsound Investment

Recorded in fall 1981 by Ellen McDonald from her father, Jerry McDonald, of Thomaston, Upson County; he learned it from his grandfather, Charles Brown.

These two old country boys got 'hold of a dollar apiece for the first time. And, of course, they never had any money to spend, and they really felt wealthy with having a dollar apiece to spend. And so one says to the other, "What are you gonna buy with your dollar?"

And he said, "Well, I'll tell you. I've always wanted one of those dollar wristwatches that you wear around. I've always thought that was just the height of wealthy to have a wristwatch." And he asked the other one what he was going to buy.

And he said, "I'm gonna buy me a pair of underdrawers. Living in the country I've never had a pair of underdrawers before."

So they went into town, and the boy bought his watch and the other bought his underdrawers and sneaked out back of the store and put them on, and they really strutted around town.

It came time to go home that night, and they took the old backwoods road to the house. They had to cross a log over the creek to get home, and they always stopped on this log that crossed the creek and took a shit before they got home.

So the old boy that had the watch, when he unhooked his overalls and squatted down on the log to take a shit his watch fell off in the water and it went kerplunk! And the boy turned to his buddy and said, "You know, there's something wrong here. I just heard a kerplunk but I ain't shit, yet."

And the boy that had bought the underwear said, "Boy, something really is wrong, 'cause I just shit and I ain't heard a kerplunk yet!"

A Hazardous Journey

Recorded in fall 1981 by Marjorie Thomaston from her grandfather, Royce Veal, seventy-seven, of Deepstep, Washington County.

Well, my cousin, he's got a good memory, and he can remember these stories. And he said there's two fellows up there at Milledgeville decided that they wanted to go down there on the river where they made good whiskey and good ribbon-cane syrup [molasses]. So these fellows borrowed a Model T Ford five-passenger and they went down on the river. And they got 'em a half gallon o' white lightnin' apiece and they got 'em a gallon of the syrup.

So one of 'em was in the back seat, and naturally he's gonna top that half a gallon, you know, along; the other one done drank a little bit of it. So up on the road there's a bad sand bed, you know, and if you didn't hit a sand bed right with a Model T it cut in that rut and would flip it over quick. And so they turned it over. And the driver got out, said, "Hey, fella, you hurt?"

He said, "I'm bleedin' to death"; said, "I got blood all over me." Said, "I'm bleedin' to death; I'll be dead in a minute." Said, "How you?"

Said, "Well, I'm crushed in my chest and just burnin' up."

'Bout that time a fellow walked up—neighbor heard it—and he come up there with a lantern. Passenger was crawlin' out from under the car with an inner tube in his arms. The neighbor said, "Turn loose of that inner tube, fella; you ain't got nothin' on you but syrup and you ain't cut up at all." He thought that inner tube was his guts, you know. Little ol' inner tube on a Model T Ford wadn't no bigger than that, you know, just a little bit of air. And when he turned over he broke the gallon of syrup and that spilt all over him. And he grabbed up the inner tube [laughs] when he got out.

The other fellow then coughed, and he coughed up the little stub of cigar he'd swallowed; and that's all that was the matter with him. So they turned the Ford back over and went on in.

TALL TALES

The Wonderful Hunt

Recorded in winter 1967 by Marcia Horne from her father, E. W. Horne, fifty-three, of Atlanta, who was reared in Americus, Sumter County.

Well, the colored fella that my daddy used to have go with him when he's settin' monuments; my daddy and my mother'd go off to church or somethin' an' they'd leave this ol' man, he'd stay there an' baby-sit with us. An' he said that one time when he was young that times got real hard and they had a bad drought an' they couldn't make any crop, an' so they all about to starve to death. So he had an ol' shotgun an' he had one ol' solid ball that he could put in it, an' he decided he'd go off down there an' see if he couldn't kill a rabbit or somethin'. And they'd eat that, an' then they'd die.

So he took the shotgun an' loaded it up with that one solid ball an' went off down in the woods. He got down in the woods and he looked up in the ol' dead tree and there were seven turkeys settin' on a limb, and he got to trying to figure out how he's goin' to kill 'em all at one shot. An' he heard a little noise in the bushes, an' he looked over there an' there's a great big deer standin' over there. So he decided he'd kill the deer, 'cause there's more meat in the deer.

So then he looked down at the foot of the tree that the turkeys sittin' on, an' there's an ol' ax down there. So he set the ax up with the blade to him, an' shot the edge of the blade and split the bullet in half. An' half of it went over and killed the deer and the other half flew upside of the tree and split the limb, and all the turkeys' toes were slipped in the limb. And then when the bullet went through the limb, closed up on the turkeys' toes and caught 'em all!

So he climbed up on the tree and killed all the turkeys and dropped them down an' got down, and had to go across the creek to get his deer. So he went over there to get his deer, and said he had an ol' pair o' rubber boots on and had his britches leg down in the boot. An' when he got his deer and got back across the creek, said his britches felt real heavy, an' he looked an' he'd got in a brim [bream] bed an' he had both britches legs full of brim!

So he piled all that stuff in a pile, an' he saw he wasn't goin' to be able to carry it back to the house. So he skinned the deer, 'cause all the old harness done rotted off his wagon. He took the hide back up there and made him some harness and hooked the mule to the wagon, went down and loaded all his stuff up on it and started back to the house. An' when he got to the house, why, he looked around and his wagon hadn't even moved it 'as so heavy loaded, an' that green deerhide jes' stretched an' left the wagon down there in the woods and the mule was standin' up there at the house!

So he was tired and he put the mule up, tied him to the post there an' went on in the house. And said in a little bit he heard a wagon comin' up the road, an' he wondered who it was. An' he looked out there, an' the sun had dried the deerhide an' was pullin' the wagon up the road. An' got home, and they had enough meat to last 'em until they had a good big rain an' got a garden in.

Lucky Shots

Recorded in spring 1967 by Marion Brasington and Edward Prince from Roy Cook of Ball Ground, Cherokee County.

Oh, just like the old guy was way back yonder in the old times. He went huntin', and so he found him a deer, and he shot at the deer, and the bullet went on through the deer and went on into a tree over across the creek. And he goes over there where he hears something: "Glugle, glugle, glugle," went to see and he'd shot into a bee tree, and the honey was a-runnin' out.

And he had a bottom [creek bottomland] in there, and he had his bottom planted in corn and pumpkins; and the pumpkins was so rank 'til . . . he didn't have nothin' to catch this honey in, so he just went to cuttin' these leaf stems off and pluggin' 'em and catchin' 'em full o' honey and totin' 'em back across the creek where his deer was. Why, he had piled so much of these pumpkin stems full o' honey 'til he couldn't tote 'em. So in crossin' back and forwards across the creek, why, water come up over his boots. And he felt somethin' agin his leg an' feet; looked down, he had his shoes full o' fish! And so he caught him a good string o' fish, laid them down there.

And way back before they made trace chains outta metal had ta make the traces [the lines that connect a beast of burden to a vehicle or plow for pulling] outta rawhide, so he goes to the house and gets the mule and sled and brings 'em back down there. And 'bout the time he got loaded, came up a shower of rain an' got his rawhide traces wet and they 'gin ta stretch. So when he got up to the house, why, his sled it wasn't in sight; and so he jest undone his hame

strings, just hung his hames [to which the traces and sled were connected] over the gatepost. Well, the sun shined out then; said just soon as it dried out his traces, said it come a-drawin' in. He looked 'roun' an' here come the sled, comin' on up to the house [loaded with the deer, fish, and honey]!

Then one time way back yonder, I went out huntin'; had an ol'-time muzzle-loadin' shotgun. So I got near this deer, and I wanted to be sure an' kill it, so I loaded it pretty heavy. And so when I shot the deer, why, it just busted my gun all to pieces; flew around the hill, and I took out after it, run around the hill there. And I got around there and my ramrod had three turkeys whipped to death. And then I went on 'round the hill a little further and there was my hammer, had this here deer up agin a rock just a-peckin' 'im in the head. So I got my three turkeys and my deer all right, all with one shot; but I lost my gun and the ramrod.

The Indian's Lucky Hunting Feather

Written in winter 1967 by Keith Nicholson, a student at Towns County High School, Hiawassee; collected by Michael Moss.

Once there was an Indian boy who believed that an eagle feather would bring him good luck in hunting. The boy started out and found an eagle feather and put it in his hair.

The next morning he went hunting with his bow and arrow. It was not long until he saw three turkeys sitting on a limb. He pulled back his bow and let an arrow fly. It hit the limb and split it and caught every one of the turkeys by the big toe. The arrow had broken and one end killed a rabbit; the other end stuck in a tree, and when he pulled it out honey started pouring. He went and got some hide barrels and caught three barrels full.

When he come back he made another arrow out of a peach tree and shot a deer with it. Next year he saw a deer with a tree on his back. He tamed the deer and from then on all he had to do was to call his deer and pick all the peaches he wanted!

The Unlucky Hunt

Recorded in fall 1976 by Cindy Axelberd from Minyard Conner, seventy-six, of Dillard, Rabun County, who was reared at Stonemont, North Carolina.

Way back, way back in the old days when you had nothin' but the great rifle—you know, the one-shot gun, just shot one time—I got that gun and started to hunt. Gettin' 'long about Thanksgiving, and went away back in the mountains [motions away with hand]—the Smoky Mountains—up there among the Indians.

Goin' tuck up a big holler and went over a ridge, and over the ridge was a big gang of turkeys flew up on the trees just pretty high up, you know; and just had one shot. And I thinks to myself, "Boy, would I love to have more'n one." And directly I decided—they's all sittin' up thar lookin' down at me—I decided ta shoot up thar and split that limb and let their toes go down in thar, you know, and catch 'em. Well, I just aimed right at the center of that limb, you know [makes aiming motion with hand, as if he is holding a rifle], and my gun fired and the limb sprung open, and their toes went in thar.

Thar I had 'em, all on that limb; and it made me wonder again how I's goin' to get 'em. So I just throwed off my coat—and I had a rope in my pocket—and I clumb that tree and went up thar. I'd slide out that limb, you know, towards 'em, reach and git one and tie a good hard knot in it, you know, and I'd move to the next un and I'd slip up a little more and I'd tie another un [makes tying motion with hands].

After awhile I got the last one loose, you know, and I'd jerk him up and they'd all commence floppin' their wings, just flop, flop, flop, flop, flop, flop [puts hands under arms and makes flapping motion with arms, as if to fly]. Well, they begin to carry me! I 'as up in the air [eyes grow wide with excitement], just a-goin', and went over one big mountain, went over another un and on and on. And directly I got to thinkin' about home—they's just a-takin' me further away from home—and thinks to myself, "What will I do?" And I thinks to myself, "If they don't light on that next ridge I'm goin' cut loose when it goes to the top of the trees." An' they come sailin' right over the top of the trees, an' I just took the knife and cut loose.

When I cut loose, come right down on top of a big tree—it was a big old holler tree—and I hit that tryin' to catch it, an' chunks broke off with me, and in place of comin' down on the outside of it I went down in the center of it, you know. I didn't get hurt bad; and I looked up and I just seen a little light hole at the top and I thinks to myself, "Well, this here'll be the last ta comin'!" And my feet felt a little bit warm, and I thinks to myself, "They's somethin' down in thar!" I felt around and felt around, and by jugs, they's two little [bear] cubs down in thar [eyes wide with excitement], just small ones. And I thinks to myself, "Now, Lawd, what will I do?"

After awhile I heard somethin' on the outside of the tree: "Rap, rap, rap, rap!" His claws comin' up, you know: "Clap, clap, clap!" I jes' folded up my arms [folds arms] and thinks to myself, "Well, I'm a goner." I 'as a-lookin' up and I seen the light went out on top and I jes' shut my eyes, and I opened my eyes agin and I could see the form of it comin' down the tree; he's backin' down in thar, you know, backin' down in thar.

I had my knife; I jes' grabbed my hand into the fur of that little short tail [makes grabbing motion], and I commenced sticking him with that knife [makes jabbing motion], and up he went. He was carryin' me right back up outta thar, you know, with the limbs and bark jes' flyin'. And the bear went up over the side of the tree, and I fell off and hit the ground, jumped up and started to run.

And they brought the old white mule, and that's the end of the tale. [Laughs]

Hunting and Fishing Yarns

Recorded in spring 1978 by Bill Powers from Zenus Windsor, forty-three, of Cragford, Alabama.

Probably one of the best huntin' tales that I ever heard was this man was going squirrel huntin' with this fella he heard about. And so he got to the house and there was the ugliest man he thought he'd ever seen in his life. And so they started to leave the house and the fella says, "Aren't ya gonna carry a gun with ya?"

And he says, "Naw."

He says, "Well then, how ya gonna get the squirrel when the dog trees it?"

He says, "Well, I just ugly 'em to death."

And so they got to the tree, and sure 'nough when they got there there was a squirrel up the tree. And the man looked up the tree and just begin to make faces, and the ol' squirrel just fold up [makes folding motion with hands] and just fell out dead!

The man thought, "Well, he is so ugly, wonder what his wife looks like?" And so he asked the fella, said, "Do you ever take ya wife with ya huntin'?"

He says, "Naw," says, "she tears 'em up too bad!"

Another'n: This fella wanted to go bird huntin', and he went by this old farmer's house and asked him if he could hunt. The farmer said, "Yeah," says, "I got a lot of birds here."

The fella said, "Oh, well, I ain't got a bird dog."

The old fella said, "Well, I ain't either, but I got a mule."

Fella said, "What you mean, a mule?"

He said, "Well, my mule will point birds better than any dog that's ever been."

The fella says, "Well, I'll take him, then, and see about that."

So the old fella told him, he says, "Well, all right, you can take him huntin'. But I'll tell ya what"; says, "if you're goin' bird huntin', don't carry him down by the river."

He says, "Whatcha mean?"

He says, "Well, he'd rather fish than hunt!"

And while we're along the huntin' and fishin', maybe some tall tales'll do you some good about fishin'. Now that's really where your tall tales exist, is among fishermen, as you know.

This man said he had a farm down by the river, and there was deep water there. And they'd been hanging a fish out there that nobody could ever catch.

And so this other man decided he was going to catch him. And so he made him a fishhook

Marvin Junia Hillsman at Barnett Shoals. Roy Ward.

out of a cant hook—a cant hook is the thing you roll logs with; great big hook. So he decided he'd make him a hook that would hold him, ya know. And said he tied a great big log chain to that cant hook, and he put a ham of meat on it for bait. And so he went down by the river and threw that ham of meat out on that hook, and tied it to a tree.

And he was plowing a pair of big mules, weigh about two thousand pounds apiece; and so he came to the end up there. And that tree that he had the log chain tied to was just about to be pulled up where the fish was pulling on it; it'd gotten on his hook and was pulling so bad. And so he just quickly snapped his mules' singletree into that chain and took it loose from the tree, where those big mules would pull this big fish out. And said he turned around to cut him a limb, ya know, to whip his mules with where they would really pull; said when he turned back around, that all he could see was four ears goin' under the water! Never got that fish.

Liars' Deal

Recorded in fall 1968 by Linda Mitchell from R. E. Faulkner, seventy-three, of Bartow County.

In Guntersville, Alabama, they built a bridge where the ferry used to be over the Tennessee River. One feller said that he was fishin' under this bridge and caught a fish so big the shadow weighed fourteen and a half pounds!

And the other feller said, "Well, I was fishin' right there few weeks ago and caught a lantern." What we used to use, you know, to make lights? Kerosene lantern. Says he caught a lantern and pulled it up, and says it was still burnin'! So he

turned it up and looked at the date under it and it was 1874.

And that first feller looked at him and says, "Well, I'll tell you what I'll do." Says, "I'll take a hundred pounds off my fish if you blow your lantern out!"

The Hoop Snake

Written in winter 1967 by Joel Rogers, a student at Towns County High School, Hiawassee; collected by Michael Moss.

My granddad said about forty years ago they would go back in the mountains to cut logs and snake them out with a horse.

One day he and two other men sawed down a dead oak tree. There was a hollow knot in the tree, and as it fell to the ground out crawled a funny-colored snake. My granddad said he had never seen one of such outstanding colors. Back then all snakes were poison to them except a black snake. So one of the men took his ax and cut the snake's head off. Just as he backed away from the snake there was a loud hissing sound. My granddad and the two other men looked up the hill and there was another of those snakes. It was winding itself up in a hoop like a car wheel. Before they knew what was happening, here it came rolling toward the man who had just a few minutes before killed its mate. My granddad said he threw a limb in its path to keep it from hitting him. It hit the limb, bounced over it, and struck a tree. The snake let go of its tail; on the tip end of its tail it had a stinger about one inch long.

Granddad and the men went back in a day or two to the same spot where the incident had occurred, and the tree which the snake had struck was dead.

Did this really happen? If I were you I wouldn't be playing around with hoop snakes to find out. By the way, my granddad was a pretty truthful fellow.

Friendly Snakes

Recorded in spring 1968 by James R. Hunter, Jr., from his father, Dick Hunter, of Marietta, Cobb County.

This fellow was out huntin' in this real desolate area, and he'd been huntin' all day. And he saw this rattlesnake layin' there, and he thought he's gonna kill him. And then he decided, "Aw heck, I won't shoot ya, I'll just let you live."

So he walks on for a ways and he comes to this railroad crossing, and he thought, well, he'd just sit down and rest a little while. But he was pretty tired, so he just laid back over, put his head on the steel [rail], and went to sleep.

After awhile there's a fellow wakin' him up there, shakin' him. And he says, "Fellow, how about gettin' off the rails, because I wanta bring the train on through here."

So he says, "How come you stopped the train?"

He says, "Well, 'bout a quarter of a mile down the track down here was this rattlesnake with your red bandana, had come and was flaggin' us down! So he saved your life."

Another one of the old stories they used to tell around the house when I was a kid was about this old man who went off down the creek to fish. And he got down there, happened to realize

he didn't have any bait. And so he got lookin' around for something he could use for bait, and he saw this snake layin' there with a frog in his mouth. So he took a forked stick an' reached down, put it around the snake's neck and got the frog out of the snake's mouth to use that for bait. And he looked down at the poor old snake, and he looked so dad-blamed pitiful he took his pint bottle out and give him a little shot of whiskey. And so the old snake wiggled off, and the old fellow cut the frog up, went about his fishin'.

And after he'd been fishin' for a little while, he felt something tappin' him on the leg. And there was that old snake back again with a bigger frog in his mouth!

Big Kettle for a Big Turnip

Recorded in spring 1967 by Marion Brasington, Edward Prince, and John Burrison from Roy Cook of Ball Ground, Cherokee County.

Feller he was a traveling man, and he stopped and stayed all night with this other feller. He [the host] was tellin' 'im about cleanin' him up a turnip patch, and he just had a quarter of an acre. And way back yonder we had split rails, you know, when we built a fence around anything, patches and anything like that. So he'd went and split him rails, you know, and fenced this off—which you know the cattle all run outside. Said it happened that one [turnip] come up right in the middle of this lot. And said it grew so large 'til it just pushed this fence down all around it!

Well, he [the traveler] went on this trip then; and he come back through and stopped and stayed all night with him again. Said, "You know, I seen the awfullest kittle while I was gone that I ever seen in my life." And said, "They was a-workin' on it 'bout fixin' the head"; and said, "feller he dropped his hammer just as he was fixin' to quit"; and said, "the next mornin' when they got back they heared the hammer hit the bottom of this kittle."

That feller said, "Well, Lordy mercy. What did he want such a kittle fer?"

He said, "To cook your big turnip in!"

A Trip to the Moon

Recorded in spring 1970 by Nancy Lee from Mrs. Casto (Elizabeth) Wallace, fifty-nine, of Sparta, Tennessee.

When I was a child I'd always heard, you know, that the moon was made of cheese; so I decided I'd see. There was a large mountain close to where we lived and I could see the moon as it would come up at night. It just come right over that mountain, and I thought I could just reach right over and touch it. And I'd heard people say that you could. So I decided that I'd go to that mountain and see.

Well, I started out walkin'; packed me a little lunch, you know, and put it on a stick across my shoulder. I walked and I walked, and oh, I got so tard. And I come to a pasture, and there was an old gray mar' grazin' thar in the field. So I had a rope in my pocket that I could tie to a tree so that when I jumped off on the moon, if I didn't land thar it would hold me, you know, and I wouldn't fall and kill myself. Well, I put that on the old gray mar' and made me a halter out of it.

I got up on her and went to ridin', and not far from the foot of this mountain, why, her back broke in two. I got off and I cut me a hickory limb and stuck it each way in her back and shoved it up her backbone and that fixed 'er up, you know. And I got back up on her and I rode to the foot of this mountain.

And I started up the mountain, and when I got almost to the top I saw a b'ar a-comin'; and Lawd, you can't imagine how fast I finished a-goin' up that mountain! But just as I got to the edge of this bluff, why, that b'ar was right thar behind me. And I grabbed hold of its tail and turned that b'ar wrong side out. And that b'ar went back down that mountain just a-laughin' itself to death, because all that fur was ticklin' it on the inside.

And about that time, why, here come the moon. And it was close enough that I tied my rope to the tree, you know, and as it came by I jumped off on it and I got up on thar. And in a little bit, why, I thought how far that I was from it [the bluff]. And it was a little farther the next night, and the next night; so I knew that, well, maybe I couldn't never get back on that rock anymore.

And I soused [plunged] my fingers down in the moon, and found out it *was* really cheese. And it was just full of skippers—like cheese skippers [insects], you know, that gets in old cheese—it was so old. Well, those skippers, they were larger than any huge rats we have here. I set about skinnin' those skippers, and I skinned, and skinned, and skinned. And then I tied those skippers together until I made a rope long enough that I skinnied down it, and come back to Earth!

RELIGION

Preparing for the Preacher

Recorded in spring 1975 by Michael Adams from Robert Johnson, a black resident of Atlanta.

Ol' Eugene's out in the field plowing. The little boy come running. "Hey, Daddy, Daddy!"

"Whoa! What is it, boy?"

"The preacher's coming to the house."

"Whatta you say, boy?"

"The preacher's coming. What must I do?"

"I tell you what you do, Son. Go home, lock up all the chickens, sit in ya mama's lap and wait 'til I get there!"

The Right Stuff

Recorded in spring 1969 by Barbara Lanier from Bill Emmett of Scottdale, DeKalb County.

This colored preacher went to a new church, an' that mornin' he said, "Now I want all you brethren t' come out here this aftuhnoon t' a special meetin' we gonna have."

So about two o'clock they all gathered in the church for a special meeting. He says, "Brethren," he said, "I call us uhgethuh here so dat we can git evuhthing straighten' out, an' you can unduhstand-a me, an' I kin un'stan' you." Said, "What I wanchoo t' do," said, "evuhbody what loves-a de Lawd t' get ovuh here on my right, an' evuhbody wha' loves-a wine an' de women t' get ovuh here on my left."

Well, everybody started getting to their right places. He noticed one nigra man settin' there in the back lookin' real puzzled all by himself. He said, "Say there, Brothuh"; said, "din' ya undastan' what I said? I said evrabody what loves de Lawd to get ovuh here on my right, an' evuhbody what loves-a wine an' women t' get ovuh here on my left."

He say, "Yazzuh, Pa'son. I unnastan's that, but I's a-wonderin', suh, uh, I don' know"; says, "you see, I loves de Lawd, an' I loves wine an' de women too."

Said, "Hmm"; said, "well, son, you jest come up here in de pulpit wi' me. You's been called t' preach!"

The Preacher's Bicycle

Recorded in spring 1974 by Lori Dinerman from her father, Sam Dinerman, fifty-four, of Atlanta.

This concerns two preachers—rather young men—who were ardent bicyclists. And every Monday morning they met at six o'clock sharp and they would ride their bicycles for miles and miles through the city. And this went on for several years. But one Monday morning at six o'clock, one of the preachers was there waiting, and finally here comes the other one without his bicycle, walking. He says, "Good gracious," he says, "what happened? Where's your bicycle?"

Says, "Well, I'm rather disillusioned. I'm pretty sure that a member of my congregation stole it at the church meeting last Sunday," he says, "but I'm not sure."

So his friend says, "Well, have you considered giving a sermon, and perhaps you could touch the conscience of this guilty person if he's in your congregation and prod him to return the bicycle."

So he says, "Well, that's an excellent idea."

So the next Monday morning at six o'clock he appeared with his bicycle.

Says, "Oh," says, "I see you were successful in recovering your bicycle."

Says, "Yes," says, "I sure was. I took your suggestion and I gave a sermon, and I used the Ten Commandments as a basis."

Says, "Well," he says, "you must have really touched the member of your congregation"; he says, "it really must have hit his conscience hard."

He says, "No, I wouldn't say so," he says. "I gave the sermon on the Ten Commandments, and as I was going down the list of commandments I got to the one that says, 'Thou shalt not commit adultery,' and I remembered where I left the bicycle."

The Preacher's False Teeth

Recorded in spring 1969 by Barbara Lanier from Don Buchanan of Decatur, DeKalb County, who heard it from his father, a Baptist minister of Leesburg, Virginia.

Once there was this preacher who *loved* fried chicken, as all preachers are supposed to love fried chicken. And he was invited to eat at the house of one of his parishioners one Sunday. After church he made his way through the country to this house, and it so happened, as he was crossing this particular creek, right in the middle of the bridge he stumbled and he lost his false teeth, and they fell in the creek.

Well, 'course he couldn't eat, but he couldn't turn down this invitation either, so he went on to the house. And, as they ate dinner, he ate what he could eat—mash potatoes an' things that weren't hard to chew—but he didn't touch the fried chicken. Well, he had a great reputation for eating fried chicken, and so, of course, everybody at the table was amazed and couldn't understand why he wasn't eating any fried chicken. So finally they asked him. And he said, "Well, I just have to tell you the truth. I lost my teeth goin' across the creek down here, an' I just can't eat any."

Well, he no sooner got the words out of his mouth than a little boy 'bout twelve years old jumped up from the table, grabbed a chicken leg from off the platter, got him a piece of string, and went out the door.

'Bout half an hour later he came back in, and he had the teeth in his hand. An' the preacher said, "How in the world did you get those teeth out of the creek?"

He said, "Well, I just took this chicken leg and tied the string on it and dipped it down in the water, and those teeth bit right on it!"

The Preacher Who Loved Rabbit

Recorded in spring 1977 by Patricia Bell from Sherry Camperson, twenty-three, of Atlanta, who heard it from her evangelist father.

There was this preacher, and they all knew that he loved rabbit to eat, you know. In the past they didn't have preachers stay in motels, they had 'em stay in their homes, and the people cooked for them and things like that. So, this preacher let the people know that he liked rabbit.

So, the first night he went out to dinner—on Monday night—and this lady fixed rabbit; fried it up and everything. And he was so excited 'cause it's just his favorite food. And he goes, "I can't believe it; this is my favorite food!"

And on Tuesday night he went again, and he had stewed rabbit this time. And it was great and he loved it—I won't drag it out—on through the week until it came on down to Friday; he had it again. And he says to himself, "I'm gettin' sick of rabbit."

So, on this last night of the revival he was goin' to somebody's house, and he was hoping they wouldn't have it [rabbit]. And the lady had a meat dish all covered up, you know, and she pulled off the top and there was a beautiful rabbit with all the trimmings. And somebody said, "Preacher, would you please say the blessing?"

And he bowed his head and he said,

"Lord, we've had rabbit hot, and we've had it cold,
We've had it young and we've had it old,
We've had it tender, we've had it tough,
But now, dear Lord, I think we've had rabbit
enough!"

Preacher Tells a Lie

Recorded in spring 1979 by Pamela Roberts from Hattie Mae Dawson, sixty, a black resident of Atlanta who heard her stories at Gibson, Glascock County.

This is a li'l story about three li'l boys. An' one of 'em had a dog, an' the othah two they didn't have a dog but they wanted one. An' every Sunday mo'nin' their parents would get 'em up an' get 'em ready ta go ta Sunday school. So, this particular Sunday they didn't want ta go ta Sunday

school. So. They got 'longside the road an' one said, "I don' wanna go ta Sunday school."

Othah un say, "Me neither."

Othah un say, "Me neither." He say, "What can we do?"

One say, "Oh, I know what we can do." Say, "We can tell a story; one tell the biggest story gits the dog."

The othah un say, "Yeah!"

The othah li'l boy he say, "Yeah!"

So. By that time the preacha come along. The preacha got there, he says, "Why-h-h-y, son. Why ain' y'all in Sunday school? Sha-a-ame, sha-a-ame! Mmm, mmm, mmm!" [Clicks tongue after each "mmm"]

An' says, "Well, Preacha, we 'as sittin' here an' the one tell the biggest story gits the dog."

He says, "Mmm, mmm. Sha-a-ame, sha-a-ame. Why, I never tol' a lie in my life."

One of 'em jump up an' say, "Give 'im the dog!"

The Corpse Popped Up

Recorded in fall 1976 by Frances W. Hall from L. C. Davis, forty-four, of Smyrna, Cobb County.

This Negro preacher had preached at this church for about fifty years, and he was about eighty years old and he died. He had a stroke, and when he died the stroke had drew him up double and he died like that. So when they laid him out in the casket they had to strap him down, because it was about seventy-two hours before they got to him and rigor mortis had set in, and they literally had to rebend him out straight [gesture with hand to indicate straightening body] to keep him flat in the casket and put straps on him. So they had their services at the church.

Durham's Chapel, Scott County, Virginia. Kenneth Murray.

After the services, after the burial ceremony, the board of deacons met the next weekend to pick a new preacher. So one of the deacons got up and he said, "I nominate Reverend Smith that preached the pastor's funeral"; said, "he preached an awful good funeral."

The other deacon got up and he said, "I objects to that nomination." He said, "Reverend Smith uses profanity."

And the chairman of the board of deacons he says, "Brother," he said, "that's a serious charge, now, to say that a man of the cloth will use profanity." He said, "How do you know that Reverend Smith uses profanity?"

And he says, "Well, brothers, I heard him."

And they said, "Well, when was this?"

"Well, do you remember the day that the pastor died?"

And they said, "Yeah, we remember."

Said, "Do you remember the day of the funeral?" They said, "Yeah, we remember."

Said, "Do you remember when Reverend Smith was preaching the funeral, and the straps broke and the pastor sat up in the coffin [hand gesture to indicate body sitting up]?"

Said, "Yeah, we remember."

He said, "Well, Reverend Smith passed me going across the creek down there in the woods with the window frame around his neck saying, 'God damn these one-door churches!'"

The Religiously Trained Horse (1)

Recorded in spring 1975 by Jean Bieder from her brother, Rev. Robert Green, forty-nine, of Dahlonega, Lumpkin County.

This preacher had a horse he wanted to sell, and he advertised it. And one day a deacon came up and said he'd like to buy it, and they talked about the price and they agreed.

After they'd settled on the deal, the preacher told the deacon, he said, "Now, this is a good horse, but I've trained him a little different from the usual horse." He says, "Instead of, you know, 'giddy-up' and all like that and 'gee' and 'haw,'" said, "I've used Biblical terms. When you want him to get started all you gotta do is say, 'Praise the Lord.' You want him to go faster you say, 'Hallelujah.' If you want 'im to stop you have to say 'Selah.'" That was the word: "Selah." And so said, "Can you 'member that?"

And the deacon said, "Oh, yeah, I can remember that." So he got him and took him home, and the next day he was gonna take 'im out riding.

He got on 'im and he says, "Praise the Lord." And the old horse started up, just going along nicely. And he said, "Boy, that's great!" He tried out "Hallelujah" on him, and the horse began to just trot along nice. They were riding along this mountain road, and the old horse kept gettin' faster and faster. The deacon got a little bit worried, and he couldn't think of the word to get him to stop. The old horse kept picking up speed, and they were headed right toward the jumping-off place. And just at the very last minute he thought of the word and he said, "Selah!" And the horse put on his brakes and came to a stop with his front hoofs right on the edge of the precipice!

And the old deacon was so thankful he took off his hat, wiped his brow, and he says, "Praise the Lord!"

The Religiously Trained Horse (2)

Recorded in spring 1978 by Thelma Shoate from W. B., a young black Atlanta man.

Say once upon a time, this old Methodist preacher was out making a circuit, you know, in the country, and he was going to get 'im some. Going out 'round Lookout Mountain in Chattanooga. So his goddamn hoss fell dead, right out there in the midst of nowhere. And the closest place he could go was to a Baptist preacher's house, ya know. So he walked up there and knocked on the door. He say, "Now listen, Rev, you know we're both men of the cloth, and I got to go up here on the mountain and get this good sister. My goddamn hoss died; could I borrow yo' hoss?"

So the Baptist preacher told the Methodist preacher, say, "Listen, man," say, "you can't ride my hoss, 'cause this is a Baptist hoss."

He say, "Now, listen, I got to go up dere and get dat sister; now ain' no need o' you starting nothin' wid me." Say, "Now jist let me have it."

So the Baptist preacher say, "Okay, I reckon." Say, "Now, the way you do to handle dis hoss— 'cause he run like a damned scalded dog—you say 'Praise the Lord,' that'll make him run; and when you get ready for him to stop you say 'Amen.' Do you have that?"

He say, "Yeah, I got it."

So the Methodist preacher went on up Lookout Mountain thinking 'bout that sister he was gonna git. He say, "Praise the Lord!" That got that hoss a-flying, man. [Laughs] Gittin' up there, you know. So he got up there on Roofer Falls and screw the woman; she wore him out. It was good to 'im, ya know.

He was thinking about how good it was while he were headed back down the mountain. He say, "Praise the Lord, praise the Lord!" The more he say "Praise the Lord," the faster the hoss would gallop. So when they got over there by Lovers' Leap, he saw the goddamn hoss running so fast he say, "Oh my goodness, I forgot; de man told me, say, 'Praise the Lord' makes the hoss run, but I forgot what you say to stop 'im!" So the hoss just running: "Pougadee, pougadee, pougadee, pougadee, pougadee!"

So all of a sudden, before the goddamn hoss got ready to fall off the mountain, he thought of what he said, ya know. He say, "Amen!" The hoss stopped on a dime, just before they get to the cliff.

He say, "Whew! Praise the Lord!"

So that hoss took his ass right on over the cliff!

The Chandelier

Recorded in spring 1971 by Henry See from Samuel Carson, ninety, of Atlanta. The story was taken down by hand during a power failure when the tape recorder could not be operated.

There was a country church that had been more or less abandoned over the years. And new residents near the church decided to renovate the building, get themselves a preacher, and begin to have services.

There was a meeting of a committee appointed to attend to the building and the furnishings, and to begin a search for a suitable minister. At this meeting everyone was expected to offer such suggestions as might be helpful.

An old lady said she had been to Atlanta to visit her boy, and that he had taken her to his church one Sunday night where they had the prettiest chandelier that she had ever seen in all of her born days. And she wanted to suggest that they get one for the church.

One old hard-boiled fella sitting in the extreme rear said in a very loud voice, "I am positively agin that there thing." When asked why he opposed the suggestion of the sister, he said, "In the first place there ain't anybody here what can spell it, and I'm sure there ain't anybody here what can play it. What we want is some kind of something we can use for lighting up the church on Sunday night."

The Old-time Religion

Recorded in spring 1978 by Linda Green from Grace Calhoun, thirty-nine, of Marietta, Cobb County, who was reared in the mountains of North Carolina.

This old man in our church, Uncle Robie Hicks . . . well, not only him, but a lot of mountain people, you know, they'd just say "amen" to everything that the preacher said. "Amen, Brother, amen! Preach it, Brother, preach it," you know.

And one of the things that mountain people did not believe in and many of them still don't today is they didn't believe in preachers usin' notes to help them in their sermon. They'd say that if a man were really called by God, that he oughta be able to just get up and preach a sermon without havin' to use notes, you know. And they would think that if an educated man came and used notes, that he wasn't really called by God; that this was just the work of the Devil. And so over the years this changed, too; but way back in some of them old areas, some of the people still hold these beliefs.

But I remember this one preacher came from Johnson City in Tennessee. And, of course,

Johnson City's a good-size town, you know. So the deacon board got Uncle Robie off and they told him, "Now, this fella's a city preacher." And said, "He's a real good preacher, but," said, "he's not used to this business of somebody sayin' 'amen' all the time. See, they don't do that in city churches." And said, "You may distract 'im," said, "get him mixed up in his sermon."

Old Robie said, "Now, I say if the Lord's givin' it to 'im, he'll say it regardless of what's goin' on out there."

And they said, "Well," said, "we just don't want you to be carryin' on like you usually do." And said, "Tell you what. If you won't say 'amen' and all while he's here," said, "we'll make up and buy you a pair of boots."

And old Robie said, "Now, boys, I don't know if I can quanch the Sperrit or not"—meaning quench the Holy Spirit, you know. And he said, "But I'll shore try."

So the first night old Robie sat there on the front pew, and he squirmed and twisted. And the second night, he did the same thing. He'd get out on the edge of his seat and he'd wanna say "amen," you know, and make gestures eggin' him on. So, the third night the preacher musta been suitin' him pretty well, because right in the middle of the sermon, old Robie got out on the edge of his seat and he jumped up all at once and he said, "Amen, Brother! Preach it, boots or no boots!"

Getting Too Personal

Recorded in spring 1981 by Ethel Henderson from Lucy Gibson, a black resident of Conyers, Rockdale County.

The preacher was preaching. And he got to preaching and he say, "Yeah," say, "all you backsliders."

And a lady she was sitting on the amen bench and she go to hollering, "Amen, amen! Tell the truth!"

"Yeah, and all you whoremongers."

"Oh, amen, tell the truth; say it good, Preacher!"

"Yeah, and all you backstabbers."

Oh, man, she jumped up and said, "Yeah!" And, "Talk about it, tell it, talk about it, Rev!"

And he say, "Yes, and all these young ladies wearing they dresses too short."

"Oh," she say, "talk about 'em, talk about 'em, tell the truth!"

He say, "Yes, and all of you snuff dippers."

Say she say, "Oh hell, he done quit preaching and gone to damn meddling now!" [Laughs]

Adding Insult to Injury

Recorded in spring 1980 by Arthur Holt from Joe Jones, sixty-five, a black resident of Atlanta.

An old fella he done lost his job an' wadn't making no money; and his wife wanted a whole outfit for Easter. She say, "You the sorriest man I ever seen." Say, "Everybody else getting a new dress." Say, "If I don't have a new outfit for Easter," say, "I'm 'oin' quit you."

He says, "Honey, you goin' leave me?"

She say, "Yeah, I'm 'oin' leave you an' git me that dress."

So he went out in the woods, you know, got down on his knees, an' he pray. He put his hand out, say, "Lawd, put some money in my hand, where I can get my wife some clothes for Easter."

So a little bird sittin' up in the tree, an' the little bird shit in his hand. He say, "Lawd, I don't want no shit out you!"

MARRIAGE

The Taming of the Shrew

Recorded in spring 1978 by Joy Breedlove from Randy Picklesimer, twenty-one, an Atlanta college student reared at Culbertson, North Carolina.

This couple had just gotten married; this was back before they had cars, and they had their own horse an' wagon, an' everything. And they left the church and they were going towards their new home, riding along in matrimonial bliss there; and the horse stumbled. Farmer said,

"Whoa." Horse stopped. He got out, walked around in front of the horse, looked him right in the face and says [shakes finger], "That's one!" Got back in the buggy and started up. And the wife's going, "My God," you know, "what's going on here?"

So they go on down the road a little farther and the horse stumbles again. Guy says, "Whoa," stops the horse, gets out, walks around in front of the horse, looks the horse eye to eye and says [shakes finger again], "That's two!" Gets back in the buggy. And the girl's beginning to wonder what kind of guy she's married here. So he takes off on down the road.

Well, everything's fine for a few miles there, but the horse stumbles again. Farmer says, "Whoa; stop, boy." Then he jumps out, walks around in front of the horse, says, "That's three," pulled out his gun, and shot the horse in the head; horse fell over dead!

Woman jumps up, says, "What are you, some kinda idiot? What are you doing?" Said, "This is our only horse; now we're gonna have to walk five more miles home. What's wrong with you, you crazy?"

Guy looks up at her and says, "That's one!"

The Synthetic Bride

Recorded in spring 1967 by Michael Moss from Harrison Barrett, Jr., seventy-four, of Hiawassee, Towns County.

I 'as out a-loafin'; I'd been out 'bout thirty days, loafin'. An' I stopped at a little country church. An' there's a girl in there just as purty as she could be. Oh, she had on a silk dress; she 'as absolutely as purty a thing as I ever seed. An' I made a date with her; me an' her fell in love an' got married.

Went t' her house that night. She wouldn't go t' bed. Atter 'while I got tard an' I went t' bed, an' atter 'while she decided she'd go t' bed.

She reached down an' pulled off an ol' wooden leg an' stuck it under the bed. Reached over here an' got another'n an' stuck it under the bed. An' reached up an' got a glass eyeball an' laid it on the table; reached over an' got another, laid it on the table.

I jumped outta bed an' I didn't stop runnin' 'til

I give out. That 'as the awfullest lookin' thing I ever seed in m' life.

An' ever since that time I ain't took off after nothin' that looks real purty, she fooled me s' bad.

Fair Exchange

Recorded in spring 1981 by Ethel Henderson from Dorothy Rome, a black resident of Conyers, Rockdale County.

One time there was a man and wife had a crowd of chillen, and he used to have a big crop. He'd pick four or five bales of cotton and he'd go off and get the money, and go get his girlfriend and go off and stay a week at the time with her. Tell his wife he was going to a association, a big meeting.

And when they got old, they was walking one evening and he told his wife, say, "Honey, I just got to tell you." Say, "My conscience just keep whipping me and whipping me"; say, "I just got to tell you." Say, "You know all them big crops we made, and all that money I got and told you I was going to a big meeting?" Say, "I didn't go to no big meeting." Say, "I went and got my girlfriend and went and stayed with her."

Say she told him, "Well, Honey, don't feel bad about it; all them chillen I had," say, "you ain't the daddy of no one." [Laughs]

Dueling Tombstones

Recorded in spring 1978 by Bill Powers from Zenus Windsor, forty-three, of Cragford, Alabama.

They said that it was true, I don't know; said this man's wife and he never really got along, ya know. She was very self-righteous and he was just a, ya know, plain ol' sinner. And she tried to inspire him down through the years, ya know, to change. And so she thought best thing she could do was to speak to him even beyond death. And she knew she was gettin' sick and she wasn't goin' to live long; so she had her own tombstone made and put her own epitaph on it, ya know, for him.

And so whenever they put her tombstone up, he went over to read it. And it said this:

"Husband, think of me as you pass by;
As you are now, so once was I.
As I am now, someday you'll be.
Prepare for death and follow me."

So the husband he looked at that, ya know, and he studied it. And so he fixed his tombstone and answered, ya know, what she had to say. And when he passed away they put up the tombstone, and it read like this:

"Wife, unto your wish I'll not consent,
'Cause I just don't know which way you went."

Rapid Turnover

Recorded in spring 1974 by Carol Ann Turner from Augusta White of Slocomb, Alabama.

Now, the preacher told this joke in church. And he said one time they was a man and a woman, and they'd lived together quite a long time. And this woman wasn't ready to settle down, you know, like the man was, and so she just decided she'd like to get out and have her a good time.

In the meantime this man got sick, and she waited on him, being real good to him, but hopin' every day that he'd soon pass on, you know, so she could get out and have her a good time. And he finally died. And she got out and she had her a good time then.

Well, her good times lasted a right-smart while, until she got sick herself and she died. But before her husband died he'd told her, he says, "Now, I'm goin' to die and leave you." He says, "I want you to be true to me and come to heaven, because I'm goin' to heaven." And he says, "If you don't live true to me after I'm gone," he says, "I'll turn over in my grave."

So when she died she went to heaven, you know, and old Saint Peter met her at the gate. And he says, "Oooh, Sister Jones," he says, "just welcome into heaven."

She said, "Just wait a minute before I go on into there"; she says, "I wanta find John."

He says, "Well," says, "you'll have to describe him"; says, "we got ten million Johns here."

She says, "Well, he's tall and handsome."

Said, "Well, we got five thousand Johns here that's tall and handsome." Said, "Can't you give us another description of him?"

Said, "Well now, he was blond, had blue eyes."

Said, "Well, we got five hundred men here that's blond and blue-eyed named John. Don't you know somethin' else about him?"

She said, "Well, I just can't think of nothing else, only he asked me to live true and come to heaven, and if I didn't he'd turn over in his grave."

And old Saint Peter said, "Oh, I know who you talkin' about now." Said, "Up here we call him Whirlin' John."

Summer Bed. Jack Leigh.

DOWN ON THE FARM

The Brush Peddler and the Farmer's Daughter

Recorded in winter 1967 by Adrina Grayson from Ed Davis, twenty-two, a black college student in Atlanta who was reared in Birmingham, Alabama.

This farmer lived way out in the country, and he had a pretty daughter.

So the brush peddler say—he was in town—"I got to sell my brushes"; he say, "which way are most o' the houses?"

So the old man in town say, "Down this street, to the left, just follow that road." He say, "But don't stop by ol' man Gabber house, 'cause he got a pretty daughter, an' he sure kill ya."

So the brush peddler went on down the road. He had been to all the houses; so about evening, almost dark, he came by ol' man Gabber's farm. His daughter was out there an' the wind was just blowin' her dress up; he was just standin' there lookin'. Dropped all o' his brushes an' just standin' there lookin', wind blowin' her dress up. Countin' the fringe on her pants; he was nervous. So he went up to the old man, he told him, say, "I got some brushes"; say, "I got any kind o' brush you can name, from brushin' your teeth to brushin' your ass, I got all kind o' brushes."

So the ol' man say, "I don't need no brushes; I got a sweet little daughter."

So he say, "Yeah." The brush peddler started again, say, "I got any kind o' brushes you want from brushin' your teeth to brushin' your ass."

And the old farmer say, "I don't need no brushes; I got a sweet little daughter."

So by this time the brush peddler wonderin' what the farmer's daughter doin', bein' he didn't need nothin' but his sweet little daughter. So a storm came up. The brush peddler say, "I can't leave in that storm"; say, "I ain't got no umbrella." Say, "I'm walkin'"; say, "I'm miles from the city."

So the farmer say, "Well, you can stay here"; he say, "we ain't got but two beds, an' I ain't no sissy an' you sure can't sleep with me."

He say, "I can't sleep on the floor, I got a bad back."

He say, "Well, I'll put you up with my daughter."

So the farmer got an ironin' board, an' put the ironin' board between the brush peddler an' his daughter. The daughter, she knew he was gonna sleep with her. So she went to bed nude that night, in the raw. She was layin' over there on her back with her hair all down to her shoulders. The brush peddler was on the other side of the ironin' board. Every time he reached across the ironin' board under the cover to touch her, the farmer would swing the door open. "Don't do that, son!" He snatch his arm back.

So this went on all night. She was layin' over there whisperin' to him, "Brush peddler, brush peddler." He was layin' over there an' broke out in a sweat, wringin' wet. Just sweatin'. Anyway, every time he'd reach across, every time he'd raise up a little bit to get over that ironin' board, that ol' man would swing that door open, had that shotgun in his hand. The brush peddler could hardly stand it.

So the next mornin' after breakfast he say, "Farmer, let me see your farm"; says, "I can't sell you no brushes, just let me enjoy the view an' walk this big breakfast down your daughter give me here."

So he say, "Okay, I'll get my daughter here to show you around."

So the farmer's daughter had on a pretty yellow print dress, an' she had on a sunbonnet, a white sunbonnet. So they went out to look things over, you know; they were walkin' around. So the brush peddler had it on his mind. He say, "Well, now I got it made." He had picked him a spot in the weeds an' everything. So a brisk wind came up an' blew the farmer's daughter's bonnet off her head over the other side o' the fence. So the brush peddler jumped around, said, "Hold it, hold it"; said, "don't move, I get it." He jumped up on the fence, figurin' to go across the fence.

She told him, she say, "Hold it." Said, "Ain't no need. I know if you couldn't get across that ironin' board last night, you can't get across that fence!"

No Eggs for Breakfast

Recorded in spring 1978 by Joy Breedlove from Randy Picklesimer, twenty-one, an Atlanta college student reared at Culbertson, North Carolina.

There's this traveling salesman [laughs] travelin' through North Carolina selling vacuum cleaners or something. And it was gettin' dark, and it's pretty far between them farms, and he didn't have no car or nothin'. And he come up on this one farm and he says, "Being as I'm already here, old-timer," says, "how about lettin' me spend the night?"

The farmer says, "Well, I reckon it'd be all right"; he says, "but you'll have to sleep with my daughter."

And the travelin' salesman says, "Well, that's all right!"

And the farmer says, "But you better keep your hands off of her or I'll kill you." So he says, "Now, just to make sure that you're gonna be faithful and not mess with my daughter, I'm gonna put a row of raw eggs between the two of you in the bed." He said, "If any of them eggs is broke, you're in trouble."

So the fella says, "Well, I don't care." He'd never seen the daughter or nothin'. So the farmer goes up and puts his daughter to bed, you know, and he lays the eggs out.

And the travelin' salesman walks up there to get in bed, and he looks at that girl; and she's about twenty years old, and she is the most beautiful young thing he has ever seen in his life, just a specimen of country beauty. He says, "Oh my God, I can't stand this." So he lays down, and he's looking over at her, and he can feel her soft breathing, and he just can't take it. And he just flies over there and just ravishes her, eggs just flying everywhere [laughs]; just a mess, you know—shells, yellow—aw, it's just terrible. He breaks every egg in the bed.

So finally, about three hours later, he's laying there and he looks down and he says, "Oh my God, that farmer's gonna kill me in the morning." So he says, "I gotta do something." And so he remembered he's got some Elmer's Glue-All in his kit there, so he gets it out and he starts gluing them eggshells back together. So he stays up all night, but just as dawn's breakin' he got the last one glued back into place.

So the farmer comes up there and the guy's just covered himself back up, you know, and the farmer looks down and sees all them eggs laying there and says, "Aw, son, I'm proud of you." Says, "I'm glad you didn't let me down."

Salesman says, "Yeah."

So the farmer says, "Since you didn't mess with the eggs, I think we'll have a few of 'em for breakfast." So the farmer reaches down, gets four of the eggs and takes 'em downstairs.

The salesman says, "Oh God, I'm in trouble now."

So he hears the farmer crack one of 'em and go, "My God!" and throws it down. And he hears the farmer crack another one of 'em and go, "Oh, my God!"

And he hears the farmer run in there to get his shotgun, and he says, "Oh, I've had it now."

The farmer goes tearing out the back door and the fella hears him screaming as he's running out in the back yard, "I'll teach 'em damn roosters to use rubbers!"

Mustard and Custard Make Fruit Salad

Recorded in fall 1978 by Betty Jones from her brother-in-law Robert Akers, Jr., thirty-seven, of Lithia Springs, Douglas County, who has lived in a number of southern states.

Mustard and Custard was s'posed to spend a weekend or somethin' like that on the farm. And wasn't no place for them to sleep, but, of course, with the farmer's daughter. And the farmer told 'em, says, "Look here, boys"; says, "now, I'm gonna let you sleep with my daughter." Said, "But if you get to foolin' around," said, "there's gonna be hell to pay."

Said, "Oh," said, "we won't mess with her." But you know what a lie that was.

So the next mornin', the old farmer found out they'd been foolin' around with his daughter. So

he said, "All right, you two characters, I want you to go out in the orchard and pick your favorite kind of fruit."

So they's gone about a half hour, and ol' Custard come back with a handful of grapes. Well, the ol' farmer just stripped his overalls down around his ankles and turned his behind up to the sun, and started feedin' him them grapes through the butt end! Well, he started off hollerin' and squallin' there, but then he started laughing. And the farmer said, "What the hell are you laughin' about? This is s'posed to teach you a lesson."

He said, "Mustard got a watermelon!"

A Rough Night on the Farm

Recorded in fall 1981 by Ellen McDonald from her father, Jerry McDonald, of Thomaston, Upson County; he learned it from his grandfather, Charles Brown.

The traveling salesman had to put up with this old man and this old woman. And they had had peas for supper, and the traveling salesman just couldn't get enough of those peas. He just kept eating those peas and eating those peas, and the old farmer finally walked over and grabbed the bowl and put it away; said, "That's all you can eat tonight."

So that night the traveling salesman had to sleep with the farmer and his wife. And the old farmer, of course, he just went right off to sleep. And the farmer's wife kept nudging the traveling salesman and said, "I know what you really want. I know what you really want, and now's your chance to get it."

So the traveling salesman says, "You know

what? You're right." So he jumped out of bed and ran to the kitchen and just got that bowl of peas and started eating them, just scarfing them down!

Well, the old farmer's wife she got so mad she ran in there and grabbed that bowl of peas from the man and tried to pull him back to the bed. Well, in pullin' him back to the bed he brought the peas with him, and as she tried to throw him in the bed, why, he just spilled the peas all over the old farmer that was laying there asleep.

Well, the farmer, feeling something all over him, just jumps up and runs out the door. And the traveling salesman sitting there with his empty bowl of peas runs out behind him and just takes the bowl and breaks it over his head. And the farmer comes back in holding his head, and he's covered with those peas. And his wife says, "Honey, what's wrong?"

And he said, "I'm having an awful time. First I shit all over myself, and now I've been struck by lightning!"

The Long-Handled Spoon

Recorded in spring 1973 by Linda Clement from her mother, Roberta Mae Burnette Clement, fifty-six, of Mineral Bluff, Fannin County.

They's this woman been goin' to church fer years praying that somehow or other the Lord'd touch her husband to make him quit drinking. Said that ever' weekend of the world he'd just come home so drunk, and said just made their life miserable. Said ever' time he'd get drunk that he just got deathly sick and just vomit something awful! And she told him, she said, "Some of these times you're a-gonna get a overdose of that"; and says,

"it's a-gonna kill ya, you're gonna vomit yer insides up!"

He says, "I know it, Honey, I know it; I'm a-gonna quit." And he'd promise her he wouldn't take another drink, ya know.

And it's back in the days when ya couldn't buy chickens already dressed, and if ya had any, ya had to dress your own. So it's on a Friday—a weekend—and she decided that she'd cook a good supper that night because maybe he wouldn't come in home drunk for one time. And she got out and she caught her two of her fry chickens and she was dressing them [outside]. And just when she got ready to take the entrails out of the chickens, why, it started raining. So she had to finish up, and she came in the house and laid 'em up on the sink to finish up. And she'd just got through when somebody called her from the back and she had to go to see who it was at the door.

And meanwhile, while she's in the back a-talkin' to whoever it was, why, her husband came in. He come in at the door just a-staggerin' and a-vomitin'. And he come on through to the kitchen and there he was at the sink, just a-gaggin' and a-vomitin'.

And in the meantime she finished talking to the neighbor. And she come in; there he was a-leanin' over the sink. And he says, "Well, Honey," he says, "what you said'd happen sure has happened."

And she says, "Whatta you mean?"

He said, "Well," said, "you told me if I didn't quit that drinkin', sometime I's gonna vomit up my insides"; and he said, "Honey, I did! But," said, "with the help of the Good Lord and that long-handled spoon," says, "I got all my insides back in!"

And ya know what had happened: he saw

those chicken entrails there and thought he had vomited up his insides, so he got 'em all back in by the help of that long-handled spoon!

Slaughter in the Chicken House

Recorded in spring 1974 by Charlotte Abrams from Gerald Holder of Chapel Hill, North Carolina, a man in his thirties who was then living in Atlanta.

The story has to do with an elderly couple, namely old Grandpa and my grandmother. And, uh, my grandfather had been known to drink a little whiskey in his day. And my grandmother always said she could tell when he was about half crocked, 'cause when he came home he inevitably would strip nude; otherwise he would sleep in some kind of undergarments.

But in the interim, my grandmother had always raised a lot of chickens, and sold eggs and whatnot. And she'd been having some trouble with some kind of varmint that had been killing her chickens at random at night, and she was very concerned about it.

And, as the story goes, one night Grandfather came in and he was about half crocked and stripped off and climbed into bed. And by the time he got to sleep, a terrible commotion arose in the henhouse—screaming chickens—and my grandmother jumped up and was pounding my grandfather to wake him up to get outside to see what the hell was going on in the chicken house. And he woke up with a start, forgot to put any clothes on, grabbed the double-barrel shotgun out of the closet and a lantern, and out the door he went.

He approached the chicken house and pushed the door open very carefully, holding the lantern out in front of him in one hand and holding the shotgun at ready in the other hand. And as he was peering around trying to find out what was after the chickens, his old hound dog by the name of Major came up behind him. And I don't have to say where old Major shoved his cold nose. And with that Grandfather cut loose with the shotgun and murdered fifteen chickens who were sitting very peaceably asleep in the coop. And it almost caused a divorce after forty-five years of marriage.

The Frustrated Rooster

Recorded in spring 1969 by Rick Smith and Ann Adams from P. H. Gibson of Monroe, Walton County.

A young couple was married, and hadn't been married long. And one day the husband called his young wife from the office and said, "Gonna have a couple to eat supper with us tonight."

And she got worried; didn't have nothing much to eat in the house. And they had one big young rooster in the yard, so she decided she'd kill that rooster and cook him for supper. But she'd never killed nor dressed one. So she went out and caught him and picked him before she killed him. And then the phone rang again, and it was her husband and he said, "Don't fix supper for 'em, they decided not to come."

So then she was worried about that rooster over his feathers, and he'd freeze to death. She went and made him a little suit of clothes and put on him and turn him loose. And her husband comes in later and he laugh.

And she said, "What ya laughing at?"

Said, "That rooster out there in the yard. He look so funny."

She says, "Well, I know his clothes don't fit good, but was the best I could do."

He says, "Clothes was all right; but when I saw him he's chasing the hen around the house on one foot, trying to unbutton his britches with the other."

Brewster the Oversexed Rooster

Recorded in spring 1978 by Joy Breedlove from Randy Picklesimer, twenty-one, an Atlanta college student.

Okay, this is the story of the famous Brewster the Rooster. Now this joke, I remember where I heard it: a guy from I think it was Lavonia, Georgia, was in Army ROTC with me, and we used to go down to Fort Gordon every year. And on the way back on the bus we'd all tell jokes. And this joke won the Best Joke Contest two years running.

One time there was this fella in the army—we was all in the army, see—and he says, "Look, there's gotta be an easier way of makin' a livin'." So he saved up about three thousand bucks, he got out of the army, and looked around at business investments he could make. And he found that people were makin' a pretty good livin' havin' chicken houses, you know, and sellin' the eggs from the chickens. So he figured he'd go into this. He sunk most all of his money in the chicken house, bought him three thousand chickens, and set him up that chicken house there.

So, he'd had it about two weeks, and betwixt all them three thousand chickens they'd laid about five eggs. And he said, "Somethin' is wrong; I haven't made fifty cents in two weeks. This ain't gonna cut it."

There was other chicken houses around there, so he went down to one that was nearest him, said, "Look," said, "what are you supposed to do here?" He says, "I'm just new in this business, and my chickens ain't laying eggs." He said, "What's wrong?"

The other farmer says, "Well," says, "how many chickens ya got?"

He says, "I got about three thousand hens."

And the guy says, "Oh, well," says, "how many roosters ya got?"

And the guy says, "Roosters? I ain't got no roosters."

And the guy says, "Oh, my God," says, "you dumb or something? That's the problem—them hens ain't happy. You gotta have some roosters to keep 'em happy so they'll lay them eggs, satisfy 'em."

Guy says, "Oh, okay." Says, "Where can I get some roosters?"

Fella says, "Well, I don't rightly know; there's kind of a rooster shortage right now. I don't know whether you're gonna be able to find none or not."

Guy says, "Aw, please, I'm desperate. I got my life's savings sunk in this chicken farm." Says, "I gotta have some roosters."

The fella thought for a minute and says, "Well, I do know of a fella around here that's got this rooster. He calls him Brewster the Rooster, and says he's the most oversexed rooster he's ever seen. You just can't stop him; he has to keep him in an iron cage, he says he's uncontrollable."

And the guy says, "Oh, well," says, "reckon he could take care of my three thousand hens?"

The guy says, "Aw, Brewster wouldn't have no

Free Hill, Tennessee, 1983. Tom Rankin.

problem takin' care of your three thousand chickens; that wouldn't be a strain on him at all."

So the guy says, "Well, I'll buy him."

So they went down an' talked to this farmer. Brewster was kind of a rare thing, and the farmer says, "Well, I'll need about five hundred dollars for him."

The guy says, "Well, that's a lot of money, but I gotta have 'im." So he goes in there and gets Brewster the Rooster, and he's in this huge iron cage and he's squallin' and beatin' at the bars, you know, just running around screaming; aw, just pitiful, you know. So he puts him in the back of his pickup truck and drives him down; the rooster's jumping up and down, he knows somethin's about to happen.

So the fella backs that truck up to the doorway of that chicken house and lets down the tailgate, and Brewster's lookin' in there, seein' all them hens—he's just going wild! And the guy says, "Okay, Brewster," says, "do your stuff, boy!" So he jerks that cage open.

Brewster goes "Nnmannn," tearing into that chicken house. Wham bam, wham bam, wham bam, one right after another; "Brawk, buck, buck, buck, buck" [noise like chicken], chickens flying all over the place. Brewster is just rapin' every one of them, one right after another; three or four times, some of 'em.

The farmer, he walks in there and he sees feathers flyin', you know, and chickens squallin', smilin' and grinning all over the place, Brewster just going from one to another. Says, "All right now, take it easy, Brewster." Says, "You got a long time here. I paid five hundred dollars for you; I don't want you to hurt yourself."

Brewster don't listen to nothin'; he keeps on enjoyin' the chickens. He goes through all of 'em once, twice, three or four times, and some of 'em's dying. Them hens just can't take it. I mean they're laying there with their poor little legs stuck up in the air, big ol' smiles on their faces, and they're dead, you know.

So the farmer's going, "Brewster! God, take it easy, son, don' kill yourself; I got all my money invested in this, don't ruin it for me."

Brewster didn't listen. Three or four hours, every one of them hens was dead; it was pitiful. Brewster goes tearing out of the chicken house and looks around, looks up on the hill and sees the cattle grazing up there. Well, you know what happened next. He rapes the cattle, the bulls, the sheep, pigs, everything. He gets the snakes, grasshoppers, anything he can find; it's just a pitiful sight. Farmer's following him around saying, "Brewster, for God's sake, you're ruining me. All this livestock, my life's savings; what are you doing?" Brewster's killed chickens, pigs, cattle; everything laying around dead. Big smiles on their faces, but dead. It's getting dark. Farmer can't take it no longer; he goes inside and throws the covers up over his head so he won't have to listen to the pitiful moans of the dying animals.

Next morning he wakes up, says, "Oh my God, he's ruined me. I bet ya everything is dead." He throws back the covers and sits up in his bed, and where yesterday the pleasant sounds of all the livestock had flowed in through his bedroom window, there's dead silence today. He crawls out of bed and he walks out the door, and it is a pitiful sight to behold. Dead chickens, pigs, cows, grasshoppers, ducks, guineas, fish, anything you can name laying there dead; big smiles. So he says, "Oh my God, that stupid rooster's killed himself." He looks down the road and he sees some buzzards circling overhead, an' he says, "There's Brewster."

Shore enough, he walks down the road and

where them buzzards is flying around, there's ol' Brewster, just layin' down in a ditch, layin' on his back with his poor little feet stuck up in the air an' his head laid back. He says, "Brewster, you stupid rooster, I paid five hundred dollars for you, got all my life's savin's sunk in this farm; you've ruined me!" He just rants and raves and he looks down at Brewster.

Brewster raises his head up, opens one eye and looks up at them buzzards and says, "Shh! They're about to land!"

Poor Old Trailer

Recorded in fall 1978 by Betty Jones from her brother-in-law Robert Akers, Jr., thirty-seven, of Lithia Springs, Douglas County, who has lived in a number of southern states.

I heard this in Kentucky. Dogs out in Kentucky have real strong names, like Trailer, or Bugle, or something like that. You know, you name your city dogs Lassie and Fifi, but dogs where I come from have real good names.

Well, it seems like this fella had come courtin' this gal one day, and out in Kentucky the central heat is the fireplace. You know, when the guy comes sparking his girl, they have to spark in front of the whole family. So Grandmaw and Grandpa and Mom and Dad and the girl and the boy was all sittin' around the fireplace there, and ol' Trailer was layin' down by the fireplace, you know. And everybody just havin' a nice evenin', eatin' popcorn or something.

And all of a sudden, this guy had to break wind—this guy that'd come a-courtin'. Well, I don't know if you've ever been in a crowd and had to do that, but you know how you can just

kinda squirm around a little bit and ease one out. [Laughs] That's what he did.

Well, it kinda drifted around the room there for a minute, and Grandmaw got a whiff. So, she reached out with her cane, and pecked ol' Trailer on the head with that cane. "Trailer!"

And the ol' boy started laughin' up his sleeve, 'cause the dog got the blame for that. So they sat there for a while, and pretty soon, sure enough, there come another one. So he kinda squirmed back around his chair there a little bit, squeezed another one out.

Coupla minutes Grandmaw got a whiff again, and she reached over there with the crook of her cane this time; boy, I mean, she pecked ol' Trailer on the head, wop! Said, "Trailer!"

The guy he just thought that was the funniest thing he'd ever seen in his whole life, you know. Here he was, gassin' 'em up, and the dog was gettin' the blame for it. Well, he felt one comin' there, and he's gonna try to hold it 'cause he knew it was gonna be a whopper. And he was holdin' it and holdin' it and holdin' it, and finally it just got too much for him and he squeaked it out. [Laughs]

Grandmaw got a whiff of it and she got up and she kicked the ol' dog in the side. "Trailer! Damn it, move before that man shits on you!"

The Stood-Up Sleepers

Recorded in fall 1967 by Lynda Carriveau from her grandmother, Lottie Fraser, seventy-nine, of Statenville, Echols County. The collector states, "I wanted her to start with this story because it's my favorite. I've heard her tell it many times on the occasions when a bunch of us grandchildren would spend the night with her. The whole floor would be covered with mattresses she would lay down for us to sleep on, and then she would say with a laugh, 'Reminds me of the story about . . .'"

One time there was a man. He went to a place to spend the night. And the feller saw they didn't have but jist one bed, but they had seven children. And he looked around and he said, "Well, I wanted to spend the night, but you haven't got but one bed."

But he said, "Oh, that's all right. You're plumb welcome to spend the night."

So he wondered where in the world would he sleep at—the house was so small. So ever' time one of the little children went to sleep they'd lay him on the bed, and finally they all went to sleep. And him and the man set and talked and talked and talked, and after 'while he taken the children and stood 'em upside the house! And he says, "Mister, you can occupy the bed." Says he went to bed and wondered where they went.

Said next morning, when he got up, he was a-standing upside the house, and the old man and the old lady was in the bed!

The Last Biscuit

Recorded in spring 1978 by Joy Breedlove from Randy Picklesimer, twenty-one, an Atlanta college student reared at Culbertson, North Carolina.

I think my uncle or my aunt told me this. You know, in the country, it's bad manners to take the last of whatever is left on the table. Last biscuit, last pork chop, last anything: nobody touches it. If somebody wants it they sneak back down in the dark o' night an' eat it, or let the rats get it.

Well, this family's all sittin' around eatin' one

night. And there's Grandpa, Grandma, a bunch of grandkids, you know, an' Ma and Pa—about eight of 'em—and they're just eatin' like crazy; and they had a good bunch of biscuits there. And they got down to where there wasn't but one biscuit left. So, they's sittin' there and they'd finished eatin', and they's all lookin' at that last biscuit; God, they's wantin' it so bad they just couldn't hardly stand it. And it's sittin' right in front of Grandpa. So they's all jus' sittin' there, their mouths waterin'.

Well, about that time this big wind come by and the door blew open, and it blew the lantern on the table out. Pitch darkness! Well, things was quiet for a minute, and then there was this bloodcurdling scream—it was terrible! So Grandma got up and lit the lantern, and she looked down, and there was Grandpa's hand clenching that biscuit and there was seven forks stuck in it!

Old Enough for Britches

Recorded in spring 1980 by Wanda Patterson from Forrest Sawyer, forty-eight, of Canton, Cherokee County. He learned it from his foster father, the late Homer Cable, a noted local jokester.

There was a good one about the child who outgrew the dress. Back in the old days, they put dresses on little children, boys and girls—little long dresses—up 'til they was pretty good size; and then they'd put boys' clothes on boys and girls' clothes on girls.

He said he was eating with this family one time, back up in the mountains. They's all around a big, long table like families used to have. This little boy just half reached and half dove across the table, reaching for him a biscuit, and there's a bowl of gravy sitting there. Said the little boy straightened up and set back down after he'd got his biscuit.

The father looked over at the mother and said, "Annie, looks like we're gonna have to put britches on that boy." Said, "You see what he drug through the gravy?"

Remarkable Longevity

Recorded in spring 1975 by Jean Bieder from Walt Grindle, sixty-eight, of Dahlonega, Lumpkin County.

They used to have a saying here that people who lived back in the mountains where there was no worries or nothing would live on and on, just live for years and years. So this man was out taking the government census, and he got way back up in the mountains. Went up to this pore house sitting up on the hillside, with the bottom [land] down in the creek there.

This old man was sitting on the porch stringing beans; had a long beard. He went up to 'im an' begin to ask 'im a question about his name and how many were there in the family.

He said, "Well," said, "just my dad and me here now."

Said, "What? Your mother dead?"

He said, "No," said, "she got jealous of Dad and they separated. Dad and me's been living here."

Said, "Where is your dad?"

Said, "Well, he's down in the field plowing."

Said, "How old are you?"

Said, "I'm seventy-eight."

"Well, how old is your dad?"

"He's ninety-eight."

"And just you two live here?"

"Well," said, "Granddad's been living here with us, but he's not here today."

Said, "Well, where is he? And how old is he?"

Said, "He's a hundred-and-seven."

Said, "Where is he?"

"He's about a mile up the road here, at the justice of the peace." Said, "He's gettin' married this evening."

Said, "Can you tell me what a man a hundred-and-seven years old would wanna get married for?"

He said, "He didn't want to; they're making 'im!"

The Laziest Man

Recorded in spring 1972 by Ruth Cipolla from Louise Brewington, a black resident of Atlanta in her sixties.

There was a man—lazy. But, oh, he was the laziest man! And some of 'em, they decided they would bury him alive, because he was so lazy. So, they had him in the wagon, goin' on with him.

Say, "What you gonna do with him?"

Say, "We gonna bury him alive. He's too lazy to cook and eat."

So one lady said, "Well, don't bury him alive." Said, "I'll give him [food]; he won't work." Say, "I'll give him a bushel of corn."

He raised up and said, "Shelled?"

So she said, "No."

So he say, "Well, drive on."

So another one wanted to know and they told her, say, "Well, he just is so lazy he won't work, won't do anything." Say, "He too lazy to even eat."

So she said, "Well, I'll give him a peck of meal." Say, "Don't bury him alive."

He raised up again, said, "Is it cooked?"

Say she said, "No."

Say he said, "Drive on."

And so it went on 'til he got near 'bout to the cemetery. And they asked what they were gonna do with him. And said, "He's just so lazy, he won't do anything. Too lazy to cook. You give him food, he's too lazy to cook it."

Say the one said, "Well, I'll give him some food that's already cooked." Say, "I got cornbread, black-eyed peas, and baked potatoes." And say, "The potatoes is peeled, and the bread is broke." And say, "I'll give him all of that if you don't bury him alive."

And say he raised up, said, "You gonna chew it?"

She said, "Man!" Says, "No."

Say he take that a little while, he say, "Well, all right. Bring it on, then. I guess I can chew it."

Now do you know that was some lazy!

CHAPTER TEN

Instructive Tales

The Crow and the Water Jug

Written in spring 1974 by Mattie Mitchell, seventy-nine, a black resident of Zebulon, Pike County; collected by her granddaughter, Eleanor Mitchell.

There was once a old man who liked to farm and raise his food. He enjoyed raising peanuts. He worked very hard. One day as he was pulling up peanuts, the weather was hot and dry; he was tired and went and sit down under the shade of a tree to rest nearby.

He saw a lonely, hungry, and thirsty crow flying around searching for food. It was easy for him to get full of peanuts that was left in the ground where the farmer had left them after they was pulled up. So after he had eat and was full he was thirsty, but no water could be found; the lonely crow continually flying around by himself.

At last he spied a water jug, but the water was too low in the jug for his bill to reach. The farmer sit quiet and watched the lonely crow as he worked. And so the crow began to pick up small pebbles, dropping them one by one in the jug until the water rose near the top; then he could reach the water with his bill. Oh, how glad was he! He drink water until his thirst was quenched. The hungry and thirsty crow flew away, refreshed and renewed.

This helps us to know that wherever there is a will, there is a way.

The Lion and the Bull

Written in spring 1980 by Cindy Jackson, sixteen, a student at Riverdale Senior High School, Clayton County; collected by Holly Carver.

One day there was a lion that lived in a dark part of the jungle. He was so hungry he then went to look for something to eat. Suddenly he hears a noise. It's a wild bull running through the jungle. The lion decides to jump on the bull. He jumps on him and eats him all up. The lion felt so good about the kill he roared as loud as he could.

Meanwhile, a hunter hears the lion and runs to shoot him. Bang! The lion dies.

Do you know what the moral of the story is? When you're full of bull, keep your mouth shut!

The Little Bird

Recorded in fall 1976 by Frances W. Hall from L. C. Davis, forty-four, of Smyrna, Cobb County.

Okay, I'll tell you the story about the little bird. This little bird was up in his nest, sorta adventuresome, and each day he'd look a little farther out over the nest to see the world. The third day he fell out and he hit the ground [hand gesture of falling and hitting]! He couldn't fly; he couldn't walk—freezing to death. And he lay on the ground, just chirping.

And this cow came by. So the cow looked down and she saw the little bird, and so she just turned around and dropped a cowpod on him. Well, it was warm, and the little bird lay there in the cowpod and got nice and warm. But he got to worrying, and started chirping again.

Along came the wolf and he heard the little bird chirping, so he kept looking and he found him. So he reached down and picked him up out of the cowpod [gesture of reaching and picking with hand] and dusted him off and cleaned him up, and then eat him [hand gestures of dusting, cleaning, and plopping into mouth]!

Now, there's three morals to this story. The first moral is that anytime somebody throws a little shit on you, that doesn't necessarily mean they're trying to do you a whole lot of harm. The second one to remember is that anytime somebody picks you up and dusts you off, that doesn't necessarily mean they're trying to do you a whole lot of good. And the third and main moral you should always remember: anytime you're up to your mouth in shit, you keep your mouth shut!

The Boy Who Went Hunting Alone

Recorded in spring 1974 by Charlotte Abrams from Gerald Holder, an Atlanta man in his thirties who was reared near Chapel Hill, North Carolina.

As a young lad of eleven or twelve I had my first gun, and I was consistently and constantly pestering my father, who was a farmer and had other things to do, to take me hunting every afternoon when I got home from school. He frequently could not do this, and so I began to pester him about going by myself. And, of course, he was very apprehensive about that for any number of reasons, and he related this tale to me about what happened to a young boy who wouldn't listen to his father and he went off into the swamp hunting by himself.

And this lad apparently had been pestering his father, and so one day he decided he would go by himself. And his father had told him that there were vicious bears in the swamp, and that a young boy shouldn't go off by himself because the bears would get him. But, nevertheless, he took his gun and off to the swamp he went.

He was having a fine old day of hunting until sure enough, as fate would have it, he encountered this rather disgruntled bear. And the bear scared him to death. And the first thing he did was to throw his gun down, and off he went hard as he could go, the bear after him. And the chase was on through the swamp.

And in the meantime, back at the farm, the father was out in the yard. And he heard way off in the distance this "help, help," and it got louder and louder. And he looked and he saw his boy coming, and then he saw the bear.

So the old man went back to the house and he opened the door up, and the boy shot through the door and he circled the room. And the bear came in behind and the boy went out the door and closed the door, leaving the bear in the house with the father. And as he was out in the yard the father raised the window and said, "Hey, Son, what do you want me to do with this bear in the house?"

And he said, "You skin him, Pa, while I go get another one!"

Challenging God's Will

Recorded in winter 1967 by Marcia Horne from her father, E. W. Horne, fifty-three, of Atlanta, who was reared in Americus, Sumter County.

My mother tells a story about the fella that planted in a crop o' corn, and when it got up pretty good, why, there came a drought, an' his crop began to dry up. An' he prayed for rain, an' everybody prayed for rain, but no rain came. An' so he got real upset about it, of course, 'cause he's gonna lose his crop.

So 'bout the time his corn got really past any good at all, why, there came a big cloud. And he saw that it was goin' to rain, but he knew that it was goin' to be too late to do his crop any good. He had slaves; he called them all out and made them go out an' pull up every bit of that corn. Said that if God wouldn't let it rain when he needed it, he certainly wasn't going to let God rain on it when it didn't need it.

So after they got it all pulled up, he went back to the house. And they had one of them ol' clocks on the mantelpiece—it was just the case, the clock was out of it—an' he kept receipts an' everything in there. An' he was in there mouthin' about what he had done, an' this ol' clock case struck twelve times! So that made 'im mad, an' he ran out in the yard. And just as he ran out in the yard lightnin' struck him and killed him.

That's it.

Blasphemy Punished

Recorded in spring 1973 by Deborah Hudson from Grace Ledford, forty-six, of Tucker, DeKalb County, who was reared in Franklin, North Carolina.

Do you remember that story, or did you ever hear that tale about—now I don't know who that ol' man was that told me that—this very mean man, and he sort of defied God in every respect. And one day it was thundering and lightning and the wind was blowin' and his corn was just laid down to the ground. And it made him mad because God had sent this storm. And he walked out and said [in a defiant voice], "Try *me* a shot, Ol' Man!" You know, like that.

And the story was that the lightnin' came down—shhuu—like that and just scalped him, took a streak out of his hair!

A Humbling Experience

Recorded in spring 1967 by Michael Moss from J. Ross Brown, sixty-five, of Hiawassee, Towns County.

Widder Turnipseed, she lived way down in the valley, down in lower land. And I lived up on higher land where it never did come a flood.

One Sunday I went over t' the little country church. They's takin' up a collection for Sister Turnipseed: a flood washed ever'thing away that she had, she didn't have anything left. An' I just said t' myself, "Well, now, I live up 'ere on higher land an' it won't have any effect on me." An' I reached m' great big hand down in m' pocket an' fumbled aroun', an' I finally got ahold of two or three pennies. Reached over right easy an' slipped it down in the hat; I didn't want anybody t' see these pennies, ya see. I didn't think a storm would ever bother me or any flood, me a-livin' up on higher groun'. Preacher preached an awful good sermon, seem like ever'body enjoyed it.

After services I started home, back through the

The Convict Camp. Roy Ward.

woods. On the way home it come up a terrible 'lectric storm—wind a-blowin' ever' way, lightnin' a-poppin' an' a-crackin'. There's a big ol' holler tree standin' there, just big enough fer me t' crawl in t' wait 'til the storm got over. An' lo an' behold, lightnin' struck this damn tree!

Well, there I was, fouled in this tree, couldn't move no way in the world, a long ways from anybody. An' I got to thinkin', what in the world I's gonna do? I got t' thinkin' about all the bad things I'd done an' what few good things I'd ever done in m' life. An' the worst thing I could see was my big han' a-droppin' those two or three pennies in fer the collection of Sister Turnipseed down at the church.

An', ya know, I got t' feelin' so doggone little, I saw a knothole right on up in that tree an' I just crawled up t' that knothole an' crawled out an' went straight on home!

Between the Saddle and the Ground

Recorded in spring 1973 by Deborah Hudson from her aunt, Willene Long, fifty-four, of Lilburn, De-Kalb County.

Bill Erwin told this story, and he said it was true. Said his parents had told him, and his grandparents before 'em. He was raised in the north Georgia mountains around Dahlonega, up in that section.

Said that, way back years ago, this boy was up there; well, everybody thought that he was a sinner, you know. He would drink, and didn't live just like people thought he ought to to be a Christian. And he'd ride a horse, and he was out one night a-ridin' and, uh, somethin' happened. I don't remember what it was that happened; the horse throwed him, or he fell off the horse, or something. And he hit into a bank, you know, on his head, and it broke his neck—killed him. And said that they had his funeral and all. Everybody talked about it, just wondered if he was saved, you know. I guess people back in them days were more conscious of things that way than we would be now.

Said that in a few years they went to clean off the cemetery and clean off his grave, and there was some kind of a little vine had grown up on his grave or by the grave or something. And said it was just wrote as plain as you've ever seen: "Between the saddle and the ground salvation was found."

Simon and the Talking Fish

Written in spring 1974 by Mattie Mitchell, seventy-nine, a black resident of Zebulon, Pike County; collected by her granddaughter, Eleanor Mitchell.

This is a old slavery-time story that my grandmother told that happen soon after slavery was ended and the poor old Negroes was free to go about to different places by themselves. Some would like to go where they could sing and pray together. There was a old man that would go to fishing most every Sunday; they could not talk to him and get him to take time to worship with them anytime. His name was Simon. All his friends and loved ones was having a good time at the place they would have their meeting, which they called their church. It was a bush arbor. They would keep it clean; the mens cut small trees of wood and made benches to sit down on, and the women would carry cloth and spread it over their seats to make them look clean and nice. And they would have a good time together, giving thanks and praises to God and Jesus Christ our Saviour, for freedom.

And so it happen on one beautiful Sunday, as the old man name Simon was fishing as he always had been doing most every Sunday, all of a sudden a big fish swallowed his hook. The fish was so heavy and strong he could not hardly pull the fish out of the water, but he finally got the fish to the bank. Then the fish said, "Carry me to the house now, Simon." The poor man was so afraid; he carried the fish to his home.

Then the fish said to Simon, "Clean me and put me in your frying pan, Simon; I ain't quite dead yet." Oh, Simon was so afraid. He went on and clean the fish, and fried it brown.

Then the fish said, "Take me out of the pan, Simon, and eat me up." Poor old man Simon, he went on and eat the fish up. As soon as he had eat the fish up, the fish said, "Belch me up, Simon, I ain't quite dead yet; Yankee Dilly you, Simon."

"I can't, oh I cannot belch you up."

"Bye bye," said the fish to Simon. "Yankee Dilly, Yankee Dilly."

Poor old man Simon burst wide open. There laid Simon and the fish together, on the ground.

Granddaddy Glenn and the Devil

Recorded in spring 1974 by Charlotte Abrams from Carroll Glenn of Chamblee, DeKalb County, who heard it as a boy from his grandmother in Albany, Dougherty County.

It seems that Great-granddaddy Glenn—Will Glenn, deputy sheriff of Mitchell County at the time—belonged to a very conscientious Baptist family, and church life was the most important function of their lives outside of their jobs. But my great-granddaddy had a very strong lust for fishing, you might say, and very often he would skip social functions and church functions to go fishing.

But one Sunday morning—it was in early May in the late 1800s or early 1900s—Granddaddy elected to go fishing instead of going to church that Sunday. So he went fishin' and had a very good day of fishin', but during the day it began to bother his conscience somewhat that he had skipped church, and he knew that the family would be upset with him. He was a little concerned with what God might think of him too, I believe.

But anyway, toward dusk he was beginning to wrap up his fishing trip. He heard something behind him and he turned around, and there was the Devil himself standing right behind Granddaddy! Well, it startled him tremendously. The Devil spoke to Granddaddy and told him that, because of his skipping church, he was going to take him with him to hell this very day. Well, this upset Granddaddy to no end, and of course he began to plead for his life and for the Devil not to take him with him. But the Devil said no, that even though he was a good Baptist he had now broken his faith with the Baptist church by skipping church and going fishing, and he was gonna take him today.

Granddaddy pleaded more and more, and finally the Devil decided that perhaps maybe he might bargain with him. So the Devil told Granddaddy that he would enter a contest with him and, if he [Glenn] won, he would not have to go to hell with him. Granddaddy asked what the contest might be, and the Devil told him that the contest would be who could tell the biggest lie. So the Devil said, "I'll tell the first lie, since I'm a expert at lying and deceiving." And Granddaddy agreed. So the Devil said, "Okay, my lie is that I caught a fish today as big as the world."

My granddaddy thought this was a lie that couldn't be topped, but he thought for a few minutes and then retorted with his answer. He said, "That's a good lie; but I have a frying pan that will hold two fish the size of the one you caught."

This, of course, was a bigger lie than the Devil told, so the Devil allowed Granddaddy to go on home and not have to go to hell.

CHAPTER ELEVEN

Anecdotes

The Uncle Tom Anecdote Cycle

Recorded in fall 1971 by Sharon Mattox from Alma Watkins, forty-five, of Atlanta, who was reared in Madison County, the setting for the stories.

These are the stories I heard my daddy tell about my great-uncle Tom. He was real stingy. He was accounted as pretty well off for that time, and I suppose how he got his money was that he was so stingy that he wouldn't ever spend anything.

He had a fence around his property, and he wouldn't let you go in and out the gate. He'd make you climb over the fence to keep from wearing out the hinges.

And another one of the stories was he had a spring; you know, before they even had wells they had these springs. So he had a real good spring and he wouldn't let anybody drink out of it. He'd make you catch the water that was running off and wasting.

Let's see; oh, there's quite a few stories about 'im. When he'd go to church, he would have his wife to ride in the buggy and he would go along beside of the buggy and carry his shoes in his hands, and then when he got in sight of the church he'd put his shoes on. That was to keep from wearing out his soles.

And when he hauled wood—you know, they had to haul the wood up to burn in the fire-

places—he would haul a load of wood and then he'd walk along by the side of the wagon and carry one on his shoulder. That was to save steps, you know; if he brought an extra one that would save a little bit more on the next load.

They tell the story about when his wife died. He was in the field pulling fodder, and they didn't have a doctor. Some of the neighbor women were in, you know, takin' care of her. So they saw that she was what they call on her death bed, and so they sent some of the men to the field to tell him that his wife was dying. By the time he got to the house his wife had already died, and he went to the bed and looked at her and said [lowers voice], "Well, she's dead. Ain't nothing I can do." Started back to the field to pull fodder!

And after she died, though, he paid his brother Thornton a thousand dollars to take care o' him the rest of his life—you know, at that time a thousand dollers was considered a lot of money. And he wouldn't eat anyplace else. He had his place at the table; nobody dared get in his place at the table! They said if he went somewhere and stayed all day he wouldn't eat anything. He'd say [lowers voice], "I's paying Thornton to feed me."

And another thing about him being so stingy—this sounds terrible, but anyway they said it was the truth—that he used to take two mouthsful of water—he'd take one mouthful of water and spit it in his hands and wash his face, then he'd take another mouthful of water and spit it in his hands an' wash his hands with it. Said, "Two mouthsful of water is enough to wash anybody's face and hands."

And then on Saturdays he'd take one pan o' water and take a bath. He would shave and take a whole bath in that one pan o' water.

And his brother's wife saw him going around one day holding up his pants, and she said, "Uh, Tom," said, "why didn't you tell me you had the buttons off your pants?" You know, they had their suspenders buttoned to their pants.

He said [lowers voice], "There's nothing wrong with my pants"; said, "I hadn't got anything else to do but go around holdin' 'em up." He didn't want to wear out his suspenders!

The Meaning of Friendship

Recorded in spring 1975 by Jean Bieder from Jack Carpenter, fifty-seven, of Dahlonega, Lumpkin County, who was reared in Franklin, North Carolina.

Well, Snipe and Boney were two very colorful old men. They weren't too reputable, though. They came in one Saturday night, both of 'em pretty well drunk. It was raining, and Snipe fell in a ditch—in a big mudhole—just close to Boney's house. And he couldn't get out; he was so drunk he couldn't get out. And Boney tried to help 'im. Boney reached in there, and he couldn't pull Snipe out at all. And he said, "Snipe," he said, "we've been friends for many years, haven't we?"

Snipe said, "Yes."

Said, "Snipe, I've always stood by you, haven't I?"

Snipe said, "Yes, Boney, you sure have."

And Boney said, "Snipe, this is a dark moment in your life and mine." And he says, "You're in trouble and I can't help you. But I'll do the next best thing. I'll jump in there with you." So he jumped in with Snipe!

Their wives pulled 'em both out.

Fruitless Prophesy

Recorded in spring 1975 by Jean Bieder from Walt Grindle, sixty-eight, of Dahlonega, Lumpkin County.

Great-uncle of mine, he liked pepper—any form of pepper. He 'as crazy about pepper. And his name was Hiram, and his wife was named Elizabeth. So she was always grumbling; she 'as just a chronic grumbler [hypochondriac].

Come spring of the year, and he told her one day, he said, "Elizabeth," said, "it's time you's sowing pepper seeds now."

She said, "Oh, Hiram, it's no use"; said, "I won't live to see no pepper grow this time."

He didn't say any more about it.

So after wadn't no pepper come, that fall, when he had something he 'specially wanted pepper with, they set down to the table and he looked around, said, "Elizabeth, here you are still a-living, and no pepper."

A Slow-Grinding Mill

Recorded in spring 1973 by Rebecca Morrison from her grandmother, Mollye Shook Gillespie, sixty-eight, of Atlanta, who was reared at Clyde, North Carolina.

This is a story about two members of my family, Uncle Holden and Aunt Mahala Evans. They lived long ago on a little farm in the mountains. They had seven children, and they were very poor.

And late one afternoon, after the day's chores were finished, Uncle Holden got on the ol' mule with a bushel of corn to go to the mill for meal. He didn' come home that night, and he didn' come home the next day. An' nobody had seen him an' nobody knew what happened to him.

And time passed on—days, weeks, months, and years. An' Aunt Mahala did the best she could to raise the seven children. They all grew up, married, and left home, and nobody had ever heard of Uncle Holden.

And one afternoon she was sitting on the little cabin porch in a rockin' chair, and she saw this man coming up the road on a mule. And he rode into the yard and he said, "Mahala, I'm back."

She said, "Yes, Holden, you're back."

And he said, "Mahala, I've brought your meal."

And so he had! [Laughs]

The Buzzard Eggs

Recorded in spring 1976 by Anita Anderson from Zelma Hall, fifty, of Atlanta.

My aunt's father-in-law was with the railroad in the early 1900s. And they lived somewhere below Griffin, Georgia. He was a fireman, and the train would stop at all of these little places, you know, along the way. And they'd sell things to the passengers on the train; people'd be lined up and down the tracks.

And, one morning, Papa Jones's wife told him, says, "Now look, I've got a turkey out, and she's wantin' to set. And she needs some eggs to set on, and I don't have any turkey eggs; I need some to hatch. So, along your run this morning, if you see anybody selling any turkey eggs, buy me some."

So they was goin' along there, you know, and they stopped at this little ol' station. There was a bunch of little boys out there, and they were sellin' eggs. He says, "Hey, boys! What kinda eggs over there?"

They had different kinds o' eggs, and there was a couple little boys said, "We've got some buzzard eggs. I bet ya never saw any buzzard eggs."

He says, "I'll take the buzzard eggs. I'll get my wife this time; boy, I'm gonna pull a joke on her, good and proper." So, he takes the buzzard eggs home.

Couple o' weeks, he says, "Mamie, how are your eggs comin' along that I brought you for the turkey to sit on?"

And she says, "Oh! I forgot to tell you about those turkey eggs." She says, "I had to cook 'em and put 'em in your lunch one mornin', 'cause I was plumb outta eggs."

Doody's Escape from the Revenuers

Recorded in spring 1974 by Jack Beckman from his father, Guy Beckman, fifty-three, of Smyrna, Cobb County, who was reared in McClellanville, South Carolina.

This is supposed to be a true story, an' it's about a man by the name of Doody Snyder. Doody was known to be a man fast afoot, but he couldn't swim. And this little instance happened in the

Roadside Vendors, Georgia. Al Clayton.

Hellhole Swamp in Berkeley County over in South Carolina. And it was down around the Wambaw Creek area, which has heavy foliage, underbrush, and in that area is called a thicket, where the undergrowth is heavy and dense. And back in this swamp, Doody was workin' for this man that had a whiskey still. And the revenuers for a long time had been tryin' to catch Doody and the man [who] owned this still.

It was late in the afternoon, and this man that owned the still carried Doody out to the area an' dropped him off. So he made his way through the woods to the still. Doody was goin' about his chores out there at the still, and he had another man that was working with him. And, while they were workin', Doody had a very strong sense of sound, and he heard some noise off in the distance; it happened to be these revenuers.

And so Doody and his friend started runnin', and revenuers started firin' at 'em and hollered "Halt!" Doody didn't stop runnin'; he kept goin'. And bullets were just whizzin' all through the underbrush.

And Doody got to the Wambaw Creek, and then he decided, "Well, now, it's either get caught or get across this river one way or the other." And so he decided, "Well, there's only one way to go; I can't swim." So he walked it, walked underneath about thirty-five feet! After he crossed this thing, he didn't stop running; he kept on runnin'. He was about five miles from his home.

And the revenuers decided, "Well, we know we can catch him at his home. We'll be there before he will." And so they went back and destroyed the still.

In the meantime, Doody kept runnin'; and he ran all the way home. And when the revenuers got to his house they knocked on his door, and who should come to the door but Doody, all dressed up, cup of coffee in his hand.

And they were really shocked to know that he could get there that quick. And they asked him why did he run when they hollered "halt" up the woods at him. An' Doody said he hadn't been anywhere; he'd been home all day. And he called his wife, and his wife came to the door and verified the fact that Doody had been home all day.

And he got out of that jam.

The Eyeballs and the Cannonball: Two Cobb Family Anecdotes

Recorded in spring 1973 by Lamar Blaylock from Junior Pierce of Dalton, Whitfield County.

Now, you know, they called yo' great-uncle Ty Cobb "The Georgia Peach." Ty was a famous baseball player, and finally they made him quit because he was too old. And that kinda hurt his pride a little bit. Pride's a bad thing, Lamar. Well, ol' Ty he came home feelin' awful bad.

And there was this fella in town—he was no good. Lemme tell ya, he was no-o-o good. He was the rottenest, drunkenest fella you ever met. He just laid around town all day looking for something mean to do to folks. Well, after church one Sunday he says to Ty, "Ty Cobb, I don't think you're that good." And he says, "We're gonna have a ballgame this afternoon, bein' it's Sunday, and we want you to come out to that ballfield and we want you to play with us."

Well, you know Ty—well, you didn't know Ty—but Ty just couldn't let that go by; it's in the Cobb blood, son. So, ol' Ty he says, "All right," and he went out there.

Well, this "smart" fella—we called him somethin' else—this smart fella he says, "Now I'm gonna pitch to Ty Cobb, and I'm gonna strike him out."

Ty he gits himself a bat there, and he steps up to the plate. Mind ye, now, he was pretty old; and a lot of us, even Cobbs, we was doubtin' that he was gonna hit. So he steps up there, and the first pitch he hits right back; hits that man right between his eyes—right there on his forehead—and lo and behold if that man's eyeballs didn't fall out, he hit him so hard!

That man, he's the blind man now in town. He used to be the town drunk that laid on the sidewalk; now he's the blind man, sits and begs for money, and they tell me he's a humble fella now. But they tell me that to this day he's crawlin' around on that baseball field, every Sunday afternoon, lookin' for them eyeballs.

Now, what he don't know is that your great-uncle Ty he picked 'em up, put 'em in his pocket, and put 'em with all the rest of his baseball trophies.

Now that you understand a little bit about the Cobb blood, this is about yo' great, great, great—and a few more greats thrown in there—grandpappy. He fought in the Civil War. Now, you see, the Cobbs they always been pretty well off in these parts; but he was the first one to come here, and he was a German. And he set up all these carpet mills; they are still here today—they were called thread mills back then—but he owned 'em all. And he built himself a big plantation; grew his own cotton for his thread mills; had a lot of slaves. Anyways, the Yankees didn't like it, and they started the war.

Now, all the rich folks, like your great, great, great-grandpappy Cobb, they made officers because they were gentlemen. And regular folks they made the privates. So your great, great, great-grandpappy Cobb went off to war; left be-hind his plantations; left behind his thread mills; fought through the whole war, fought well. Then, in the battle of Atlantee, they shot a cannonball right through his stomach. And it stayed there, right in his stomach. Well, they knew he was gonna die; and he did.

And your great, great, great-grandmama Cobb went down there and had him brought back to the mansion—and that mansion it's still there today, right there in the middle of where them old cottonfields used to be. She brought that body back with the cannonball still in the stomach, and she put him up in his big bed. And while he was lying in state, that cannonball fell off his stomach and rolled down the stairs in the middle of the night. And it scared all them slaves to death that was in that house; they went runnin' out, and they never would go back in.

Well, they had the funeral and they buried him; and they say they buried that cannonball, too, with him, but nobody ever saw it. And now everybody's scared to go back in that mansion at nighttime. But some of the Cobbs, they still live there. And they say that once a year, on the anniversary of his death, late at night, they can hear that cannonball roll down them stairs. And they believe it's the ghost of your great, great, great-grandpappy Cobb, tryin' to git rid of that thing. He don't want it; that's why, when he was dead, he pushed it off his bed—it couldn't have just fell off, he must have pushed it off—and rolled it down them stairs. They went against his will when they buried that thing with him. And I believe that he's tryin' to git rid of it to this day.

Well, it went a little farther than that; on the anniversary of his death, everybody that worked for him at the carpet mills got a terrible stomachache; and all his relatives git it—every one of us, to this day—we git that stomachache, once a year, on the anniversary of his death.

CHAPTER TWELVE

Legends

SUPERNATURAL

Mary the Wanderer

Recorded in spring 1972 by Virginia Diane Morris from Marianna Lines, an Atlanta woman in her late twenties, who, according to the collector, "spends most of her summers at St. Simons Island, Georgia. She has been going there since a small child. Her parents and grandparents spend a great deal of time on the island and have learned a good many stories and legends which they have passed on to her."

Well, the one that everybody tells that I guess everybody has their own version of, but I've heard ever since I was a little girl, is the story about Mary the Wanderer. I think the black people on the island refer to her as Mary de Wanda.

Anyway, the story as I heard it is that Mary the Wanderer was a young girl, engaged to be married. And her lover was out in the sound on a fishing boat at night, and it was near Retreat Plantation—which is now where the Sea Island Golf Course is. It was, I guess, around midnight when the ship was supposed to come in; and a storm had been brewing and it was very windy. And as she was standing there on the point looking out and waving to him, waves started just enveloping the boat. And pretty soon the boat just

completely turned over, and he was drowned. And she swam out to try to get to him in time to save him, and she drowned too. So I guess that was some poetic justice that they both could die together.

But ever since then, the story goes, Mary the Wanderer wanders up and down the island there on the Retreat Point looking for her lover, and she's never been able to settle into her grave—wherever that may be—because this great loss wouldn't allow her soul to rest. And you can see her, they say, on a moonlit night, usually when it's windy and about the same conditions it was back during the days that this happened. And there's rows and rows of ancient live oaks that are covered with moss, and these form an archway; and they say that if you drive down there or walk down there on this moonlit night you will see Mary the Wanderer clothed always in white holding a lantern up in the air, looking for her lover, and that she wanders there only at these hours.

Ebo Landing

Recorded in spring 1971 by Julia Wilson from her cousin, Jim Wilson, of Atlanta.

207

This is the story of Ebo Landing. Ebo Landing is located in St. Simons, Georgia, which is near Brunswick. The story that we're dealing with occurred during colonial times. The slaves being brought from Africa were being let off the boats here at this landing, and then would be shipped to wherever they were to be sold. And so they had lots of slaves coming in every day, and there was one boat bringing this group of slaves which were the Ebo tribe from Africa. And this Ebo tribe was a very proud and very self-righteous tribe, very difficult for the slave drivers to handle, and they gave the people a lot of difficulty in coming across the ocean. They'd have people trying to jump overboard, and this kind of thing.

And so finally, when they arrived at the landing, the Ebo slaves walked off the boat; and when they were standing on the shore near the landing, proceeded to march into the water. And as they marched in they chanted a chant from their African ancestry which went, "The water brought us and the water shall take us away."

Now, I've been going down to St. Simons since I was sixteen months old every year, and stayed on Sea Island. And recently it's become a big thing with the kids to go to the Ebo Landing. And the most magnificent thing about it is that it's not industrialized, and people don't try and make a big gimmick out of it. And a lot of people when you tell 'em about it say, "Oh, that's a bunch of bull." But I've been down there before, and if it's a real clear night, a little breeze coming off the marsh—this is located right on a marsh with a channel coming in so the boats could come in—if you sit there for . . . it took me about an hour before I heard anything. Maybe that's enough time for my imagination to kinda go wild. But after I had been there about an hour, I began to hear what sounded like just a

faint mumble that kinda grew, and got a little louder [supposedly the murmur of the Ebo ghosts chanting]; and about that time I left rather quickly!

The Lone Grave

Recorded in spring 1971 by Julia Wilson from her cousin, Jim Wilson, of Atlanta.

Well, this is a story which occurred in St. Simons, Georgia, and this was told to me by a native of the area, and I went to see this. The story concerns a lone grave which is about five hundred feet off the main highway on St. Simons. You can't see it from the road unless you know exactly where it is, and you have to step down and really look for it. But once you find it, you'll find that this grave is . . . nothing grows around it; there's trees all but five feet up to it, and then there's nothing really on top of it. And it's been there for over a hundred years. It is the grave of a schoolteacher, and on the grave it says, "A Beloved Teacher," and the name and dates of her birth and death.

And the story behind this grave is that this schoolteacher had been teaching her kids and performing the normal roles of a schoolteacher, and yet after school a small group of black children would come in and she would help 'em. And the white plantation owners in the area didn't like it, but they put up with it. And there was one exceptionally bright young black child that she was really, ya know, hoping could advance, and he was advancing quickly and really a smart kid.

But during a slave uprising during that period, the small child was killed when his house was burned down by a mob of white people that were trying to kill the people that were causing the slave uprising. And so after this the school-teacher was real upset, but she couldn't do any-thing and nobody else did anything, so it just kinda blew over; and her classes with the black children had to end. And this upset her a great deal, but she was paid by the plantation owners and this is what she had to do.

Well, about several months after that, it's said that one of the white children that went to the school passed by the schoolhouse after class and saw the teacher talking to what looked like a raven—a big, black bird—just conversing with it. And he went home and told his parents, and his parents were very superstitious, and decided that this was the black child reincarnated, and decided that his teacher was a witch. And so a wild mob approached her home, which was next to the schoolhouse, and she was killed by this mob. And nobody wanted to bury her. They just thought she oughta be left there, and the school just be closed down, and wait 'til they could get somebody else to teach.

And so there was one plantation owner that she had done a great deal for, and he felt he was obligated to do something with her, to bury her. So he had a coffin made and had a tombstone made with the inscription, "My Beloved Teacher." And he wanted to bury her in the Christ Church graveyard where John Wesley had preached and the big church for the whole area, which was the Methodist Church there. But the other white people in the area didn't allow anybody that wasn't white to be buried there, and they cer-tainly didn't allow any witches to be buried there, so they said this was absurd. So he buried her about three miles away from the church and not very far from his plantation, just off one of

the roads toward his plantation and from the church.

Nothing else happened about it, and he was kinda condemned by the community for doing it, but that kinda blew over. But it still remains today, this perfectly white gravestone with noth-ing growing around it, no moss, no vegetation of any kind growing around it. And all the grave-stones at the church have all grown over, and have to be groomed quite often. But this one gravestone is never groomed. You can go up to it, and there's no cut-back branches where some-body is trying to make it a good tourist attrac-tion. And very few people who are from outside the area know it, but there it is, just this one lone grave all by itself with no other graves around it, with no vegetation growing on it.

The Grateful Headless Ghost

Recorded in fall 1967 by Lynda Carriveau from her grandmother, Lottie Fraser, seventy-nine, of Staten-ville, Echols County.

One time they was a pore man married a rich girl. And the girl's parents weren't willin' to it, and they lived off a little piece; and every time they'd come to see her they'd throw off on him—make fun of him, ya know.

And he come in at dinner one day and she was tellin' him about it; and he says, "You jest bundle up what clothes you can tote in a handkerchief and I'll bundle up what I can tote, and we'll leave, and we'll travel just as long as we got land to travel on." Says, "We're leaving."

So they done that. And they traveled fer miles and miles and miles. And they passed a house that was empty—looked like—and went to another house that was close by, and asked if they could spend the night. And says, "It looks like it's goin' ta be bad weather, and I don't want my wife to get wet."

He says, "Mister," he says, "that house right down yonder that you just passed," says, "is well furnished and everything; stay there just as long as you want to. But I haven't got room enough here in this house; my family's too big." He says, "That is, if you can keep the door shut." Says, "That's the reason I left everything just like it is."

So they went in and got 'em some splinters and made 'em up a little fahr. And they was sittin' there talkin', and terec'ly a cat walked in. And he says, "Well, that is a purty cat, itn't it?" It got up and walked out. And a big ol' cat walked in. He says, "Well, that's the biggest cat I ever seen." He turned and walked out. And a little dog walked in, and he says, "Well, all these animals must belong to that man down there." And he walked out. And direc'ly a *big* ol' dog walked in and stood there, and he says, "I know that's where they come from is from that house down there." So he went on out.

And the wind begin to blow, an' it begin to drizzle rain. And so he went to the door and shut it. An' time he sat down, it flew open. He got up an' fastened it, an' it flew open. Says, "Well, if we could keep the door shut." So they just left it open.

And terec'ly a man walked in with his head off! An' he stood there and looked at 'em. But when he walked in, this girl's husband jumped up and run out. He didn't wanna leave his wife but he couldn't stay in there, so he run around and hid in the chimney corner. And while he was outside, she sat there and studied what to do, and terec'ly she says, "What in the name of the Lord are you here fer?"

He says, "Lady, you're the first person that's ever spoke to me since I was killed." He says, "Don't be worried, now." He said, "Listen to what I'm a-tellin' ya now, careful." Says, "Don't worry. Your husband ain't gone nowheres; he's around there in the chimney corner." Says, "My brother killed me fer my money, but he couldn't find it." And says, "I want you to have it." And he says, "If you'll come an' go with me, I'll show it to ya."

So she got up and walked out with him, and when she did, her husband walked along. So they all went on. And he went in an old buildin'—an ol' log house—and he went to one of the logs an' he pulled out a plug, you know, pulled it out and hand her so much money. An' he went to another place an' he pulled that out and hand it to her. An' he says, "Now come and I'll show you my grave, and you do what I tell ya. This money is yours."

So they started back to the house, and there was just a little [pine] straw ever'where, and leaves. He walked to a place; says, "Right there," says, "you see, is where my brother buried me at." An' says, "Nobody ain't never found me. They don't know what went wi' me." He says, "All I ask ya t' do is go git the sheriff tomorrow." And he told her how fur she'd have to go to git him. But says, "You git him an' bring him here time the sun rises good. And tell him I says if he didn't believe it, to git my brother and bring him here and let him touch this grave with his fingers like *that*" [taps the chair where the microphone is with finger]. An' says, "It'll bust into a glory o' blood."

And they said when he done that that there was fresh blood there. He done that to convict his brother, ya see, fer murderin' him. He murdered him, ya see, fer his money.

The Crying Ghost Baby

Recorded in fall 1967 by Richard Brown from Mrs. Paul (Lovey) Brown, forty-nine, of East Point, Fulton County, who was reared in Montgomery, Alabama.

My grandmother used to tell us many ol' tales, and kept us spellbound for hours. She said she lived in what she called a stone house in Atlanta, Georgia. She said it was supposed to be haunted, an', sure enough, every time it stormed she would hear this baby crying, and it would just terrify her.

An' she had an old-maid aunt; she was cynical—anyway she called her a mean ol' thing, didn't believe anything. An' she came to visit her, an' she told her about it—how terrified she was ever' time it stormed: when a storm came she heard this baby cryin'.

And she said, "Oh, that's a lot of poppycock. I don't believe a word of it."

An' my grandmother said, "I hope and pray it storms while you're here, so I can prove it."

So she stayed a few days, an' it came up a thunderstorm one night. An' she said, "All right, Elizabeth, it's stormin'; I don't hear any baby cryin'."

She said, "You will."

So they all went to bed, and the storm let in like crazy. An', sure enough, that baby started cryin'. So the old-maid aunt got up—my grandmother didn't say cussin', but I imagine she was by the way she describes her. She lit the kerosene lamp, and went all over that big ol' house looking for that baby, that noise. So she came to the fireplace in one of the rooms—back then they had fireplaces in the bedrooms—an' she located the sound. An' my grandmother said she

was just so hateful, the way she put it, she went outside and got the hatchet that they chopped splinters with to start fires, and come in there an' *tore that fireplace apart.* She said, "It's coming from here, an' if there's anything under there, I'm gonna find it." An' she took that hatchet and she tore that brick hearth up, an' there was a baby skeleton underneath there! She said, "Well, here's the source of your trouble; somebody's killed a baby an' put it down there, and this is the ghost of it." She said, "I never believed in ghosts before in my life."

But they took that thing out of there, and my grandmother never heard that noise again.

Ghostly Sounds of a Murder

Recorded in winter 1981 by Wanda Simmons from Teressa Hamrick, twenty-six, at Gainesville, Hall County.

When she [teller's grandmother Fanny] was young she was real talented on the piano and the organ. This would have been about 1915–1920. And back then you just didn't go take piano lessons each week or something, you had to go live with your teacher, 'cause there was no way you could really travel back and forth unless it was right in your community—or, as my grandfather calls it, the settlement. And so she went up to live with this family in Blairsville and, you know, she stayed and helped with the housework and stuff and got piano lessons in exchange.

And she said the first night she was there she heard a noise like a spinning wheel spinning, and then she heard all this crashing like dishes breaking and stuff like that. And she ran out in the hall and, you know, was scared to death; she didn't know what was going on. You know, Fanny she is real flaky anyway; anything scares her.

And the people that lived there came out of their rooms—they were acting real unconcerned—and told her that that happened now and then. That before they bought the house a woman had been murdered there; that somebody had come in while she was spinning, and from the way my grandmother talked—she never actually come out and said it—apparently the woman was raped and murdered. And she put up a big fight before she was killed and, you know, drug down everything off the cabinets and stuff and knocked over the china cabinet and everything. And now and then again they'd just have those sounds.

My grandmother said she didn't stay another night in that damned place; she hit the road for home!

The Covers

Recorded in fall 1978 by Danny Fowler from Estelle Campbell, fifty-six, of Stone Mountain, De-Kalb County, who was reared in Villa Rica, Carroll County.

My grandfather told me a story one time about these people back in the 1800s. They would go to Carrollton to trade horses, and it would take two days. And then they would have to stop and spend the night on the way.

So they stopped at this house and spent the night. And they couldn't keep the covers on the bed. Every time they'd put the cover back on the bed it would slide off.

So they found out that there had been a

murder in that room. Some lady had shot her daughter-in-law; they were fighting over some quilts. And that's the reason they couldn't keep the cover on the bed; it was haunted.

The Dead Lady's Baby

Recorded in spring 1979 by Pamela Roberts from Hattie Mae Dawson, sixty, a black resident of Atlanta who heard her stories at Gibson, Glascock County.

I heard my grandmama, now, useta talk about they was a lady had a li'l newborn baby, an' she [the mother] died. But she stayed sick a good while. An' she didn't have no sista, but she had some brothers. An' she didn't like one of her sista-in-laws, an' so she called for 'em ta come. They were livin' in the country. An' so she tol' her sista-in-law Ruth, say, "When I'm gone, I want you ta have my baby." Say, "I don' want Lou ta have it; I want you ta have it."

An' so, she died. An' afta she died Miz Lou she say, "I don' care what y'all say; I'm goin' take that baby. An' I'm goin' raise it, 'cause that's a purty baby."

An' so they was there cleanin' up; ya know how folks . . . well, you don' know 'cause you ain' nevah live in the country. But 'long back then, when a person would die in the country, afta the funeral an' ever'thing, ever'body in the neighborhood would git together an' go down an' they'd take down the curtains, an' they take ever'thing off the bed an' they wash the bed an' put it out an' let it dry, an' then they take an' wash down the wall an' clean the floors up an' ever'thing; then they'd put ever'thing back.

An' so they had did that an' they was through,

an' they 'as sittin' down under a tree. An' Miz Lou had the baby in her lap. An' ever'body jes' sittin' there laughin' an' talkin'. An' somethin' come down an' took that baby outta Miz Lou's lap an' put it in Ruth's lap!

An' say that like ta scared 'em ta death! Say everybody they was up an' runnin'! But they know, then, who that lady wanted to have that baby.

The Phantom Lantern Man of Ray City

Recorded in spring 1978 by Gay Nix from her husband, Bill Nix, thirty-one, of Decatur, DeKalb County, who was reared at Valdosta, Lowndes County.

This story comes from right near my home town of Valdosta; it's really not much of a story. But the Southern Railroad runs right through Valdosta and just before coming to Valdosta goes through a real small town called Ray City. There was a certain dirt road that ran parallel to City Hall in Ray City that went back to the swamps by the railroad tracks.

Growing up around Valdosta we were always told that at one time a Negro man who used to work for the railroad had been out on the tracks swinging his lantern and trying to get a train to stop because there was a school bus broken down on the tracks right there at Ray City; and that he stood on the tracks so long that the train hit him, and he gave his life for these school-children. And that today if you drive down the dirt road to the end of it—which is right by the track—during a full moon, and if you look off to the railroad tracks, you can see this old Negro man swinging his lantern. And I've been down

there myself on many an occasion and I've personally seen that light.

Ghost Light Disproven

Recorded in fall 1967 by Carol Sanders from a Mr. Watson of Cherokee County.

There ain't no such a thing as a haunt. When I was out a-courting, they used to tell me that the Liberty Grove Church cemetery was haunted; they'd see a light there. So I was going with a girl back over the other side of there, an' I had to go right back down by there, me an' another boy.

An' we was coming over the hill one night [on horseback]. He says, "Look yonder at that light down there at the cemetery!" Boy, my hat jus' riz plumb up on my head. There it was, looked like it was a-settin' right by the side of the monument jes' as pretty as you please.

Well, we had to come home, an' he wanted to know what we were going do, was we goin' turn 'round an' go back. Would've been about seven or eight miles back around to miss the cemetery. I says, "No," I says, "I don't believe that there's anything can catch me if I git started."

An' he says, "Well, I just don't much want to ride down by there."

An' there's a house right straight direct in line with the cemetery. An' I was in front, it happened. An' I told him, "I tell you what let's do. Let's jus' find out what that thing is. It cain't hurt us."

And he says, "Uh uh! I just don't want to be fooling around no cemetery."

An' I says, "I ain't going to the cemetery." We rode on down just a little piece, an' that light got out of line with us an' went out.

An' so he says, "Now what went with it?"

An' I says, "I couldn't tell you." I says, "I'll tell you what we'll do; you just sit where you're at, an' I'll turn my horse around an' go back up and see if I can see it." An' I got back up in line with that house an' I told him, I says, "Jus' wait a minute. I found that thing."

An' he says, "What?"

An' I says, "I sure have." I says, "Now, I'll pull my horse on down there next to you, and I'll walk back up there, an' I'll stay in line, an' come right down." An' when I got to the monument, why, that light from that house was a-shinin' on that monument. Make it look like it was settin' right there by that monument. An' that's everything in the world it was.

And they'd tol' for years that they was somebody that set out there with a light in the graveyard. They said it was haunted; it jus' wouldn't do to go by there. An' it wasn't a thing in the world but light reflected from that house. It got to the place where it got interesting; it just got interesting to think about. You'd get so far and it'd go out. I wanted to learn where it was comin' from.

Grandpa and the Ghost

Recorded in spring 1974 by Louellen Wright from Tom Quinton, forty-three, of Talking Rock, Pickens County.

I'll tell you one about Grandpa. You know, all the cattle just ran out. And 'course the cow, because of habit, would come to be milked at night, you know. One night, Grandma's old cow didn't come in—now this was Great-grandma W.—so Pa John had to go looking for it. It 'as already gettin' dusky-dark when he started out lookin' for the cow. You know, they'd call, "Sook, heifer, sook, heifer," and the cow would usually hear them callin' and think of the good food she's gonna get. As the usual thing she just foraged for food, but when they were milkin', why, they gave her corn or nubbins. Do you know what a nubbin is? It's the little ears of corn that don't fully develop, you know; it has some kernels of corn, but not much.

Well, Grandpa, he called and called. Nothing. He was gettin' away, and he went even farther than he usually had to go; and he's gettin' close to the cemetery. Most youngsters didn't like to go close to the cemetery at night. And Grandpa, he's gettin' a little more nervous and a little more nervous about this thing. And he came around the curve in the path, and here was something big and white. All he could see was just something white there, you know, where all the rest of the things were dark or dark green. It was gettin' so dark that all he could tell is that there was just something white there. Scared Grandpa pert'-near to death, I guess.

And they had an old saying, that if you ever saw a ghost or something unnatural—a ghost was somebody who couldn't rest, you know, in death, that they were searchin' for something, something had been wrong when they died; they even said that if they'd left money buried, why, the ghost'd come to show where it was—you were supposed to say, "What in the name of God are you doing here?"

So Grandpa, here he was, shivering and shaking, you know, and he said, "Wh-wha' in the name of God are y-you doing here?"

And he said just about the time he said it, the

Wheat Field, Oglethorpe County, Georgia. Doug Brown.

old cow moved, and he heard the bell tinkle; and he had been scared by a cow! But he did find the cow to go home. [Laughs]

The Man Who Thought He Was Brave

Recorded in spring 1969 by Maureen Crawford from her sister-in-law, Julie Crawford, thirteen, of Atlanta. She heard this story at a spend-the-night party.

There once was a man that thought he was real, you know, hot stuff, and real brave, and he was always bragging about all the things that he was doing, how brave he was. So one night one man decided to, you know, get the better of him. So this farmer, this man, was coming along with a load of watermelons, and he met the other man who was always bragging. Now, in this town there was a haunted house, and nobody had ever slept there, because there was horrible tales told about it of strange things that had happened there. So he says, "I'll give you this wagon of watermelons if you'll sleep one night in this house."

So the man says, "Okay. Nothing scares me, you know, ghosts or nothing." So he went home and he packed his things, and he told his family that he was gonna sleep in a haunted house. Of course, they begged him not to go, but he went anyway, just laughing.

So he got there and it was sorta eerie and kinda spooky, but he didn't pay any attention to it. He made himself a fire and he sat down and read a book. Well, after awhile he got sleepy, so he decided to go to bed. Well, it was a warm night, yet it was still a little cool, so he needed a sheet. And he let the windows open and the moonlight was streaming in, because there was a full moon that night. So just to be on the safe side against practical jokers, he took a gun with him to bed. So anyway, he covered himself up with the sheet and he went to sleep.

But later that night he woke up and there he saw it, at the foot of the bed! There were two bright shining eyes staring at him. At first he thought he was half asleep or having a dream, so he pinched himself. But he was wide awake. He didn't know what to do at first, and he sat there and shook real good. And the funny thing about it was that it seemed that when he moved those eyes moved. So finally he decided he better shoot it—whatever it was—before it got him. So he got the gun, and he was shaking so bad he could hardly do it; but finally he squeezed the trigger. And then there was a loud yell. For you see what had happened: it was his toenails shining through the sheets with the moonlight on them. And the man that was so brave and wasn't afraid of ghosts had actually shot his own toe!

The Fork in the Grave

Recorded in fall 1979 by Janna Nelson from John Henry Holliday, sixty-five, of Irwinton, Wilkinson County.

The story I'm fixing to tell is supposed to be a true story; as to whether or not it's a statement of fact I don't really know.

Seems like maybe five or six boys and girls was sitting around one night, talking about ghosts, spirits, cemeteries, things that would strike terror in the hearts of most people. One young lady, among the people there, said she wasn't afraid to go up to the cemetery alone.

And they told her, "All right, we'll see if you'll go up there by yourself." And as proof that she had been to the cemetery, they asked her to take a common kitchen fork, like you eat with, and said, "Now, when you go up to the grave"—'course the graves at that time and age was just mounds of earth, no slab, no cement, just a mound of earth there in the cemetery—say, "as proof that you go up to the cemetery we want you to take this fork and stick it in the mound of dirt and leave it there and come back. And then we will go up there, and if we find the fork sticking in the grave we'll know that you have been there." She agreed to the terms.

So she left with a fork and she stayed gone for a considerable time and hadn't come back, and they decided they'd go and see what had happened—if she had changed her mind and went some other way. But anyway, they went to the cemetery to see if the fork was there in the grave.

When they got to the graveyard everything was still and quiet. And they proceeded to search for her. And they found her. She had fell over this grave, and they picked her up to see what was wrong. She wore a apron or long piece of clothes of some kind that fell over the grave as she stooped down to stick the fork into the grave, and she stuck the fork through her apron, kinda pinned the apron down to the grave. As she started to arise from the position she was in when she put the fork in the mound of earth, this apron pulled on her, which to her way of thinking might be something that grabbed her or caught her. And when they found her she was dead from shock; but they found her over the grave with this fork that was stuck through her apron to the mound of earth.

This is a story been told to me for at least fifty-five, sixty years. As to whether there's any truth to it, I don't know, but I've heard it many a time.

The Vanishing Hitchhiker (1)

Recorded in spring 1971 by Debby Creecy and Sharon McParland from Joy Hendrix, forty-five, of Metter, Candler County.

My husband and I were living in Savannah, where we had lived since we were married. Since we loved the beach so much, it was always the case, if someone should drop in from out of town, that we would want to take them to the beach. On this particular occasion, a friend of his in service came to visit. After he had arrived at our house and we had had dinner, we decided to go down to the beach. This night they were having a nice orchestra to play and we thought we might could enjoy dancing, even though we didn't have him a date. It was always nice to walk out on the pier between intervals of the dance and enjoy the breeze.

On this night, as we were driving along—the three of us to the beach—we saw this girl standing by the road, probably a half mile before we got to her. And as we approached we saw that she was seemingly trying to stop a car. The wind was blowing, and her long blond hair seemed to flow with the wind along with the soft material of her white dress, if you could picture this. As we got to her she seemed so lonely and we knew that she needed help, so we stopped. And she asked if we could give her a ride to the beach. Naturally, we picked her up, and she began to talk with us as though we had always known her.

We had not driven more than a mile before

she said she was hot and wondered if it was all right to lower the window in the car, even though she was the only one with a sleeveless dress on. We felt that something must be wrong with her because we had on wraps, but of course we went along with her, and she did this in a jovial manner. We enjoyed her company to the beach, and when we got there we asked where she was planning to go. And she said, "Nowhere in particular"; so we asked her if she would like to join us for dancing. She immediately said she would love to.

After we arrived at the place where the orchestra was playing, we decided to walk out on the pier; but we were afraid that she would be cold, because even on a summer night it was usually cold to walk out over the water. But she insisted that she wasn't cold at all, that in fact she thought it would be refreshing because she was a little warm.

After we came back to the table where we were sitting, she excused herself to go to the little girls' room, and as soon as she left we saw this bewildered look on the friend of my husband's, who had danced with the girl. As soon as she left the table he said, "Something is wrong." He said, "As soon as I took her hand to dance, it was just like holding a piece of ice." Said, "She isn't warm, she's cold." Naturally, this stirred up a little excitement in us. She came back to the table. My husband asked her to dance, and he came back to the table and related the same thing to me, that she was so cold: her hands were just like ice.

So, shortly after this, we decided to leave to come home, and we asked her if we could carry her someplace. And she said no, that she was just coming down to enjoy the night, that she would go back with us. And the boy thought that

she was very charming, though, and he had asked her where she lived, and she gave him her house number and the street she lived on and told him that it would be all right for him to call if he liked someday. So he wrote her name down; he thought as we came back that when we carried her home he would know how to get back to her house so that he could look her up. But as we approached where we had picked her up, she said, "You can stop here." And of course the men just thought that this would be terrible to put a young, charming, beautiful girl out by the road, and they insisted on carrying her home. But she said, "No, put me out right where you picked me up." And she made this so definite that there was no other way out.

And of course she was the conversation all the way home: the strangeness of her being 'side of the road, going down and enjoying the evening with us, and then coming back and wanting to be put out by the road again. But we left her, and the last sight that we saw was the wind blowing her long blond hair and the beautiful white silk dress that she had on.

So we got back to our place and started to get out of the car, and my husband's friend realized that the girl had left her glove. Her name was a strange name, and yet it was one you couldn't forget. Her name was Rose White. And he said, "Rose left her white glove." So we decided to go on in and the next day we would go back to her house and return her glove. I guess, partly, that we were interested in knowing if she got home or finding out a little more about Rose White. But now we had a good excuse to go back, and he had her house number and the street that she lived on.

The next day, shortly after church and we had had dinner, of course, we ventured off to Rose

White's house. We wanted to see what she was like in the day. And if the others were like I was, we hardly knew what was going on in church and even eating our lunch was just a procedure that we went through. Hurriedly we got into the car and we started back on the road to Savannah Beach. We got to the place where we picked her up, and, sure enough, this was the name of the street that she lived on. But when we drove up about a mile off the highway we saw the number of the place, and it was a convent. Then we began to wonder if she had slipped out of the convent; maybe this was why she was so mysterious about getting out. Then we thought, "No, this couldn't have been true," and after wondering really if we had taken the right number down we decided the only thing to do was to go and ask one of the sisters.

The friend and my husband went to the door, and they asked if this is where Rose White stayed. And the elder sister looked at them, not with wonder, they said, but with concern. And she said, "Rose White? Yes, come in, my friends." So they came back to the car to get me, and the three of us went in. And the sister said, "Where did you know Rose White?"

And we said that actually we did not know her before the night before, that we had met her just the night before.

And she said, "Would you recognize her picture?" And of course we would. She took down this old album and she said, "Thumb through here, and find a picture that you think is Rose White."

So immediately the three of us, still with curiosity, flipped through the pages, and then we saw the beautiful eight-by-ten picture of Rose White and there was no mistake, we knew this was she. We told the sister, "This is Rose White, that we met last night."

Then she said, "My friends, you aren't the first ones who have come here looking for Rose White. But I'd like for you to go with me to where she is." And she came out and got into the car with us and directed us down the road. We turned off to the left and then we could see this cemetery. We got out, without a speech of thought from anyone; we walked through the cemetery and she came to this tombstone and she said, "My friends, there is Rose White." And we saw on the tombstone, "Rose White." She had died on the day of her graduation from high school. The day that she died was the very date of the day before. We were so lost in thought, we were so bewildered, until we all just bowed our heads.

We went back to the car, the sister followed, and on the way she told us, "Yes, Rose White has been seen three other times, and it's always on the date of the day that she was buried. She doesn't come back but once every fifteen years." And that happened to be the day that we passed.

This next September will be fifteen years ago that we picked Rose White up on the road, the Old Savannah Road between Savannah and Savannah Beach. I'm not sure that I'll go back down the road next September; but if anyone would like to see if Rose White is there they might just travel down that road, because this will be the year that she should return, according to the last three times.

The Vanishing Hitchhiker (2)

Recorded in spring 1978 by Gay Nix from her husband Bill, thirty-one, who had been a student at Berry Academy, the high school connected with Berry College near Rome, Floyd County.

This story was widely circulated among the freshman class at Berry in 1962. Understand, now, that this was an all-boy school. Berry Academy is about twelve miles from the college campus. There's about an eleven-and-a-half-mile stretch of nothing but road and woods coming from the college campus which is on the main road there out of Rome.

The story goes that on rainy nights when there was a dance at the academy there was a girl who used to stand by the road several miles from the college and try to board the bus coming from the college campus to the high school campus for the dance. The story was that at least once every two years she would try to hitchhike or get on the bus there. She was alleged to have been dressed in a very beautiful evening gown, and the story was told to me that the year before I arrived at Berry she was picked up on the bus and brought to the school campus for the dance—girls were not allowed to drive cars back to the high school campus at that time.

The girl was alleged to have danced and danced with several of the more popular boys at the school and returned with these boys on the bus on the way back to the college campus—the students were allowed to ride back on the bus with their girlfriends at that time. As the story goes, just about three miles from the campus she asked the bus driver to stop—which he did—and she jumped off the bus and ran into the woods.

One of the students who had danced with her that night and was bringing her back to the college campus to catch her ride home had let her wear his varsity jacket, and he was extremely upset when she jumped off the bus and ran into the woods. He, along with several other students, chased the girl through the woods for several miles and were unable to catch her. In fact, they

followed her back to the college campus and on down the road from what we called Possum Trot—which was the original high school there at Berry. They lost her there at Possum Trot.

Several days later the student and his buddies were searching the woods trying to find the girl or his jacket—that seemed to me to be what he was more concerned about. And there's a graveyard there on the other side of Possum Trot, and the student noticed a varsity jacket on a gravestone. He went to it and it was the gravestone of a girl named Sara Smith; at that time he really didn't pay that much attention to her name.

Several weeks later they were back out at Possum Trot during one of the festivals there at the school and were talking to some of the older people who lived in the mountain area around there. And these mountain people revealed to the student that back during the 1890s or early 1900s this girl along with her family lived in that area, and that Sara Smith's family was a very proud family although extremely poor. And some good people from up in Chattanooga or either Atlanta—that was never clear—had brought several loads of clothes to these poor mountain people. Sara's family, being so proud, refused to take anything; however, after begging from Sara and her brothers and sisters—who were all blond-headed, as I remember—her parents finally agreed to allow them each to take one article of clothing from the boxes. Sara picked this evening gown which she was allegedly supposed to have been wearing at all these parties and dances that she attended.

Sara refused to wear anything except this evening gown, and after several weeks of owning it she was out in the yard during a fall storm and was struck by lightning and killed. And as the legend goes, on a stormy, thunder-showery night, Sara will come up out of her grave and go directly to the point where she catches or tries to stop the bus going to the school so she can dance in her evening gown again.

Escape from the Devil

Recorded in fall 1968 by MaryAlice Toomey from Carl Black, seventy-six, of Augusta, Richmond County. The setting of the story is Gibson, Glascock County.

My grandfather loved dancing, and he'd get on a horse and go for ten an' fifteen miles to a dance. And he drank a little bit, he said. An' so he stopped that night before he got to where he was supposed to go, because there was a house lit up and they was callin' the sets of dancing an' the music and everything. An' he just hitched his horse to a limb, an' when he walked up on the doorsteps all the lights went out and all the music stopped! He stood there for a second, and nobody made no fuss nor nothin'. He turned around an' went back to his horse.

And when he went back to his horse the music come back on again, see, an' so he turned around an' went back to the house an' caught hold t' the door then to go inside an' all the music stopped, see, an' he got skittish then about it.

An' he went back to his horse an' untied the horse, an' as he untied the horse, the horse snorted two or three times. An' he jumped on the horse an' tore out back towards home. So when he come to this little creek—it was just one mile from home—the horse snorted, an' he stopped an' looked up an' this Devil was on the side o' this tree with a fat light o' smoke comin' out of his eyes an' nose! I've heard him tell it many times, see: comin' out o' his eyes an' nose.

An' he said that to go by it he'd have to take a chance, an' he thought one time to go back around six miles further out o' the way to keep from goin' by the Devil, see. An' he said, "Naw, I'll just kick the horse in the side an' run by him," see; so he kicked his horse in the side with the spurs an' run by it, an' when he got even with it it jumped on the horse behind him an' helt to him! He said he was scared to death, just about, an' the horse was, too.

An' Grandmother heard the horse comin' an' she knew there was somethin' wrong. An' she run opened the locked gate, an' as this horse started in the locked gate it th'owed him off. If it hadn't the piece across the top o' the gate woulda hit him about his head an' nose, see. And so the horse run on in the stable, an' how the horse run in the stable an' stopped as quick as it did they don't know. But they never did know what become of the Devil. See, he was on the back o' that horse, on the back end.

And so after that he went to town and bought him a Bible the next day, an' the first page he opened had that Devil on the side of a tree just like he saw the night before, see. And from that day on he never touched a drop o' whiskey of no kind, not even wine nor nothin', see.

The Neighbor Man
Who Became a Witch

Recorded in winter 1969 by Nancy Foote from Elias Moore, fifty-seven, of Ambrose, Coffee County.

I don't know the man's name, but he was a neighbor to my father. An' he told my father that he'd made himself a witch by shootin' at the sun

Kitchen Table, Jackson County, Georgia. Doug Brown.

nine times early each mornin' for nine mornings, with a gun. An' said the ninth mornin' the sun went ta bleedin' to him, the sun was a-bleedin' blood.

An' said he never could play a musical instrument—this man couldn't—until that day. An' said he went by a little ol' empty house, said there was the most people there he had ever seen; said he knowed no one lived there. Said he stopped there. Wadn't no cars or anything; people rode horses an' mules. Most prettiest music! Said he went in an' some o' 'em told him he played the fiddle. [He] told 'em, "I never could play anything."

Others said, "Yes, you can." He wadn't acquainted with the people, you see, but [they] said, "Yes, you can play."

Said he picked up a fiddle; said he could play anything he wanted to!

My father was old when I was born; he must have been fifty-six or -eight years old when I was born. An' some of the stepchildren that were older than I were, they told that this man would come over to the house—Daddy's house—an' say, "Well, come an' spend the night with me."

"I can't; I'm busy."

"Well, you won't sleep much tonight."

An' after they go to bed, said the doors would rattle; the doors would open. Said their stepmother woke up one night an' a small cow was standing there, buttin' the cover off of her!

Said he [the witch neighbor] could take a pail an' go out to milk the cows, an' come back; instead of milk, he'd have a pail full of butter! He'd turn it to butter while he was coming back to the house.

An' he could stand by the fence around the yard an' just call up a bunch of hogs inside the yard, out of nowhere!

Married to a Witch

Recorded in spring 1976 by Ray Edwards from James Kemp, in his sixties, of Rosalie, Jackson County, Alabama.

Well, this is an ol' story my grandmother useta tell me: story 'bout a witch. My grandmother useta tell me this story when somebody was havin' marriage problems; you know, when the husband and wife weren't gettin' on together.

One time this country fella got married, and he married a witch. Of course, he didn't know she was a witch before he married her and didn't know it immediately thereafter. As you can perceive, this fella wasn't terribly smart, but he begin to suspect that somethin' was wrong on his honeymoon when he'd reach over to where his wife was supposed ta be and she wadn't there. Well, this went on for 'bout a week; 'bout five nights in a row he'd reach over there to touch his wife and she wadn't there. Well, this kinda disturbed 'im as you can imagine, especially on his honeymoon.

Well, his sister was kinda the bright one in the family, so this ol' fella goes to his sister and explains the situation to her. He tells his sister how, on his honeymoon, he reached over ta find his wife and she wadn't there; and he asked his sister if it was supposed ta be that way on his honeymoon.

And his sister said, "No, that's not how it's supposed ta be; your wife is supposed ta be there." The sister said, "Somethin' is wrong, and you gonna have to find out what it is." She said, "Tonight when you go ta bed you jes' pretend like you goin' ta sleep; don't really go ta sleep, jest kinda make out like ya goin' ta sleep, and close one eye and keep the other eye open watchin' her and see what happens."

So, this ol' fella did. He gets in bed and turns out the light and makes like he falls immediately asleep, but of course he's got this one eye open, watchin'. Well, a couple hours later, close to midnight, the wife gets outta bed and looks over to her husband. She sees or believes that his eyes are closed, so she walks over ta the corner and takes off her skin and leaves it layin' over in the corner. And then, she flies out the winder ta meet up with another witch.

Well, this ol' fella, he's kinda disturbed at all these happenin's, so he lays awake an' concerns himself with what's goin' ta happen. Well, 'bout dawn he gets back in bed, 'cause he knows his wife's gotta come back in the mornin' and she's goin' ta know that he suspects. So he gets back in bed and closes his eyes, and, sure 'nough, in comes the witch—zip—went right through the winderpane, didn't even raise the winder sash. She went over ta the corner and says, "Skin, get back on me," and the skin went "zip," slipped back over her, and she got back in bed.

Well, later on that day this ol' fella goes back over ta see his sister again. His sister says, "Yep, you've done married a witch."

The fella said, "What am I gonna do 'bout it?"

Sister says, "Well, I'll tell you what you can do; you can do a number of things." She said, "A lot of people are troubled 'bout witches; you proba- bly have been yourself in the past and jest didn't know it."

This ol' fella's not havin' any of this. He said, "No, I ain't never been troubled by any witch before."

His sister says, "Aw, I bet you have." She said, "Have ya ever woke up at night all sweating?"

The fella says, "Yeah!"

The sister says, "Well, a witch has been ridin'

ya. And when ya have nightmares witches are ridin' ya. And they don't just ride people; they ride animals too. Have ya ever gone out ta the pasture ta catch your horse in the mornin' and find his mane all done up in knots?" She said, "Well, that's an indication that a witch is been ridin' the horse all night." She said, "Now, I've never been troubled with those things 'cause I got a solution, and I'm gonna tell ya how ya can get your solution too." She said, "I put a sieve under my bed. One thing 'bout witches, when they come to ride you they've got to go in and out all those holes." She said, "Of course, some people put a Bible under the bed, 'cause a witch is gotta read every chapter in the Bible before they can ride ya."

Ol' fella said, "Well, look, I'm not concerned 'bout her ridin' me; that's not been the problem. The problem is that I don't want ta be married to her. I don't want ta be married ta no witch."

The sister says, "Okay, we can take care of that, too. What you want ta do is tonight, when she goes out and she takes her skin off and lays it in the corner, what you want to do is take some salt and pepper and sprinkle all over that skin. And when she comes in, she'll have trouble gettin' her skin on."

So, that night when the wife got up, jumped out of her skin and flew out of the winder, the ol' fella got up and sprinkled salt and pepper all over that skin inside and outside. Along toward dawn—now, he was awake and he was watchin' all of this 'cause he was interested in seein' what was goin' to happen—along toward dawn the witch comes back in through the winder—zip— and said, "Skin, get on me." The skin didn't move, jest laid there in a heap. So, she repeated her request: "Skin, get on me." The skin didn't move. So she reached down and picked up the skin and started puttin' it on, but it was very difficult to get on because it wasn't helpin' her at all; it was kinda like puttin' on wet clothes, if you ever tried that. She finally got it on, but, boy, how it was itchin' her, and she was scratchin', and she couldn't stand that so she took the skin off again and flew out the winder. And that was the last the fella ever saw of his wife who was a witch.

Did you ever hear that story before? That's an ol' one.

The Witch Mother

Recorded in fall 1969 by Cheryl Parks from Leola Newton, in her late fifties, of Ellijay, Gilmer County.

Well, this here boy, he 'as good. He had a wife and a baby. And his mother'd been a-goin' out on Wednesday nights, and he didn't know whar she was goin', and he got mistrusted that she was goin' to see witches somewhar. Said he knowed whar thar was an old house whar thar'd been witches havin' dances thar. And so this here boy said he was gonna go and find out if his mother wadn't a witch.

And he went and he clum up in this old house, up in the loft. Well, said he laid down up thar and said they went to comin' in, the witches did, jus' a-dancin' and a-goin' on; and they was a-havin' a meetin'. And said directly in come his old mother. And these here old witches was gettin' on to her 'cause she hadn't done no meanness. And she told 'em that if they'd let her off without punishin' her that night, that the next day when her boy's wife was gonna wash, she'd turn herself into an old sow—an old pig, see— and she'd turn the cradle over and eat the baby, tear the baby up. And said that he went, then.

And that night—he never told his wife nothin' about this—he went and sharpened him a butcher knife and he laid out of work the next mornin', and never let her know nothin' about it. Said his wife went out to wash. The old woman she took off up the hill, and he went and hid behind the cradle with this butcher knife. And said that directly here his mother come down the hill jus' like an old sow. Said she run in thar and rared up on that cradle to turn it over, and he jumped up with the butcher knife and he come down on her foot and cut one of 'em off. And said when he cut her foot off, thar was his mother standin' thar and had her foot cut off!

Getting Rid of a Witch

Written in winter 1967 by Linda Plott, a student at Towns County High School, Hiawassee; collected by Michael Moss.

There was once a witch with the name of Vandiver. She was very wicked, and for no reason at all she bewitched a lady by the name of Mrs. Souther, who got very sick and was on her death bed.

Mr. Souther got a witch doctor and brought him to his wife to see if he could help her. The witch doctor told Mr. Souther that in a few days she would be well again. But to be careful not to let the witch have anything from their home. Well, Mr. Souther thought he meant only until his wife got better, so until she was well again he was very careful to watch everything.

One day about three or four months later Mr. and Mrs. Souther were both out, and the daughter of the witch slipped in and stole some tobacco from the mantel above the fireplace. And the wife got sick again. No one could help her, and she finally died. The witch doctor told Mr. Souther that the girl had stole the tobacco and this was why his wife had died.

This made Mr. Souther very mad, so he painted a picture of the old witch, took it and hung it on a tree, and shot her through the heart with a silver bullet. At that instant the witch fell dead.

The people wouldn't let anyone dress her for her burial, because they knew the bullet was there and they were afraid that something might happen to them if they touched it. So they just put her in a box and then in a hole in the ground and covered it up.

The Battle of the Walking Sticks

Recorded in spring 1976 by Gordon Matthews from Mary Adams, sixty-three, of Savannah, Chatham County, who was reared at Bellinger Hill on the South Carolina coast, where this story is set.

This is true. I didn't see it, but it happened, I think, before we moved over there. There was a middle-aged colored woman and she had a little store, and people usually gathered around; and it was just a little dirt road then, just oxen and carts, or maybe a mule or a horse and buggy'd go by once in a while.

So one day there was two colored men having a terrible argument about something which didn't amount to much, but they each had a cane, and they were pointing the canes at each other and were just about to fight. And another man that was an acclaimed, so-called witch doctor came along, and he said, "Let's don't argue this"; says, "I know how to settle a quarrel."

So they said, "Well, how? Tell us how."

And he said, "Well, give me your walking sticks." So they gave him the two walking sticks, and he walked out into the middle of the sandy road and he stood them up, and told them to watch now. And so he backed off from the two sticks, and they stood there without anything holding them, and they fought—the sticks fought! That is telekinesis, I understand, in modern ESP language. And so the two sticks fought, and one of them beat the other one down, and the winning stick laid on top of the other one.

So he went over then and picked up the stick that won the fight and gave it to the man that it belonged to, and he said, "You are the winner. You won the argument."

And so several people told us that they saw it happen, about three-quarters of a mile from where we lived.

HISTORICAL

How Talking Rock Got Its Name

Recorded in spring 1974 by Louellen Wright from Tom Quinton, forty-three, of Talking Rock, Pickens County.

The funny theory about it is, that when the white settlers came in, there 'as a huge boulder where Talking Rock is now. And carved on this boulder was, "Turn me over." And it was so huge that no one man could do it, so they had to get a bunch together. And after they got this bunch together, they used poles, you know, and everything, and they turned it over. And on the other side it said, "Now turn me back and let me fool somebody else." [Laughs]

This rock has never been found, but this is what we were always told when we were growin' up, that there had been a rock there.

How The Rock Got Its Name

Written in fall 1985 by James Few, a black college student in Atlanta whose family is from Barnesville, Lamar County.

My paternal family lived in a community that was rich in historical sites. One of the most interesting is The Rock, Georgia. This village received its name from a very large rock found in the middle of the area. My great-grandfather and his friends told a very interesting story about this particular rock.

It is said that the slaves used this rock as a hiding place for a book that was shared secretly by them. They also hid notes that they had written to each other. This story states that the slave masters did not allow the slaves or their children to learn to read and write, but many of them did learn. They had a book that was passed from one to another. When one person had completed the use of the book, it was hidden by the rock for another slave. This plan was discovered when the slaves began to say to each other, "Look by the r-o-c-k and find the b-o-o-k." According to stories told by former slaves, this is how the village apparently got its name.

How Pobiddy Got Its Name

Recorded in spring 1975 by Dorothy Moye from Sam Bulloch, sixty, of Manchester, Meriwether County.

I was down in Talbot County, the adjacent county to our county of Meriwether. On U.S. 80 between Talbotton and Thomaston, there's a little crossroads store there and a community that's now known as Pobiddy. And it has been placed on the Georgia map as Pobiddy.

And the way this was told to me at that time was that this community got its name from the fact that back in the late twenties or early thirties —depression days—that a Royal Crown Cola salesman stopped his T-model Ford truck in front of this store and got out. And as you know, a little chick is not only known by "little chick," but also by "biddy." And in front of this store was a little biddy walking around that had shed its baby feathers and had never put on its other feathers, and it was very cold out there. And this Royal Crown salesman wanted the proprietor to let the chicken into the store where it wouldn't freeze, and the proprietor wouldn't agree to it. And the RC salesman made the remark, said, "Po' biddy."

And from that time on that community has been known as Pobiddy, and it has gone far enough to be carried on the map of Georgia now.

How Resaca Got Its Name

Recorded in spring 1975 by Dorothy Moye from Sam Bulloch, sixty, of Manchester, Meriwether County.

I've heard a lot of stories in my life by old people talking, but one of the things that has stuck with me the best is a story that I heard when I was traveling around with former Governor Marvin Griffin, and he was campaigning for governor. We stopped at a little town in north Georgia [Gordon County], at a store there, and was shaking hands with people. And the name of the place was Resaca. And it intrigued me where they could find a name like Resaca. So I asked the owner of this store how they came up with such a name.

And he said, "Well, the story goes that an old Indian chief that lived in this area, before the white people came in here, wanted him a young bride. So he sent his braves out to another tribe to kidnap one from the other tribe. And they brought her back. And they had stole her from the other tribe and put her in a sack and brought her back. And they sat her down in front of the old chief and pulled the sack down around her. And he looked at her and shook his head and he said, 'Resack 'er, resack 'er, resack 'er!'"

So that's where the name of Resaca, Georgia, came from, according to the old hand-me-down story.

that the girl had never lived in. And anyway, they told her when they built their cabin that panthers roamed that area. And the first year they didn't take in too much land, because of course they didn't have the tools they do now to clear with; but they had a good-sized field. And they told the girl if she ever heard a noise like a woman screaming that it would be a panther, and to pull off her clothes one piece at a time and run as hard as she could, because the panther would stop and tear whatever you put down to shreds.

And said one day she used that knowledge to very great advantage. Said she took some water down to her husband in the field, and when she got about halfway home she heard this scream and she knew it was a panther. So she had on a big bonnet. She pulled that off first and threw it down, and she ran a little further and pulled off a jacket that she had, and then she pulled off an apron, and she pulled off her skirt, and then her blouse, running just as hard as she could.

Said when she got home she was stark naked, but she beat the panther and saved her life. And she did get to see him, and he was a giant of an animal.

The Panther

Recorded in spring 1974 by Carol Ann Turner from her mother, Yvonne White Turner. The setting of the story is the Florida Panhandle.

Years ago, people would settle on what they called a section. Now, I don't even know how big that is; but anyway, it was probably over two or three hundred acres. And there was a young couple married and settled in a part of the country

The Yankee Lieutenant

Recorded in fall 1971 by Diane Toni from Robert Tomlin, sixty, of Atlanta, who was reared in Gainesville, Hall County.

Grandma tol' me when I was real young that she and her sister was out digging dirt [from the smokehouse floor] to boil it to get salt out of it, 'cause thar wasn't no salt; and that's the way they

Bureau of Memories. Jack Leigh.

used to get it in those days, during the time of the Civil War—right in the middle of it.

Well, the two of them heard a Yankee troop of soldiers a-ridin' up to the house, and both Grandma and her sister run to the house and tried to bolt the door. The menfolk had gone off to fight them, see. Well, she said she was scared to death, 'cause they could hear the bastards ridin' up closer an' closer. Well, lo and behold they got to the door and like-near busted it down, and Grandma got scared. So she went to answer the door to keep 'em from bustin' it in.

Well, she said, thar was this here Yankee lieutenant starin' at her, and she said she almost passed out, and her sister hid behind the door, see. Well, he asked her where the menfolk was, and Grandma jes' looked at him and said, "Out fightin' you bastards!"

Well, she said he looked at her and reached into his pocket, and Grandma said she thought he was gonna pull a gun on her. Well, lo and behold he pulls out this here big red apple and gave it to her, and then the troop rode off. She said her and her sister laughed and cried at the same time, 'cause they was so scared, but boy was they glad they didn't get killed.

Yeah, Grandma remembered that and told us over and over again. I thought you might enjoy that!

The Yankee Soldiers and the Baby

Recorded in fall 1978 by David Brogdon from Retha Payne, twenty-six, a resident of Atlanta who was reared at Piedmont, Alabama.

My great-grandfather told my grandmother something that happened back during the Civil War. A lady he knew that lived down the road from them was in her cabin with her baby, and some Yankee soldiers came riding up. She started to hide [in the loft], and she didn't have time to hide the baby. She figured that the soldiers wouldn't bother the baby, so she left it down there.

And she could hear them; and she heard the baby laughing, and after a little while she heard it crying, and then it didn't make any sounds at all and she could hear it kicking.

So when the soldiers left she came out of her hiding place. And they had been throwing the baby up, and that was causing it to laugh; and one of them had taken a bayonet and stuck it through the baby and pinned it to the ceiling, and the baby was kicking the ceiling as it was dying. And that's what she heard, the kicking.

Inn of the Nine Murders

Recorded in spring 1975 by Donna Manth from Lurline Howington, seventy-three, of Macon, Bibb County.

My great-grandmother lost her husband, and he owned some land in another county. They had several children, and she had to go on horseback to this county to sell some land. So, dark overtook her on her way back home. So she stopped at a little inn on the road and asked if they had a room for the night, and they said yes. So they asked her would she like to eat and she said no, that she had a lunch with her. And she was very tired and would like to get on to bed, and left the time for them to wake her the next morning.

So, she heard a noise in the night. And she got up, and there was a cloth draped over the mantel. So she raised the cloth and looked through into the next room; there was a knothole that she could see through. So she saw them take this dead man and turn his pockets wrong side out; they had him on the bed. And when they robbed him they took his watch and his money. And they wrapped him in a sheet and put him up under the bed. So she became very frightened, and she just put her clothes on and got back into the bed. So she said someone turned the doorknob three times in the night, very easily. Of course they couldn't get in, because she had it locked from the inside.

They knocked on the door the next morning and told her it was time for her to get up. So she did, and they asked her would she like breakfast. And she said, "No, because I'd like to get back to my children. Some of them are small and I need to get back as quick as possible." And she was afraid that they might poison her. So she said, "Just get my horse and saddle the horse, and I'll be ready." And she paid her room rent and left.

So about three miles down the road there was a man that overtook her. He was also on horseback. And he said, "Good morning. What is bringing you out so early in the morning?"

She said, "My husband died and I had to go over to a certain county and sell some land I had over there. And dark caught me on the way back, so I stopped over at the inn and spent the night."

He said, "Did you have a good night's sleep?"

She said, "Yes, I didn't know a thing from the time I hit the bed until I was called this morning."

And so he grazed his horse over to the side and bid her good day. And so she said she turned back and saw that he was still grazing the horse on the side of the road.

So about three more miles down the road, another man overtook her and asked her practically the same questions. And she answered him the same way.

And so when she arrived at the next town she notified the marshal. So they went out to the inn and they searched the place. And way out on the land they found nine bodies in a well, wrapped in sheets, where they had robbed them and murdered them.

So they would have gotten her, I suppose, with poison or some way, you know, if she had eaten; or maybe because she was a woman they didn't take her, 'cause they [the corpses] were all men.

The Cannibal Couple

Recorded in fall 1967 by Claudia Wells from Suzie Petty, fifty-five, of Atlanta. She was reared on a farm near Adamsville (formerly Lickskillet), Fulton County (now incorporated into west Atlanta).

When I was a little girl, my mother used to tell us stories. She told me one time about her grandmother, her mother, and her great-grandmother having to travel for miles and miles and miles from one "country" to the other, because they were trying to get to Atlanter. My grandfather and my mother's grandfather had died, and they just traveled and traveled.

So, one night they stopped at this farmhouse, and they asked could they work, you know, so that they could get food and travel on the next day. And said they stayed there that night, and got food fer to go on to the next li'l farm.

Said when they went to the next farm it took 'em days and days to get there, because houses wadn't close together. She said she got to the farmhouse an' she knocked on the door, an' said a man came to the door, and she asked could they spend the night. And they told her to come on in. Well, she went on in, and Great-great-grandmother and Great-grandmother all went on in. Said she set down; the old lady was cookin' supper, said she had collards. And said Grandmother had a little apron on; and said she was eatin' away on them collards, and said she found a forefinger in the collards! Said she didn't say nothing to nobody; said she just raked it out in her lap, and wrapped it up in a little handkerchief she had, and stuck it in her apron pocket.

So the man and woman got ready to go to bed, and said when they went to bed there were two teenage boys there who stayed to wash the dishes. The two teenage boys told 'em, "Don't y'all stay here tonight"; say; "they'll kill y'all like they did our mother and daddy, and salt ye down like hogs!"

So the grandmother and them got so scared; they told the two boys, said, "Well, we'll hitch up and we'll leave, and we'll take you with us." And they was afraid, you know, that they make enough noise to get the people up; so they slipped out and went on to get the mule and wagon, and they drove on off.

They rode for days and days and got to the next farmhouse, but the next farmhouse was a sheriff—he lived there. And on that plantation it was four or five houses, you know, that the farmers lived on. So, Grandma she walked up

and knocked on the door, and the man came to the door. She was kindly scared then, but when he told her that he was a sheriff she wadn't scared anymore. So she said that Great-grandmother an' all of 'em got out of the wagon, and they told the man what had happened. And the little boys told about them killing their mother and their daddy, and they had 'em down in the basement, salted down; just had a lot of people down there, salted down like hogs.

And said that he had a horn—they called it bugles back then—and he blowed it, and when he blowed that bugle the men and women knew some'in' was wrong and they all came, and they got on mules. They went and took Grandma and the two boys and all of 'em back to the farm where they had come from, and the old lady and the old man was there. When they went to searchin', they found all these bodies where they had salted 'em down and put 'em in the basement. They found even little babies; they had killed little babies and salted them down. They said that was the "young meat," and when they killed old people they called it "old meat," see.

And she said that when they found all that, this woman and man tried to get away, but they couldn't get away because it was so many there. And they caught 'em and they tied 'em up, and then they tarred and feathered 'em, and took 'em to a stake, and burnt 'em, just set fire to 'em. Back then, they did that.

And that was it. They come to Atlanter, where they had started.

Notes

Notes for the tales are intended not to be bibliographically exhaustive but to place the stories within a framework of folk-narrative scholarship by referring both to the major reference tools of the field and to published examples from the region. Citing other reports helps to establish a tale's folkness (i.e., is evidence of its oral circulation), but the lack of such reports (or the failure to discover them) is not proof of the tale's nontraditionality. Unless otherwise indicated, the motif numbers refer to Stith Thompson's six-volume *Motif-Index of Folk-Literature,* a catalog of international narrative building blocks especially useful for legend and myth research; type numbers refer to Antti Aarne and Stith Thompson's *The Types of the Folktale,* a one-volume compendium of plots and supporting bibliographic references for folktales collected mainly in the Indo-European culture area. Ernest Baughman's *Type and Motif Index of the Folktales of England and North America* is a valuable research tool for narratives of the English-speaking world.

Introduction

1. Theodor H. Gaster, *The Oldest Stories in the World* (New York: Viking Press, 1952).

2. H. Munro and Nora K. Chadwick, *The Growth of Literature,* 3 vols. (1940; reprint, Cambridge: Cambridge University Press, 1968).

3. Walter J. Ong, *Orality and Literacy: The Technologizing of the Word* (New York: Methuen, 1982).

4. Stella Brewer Brookes, *Joel Chandler Harris—Folklorist* (Athens: University of Georgia Press, 1950); Florence E. Baer, *Sources and Analogues of the Uncle Remus Tales,* Folklore Fellows Communications, no. 228 (Helsinki: Academia Scientiarum Fennica, 1980); John A. Burrison, *"The Golden Arm": The Folktale and Its Literary Use by Mark Twain and Joel C. Harris,* Arts and Sciences Research Papers, no. 19 (Atlanta: Georgia State University, 1968); Bernard De Voto, *Mark Twain's America* (Cambridge, Mass.: Houghton Mifflin Co., 1932); Kenneth S. Lynn, *Mark Twain and Southwestern Humor* (Boston: Little, Brown & Co., 1959); Thomas L. McHaney, "What Faulkner Learned from the Tall Tale," in *Faulkner and Humor,* ed. Doreen Fowler and Ann J. Abadie (Jackson: University Press of Mississippi, 1986), pp. 110–35. See also Paula H. Anderson-Green, "Folklore and Fiction in Nineteenth-Century North Carolina: Taliaferro's *Fisher's River* and Chesnutt's *The Conjure Woman*" (Ph.D. diss., Georgia State University, 1980), and, for further references, Steven Swann Jones, *Folklore and Literature in the United States: An Annotated Bibliography of Studies of Folklore in American Literature,* Garland Folklore Bibliographies, vol. 5 (New York: Garland Publishing, 1984).

5. Baer, *Sources and Analogues.*

6. SHE FLUNKED THE FIDELITY TEST. Vance Randolph, *Who Blew Up the Church House and Other Ozark Folk Tales* (New York: Columbia University Press, 1952), pp. 11–13; G. Legman, *No Laughing Matter: An Analysis of Sexual Humor,* 2 vols. (1968 and 1975; reprint, Bloomington: Indiana University Press, 1982), 1:409–10; cf. motifs H466.1, J1142.3, K1550.1.1, and

Ronald L. Baker, *Jokelore: Humorous Folktales from Indiana* (Bloomington: Indiana University Press, 1986), no. 55, p. 29.

7. Wayland D. Hand, ed., *American Folk Legend: A Symposium* (Berkeley and Los Angeles: University of California Press, 1971).

8. Jan Harold Brunvand, *The Vanishing Hitchhiker: American Urban Legends and Their Meanings* (New York: W. W. Norton & Co., 1981); idem, *The Choking Doberman and Other "New" Urban Legends* (New York: W. W. Norton & Co., 1984); idem, *The Mexican Pet: More "New" Urban Legends and Some Old Favorites* (New York: W. W. Norton & Co., 1986).

9. THREE WHITE ANGELS. Motifs V235, V234, V245, V522.

10. A DEVILISH STATE OF MIND. Motif J1785. Cf. Mariella Glenn Hartsfield, *Tall Betsy and Dunce Baby: South Georgia Folktales* (Athens: University of Georgia Press, 1987), no. 22, pp. 91–92.

11. John Greenway, *Literature among the Primitives* (Hatboro, Pa.: Folklore Associates, 1964), p. 40.

12. CREEK ORIGIN MYTH. Motif A1631. Albert S. Gatschet, *A Migration Legend of the Creek Indians,* Brinton's Library of Aboriginal American Literature, vol. 4 (Philadelphia: D. G. Brinton, 1884), pp. 244–45.

13. GIVING CREDIT WHERE IT'S DUE. From the Atlanta *Constitution,* 29 August 1938, p. 4. Motif J1260. Vance Randolph, *Hot Springs and Hell and Other Folk Jests and Anecdotes from the Ozarks* (Hatboro, Pa.: Folklore Associates, 1965), no. 236, p. 84; J. Mason Brewer, *The Word on the Brazos: Negro Preacher Tales from the Brazos Bottoms of Texas* (Austin: University of Texas Press, 1953), pp. 9–10; cf. Legman, *No Laughing Matter,* 2:948. For the interaction of oral and printed tale-texts, see Richard M. Dorson, "Print and American Folk Tales," *California Folklore Quarterly* 28 (1964): 251–65, and, for a southern case study, Gary Holloway, "The Form and Function of Church of Christ Preacher Anecdotes" (Ph.D. diss., Emory University, 1987).

14. Elizabeth C. Fine, *The Folklore Text: From Performance to Print* (Bloomington: Indiana University Press, 1984); Henry Glassie, *Irish Folk History: Texts from the North* (Philadelphia: University of Pennsylvania Press, 1982).

15. Richard M. Dorson, "Oral Styles of American Folk Narrators," in *Style in Language,* ed. Thomas A. Sebeok (New York: John Wiley & Sons, 1960), pp. 27–51, is suggestive; see also Hartsfield, *Tall Betsy,* appendix 2, "The Oral Style of Two Narrators," pp. 168–74.

16. Recent examples are Michael Doherty of Donegal, "The Girl Too Smart for the Fiddler," *Songs of Courtship,* The Folksongs of Britain, vol. 1, Caedmon Record TC 1142, band B5; *"Says I, Says He,"* a play of the late 1970s by Ron Hutchison of Northern Ireland. Patricia Jones-Jackson, *When Roots Die: Endangered Traditions on the Sea Islands* (Athens: University of Georgia Press, 1987), pp. 142–43, notes West African parallels for *say* as an introductory verb.

17. Richard M. Dorson, *American Negro Folktales* (Greenwich, Conn.: Fawcett Publications, 1967), pp. 91, 98, 99, 111; Elsie Clews Parsons, *Folk-lore of the Sea Islands, South Carolina,* Memoirs, vol. 16 (Cambridge, Mass.: American Folklore Society, 1923), pp. 42, 43, 49, 73, 83, 94, 98, 138, 146, 147. For a wider range of formulas see Roger D. Abrahams, ed., *Afro-American Folktales: Stories from Black Tradition in the New World* (New York: Pantheon Books, 1985).

18. Hartsfield, *Tall Betsy,* p. 172.

19. Richard Bauman, *Verbal Art as Performance* (Prospect Heights, Ill.: Waveland Press, 1984).

20. Thomas H. English, ed., *Mark Twain to Uncle Remus, 1881–1885,* Sources and Reprints, ser. 7, no. 3 (Atlanta: Emory University Publications, 1953), p. 11; quoted in Burrison, *"The Golden Arm,"* p. 14.

21. EVERYTHING'S BIG IN ATLANTA. Motif J1772. Baker, *Jokelore,* no. 253, pp. 146–47, gives the usual "Everything's Big in Texas."

22. THE WITCHES' DANCE. Baughman motifs G242.7(g), G247, G242.7(d). B. A. Botkin, ed., *A Treasury of Southern Folklore* (New York: Crown Publishers, 1949), pp. 543–47; Richard Chase, *American*

Folk Tales and Songs (New York: Signet Key–New American Library, 1956), pp. 64–70; Leonard Roberts, *Old Greasybeard: Tales from the Cumberland Gap* (Detroit: Folklore Associates–Gale Research, 1969), no. 34, pp. 133–35. A third version by Conner, told in the third person, appears in Eliot Wigginton, ed., *Foxfire Two* (Garden City, N.Y.: Anchor Press–Doubleday, 1973), pp. 354–55.

23. Richard Bauman, *Story, Performance, and Event: Contextual Studies of Oral Narrative,* Cambridge Studies in Oral and Literate Culture, vol. 10 (Cambridge: Cambridge University Press, 1986), ch. 5.

24. Kenneth S. Goldstein, *A Guide for Fieldworkers in Folklore,* Memoirs of the American Folklore Society, vol. 52 (Hatboro, Pa.: Folklore Associates, 1964), chs. 6 and 7. For contextual treatments of southern storytelling, see Jones-Jackson, *When Roots Die,* pp. 99–110; Ray B. Browne, *A Night with the Hants and Other Alabama Folk Experiences* (Bowling Green, Ohio: Bowling Green University Popular Press, 1976), pp. 1–78; and Zora Neale Hurston, *Mules and Men* (1935; reprint, New York: Harper & Row, 1970).

25. James S. Lamar, *Recollections of Pioneer Days in Georgia* (n.p., n.d. [probably Augusta, ca. 1900]), pp. 18–19.

26. Harden E. Taliaferro [Skitt, pseud.], *Fisher's River (North Carolina) Scenes and Characters* (1859; reprint, New York: Arno Press, 1977), pp. 141, 148–49.

27. Hartsfield, *Tall Betsy,* pp. 31–34, 36–38, 41.

28. Caleb A. Ridley, *The Southern Mountaineer* (Atlanta: Privately printed, [ca. 1900]), pp. 82, 85–86. For the traditionality of the tales quoted, see Randolph, *Hot Springs and Hell,* no. 317, pp. 113, 241–42.

29. THE TOBACCO THIEF AND THE VOICES. Baughman motif J1811.5*(d). Hartsfield, *Tall Betsy,* no. 24, pp. 93–94.

30. THE TRESTLE GHOST. Motifs E422.1.1, E272.3, E545.12.

31. Joel Chandler Harris, *Nights with Uncle Remus: Myths and Legends of the Old Plantation* (Boston: Ticknor & Co., 1883), pp. xii–xiv.

32. LAY THERE, YOU'VE SLAYED MANY. Cf. Frank Hoffmann, *Analytical Survey of Anglo-American Traditional Erotica* (Bowling Green, Ohio: Bowling Green University Popular Press, 1973), type 1369, "The Lazy Husband Cured."

33. Robert Hellman and Richard O'Gorman, trans. and eds., *Fabliaux: Ribald Tales from the Old French* (New York: Thomas Y. Crowell Co.–Apollo, 1966), pp. 59–66.

34. Ibid., p. 184.

Chapter One. Four Storytellers of Cedartown, West Georgia

BILLY BOBTAIL. Type 130, "The Animals in Night Quarters (Bremen City Musicians)." Richard Chase, *The Jack Tales* (Cambridge, Mass.: Riverside Press–Houghton Mifflin Co., 1943), no. 4, pp. 40–46; Charles L. Perdue, Jr., ed., *Outwitting the Devil: Jack Tales from Wise County, Virginia* (Santa Fe, N.M.: Ancient City Press, 1987), no. 11, pp. 57–59; Leonard W. Roberts, *South from Hell-fer-Sartin: Kentucky Mountain Folk Tales* (Berea, Ky.: Council of the Southern Mountains, 1964), no. 1, pp. 14–15; idem, *Old Greasybeard: Tales from the Cumberland Gap* (Detroit: Folklore Associates–Gale Research, 1969), no. 2, pp.

28–32; Richard M. Dorson, *American Negro Folktales* (Greenwich, Conn.: Fawcett Publications, 1967), no. 215, pp. 350–51; Ralph S. Boggs, "North Carolina White Folktales and Riddles," *Journal of American Folklore* 47 (1934): 294 (no. 7); Arthur Huff Fauset, "Negro Folk Tales from the South (Alabama, Mississippi, Louisiana)," *Journal of American Folklore* 40 (1927): 258.

THE THREE FOOLISH BEARS. An unusual animal version of type 1384, "The Husband Hunts Three Persons As Stupid As His Wife." Cf. "The Foolish Bride" in this collection.

THE CAT, THE MONKEY, AND THE CHESTNUTS. Cf. motif K171.9.

GOING TO SQUEETUM'S HOUSE. Elsie Clews Parsons, "Folklore from Aiken, South Carolina," *Journal of American Folklore* 34 (1921): 21 (no. 25); cf. motif K526.

DRAKESBILL. Type 513A, "Six Go Through the Whole World." This tale has seldom been reported in English; the nonhuman protagonist makes this text even rarer.

THE COW GOING DOWN IN THE MUD. Type 1004, "Hogs in the Mud; Sheep in the Air"; motif K404.1. Cf. "Brother Rabbit, Brother Lion, and the Cow" in this collection for the Afro-American tradition. Betsy Ostrander recently discovered that her grandmother had learned this tale from her husband, Ira Casey, who learned it, in turn, from his uncle, Thomas Henry Casey.

THE UNTIDY GIRL. Types 1458, "The Girl Who Ate So Little," and 1462, "Clean and Tidy." Mariella Glenn Hartsfield, *Tall Betsy and Dunce Baby: South Georgia Folktales* (Athens: University of Georgia Press, 1987), no. 19, p. 87.

DIVIDING THE CORN. Type 1791, "The Sexton Carries the Parson." Known in medieval and Renaissance England with a Latin text dating to A.D. 593, this has been one of the most popular old imported tales in the South. Hartsfield, *Tall Betsy*, no. 28, pp. 103–6; Boggs, "North Carolina," no. 40, pp. 311–12; Ray B. Browne, *A Night with the Hants and Other Alabama Folk Experiences* (Bowling Green, Ohio: Bowling Green University Popular Press, 1976), pp. 172–73; W. K. McNeil, ed., *Ghost Stories from the American South* (Little Rock, Ark.: August House, 1985), no. 81, pp. 129–30; William Lynwood Montell, *Ghosts along the Cumberland: Deathlore in the Kentucky Foothills* (Knoxville: University of Tennessee Press, 1975), nos. 429–31, pp. 186–87; Vance Randolph, *Who Blowed Up the Church House and Other Ozark Folk Tales* (New York: Columbia University Press, 1952), pp. 83–84; Ronald L. Baker, *Jokelore: Humorous Folktales from Indiana* (Bloomington: Indiana University Press, 1986),

no. 218, p. 131. Cf. "Dividing the Walnuts" and "The Devil and the Lord Dividing Souls" in this collection.

THE CORNMEAL. Cf. type 1526A, "Supper Won by a Trick."

TYING THE COW'S TAIL TO THE BOOTSTRAP. Baughman type 1849*, "The Priest on the Cow's Tail." B. A. Botkin, ed., *A Treasury of American Folklore* (New York: Crown Publishers, 1944), p. 385. Botkin's popular miscellany, one of the few folklore books likely to be found in nonfolklorists' libraries prior to the 1960s, was probably the source for this and several other tales told by Mrs. Casey and her daughter. They are included here to illustrate the role of material learned from print within the repertoire of some traditional storytellers.

THE LAST WORD. Type 1365B, "Cutting with the Knife or the Scissors." Hartsfield, *Tall Betsy*, no. 49, p. 125; Boggs, "North Carolina," no. 26, p. 306.

TWISTED MOUTHS. Motif X131. Botkin, *Treasury American*, pp. 457–58 (Mrs. Casey's likely source).

WHY THE RABBIT HAS A SHORT TAIL. Type 2, "The Tail-Fisher"; motif A2216.1. Dorson, *American Negro*, no. 11, pp. 89–91; Boggs, "North Carolina," no. 2, p. 291; Joel Chandler Harris, *Uncle Remus, His Songs and His Sayings*, rev. ed. (1895; reprint, New York: D. Appleton-Century Co., 1933), no. 25, pp. 120–24; Florence E. Baer, *Sources and Analogues of the Uncle Remus Tales*, Folklore Fellows Communications, no. 228 (Helsinki: Academia Scientiarum Fennica, 1980), p. 50. Cf. "The Bear's Tail" in this collection.

THE HANGING ATTIC. Cf. Vance Randolph, *Hot Springs and Hell and Other Folk Jests and Anecdotes from the Ozarks* (Hatboro, Pa.: Folklore Associates, 1965), no. 115, pp. 41–42.

THE PREACHER WHO COULDN'T READ. Langston Hughes and Arna Bontemps, eds., *The Book of Negro Folklore* (New York: Dodd, Mead & Co., 1958), pp. 78–79; Daryl Cumber Dance, *Shuckin' and Jivin': Folklore from Contemporary Black Americans* (Bloomington: Indiana University Press, 1978), no. 59, p. 44.

TURPIE AND THE HOBYAHS. Baughman motif Z21.5*. Joseph Jacobs, ed., *More English Fairy Tales* (1894; reprint, New York: Dover, 1967), no. 69, pp. 118–24. Betsy Ostrander recently confirmed that her grandmother did own a book containing this rare Scots tale, probably Jacobs or a derivative therefrom.

THE BROWNIES AND THE BOGGARTS. Baughman motif F346(a); cf. motif J1811.1. According to the *Oxford English Dictionary,* a *boggart* is a northern England dialect word meaning a goblin that haunts a particular locale. This tale is so alien to the southern tradition that it is likely derived from a printed source.

THE LADY FROM PHILADELPHIA. Motifs J2100 and J2700. This tale is derived from Lucretia P. Hale's popular children's book, *The Peterkin Papers,* first published in 1880.

THE DOVE IN THE LOFT. Type 1837, "The Parson to Let a Dove Fly in the Church." Browne, *Night with the Hants,* p. 177.

POUND CAKE. Baughman motif J1742.7*. Botkin, *Treasury American,* pp. 412–13 (Mrs. Ellis's likely source); Vance Randolph, *The Devil's Pretty Daughter and Other Ozark Folk Tales* (New York: Columbia University Press, 1955), pp. 26–28.

UNCLE BILLY PACKS HIS GUN. Motif J1262. Botkin, *Treasury American,* p. 415 (Mrs. Ellis's likely source); Vance Randolph, *Sticks in the Knapsack and Other Ozark Folk Tales* (New York: Columbia University Press, 1958), pp. 92–93.

UNCLE BILLY AND THE VISION OF THE CORN. Baughman motif K66(ca). Botkin, *Treasury American,* p. 416 (Mrs. Ellis's likely source).

LETTERS IN THE SKY. Motif. X459.1.1. Botkin, *Treasury American,* p. 416 (Mrs. Ellis's likely source); Browne, *Night with the Hants,* p. 95; Hughes and Bontemps, *Book of Negro Folklore,* pp. 139–40; J. Mason Brewer, *The Word on the Brazos: Negro Preacher Tales from the Brazos Bottoms of Texas* (Austin: University of Texas Press, 1953), pp. 69–70; Vance Randolph, *Pissing in the Snow and Other Ozark Folktales* (1976; reprint, New York: Bard–Avon Books, 1977), no. 50, pp. 134–35.

COURTING. Cf. Baughman motif J1495.4*.

THE BOY AT THE HORSE SALE. Motif K134.

ALL OF THESE ARE MINE. Type 859D, "All of These Are Mine." Botkin, *Treasury American,* p. 450 (Mrs. Ellis's likely source), reprinted from Zora Neale Hurston, *Mules and Men* (1935; reprint, New York: Harper & Row, 1970), p. 214.

THE MULE AND THE "HIGHLIFE." Randolph, *Hot Springs,* no. 323, p. 115.

ME ALL FACE. Motif J1309.1 (Baughman motif J1309.6*). Botkin, *Treasury American,* p. 415 (Mrs. Ellis's likely source); Cecily Hancock, "The 'Me All Face' Story: European Literary Background of an American Comic Indian Anecdote," *Journal of American Folklore* 76 (1963): 340–42.

THE DEACON MEETS THE BEARS. Botkin, *Treasury American,* p. 447; Browne, *Night with the Hants,* p. 94; Dance, *Shuckin',* no. 127, p. 72; Roger D. Abrahams, *Deep Down in the Jungle: Negro Narrative Folklore from the Streets of Philadelphia,* rev. ed. (Chicago: Aldine Publishing Co., 1970), pp. 203–5; Loyal Jones and Billy Edd Wheeler, *Laughter in Appalachia: A Festival of Southern Mountain Humor* (Little Rock, Ark.: August House, 1987), p. 34.

DIVIDING THE WALNUTS. See the note to "Dividing the Corn," p. 234.

THE TWO COLORED MEN AND THE PIG. Type 1525M, "Mak and the Sheep." Dorson, *American Negro,* no. 78, p. 184; Dance, *Shuckin',* no. 354, pp. 199–200.

THE HOG THAT WORE BUTTONS. Motif X800. Randolph, *Hot Springs,* no. 402, p. 142.

THE CLEVER PEDDLER AND THE RAZOR STRAPS. Cf. Baughman motifs N81(a) and K250.1*; Richard M. Dorson, *Jonathan Draws the Long Bow* (Cambridge, Mass.: Harvard University Press, 1946), p. 80.

TAKE MY COAT TO TOWN. Cf. motif J1561.3.

RESACA. Kenneth K. Krakow, *Georgia Place-names* (Macon, Ga.: Winship Press, 1975), p. 190. Cf. "How Resaca Got Its Name" in this collection.

HOW THE DRUNK GOT OUT OF THE GRAVE. Baughman motif X828*. Jones and Wheeler, *Laughter in Appalachia,* p. 69; Montell, *Ghosts along the Cumberland,* nos. 432–35, pp. 187–90; Hartsfield, *Tall Betsy,* no. 25, pp. 94–96.

THE PIG AND THE LOCAL POLITICIAN. Motif X800. Botkin, *Treasury American,* pp. 450–51 (told of Judge Patrick of the Georgia Supreme Court); Randolph, *Sticks in the Knapsack,* pp. 106–7.

EAT 'TIL YA BUST. Motif W152.13.

THE STINGY MAN AND HIS MULE. Motif W152.13.

THE WELL-TRAINED MULE. Motif K134.6.

THE SHOE SALESMAN'S BALD HEAD. Motif J1772.1.

THE LONG-WINDED EVANGELIST. Cf. Jones and Wheeler, *Laughter in Appalachia,* p. 37.

THE WINDMILL PREACHER. Cf. ibid., pp. 36–37.

DISCOURAGING WORDS. Motif X410.

TO EAT OR NOT TO EAT. Vance Randolph, *The Talking Turtle and Other Ozark Folk Tales* (New York: Columbia University Press, 1957), pp. 151–52.

THE HAUNTED HOUSE. Baughman motif J1495.3*. Botkin, *Treasury American,* pp. 712–13; Hartsfield, *Tall Betsy,* no. 1, pp. 55–57; McNeil, *Ghost Stories,* no. 84, pp. 131–32; Elsie Clews Parsons, *Folk-lore of the Sea Islands, South Carolina,* Memoirs, vol. 16 (Cambridge, Mass.: American Folklore Society, 1923), no. 62, pp. 71–73.

THE HIGH BALL. W. K. McNeil, of the Ozark Folk Center at Mountain View, Arkansas, writes, "I first heard this story about Walter Johnson (1887–1946) told by Brooke Hays, the onetime congressman from Arkansas, at graduation ceremonies at Carson-Newman College, Jefferson City, Tennessee, in 1959" (personal communication, 1988).

THE CHURCH GHOST AND THE TRAVELER. Motif J1782.6. Browne, *Night with the Hants,* pp. 181, 193–94; Newman Ivey White, gen. ed., *The Frank C. Brown Collection of North Carolina Folklore,* 7 vols. (Durham, N.C.: Duke University Press, 1952–64), 1:681.

FIDDLER'S HOLLOW. Baughman motif E402.1.3(a). Rose Thompson, *Hush, Child! Can't You Hear the Music?* (Athens: University of Georgia Press, 1982), pp. 6–7; cf. Randolph, *Talking Turtle,* pp. 27–29.

THE GOOSE AND THE GRAVE. Montell, *Ghosts along the Cumberland,* no. 437, p. 190; Browne, *Night with the Hants,* pp. 194–95; cf. Baughman motif J1782.9*.

THE FAITHFUL GUARD DOG. Type 178A, "Llewellyn and His Dog." Jan Harold Brunvand, *The Choking Doberman and Other "New" Urban Legends* (New York: W. W. Norton & Co., 1984), pp. 31–34; Jennifer Westwood, *Albion: A Guide to Legendary Britain* (Salem, N.H.: Salem House, 1985), pp. 268–70.

Chapter Two. A Joke Session by Deer Hunters in Middle Georgia

A MONKEY HUNT. Type 1336A, "Man Does Not Recognize His Own Reflection in the Water (Mirror)." Cf. "The Looking Glass" in this collection.

A POWERFUL TORNADO. Cf. Baughman motif X1611.1.15.2*(c); "Monster Winds" in this collection.

A CHILLY CORPSE? Baughman motif X828*. Vance Randolph, *Hot Springs and Hell and Other Folk Jests and Anecdotes from the Ozarks* (Hatboro, Pa.: Folklore Associates, 1965), no. 265, p. 94; Loyal Jones and Billy Edd Wheeler, *Laughter in Appalachia: A Festival of Southern Mountain Humor* (Little Rock, Ark.: August House, 1987), p. 71; W. K. McNeil, ed., *Ghost Stories from the American South* (Little Rock, Ark.: August House, 1985), no. 85, pp. 132–33; Ronald L. Baker, *Jokelore: Humorous Folktales from Indiana* (Bloomington: Indiana University Press, 1986), no. 137, p. 85.

IS IT OUT? G. Legman, *No Laughing Matter: An Analysis of Sexual Humor,* 2 vols. (1968 and 1975; reprint, Bloomington: Indiana University Press, 1982), 2:105.

AN ILL WIND. Frank Hoffmann, *Analytical Survey of Anglo-American Traditional Erotica* (Bowling Green, Ohio: Bowling Green University Popular Press, 1973), motif X716.7.1. Legman, *No Laughing Matter,* 2:976; Vance Randolph, *Pissing in the Snow and Other Ozark Folktales* (1976; reprint, New York: Bard–Avon Books, 1977), no. 77, pp. 187–88.

BITTER LUCK. Vance Randolph, *We Always Lie to*

Strangers: Tall Tales from the Ozarks (New York: Columbia University Press, 1951), p. 25; cf. motif X1280.1.1.

FISHY FOG. Baughman motif X1651.3.1*(a). Randolph, *We Always Lie,* pp. 195–96; Baker, *Jokelore,* no. 63, p. 33.

YELLOW CHALK. Cf. Legman, *No Laughing Matter,* 1:74.

A PRECOCIOUS GAMBLER. Motif J1115.1. Legman, *No Laughing Matter,* 1:107–8 and 2:178–79, 543–44; Baker, *Jokelore,* no. 140, pp. 88–89.

IN THE DARK. Legman, *No Laughing Matter,* 2:960; cf. Zora Neale Hurston, *Mules and Men* (1935; reprint, New York: Harper & Row, 1970), p. 47.

KNEW IT TASTED FUNNY. Cf. motif J1772.9. Two other versions in the Georgia Folklore Archives make it clear that the fully developed ending should be ". . . pumpkin *pie.*" One, recorded in spring 1976 by Marion Hazelwood from Carrie Hendrix, fifty-nine, of Atlanta, has a Jewish storekeeper as the pumpkin's owner; his telephone conversation is in the form of a rhyme: "Hello, Vi, this is Si; that *vas* shit in that pumpkin pie!"

NOT SO DEAR. Cf. Jones and Wheeler, *Laughter in Appalachia,* p. 86.

WHAT A DEAL. Motif X200. Another text is in the Georgia Folklore Archives.

AN UNPROFITABLE YEAR. Baughman motif N251.7. Legman, *No Laughing Matter,* 2:248; Baker, *Jokelore,* no. 335, pp. 196–97.

TOO OLD FOR BUGALOO. Cf. Legman, *No Laughing Matter,* 1:226 and 2:248; Daryl Cumber Dance, *Shuckin' and Jivin': Folklore from Contemporary Black Americans* (Bloomington: Indiana University Press, 1978), no. 235, p. 131.

Chapter Three. Two West Tennessee Family Legends

THE GHOST STORY. Baughman motif E235.3(c); motif E423.1.1.

THE CIVIL WAR STORY. Motif K622.

Chapter Four. Lloyd Arneach: Cherokee Indian Myths and Legends

HOW THE EARTH WAS FORMED. Motifs A810, A812, A961.1. James Mooney, *Myths of the Cherokee* (1900; reprint, New York: Johnson Reprint Corp., 1970), no. 1, pp. 239–40.

THE ANIMALS OBTAIN FIRE. Motifs A1415.2, A2218.3, A2356.3.4. Mooney, *Myths,* no. 2, pp. 240–42.

HOW THE MINK GOT HIS DARK COAT. Motif A2416.2; cf. motif A2411.1.2.5. Mooney, *Myths,* no. 29, p. 277.

THE POSSUM'S TAIL. Type 8A, "False Beauty-Doctor"; motif A2317.12. Mooney, *Myths,* no. 18, p. 269; cf. Zora Neale Hurston, *Mules and Men* (1935; reprint, New York: Harper & Row, 1970), pp. 138–39.

THE BEAR'S TAIL. See the note to "Why the Rabbit Has a Short Tail," p. 234, to which add motif A2378.4.2.

WHY THE DEER'S TEETH ARE BLUNT. Motifs A2326.1.1, A2326.2, A2345, A2284. Mooney, *Myths,* no. 27, pp. 276–77.

THE FIRST PEOPLE. Motifs A1270, A1351.

ORIGIN OF THE RACES. Motifs A1614, A1610.6. John R. Swanton, *Myths and Tales of the Southeastern Indians,* Bureau of American Ethnology Bulletin no. 88 (Washington, D.C.: Smithsonian Institution, 1929), p. 75 (Seminole).

THE MILKY WAY. Motif A778. Mooney, *Myths,* no. 11, p. 259; cf. J. Russell Reaver, *Florida Folktales* (Gainesville: University Presses of Florida, 1987), no. 13, p. 16.

THE RATTLESNAKE CLAN. Motif J625. Mooney, *Myths,* no. 58, pp. 305–6.

THE LITTLE PEOPLE. Mooney, *Myths,* pp. 333–34; Ron Martz, "Legends of the Little People," Atlanta *Weekly* (*Journal and Constitution* magazine), 11 Oct. 1987, pp. 6, 14, 16; cf. motif F261.1.

Chapter Five. Lee Drake: Afro-American Tales

BROTHER RABBIT STEALS THE LARD. Type 15, "The Theft of Butter (Honey) by Playing Godfather." Joel Chandler Harris, *Uncle Remus, His Songs and His Sayings,* rev. ed. (1895; reprint, New York: D. Appleton-Century Co., 1933), no. 17, pp. 80–86; Florence E. Baer, *Sources and Analogues of the Uncle Remus Tales,* Folklore Fellows Communications, no. 228 (Helsinki: Academia Scientiarum Fennica, 1980), pp. 43–44; Richard M. Dorson, *American Negro Folktales* (Greenwich, Conn.: Fawcett Publications, 1967), nos. 1–2, pp. 68–75, and no. 4, pp. 77–79; Elsie Clews Parsons, *Folk-lore of the Sea Islands, South Carolina*, Memoirs, vol. 16 (Cambridge, Mass.: American Folklore Society, 1923), nos. 2–3, pp. 5–10; idem, "Folklore from Aiken, South Carolina," *Journal of American Folklore* 34 (1921): 2–4 (no. 1); idem, "Tales from Guilford County, North Carolina," *Journal of American Folklore* 30 (1917): 192–93 (no. 46); Arthur Huff Fauset, "Negro Folk Tales from the South (Alabama, Mississippi, Louisiana)," *Journal of American Folklore* 40 (1927): 235–39; Charles C. Jones, Jr., *Negro Myths from the Georgia Coast Told in the Vernacular* (1888; reprint, Columbia, S.C.: State Co., 1925), no. 24, pp. 59–62; J. Russell Reaver, *Florida Folktales* (Gainesville: University Presses of Florida, 1987), no. 2, pp. 3–5. Cf. "Brother Rabbit Steals the Butter" in this collection.

BROTHER FOX AND BROTHER RABBIT AT THE WELL. Type 32, "The Wolf Descends into the Well in One Bucket and Rescues the Fox in the Other." Harris, *Uncle Remus, His Songs and Sayings,* no. 16, pp. 75–79; Baer, *Sources and Analogues,* pp. 42–43; Dorson, *American Negro,* no. 16, pp. 97–98; Parsons, *Sea Islands,* no. 155, p. 137; Fauset, "Negro Folk Tales," p. 227; Reaver, *Florida Folktales,* no. 4, pp. 5–6; Daryl Cumber Dance, *Shuckin' and Jivin': Folklore from Contemporary*

Black Americans (Bloomington: Indiana University Press, 1978), no. 396, pp. 221–22; Roger D. Abrahams, *Positively Black* (Englewood Cliffs, N.J.: Prentice-Hall, 1970), pp. 51–52. Cf. "Rabbit and Fox at the Well" in this collection.

BROTHER RABBIT AND BROTHER FOX AT THE SAWDUST PILE. Dance, *Shuckin',* no. 434, p. 253; Ronald L. Baker, *Jokelore: Humorous Folktales from Indiana* (Bloomington: Indiana University Press, 1986), no. 39, p. 20; cf. Baughman motif X1218*(ab).

BROTHER RABBIT AND BROTHER FOX MEET MAN. Type 157, "Learning to Fear Men." Joel Chandler Harris, *Nights with Uncle Remus: Myths and Legends of the Old Plantation* (Boston: Ticknor & Co., 1883), no. 57, pp. 338–42; Baer, *Sources and Analogues,* p. 102; Dorson, *American Negro,* no. 18, pp. 100–104; Abrahams, *Positively Black,* p. 50; cf. Zora Neale Hurston, *Mules and Men* (1935; reprint, New York: Harper & Row, 1970), pp. 171–74.

BROTHER CROW AND BROTHER BUZZARD UP NORTH. Dorson, *American Negro,* no. 26, pp. 112–13; Fauset, "Negro Folk Tales," pp. 217–18.

BROTHER BUZZARD AND THE LAZY MULE. Motif K1047. Dorson, *American Negro,* no. 8, pp. 83–86, and no. 28, pp. 114–15; Dance, *Shuckin',* no. 441, p. 256; Fauset, "Negro Folk Tales," pp. 241–42.

WHY THE WOODPECKER HAS NO SONG. Cf. type 751A, "The Peasant Woman Is Changed into a Woodpecker"; motif A2456.1.

THE PARROT AND THE MAID. Dorson, *American Negro,* no. 34c, pp. 122–23; Dance, *Shuckin',* no. 376, pp. 211–12.

THE PARROT GOES TO CHURCH. Motifs J551.5, J2211.2. Dance, *Shuckin',* no. 430, p. 252; G. Legman, *No Laughing Matter: An Analysis of Sexual Humor,* 2 vols. (1968 and 1975; reprint, Bloomington: Indiana

University Press, 1982), 1:85, 201; cf. Dorson, *American Negro*, no. 34a, pp. 120–21.

THE DEVIL AND THE LORD DIVIDING SOULS. Here, the English tale "The Sexton Carries the Parson" has become incorporated into the Afro-American Master and John cycle. See the note to "Dividing the Corn," p. 234, to which add Dorson, *American Negro*, no. 49, pp. 146–47; Parsons, *Sea Islands*, no. 58, p. 68; idem, "Guilford County," no. 12, p. 177; Hurston, *Mules and Men*, pp. 117–19; Langston Hughes and Arna Bontemps, eds., *The Book of Negro Folklore* (New York: Dodd, Mead & Co., 1958), pp. 79–80; Harry Oster, "Negro Humor: John and Old Marster," in *Mother Wit from the Laughing Barrel: Readings in the Interpretation of Afro-American Folklore*, ed. Alan Dundes (Englewood Cliffs, N.J.: Prentice-Hall, 1973), pp. 553–55.

JOHN AND OLD MISS IN THE BARN. Motif T232.5. Cf. "The Old-time Religion" in this collection.

JOHN LEARNS A NEW LANGUAGE. Type 1562A, "The Barn Is Burning." Dorson, *American Negro*, no. 64, pp. 165–67; Hurston, *Mules and Men*, pp. 109–10; Kenneth Jackson and Edward Wilson, "The Barn Is Burning," *Folklore* 47 (1936): 190–202.

THE FOOLISH BRIDE. A combination of types 1450, "Clever Elsie," 1384, "The Husband Hunts Three Persons As Stupid As His Wife," 1245, "Sunlight Carried in a Bag into the Windowless House," 1210, "The Cow Is Taken to the Roof to Graze," 1541, "For the Long Winter," and 1386, "Meat as Food for Cabbage." Dorson, *American Negro*, nos. 204–5, pp. 338–43; Parsons, *Sea Islands*, no. 87, pp. 94–97, and no. 147, pp. 132–34; idem, "Aiken," no. 21, pp. 18–19, and no. 31, p. 22; idem, "Guilford County," no. 44, pp. 191–92; Fauset, "Negro Folk Tales," pp. 251–53; Jack and Olivia Solomon, *Ghosts and Goosebumps: Ghost Stories, Tall Tales and Superstitions from Alabama* (University: University of Alabama Press, 1981), pp. 154–58; Vance Randolph, *The Devil's Pretty Daughter and Other Ozark Folk Tales* (New York: Columbia University Press, 1955), pp. 49–51.

THE SUITOR AND THE BEAR. Dance, *Shuckin'*, no. 148, pp. 83–84; Richard M. Dorson, *Negro Tales from Pine Bluff, Arkansas and Calvin, Michigan* (Bloomington: Indiana University Press, 1958), pp. 268–70.

THE BOY AND THE WHITE DOG. Baughman motif E423.1.1.1(c). Dance, *Shuckin'*, no. 30, p. 24; Reaver, *Florida Folktales*, no. 83, p. 110; J. Mason Brewer, *Dog Ghosts and Other Texas Negro Folk Tales* (Austin: University of Texas Press, 1958), pp. 89–109.

THE FLASH OF HEAT. Ray B. Browne, *A Night with the Hants and Other Alabama Folk Experiences* (Bowling Green, Ohio: Bowling Green University Popular Press, 1976), pp. 192, 196; cf. Baughman motif E421.1.0.1*.

WHEN BOZO COMES. Type 326, "The Youth Who Wanted to Learn What Fear Is"; motif J1495.2. Dorson, *American Negro*, no. 192, pp. 320–22; Hughes and Bontemps, *Book of Negro Folklore*, pp. 171–73; Fauset, "Negro Folk Tales," pp. 258–59; B. A. Botkin, ed., *A Treasury of American Folklore* (New York: Crown Publishers, 1944), pp. 710–11; Roger D. Abrahams, *Deep Down in the Jungle: Negro Narrative Folklore from the Streets of Philadelphia*, rev. ed. (Chicago: Aldine Publishing Co., 1970), pp. 179–80; Vance Randolph, *Who Blowed Up the Church House and Other Ozark Folk Tales* (New York: Columbia University Press, 1952), pp. 163–64.

A HOODOO'S WORK? Lee Drake told this in response to a query as to whether he knew any stories about hoodoo or conjure, the Afro-American form of black magic, which can involve transferring a living creature such as a snake, frog, or insect into a victim's body. Cf. Dorson, *American Negro*, no. 85, pp. 195–96.

OLD DOCTOR AND YOUNG DOCTOR. Cf. type 1862C, "Imitation of Diagnosis by Observation: Ass's Flesh"; "How Howleglas Made Himself a Physician," in *A Hundred Merry Tales and Other Jestbooks of the Fifteenth and Sixteenth Centuries*, ed. P. M. Zall (Lincoln: University of Nebraska Press, 1963), pp. 167–70; Randolph, *Devil's Pretty Daughter*, pp. 164–65.

SHORTY, SLIM, AND THE JUDGE. Dance, *Shuckin'*, no. 514, pp. 300–301; cf. Abrahams, *Deep Down*, pp. 236–37.

ROOSEVELT AND THE LAW. Brewer, *Dog Ghosts*, pp. 37–38; cf. Hughes and Bontemps, *Book of Negro Folklore*, pp. 71–72.

ON THE COOLING BOARD. Cf. Dorson, *American Negro,* no. 162, p. 295, and no. 197a, p. 329; Browne, *Night with the Hants,* p. 198.

LITTLE BOY WHO CUSSED. Abrahams, *Deep Down,* pp. 210–11; Vance Randolph, *Hot Springs and Hell and Other Folk Jests and Anecdotes from the Ozarks* (Hatboro, Pa.: Folklore Associates, 1965), no. 353, pp. 125, 255–56; cf. motif J1321.

TEACHER AND THE BAD BOY. Motif X350. Dance, *Shuckin',* no. 372, p. 210; cf. Baker, *Jokelore,* no. 328, pp. 192–93.

JEW GIRL, WHITE GIRL, AND COLORED GIRL. Cf. Dance, *Shuckin',* no. 185, p. 99; Legman, *No Laughing Matter,* 2:243–44.

JEW, WHITE MAN, AND COLORED MAN. Dorson, *American Negro,* nos. 70c and d, pp. 174–75; Dance, *Shuckin',* no. 275, p. 153; Baker, *Jokelore,* no. 259, p. 151; J. Mason Brewer, *The Word on the Brazos: Negro Preacher Tales from the Brazos Bottoms of Texas* (Austin: University of Texas Press, 1953), pp. 88–89.

THE IRISHMAN AND THE OVERCOAT. Motif J2200; Baughman motif X621*.

THE SNEEZING IRISHMAN. Baughman motif X621*; cf. motif J2311.1.

THE TITANIC. This is one of the best-known toasts, narrative poems recited mainly by urban black men. Abrahams, *Deep Down,* pp. 120–29; Dance, *Shuckin',* no. 385, pp. 215–17; Bruce Jackson, *"Get Your Ass in the Water and Swim Like Me": Narrative Poetry from Black Oral Tradition* (Cambridge, Mass.: Harvard University Press, 1974), pp. 35–38, 180–96.

Chapter Six. Lem Griffis: Okefenokee Swamp Yarns

GOOD FISHING. Cf. Baughman motifs X1318*(a), X1303.4*, X1303.1(dd).

REMARKABLE KINFOLK. Baughman motif X921(m).

HEALTHY COUNTRY. Motif X1663.2; cf. motif X427.

AN UPPITY BLACKFISH. Motif X1303. Cf. Zora Neale Hurston, *Mules and Men* (1935; reprint, New York: Harper & Row, 1970), p. 129.

CANNIBAL SNAKES. Baughman motif X1204(b). Richard Chase, *Grandfather Tales* (Boston: Houghton Mifflin Co., 1948), p. 187; J. Russell Reaver, *Florida Folktales* (Gainesville: University Presses of Florida, 1987), no. 54r, p. 80.

THE SNAKEBIT WALKING CANE. Type 1889M, "Snakebite Causes Object to Swell"; Baughman motif X1205.1(g). Vance Randolph, *We Always Lie to Strangers: Tall Tales from the Ozarks* (New York: Columbia University Press, 1951), pp. 132–35; Loyal Jones and Billy Edd Wheeler, *Laughter in Appalachia: A Festival of Southern Mountain Humor* (Little Rock, Ark.: August House, 1987), p. 131; Ronald L. Baker, *Jokelore: Humorous Folktales from Indiana* (Bloomington: Indiana University Press, 1986), nos. 24–27, pp. 13–15. Cf. "The Hoopsnake" in this collection.

EXTRAORDINARY HENS AND HOGS. Cf. Baughman motif X1410(a).

UNUSUAL BIRDS. Randolph, *We Always Lie,* pp. 67–68; cf. Baughman motif X1611.1.13.3*.

ODD INSECTS. Baughman motif X1280.1(aa).

GOOD HUNTING DOGS. Motif X1215.7; cf. Baughman motifs X1115(a), X1215.13*(d).

JOKES ON OUTSIDERS. Vance Randolph, *The Talking Turtle and Other Ozark Folk Tales* (New York: Columbia University Press, 1957), p. 106.

HITLER'S DREAM. Evidently a reworking of a World War I poem, "Kaiser Bill's Dream," a recitation of which is in the Georgia Folklore Archives (recorded in fall 1967 by Rosa Jean Tomlinson from Mary Minter, a black resident of Atlanta in her late sixties).

ANOTHER JOKE ON OUTSIDERS. Baughman motif X1291(a); cf. Baughman motif J1499.13*(d). Randolph, *We Always Lie,* p. 144; Baker, *Jokelore,* no. 147, pp. 91–92; Mariella Glenn Hartsfield, *Tall Betsy and Dunce Baby: South Georgia Folktales* (Athens: University of Georgia Press, 1987), no. 38, p. 114; Leonard W. Roberts, *South from Hell-fer-Sartin: Kentucky Mountain Folk Tales* (Berea, Ky.: Council of the Southern Mountains, 1964), no. 72, pp. 150–51.

MONSTER WINDS. Baughman motif X1611.1.15.2*(c); cf. Baughman motifs X1205.1(f), X1623.4*(b). Cf. "A Powerful Tornado" in this collection.

COLD WEATHER. Cf. Baughman motif X1622.2.1*; Reaver, *Florida Folktales,* nos. 54a and b, p. 77.

HOT WEATHER. Baughman motif X1632.3.1*(a); cf. Baughman motifs X1632.3*(e and f), J1901.2. Roger Welsch, *Shingling the Fog and Other Plains Lies* (Chicago: Sage Books–Swallow Press, 1972), p. 32; cf. Reaver, *Florida Folktales*, nos. 54c–e, p. 77.

RICH SOIL. Baughman motifs X1402.1*(a), X1411.1.1(c). Randolph, *We Always Lie,* pp. 79, 82, 87–90; Welsch, *Shingling the Fog,* p. 61.

BIG BEAR. Cf. Baughman motif X1221(ab).

DEER HUNTER'S LOGIC. Vance Randolph, *Hot Springs and Hell and Other Folk Jests and Anecdotes from the Ozarks* (Hatboro, Pa.: Folklore Associates, 1965), no. 268, p. 96. Baughman motif X962*(b); Randolph, *We Always Lie,* pp. 177–78; Welsch, *Shingling the Fog,* p. 82.

THE BLIND CHILD. A sentimental ballad dating to the 1860s and most likely originating in print; Griffis's ascription of it to an Okefenokee author probably resulted from the localizing impulse. Vance Randolph, *Ozark Folksongs,* edited and abridged by Norm Cohen (Urbana: University of Illinois Press, 1982), pp. 472–73; H. M. Belden, ed., *Ballads and Songs Collected by the Missouri Folk-lore Society* (1940; reprint, Columbia: University of Missouri Press, 1966), pp. 275–76; for other southern reports see the notes in the above, and for a recording hear *Arnold Keith Storm of Moores-ville, Indiana: "Take the News to Mother,"* Folk Legacy FSA-18, band B2.

THE NEW ENGLAND SHORE. G. Malcolm Laws, Jr., *American Balladry from British Broadsides,* Bibliographical and Special Series, vol. 8 (Philadelphia: American Folklore Society, 1957), no. M26, pp. 192–93.

THE BUTCHER BOY. Ibid., no. P24, p. 260.

NAOMI WISE. The ballad refers to the 1808 drowning of Naomi Wise by her former sweetheart, Jonathan Lewis, in Deep River, Randolph County, North Carolina. G. Malcolm Laws, Jr., *Native American Balladry: A Descriptive Study and a Bibliographical Syllabus,* Bibliographical and Special Series, vol. 1, rev. ed. (Philadelphia: American Folklore Society, 1964), no. F31, pp. 206–7.

SMART HUNTING DOGS AND A TRAINED CATFISH. Baughman motif X1215.8(aa); Randolph, *We Always Lie,* pp. 126–27; Jones and Wheeler, *Laughter in Appalachia,* p. 84; Reaver, *Florida Folktales,* no. 54m, p. 79; Baker, *Jokelore,* no. 33, p. 18; Jack and Olivia Solomon, *Ghosts and Goosebumps: Ghost Stories, Tall Tales and Superstitions from Alabama* (University: University of Alabama Press, 1981), pp. 85–86. Baughman motifs X1215.8(ac), X1215.9(ab); Reaver, *Florida Folktales,* no. 54l, p. 79; Baker, *Jokelore,* nos. 34–35, p. 18. Baughman motif X1306.3*; Randolph, *We Always Lie,* pp. 230–31; Roberts, *South from Hell-fer-Sartin,* p. 154; Baker, *Jokelore,* nos. 51–52, pp. 26–27; Welsch, *Shingling the Fog,* pp. 97–98; B. A. Botkin, ed., *A Treasury of American Folklore* (New York: Crown Publishers, 1944), pp. 624–25.

Chapter Seven. "Ordinary" Folktales

JACK THE ROGUE. Type 1525 (especially subtypes A and D), "The Master Thief." Richard Chase, *The Jack Tales* (Cambridge, Mass.: Riverside Press–Houghton Mifflin Co., 1943), no. 13, pp. 114–26, 195–97; idem, *American Folk Tales and Songs* (New York: Signet Key–New American Library, 1956), pp. 74–79; Charles L. Perdue, Jr., ed., *Outwitting the Devil: Jack Tales from Wise County, Virginia* (Santa Fe, N.M.: Ancient City Press, 1987), no. 18, pp. 76–79; Vance Randolph, *The Devil's Pretty Daughter and Other Ozark Folk Tales* (New York: Columbia University Press, 1955), pp. 70–71; Elsie Clews Parsons, *Folk-lore of the Sea Islands, South Carolina,* Memoirs, vol. 16 (Cambridge, Mass.: American Folklore Society, 1923), no. 115, pp. 112–

13. A film adaptation of Chase's *Jack Tales* version but with black actors, "Jack and the Dentist's Daughter," was produced in 1984 by Davenport Films of Delaplane, Virginia.

CUNNING JACK. Cf. Type 1526A, "Supper Won by a Trick"; motif K842; Randolph, *Devil's Pretty Daughter,* pp. 67–69.

JACK AND THE REVENUERS. Motifs H924, H1270; cf. motif H1188.

WHISTLING JIMMY. Type 1535, "The Rich and the Poor Peasant." Chase, *Jack Tales,* no. 17, pp. 161–71; idem, *American,* pp. 79–86; Leonard W. Roberts, *South from Hell-fer-Sartin: Kentucky Mountain Folk Tales* (Berea, Ky.: Council of the Southern Mountains, 1964), no. 31, pp. 97–100; idem, *Old Greasybeard: Tales from the Cumberland Gap* (Detroit: Folklore Associates–Gale Research, 1969), no. 40, pp. 154–59; Henry Glassie, "Three Southern Mountain Jack Tales," *Tennessee Folklore Society Bulletin* 30 (1964): 89–92. For cowhide noisemakers see Mariella Glenn Hartsfield, *Tall Betsy and Dunce Baby: South Georgia Folktales* (Athens: University of Georgia Press, 1987), pp. 161–67; Randolph, *Devil's Pretty Daughter,* pp. 42–44.

THE WAYWARD BOY. Apparently a distinct Afro-American combination of elements from types 303, "The Twins or Blood-Brothers," 334, "Household of the Witch," and 958, "The Shepherd Youth in the Robbers' Power," with motifs E761.6.2, G275.2, and B524.1.2. Parsons, *Sea Islands,* no. 73, pp. 80–83; idem, "Tales from Guilford County, North Carolina," *Journal of American Folklore* 30 (1917): 189-90 (no. 39); Guy and Candie Carawan, *Ain't You Got a Right to the Tree of Life? The People of Johns Island, South Carolina* (New York: Simon and Schuster, 1966), pp. 121–23; Richard M. Dorson, *American Negro Folktales* (Greenwich, Conn.: Fawcett Publications, 1967), no. 125, pp. 249–50; J. Russell Reaver, *Florida Folktales*

(Gainesville: University Presses of Florida, 1987), no. 81, pp. 101-3; Roberts, *South from Hell-fer-Sartin,* no. 3, pp. 19–22; cf. Joel Chandler Harris, *Uncle Remus and His Friends* (Boston: Houghton Mifflin Co., 1892), nos. 11 and 12, pp. 81–100. Although the conflation of several versions of a tale is no longer regarded as the best editorial practice, it seemed the most logical solution in this case. The two variants, recorded at different times from the same narrator, were quite similar, but each contained additional details that, when combined, offer a stronger and fuller text closer to the storyteller's mental model.

NIPPY AND THE GIANTS. Type 328, "The Boy Steals the Giant's Treasure (Jack and the Beanstalk)"; motifs G610, G82, K1611. Roberts, *South from Hell-fer-Sartin,* no. 11a, pp. 46-49; idem, *Old Greasybeard,* no. 19, pp. 82–86; Glassie, "Three Southern Mountain Jack Tales," pp. 92–97; cf. Chase, *Jack Tales,* no. 3, pp. 31–39.

BLUEBEARD. Type 311, "Rescue by the Sister." Parsons, *Sea Islands,* no. 34, pp. 47–49; idem, "Guilford County," no. 22, p. 183; Ralph S. Boggs, "North Carolina White Folktales and Riddles," *Journal of American Folklore* 47 (1934): 295 (no. 9).

THE GOLDEN BALL. Type 440, "The Frog King or Iron Henry"; motifs B493.1, B211.7.1, C41.2. Randolph, *Devil's Pretty Daughter,* pp. 91–92. Normally, slinging the frog against the wall disenchants it and transforms it back into a prince (motif D712.2), who marries the girl (motif L162). In this text she's a bit too energetic; poor froggy! A film adaptation of the Grimm brothers' version but with a Victorian American setting, "The Frog King," was produced in 1981 by Davenport Films, Delaplane, Virginia.

AN IMMIGRANT'S ADVENTURES. Structured like a novella but incorporating tall-tale motifs X1133.3 and X1021.1. Cf. Randolph, *Devil's Pretty Daughter,* pp. 58–59.

Chapter Eight. Animal and Human Tricksters

THE TAR BABY. Types 175, "The Tarbaby and the Rabbit," and 1310A, "Briar-patch Punishment for Rabbit."

Joel Chandler Harris, *Uncle Remus, His Songs and His Sayings,* rev. ed. (1895; reprint, New York:

D. Appleton-Century Co., 1933), no. 2, pp. 7–11, and no. 4, pp. 16–19; Florence E. Baer, *Sources and Analogues of the Uncle Remus Tales,* Folklore Fellows Communications, no. 228 (Helsinki: Academia Scientiarum Fennica, 1980), pp. 29–32; Richard M. Dorson, *American Negro Folktales* (Greenwich, Conn.: Fawcett Publications, 1967), no. 3, pp. 75–76; Elsie Clews Parsons, *Folk-lore of the Sea Islands, South Carolina,* Memoirs, vol. 16 (Cambridge, Mass.: American Folklore Society, 1923), nos. 13–15, pp. 25–29; Arthur Huff Fauset, "Negro Folk Tales from the South (Alabama, Mississippi, Louisiana)," *Journal of American Folklore* 40 (1927): 228–31; Charles C. Jones, Jr., *Negro Myths from the Georgia Coast Told in the Vernacular* (1888; reprint, Columbia, S.C.: State Co., 1925), no. 4, pp. 7–11; Louise-Clarke Pyrnelle, *Diddie, Dumps, and Tot or Plantation Child-life* (New York: Harper & Brothers, 1882), pp. 76–81; J. Russell Reaver, *Florida Folktales* (Gainesville: University Presses of Florida, 1987), no. 6, pp. 7–9; James Mooney, *Myths of the Cherokee* (1900; reprint, New York: Johnson Reprint Corp., 1970), no. 21, pp. 271–73, the second text reprinted from the *Cherokee Advocate* of 1845 (the tale is also reported from other southeastern Indian groups, including the Creeks and Yuchis, who evidently obtained it through contact with blacks). A recorded version can be heard on *Animal Tales Told in the Gullah Dialect by Albert H. Stoddard of Savannah, Georgia,* Library of Congress AAFS L44, band B2.

BROTHER RABBIT, BROTHER LION, AND THE COW. See the note to "The Cow Going Down in the Mud," p. 234, to which add motif K581.2; Harris, *Uncle Remus, His Songs and His Sayings,* no. 20, pp. 98–103; Parsons, *Sea Islands,* nos. 18–19, pp. 31–33.

RABBIT AND FOX AT THE WELL. See the note to "Brother Fox and Brother Rabbit at the Well," p. 238, to which add type 1525D (motif K341.6), "Theft by Distracting Attention."

BROTHER RABBIT STEALS THE BUTTER. See the note to "Brother Rabbit Steals the Lard," p. 238, the ending of which is more typical.

OLD MASTER AND JOHN. A combination of several tales from the Master and John cycle. Dorson, *American Negro,* no. 40, pp. 136–37, and no. 53, pp. 151–52; Parsons, *Sea Islands,* no. 67, pp. 76–77; Fauset, "Negro Folk Tales," pp. 266–67; Zora Neale Hurston, *Mules and Men* (1935; reprint, New York: Harper & Row, 1970), pp. 112–13; J. Mason Brewer, *Dog Ghosts and Other Texas Negro Folk Tales* (Austin: University of Texas Press, 1958), pp. 9–14. Reaver, *Florida Folktales,* no. 41, pp. 55–56. Cf. motif H1151.3. Type 1641, "Doctor Know-All"; Dorson, *American Negro,* no. 35, pp. 126–29; Hurston, *Mules and Men,* pp. 111–12; Jones, *Negro Myths,* no. 35, pp. 99–100; Langston Hughes and Arna Bontemps, eds., *The Book of Negro Folklore* (New York: Dodd, Mead & Co., 1958), pp. 73–74; Roger D. Abrahams, *Deep Down in the Jungle: Negro Narrative Folklore from the Streets of Philadelphia,* rev. ed. (Chicago: Aldine Publishing Co., 1970), pp. 187–88; Daryl Cumber Dance, *Shuckin' and Jivin': Folklore from Contemporary Black Americans* (Bloomington: Indiana University Press, 1978), no. 362, p. 204; J. Mason Brewer, ed., *American Negro Folklore* (New York: Quadrangle–New York Times Book Co., 1968), pp. 80–81.

JOHN AND THE AIRPLANE. Another text in the Georgia Folklore Archives is set more logically in the twentieth century.

THE PRAYER JOHN GETS PAID BY. Cf. motif W154.1; Hurston, *Mules and Men,* p. 120.

TOO MANY "UPS." Brewer, *American Negro Folklore,* pp. 96–97; Bruce Jackson, *"Get Your Ass in the Water and Swim Like Me": Narrative Poetry from Black Oral Tradition* (Cambridge, Mass.: Harvard University Press, 1974), no. 53, pp. 197–98; cf. Dorson, *American Negro,* no. 175, p. 307.

JOHN MEETS LESTER MADDOX. Cf. type 1526A, "Supper Won by a Trick." Dr. Martin Luther King, Jr., black civil rights activist from Atlanta and follower of Mahatma Gandhi's doctrine of nonviolent protest, was assassinated in 1968. Lester Maddox, governor of Georgia from 1967 to 1969, is remembered for his defense of racial segregation, especially the 1964 expulsion of blacks from his Pickrick Restaurant in Atlanta.

BOBTAIL OUTWITS THE DEVIL. Type 1030, "The Crop

Division." Parsons, *Sea Islands,* no. 112, pp. 109–11; Reaver, *Florida Folktales,* no. 15, pp. 17–18; Dance, *Shuckin',* no. 351, p. 196; Richard Chase, *Grandfather Tales* (Boston: Houghton Mifflin Co., 1948), pp. 88–93; Charles L. Perdue, Jr., ed., *Outwitting the Devil: Jack Tales from Wise County, Virginia* (Santa Fe, N.M.: Ancient City Press, 1987), no. 8, pp. 51–53; Ralph S. Boggs, "North Carolina White Folktales and Riddles," *Journal of American Folklore* 47 (1934): 292 (no. 3);

Leonard W. Roberts, *South from Hell-fer-Sartin: Kentucky Mountain Folk Tales* (Berea, Ky.: Council of the Southern Mountains, 1964), no. 39, pp. 114–15.

WOODEN NUTMEGS. Motif K100.

ROCK SOUP. Type 1548, "The Soup-stone . . ." Leonard W. Roberts, *Old Greasybeard: Tales from the Cumberland Gap* (Detroit: Folklore Associates–Gale Research, 1969), no. 48, pp. 169–70; Jones, *Negro Myths,* no. 28, pp. 71–72.

Chapter Nine. Jests

THE IRISHMEN AND THE MOSQUITOES. Motif J1759.3; Baughman motif X621*. Vance Randolph, *Hot Springs and Hell and Other Folk Jests and Anecdotes from the Ozarks* (Hatboro, Pa.: Folklore Associates, 1965), no. 114, p. 41; Richard M. Dorson, *Negro Folktales in Michigan* (1956; reprint, Westport, Conn.: Greenwood Press, 1974), p. 183; Ronald L. Baker, *Jokelore: Humorous Folktales from Indiana* (Bloomington: Indiana University Press, 1986), no. 211, p. 126.

PAT AND MIKE AND THE HANGING JOB. Motif K841. Ralph S. Boggs, "North Carolina White Folktales and Riddles," *Journal of American Folklore* 47 (1934): 309 (no. 35); Loyal Jones and Billy Edd Wheeler, *Laughter in Appalachia: A Festival of Southern Mountain Humor* (Little Rock, Ark.: August House, 1987), pp. 101–2.

THE LOOKING GLASS. Type 1336A, "Man Does Not Recognize His Own Reflection in the Water (Mirror)"; Baughman motif J1795.2*. Vance Randolph, *The Talking Turtle and Other Ozark Folk Tales* (New York: Columbia University Press, 1957), pp. 62–64.

THE CROSS-EYED MULE. G. Legman, *No Laughing Matter: An Analysis of Sexual Humor,* 2 vols. (1968 and 1975; reprint, Bloomington: Indiana University Press, 1982), 2:941; cf. Vance Randolph, *Pissing in the Snow and Other Ozark Folktales* (1976; reprint, New York: Bard–Avon Books, 1977), no. 91, p. 215. W. K. McNeil of the Ozark Folk Center writes that this tale "appears in 'rawer' form in a number of 'dirty' jokebooks. I have also collected it a number of times

from various male narrators in the Ozarks" (personal communication, 1988).

AN UNSOUND INVESTMENT. Cf. type 1293, "Numskull Stays Until He Has Finished"; Legman, *No Laughing Matter,* 2:908; Jones and Wheeler, *Laughter in Appalachia,* p. 121.

A HAZARDOUS JOURNEY. Cf. Baughman motif J2214(e); Ray B. Browne, *A Night with the Hants and Other Alabama Folk Experiences* (Bowling Green, Ohio: Bowling Green University Popular Press, 1976), p. 73.

THE WONDERFUL HUNT. Baughman motif X1122.4.1*; types 1890A, "Shot Splits Tree Limb" (motif X1124.3.1), 1895, "A Man Wading in Water Catches Many Fish in His Boots" (motif X1112), and 1917, "The Stretching and Shrinking Harness" (motif X1785.1). Vance Randolph, *We Always Lie to Strangers: Tall Tales from the Ozarks* (New York: Columbia University Press, 1951), pp. 120–22; Baker, *Jokelore,* nos. 67–68, pp. 35–36; Roger Welsch, *Shingling the Fog and Other Plains Lies* (Chicago: Sage Books–Swallow Press, 1972), pp. 82–83.

LUCKY SHOTS. Types 1890, "The Lucky Shot" (motif X1124.3), 1895, "A Man Wading in Water Catches Many Fish in His Boots" (motif X1112), 1917, "The Stretching and Shrinking Harness" (motif X1785.1), and 1890B, "Bursting Gun and Series of Lucky Accidents." Richard M. Dorson, *American Negro Folktales* (Greenwich, Conn.: Fawcett Publications, 1967), no.

218, pp. 354-55; Zora Neale Hurston, *Mules and Men* (1935; reprint, New York: Harper & Row, 1970), pp. 151–53.

THE INDIAN'S LUCKY HUNTING FEATHER. Types 1890A, "Shot Splits Tree Limb" (motif X1124.3.1), 1890, "The Lucky Shot" (motif X1124.3), and 1889C, "Fruit Tree Grows from Head of Deer Shot with Fruit Pits" (motif X1130.2). Baker, *Jokelore*, no. 20, pp. 11–12; J. Russell Reaver, *Florida Folktales* (Gainesville: University Presses of Florida, 1987), no. 55e, p. 81; Harden E. Taliaferro [Skitt, pseud.], *Fisher's River (North Carolina) Scenes and Characters* (1859; reprint, New York: Arno Press, 1977), pp. 69–74.

THE UNLUCKY HUNT. Types 1890A, "Shot Splits Tree Limb" (motif X1124.3.1), 1881, "The Man Carried through the Air by Geese" (motif X1258.1), and 1900, "How the Man Came Out of a Tree Stump" (Baughman motif X1133.1[a]). Boggs, "North Carolina," no. 47a, p. 315; Leonard Roberts, *Old Greasybeard: Tales from the Cumberland Gap* (Detroit: Folklore Associates–Gale Research, 1969), no. 44, pp. 164–65; Michael A. Lofaro, ed., *The Tall Tales of Davy Crockett: The Second Nashville Series of Crockett Almanacs, 1839–1841* (Knoxville: University of Tennessee Press, 1987), pp. 25, 28 (1840 almanac); cf. Randolph, *We Always Lie*, pp. 122–23.

HUNTING AND FISHING YARNS. Cf. James S. French, "Crockett's Coon Story," in *Native American Humor*, ed. Walter Blair (1937; reprint, San Francisco: Chandler Publishing Co., 1960), pp. 281–82; Randolph, *We Always Lie*, p. 111; Jones and Wheeler, *Laughter in Appalachia*, pp. 100–101. Cf. Baughman motif X1215.8(ak); Jones and Wheeler, *Laughter in Appalachia*, pp. 86–87; Randolph, *Hot Springs*, no. 340, p. 121; Baker, *Jokelore*, no. 337, pp. 197–98. Baughman motifs X1302*(a), X1302*(de); Randolph, *We Always Lie*, pp. 213–14.

LIARS' DEAL. Baughman type 1920H*, "Will Blow Out Lantern"; Baughman motif X1154(c). Randolph, *We Always Lie*, pp. 231–32; Browne, *Night with the Hants*, p. 42; Reaver, *Florida Folktales*, no. 21, pp. 22–23; Baker, *Jokelore*, no. 21, p. 12; Jack and Olivia Sol-

omon, *Ghosts and Goosebumps: Ghost Stories, Tall Tales and Superstitions from Alabama* (University: University of Alabama Press, 1981), p. 86; cf. Welsch, *Shingling the Fog*, p. 97.

THE HOOP SNAKE. Motif B765.1. Randolph, *We Always Lie*, pp. 132–36; Taliaferro, *Fisher's River*, pp. 55–58; Dorson, *American Negro*, no. 143, pp. 272–73; Newman Ivey White, gen. ed., *The Frank C. Brown Collection of North Carolina Folklore*, 7 vols. (Durham, N.C.: Duke University Press, 1952–64), 1:637; Welsch, *Shingling the Fog*, p. 94; cf. Baker, *Jokelore*, no. 24, pp. 13–14. Cf. "The Snakebit Walking Cane" in this collection.

FRIENDLY SNAKES. Baughman motifs X1321.4.4*(a), X1321.4.4.2*. Randolph, *We Always Lie*, p. 226; Jones and Wheeler, *Laughter in Appalachia*, p. 136; Reaver, *Florida Folktales*, no. 54f, pp. 77–78; Baker, *Jokelore*, no. 54, pp. 28–29.

BIG KETTLE FOR A BIG TURNIP. Type 1920A, "The Sea Burns (variant: the first tells of the great cabbage, the other of the great kettle to cook it in)"; Motif X1431.1. Randolph, *We Always Lie*, p. 92; Elsie Clews Parsons, "Tales from Guilford County, North Carolina," *Journal of American Folklore* 30 (1917): 191 (no. 42); J. Mason Brewer, *Dog Ghosts and Other Texas Negro Folk Tales* (Austin: University of Texas Press, 1958), pp. 40–41; B. A. Botkin, ed., *A Treasury of American Folklore* (New York: Crown Publishers, 1944), pp. 603–4.

A TRIP TO THE MOON. Motif F16; types 1889B, "Hunter Turns Animal Inside Out" (motif X1124.2), and 1911A, "Horse's New Backbone" (motif X1721.1). Cf. *The Surprising Adventures of Baron Munchausen* (New York: Albert & Charles Boni, 1928), pp. 41–42; Edmond Rostand, *Cyrano de Bergerac*, trans. Brian Hooker (1923; reprint, New York: Bantam Books, 1959), pp. 119–25; Randolph, *We Always Lie*, p. 107; Welsch, *Shingling the Fog*, pp. 77–78.

PREPARING FOR THE PREACHER. Jones and Wheeler, *Laughter in Appalachia*, pp. 32–33; cf. Baker, *Jokelore*, no. 342, pp. 200–201; Daryl Cumber Dance, *Shuckin' and Jivin': Folklore from Contemporary Black Americans*

(Bloomington: Indiana University Press, 1978), no. 93, p. 59; Baughman motif X459.2*(b).

THE RIGHT STUFF. Cf. Randolph, *Pissing*, no. 50, p. 135; Roger D. Abrahams, *Deep Down in the Jungle: Negro Narrative Folklore from the Streets of Philadelphia*, rev. ed. (Chicago: Aldine Publishing Co., 1970), pp. 205–6; idem, *Positively Black* (Englewood Cliffs, N.J.: Prentice-Hall, 1970), p. 104.

THE PREACHER'S BICYCLE. Randolph, *Hot Springs*, no. 413, p. 146; Dance, *Shuckin'*, no. 82, p. 53; Baker, *Jokelore*, no. 289, p. 167.

THE PREACHER'S FALSE TEETH. Brewer, *Dog Ghosts*, pp. 73–76; cf. Baughman motif W153.16*.

THE PREACHER WHO LOVED RABBIT. Browne, *Night with the Hants*, p. 98.

PREACHER TELLS A LIE. Motif X459.

THE CORPSE POPPED UP. Motif J1769.2. Browne, *Night with the Hants*, pp. 99, 165; Solomon and Solomon, *Ghosts and Goosebumps*, p. 70; Dorson, *American Negro*, no. 197c, pp. 330–31; Dance, *Shuckin'*, no. 72, pp. 48–49; William Lynwood Montell, *Ghosts along the Cumberland: Deathlore in the Kentucky Foothills* (Knoxville: University of Tennessee Press, 1975), no. 463, p. 202.

THE RELIGIOUSLY TRAINED HORSE. Baker, *Jokelore*, no. 210, p. 124; F. Roy Johnson, *Oral Folk Humor from the Carolina and Virginia Flatlands* (Murfreesboro, N.C.: Johnson Publishing Co., 1980), pp. 69–70.

THE CHANDELIER. Baughman motif J1772.27*. Jones and Wheeler, *Laughter in Appalachia*, p. 34; Randolph, *Hot Springs*, no. 346, p. 123; Dance, *Shuckin'*, no. 122, p. 70; Browne, *Night with the Hants*, p. 92.

THE OLD-TIME RELIGION. Elsie Clews Parsons, *Folklore of the Sea Islands, South Carolina*, Memoirs, vol. 16 (Cambridge, Mass.: American Folklore Society, 1923), no. 154, p. 136; B. A. Botkin, ed., *Lay My Burden Down: A Folk History of Slavery* (Chicago: University of Chicago Press–Phoenix Books, 1945), p. 28. Cf. "John and Old Miss in the Barn" in this collection.

GETTING TOO PERSONAL. Dance, *Shuckin'*, no. 107, pp. 65–66; J. Mason Brewer, *The Word on the Brazos:*

Negro Preacher Tales from the Brazos Bottoms of Texas (Austin: University of Texas Press, 1953), p. 85; John Burrison, "Back to Snuff," *Folkways* 3 (1964): 13.

ADDING INSULT TO INJURY. Legman, *No Laughing Matter*, 2:778–79, 915; Abrahams, *Deep Down*, pp. 196–98; Dance, *Shuckin'*, no. 135, p. 75; cf. Brewer, *The Word*, pp. 14–15.

THE TAMING OF THE SHREW. Type 901, "Taming of the Shrew." Legman, *No Laughing Matter*, 2:723; Baker, *Jokelore*, no. 110, p. 71; Vance Randolph, *Sticks in the Knapsack and Other Ozark Folk Tales* (New York: Columbia University Press, 1958), pp. 71–73; Jan Harold Brunvand, *The Study of American Folklore: An Introduction*, 2d ed. (New York: W. W. Norton & Co., 1978), pp. 360–71.

THE SYNTHETIC BRIDE. Type 1379*, "False Members"; Frank Hoffmann, *Analytical Survey of Anglo-American Traditional Erotica* (Bowling Green, Ohio: Bowling Green University Popular Press, 1973), motifs X757.1, X757.2. Legman, *No Laughing Matter*, 1:274 and 2:649–50; Dance, *Shuckin'*, no. 232, p. 130; George Washington Harris, *Sut Lovingood's Yarns*, ed. M. Thomas Inge (New Haven, Conn.: College and University Press, 1966), pp. 276–81 (a Tennessee setting, originally published in 1867). Part of a complex of tales and ballads, including "The Warranty Deed" and "The Old Maid and the Burglar," for which see G. Malcolm Laws, Jr., *Native American Balladry: A Descriptive Study and a Bibliographical Syllabus*, Bibliographical and Special Series, vol. 1, rev. ed. (Philadelphia: American Folklore Society, 1964), nos. H24 and H23, p. 241.

FAIR EXCHANGE. Brewer, *The Word*, pp. 30–32; cf. Legman, *No Laughing Matter*, 1:444–45; Dance, *Shuckin'*, no. 264, p. 145; Randolph, *Talking Turtle*, pp. 65–66, 171.

DUELING TOMBSTONES. The inscription and its comic rejoinder are reported from Yorkshire, England, in *The Dalesman* 48 (1986): 410; cf. Legman, *No Laughing Matter*, 1:490.

RAPID TURNOVER. Dance, *Shuckin'*, nos. 262–63, p. 144; cf. Legman, *No Laughing Matter*, 1:676.

THE BRUSH PEDDLER AND THE FARMER'S DAUGHTER. Type 1443*, "The Pillow Too High." Legman, *No Laughing Matter,* 1:123; Randolph, *Talking Turtle,* pp. 99–100.

NO EGGS FOR BREAKFAST. Hoffmann, *Analytical Survey,* motif X724.5. Dorson, *American Negro,* no. 34d, p. 123; Baker, *Jokelore,* no. 316, pp. 183–84.

MUSTARD AND CUSTARD MAKE FRUIT SALAD. Type 1689, "Thank God They Weren't Peaches." Legman, *No Laughing Matter,* 2:157, 825; Baker, *Jokelore,* no. 315, pp. 182–83. Normally a traveling salesmen joke, this version belongs to a cycle of Mustard and Custard jests, the names possibly inspired by Ogden Nash's 1936 *Tale of Custard the Dragon.*

A ROUGH NIGHT ON THE FARM. Baughman motif Z13.4*(m). Legman, *No Laughing Matter,* 1:121; Vance Randolph, *Who Blew Up the Church House and Other Ozark Folk Tales* (New York: Columbia University Press, 1952), p. 16; Welsch, *Shingling the Fog,* pp. 118–19.

THE LONG-HANDLED SPOON. Baker, *Jokelore,* no. 161, p. 99.

SLAUGHTER IN THE CHICKEN HOUSE. Randolph, *Talking Turtle,* pp. 70–72; Mariella Glenn Hartsfield, *Tall Betsy and Dunce Baby: South Georgia Folktales* (Athens: University of Georgia Press, 1987), no. 41, p. 115.

THE FRUSTRATED ROOSTER. Legman, *No Laughing Matter,* 2:596–97.

BREWSTER THE OVERSEXED ROOSTER. Dance, *Shuckin',* no. 446, pp. 257–58; Baker, *Jokelore,* no. 102, p. 65.

POOR OLD TRAILER. Legman, *No Laughing Matter,* 2:337–38, 859–60.

THE STOOD-UP SLEEPERS. Randolph, *Who Blowed Up,* pp. 81–82.

OLD ENOUGH FOR BRITCHES. Hoffmann, *Analytical Index,* motif X712.6.1. Legman, *No Laughing Matter,* 1:105; Randolph, *Pissing,* no. 36, p. 108; Floyd C. Watkins and Charles Hubert Watkins, *Yesterday in the Hills* (1963; reprint, Athens: University of Georgia Press, 1973), p. 42, another text from Cherokee County, Georgia.

REMARKABLE LONGEVITY. Jones and Wheeler, *Laughter in Appalachia,* p. 95; Randolph, *Sticks in the Knapsack,* pp. 8–10. Cf. type 726, "The Oldest on the Farm"; Dorson, *American Negro,* no. 224, p. 359.

THE LAZIEST MAN. Type 1951, "Is Wood Split?"; Baughman motif W111.5.10.1. Dorson, *American Negro,* no. 223, pp. 358–59; Parsons, *Sea Islands,* no. 114, p. 112; Reaver, *Florida Folktales,* no. 47e, p. 64; Hartsfield, *Tall Betsy,* no. 39, pp. 114–15; Solomon and Solomon, *Ghosts and Goosebumps,* pp. 162–63; Randolph, *Talking Turtle,* pp. 84–86; Baker, *Jokelore,* no. 139, pp. 85–86.

Chapter Ten. Instructive Tales

THE CROW AND THE WATER JUG. Type 232D*, "Crow Drops Pebbles into Water Jug So As to Be Able to Drink." Ambrose E. Gonzales, *With Aesop along the Black Border* (1924; reprint, New York: Negro Universities Press, 1969), pp. 145–48.

THE LION AND THE BULL. Possibly a parody of the Aesop fable "The Lion and the Bulls." Cf. Loyal Jones and Billy Edd Wheeler, *Laughter in Appalachia: A Festival of Southern Mountain Humor* (Little Rock, Ark.: August House, 1987), pp. 116–17; G. Legman, *No*

Laughing Matter: An Analysis of Sexual Humor, 2 vols. (1968 and 1975; reprint, Bloomington: Indiana University Press, 1982), 2:483, 895.

THE LITTLE BIRD. Cf. type 66B, "Sham-Dead (Hidden) Animal Betrays Itself"; Legman, *No Laughing Matter,* 2:895.

THE BOY WHO WENT HUNTING ALONE. Normally told as a jest but here having a didactic function. Motif X584.1. Langston Hughes and Arna Bontemps, eds., *The Book of Negro Folklore* (New York: Dodd, Mead &

Co., 1958), p. 79; Ronald L. Baker, *Jokelore: Humorous Folktales from Indiana* (Bloomington: Indiana University Press, 1986), no. 1, p. 3.

CHALLENGING GOD'S WILL. Baughman motif N251.7; cf. Baughman motif Q582.10*.

BLASPHEMY PUNISHED. Motif Q221.3.

A HUMBLING EXPERIENCE. Baughman motif X1739.4*(a). Cf. Vance Randolph, *The Devil's Pretty Daughter and Other Ozark Folk Tales* (New York: Columbia University Press, 1955), pp. 112–14.

BETWEEN THE SADDLE AND THE GROUND. Motifs E631.0.2, F815.7, D1310.

SIMON AND THE TALKING FISH. Baughman motif Q223.6.3*(c). Richard M. Dorson, *American Negro Folktales* (Greenwich, Conn.: Fawcett Publications,

1967), no. 141, pp. 267–68; Elsie Clews Parsons, "Tales from Guilford County, North Carolina," *Journal of American Folklore* 30 (1917): 185 (no. 27); J. Mason Brewer, ed., *American Negro Folklore* (New York: Quadrangle–New York Times Book Co., 1968), pp. 53–55; Donald J. Waters, ed., *Strange Ways and Sweet Dreams: Afro-American Folklore from the Hampton Institute* (Boston: G. K. Hall & Co., 1983), pp. 289–92.

GRANDDADDY GLENN AND THE DEVIL. In addition to the didactic function of this family story, there are also elements of the supernatural legend, tall tale, and anecdote. Cf. types 1178, "The Devil Outriddled," and 1920, "Contest in Lying"; Baughman motif Q223.6.3*(a).

Chapter Eleven. Anecdotes

THE UNCLE TOM ANECDOTE CYCLE. Motif W152. Cf. type 1242A, "Carrying Part of the Load"; motifs W152.5, W152.11.

THE MEANING OF FRIENDSHIP. Snipe McCloud and Bony Ridley, residents of Macon County, North Carolina, in the late nineteenth century, became the subjects of a local anecdote cycle; see Caleb A. Ridley, *The Southern Mountaineer* (Atlanta: Privately printed, [ca. 1900]). Cf. motif J1832.

FRUITLESS PROPHESY. Cf. Loyal Jones and Billy Edd Wheeler, *Laughter in Appalachia: A Festival of Southern Mountain Humor* (Little Rock, Ark.: August House, 1987), p. 49.

A SLOW-GRINDING MILL. Vance Randolph, *Hot Springs and Hell and Other Folk Jests and Anecdotes from the Ozarks* (Hatboro, Pa.: Folklore Associates, 1965), no. 214, p. 76.

THE BUZZARD EGGS. Baughman motif K1665*. Cf. Ray B. Browne, *A Night with the Hants and Other Ala-*

bama Folk Experiences (Bowling Green, Ohio: Bowling Green University Popular Press, 1976), p. 100.

DOODY'S ESCAPE FROM THE REVENUERS. Cf. J. Russell Reaver, *Florida Folktales* (Gainesville: University Presses of Florida, 1987), no. 47a, p. 61. The moonshiner's alibi flight is reminiscent of that attributed to the seventeenth-century English outlaw Swift Nicks and later transferred to highwayman Dick Turpin and his horse Black Bess; see G. Malcolm Laws, Jr., *American Balladry from British Broadsides,* Bibliographical and Special Series, vol. 8 (Philadelphia: American Folklore Society, 1957), no. L8, pp. 169–70.

THE EYEBALLS AND THE CANNONBALL. The story about Ty Cobb (who was reared at Royston in Franklin County, Georgia) appears to be apocryphal; I could find nothing like it in his biographies. "The Cannonball" is a supernatural legend featuring motif E235.2, but the comical tone here converts it to an anecdote.

Chapter Twelve. Legends

MARY THE WANDERER. Motif E334.2.3; Baughman motif E574(ba). Burnette Vanstory, *Ghost Stories and*

Superstitions of Old Saint Simons ([Privately printed], n.d.), pp. 4–5; Kimberley Coy, "St. Simons Notebook:

You Don't Believe in Ghosts?" Atlanta *Constitution,* 27 April 1971, p. 3-B. This may be the only Georgia ghost with the distinction of having a road named for it.

EBO LANDING. Vanstory, *Ghost Stories,* pp. 3–4; Coy, "St. Simons," p. 3-B; cf. Baughman motif E337.1.1(f).

THE LONE GRAVE. Motifs E613.0.1, V62.1; cf. motif E631.2.

THE GRATEFUL HEADLESS GHOST. Baughman motifs E341.1(a), E371.6*, E545.19.2(c), E451.4(a). Ray B. Browne, *A Night with the Hants and Other Alabama Folk Experiences* (Bowling Green, Ohio: Bowling Green University Popular Press, 1976), pp. 155, 204–5; Ralph S. Boggs, "North Carolina White Folktales and Riddles," *Journal of American Folklore* 47 (1934): 300–301 (no. 17); John Harden, *Tar Heel Ghosts* (Chapel Hill: University of North Carolina Press, 1954), pp. 152–58; B. A. Botkin, ed., *A Treasury of Southern Folklore* (New York: Crown Publishers, 1949), pp. 533–35.

THE CRYING GHOST BABY. Baughman motif E337.2(d); motif E441. Eliot Wigginton and Margie Bennett, eds., *Foxfire Nine* (Garden City, N.Y.: Anchor Press–Doubleday, 1986), p. 383.

GHOSTLY SOUNDS OF A MURDER. Motif E337.1.1.

THE COVERS. Motif E279.3. Cf. W. K. McNeil, ed., *Ghost Stories from the American South* (Little Rock, Ark.: August House, 1985), no. 18, pp. 46–47.

THE DEAD LADY'S BABY. Cf. Baughman motif E323.1.

THE PHANTOM LANTERN MAN OF RAY CITY. Cf. Baughman motif E530.1.0.1(d). Perhaps the most famous southern phantom lights are those of Brown Mountain and Maco Station in North Carolina, for which see Harden, *Tar Heel Ghosts,* pp. 44–51.

GHOST LIGHT DISPROVEN. Motif E530.1.3.

GRANDPA AND THE GHOST. Cf. motif J1785.4; William Lynwood Montell, *Ghosts along the Cumberland: Deathlore in the Kentucky Foothills* (Knoxville: University of Tennessee Press, 1975), no. 444, p. 193; J. Russell Reaver, *Florida Folktales* (Gainesville: University Presses of Florida, 1987), no. 79, p. 100.

THE MAN WHO THOUGHT HE WAS BRAVE. Motif J1782.8.

THE FORK IN THE GRAVE. Type 1676B, "Clothing Caught in Graveyard"; Baughman motif N384.2(a). Browne, *Night with the Hants,* p. 53; McNeil, *Ghost Stories,* no. 27, pp. 59–60; Montell, *Ghosts along the Cumberland,* nos. 458–62, pp. 199–201; Reaver, *Florida Folktales,* no. 82, p. 103; Mariella Glenn Hartsfield, *Tall Betsy and Dunce Baby: South Georgia Folktales* (Athens: University of Georgia Press, 1987), no. 27, pp. 97–98; Vance Randolph, *The Devil's Pretty Daughter and Other Ozark Folk Tales* (New York: Columbia University Press, 1955), pp. 65–67; Newman Ivey White, gen. ed., *The Frank C. Brown Collection of North Carolina Folklore,* 7 vols. (Durham, N.C.: Duke University Press, 1952–64), 1:686.

THE VANISHING HITCHHIKER. One of the oldest "urban" legends, with preautomobile origins; Mrs. Hendrix, narrator of our first version and a schoolteacher, later admitted to casting it in the first person to make it more interesting. Motif E332.3.3.1; see Baughman, p. 148, for extensive references. McNeil, *Ghost Stories,* no. 58, pp. 95–98; Jan H. Brunvand, *The Vanishing Hitchhiker: American Urban Legends and Their Meanings* (New York: W. W. Norton & Co., 1981), pp. 24–46.

ESCAPE FROM THE DEVIL. Baughman motif E337.1.3(b). Cf. motif E332.3.1; McNeil, *Ghost Stories,* no. 69, pp. 116–17; Langston Hughes and Arna Bontemps, eds., *The Book of Negro Folklore* (New York: Dodd, Mead & Co., 1958), pp. 178–80.

THE NEIGHBOR MAN WHO BECAME A WITCH. Cf. Baughman motifs M211.10*(ca), Q386.1, D2084.2(b). Vance Randolph, in *Ozark Superstitions* (1947; reprint, New York: Dover, 1964), p. 265, reports the belief that shooting silver bullets at the *moon* was one way to become a witch. Cf. Vance Randolph, *Who Blowed Up the Church House and Other Ozark Folk Tales* (New York: Columbia University Press, 1952), pp. 168–69, for learning to play the fiddle from the Devil.

MARRIED TO A WITCH. Motifs G250.1, G229.1.1, G241.2. Richard M. Dorson, *American Negro Folktales* (Greenwich, Conn.: Fawcett Publications, 1967), no. 123, pp. 246–47; Elsie Clews Parsons, *Folk-lore of the Sea Islands, South Carolina,* Memoirs, vol. 16 (Cambridge, Mass.: American Folklore Society, 1923), no. 53, pp. 63–64; idem, "Folklore from Aiken, South Carolina," *Journal of American Folklore* 34 (1921): 10–11 (no. 9); Rose Thompson, *Hush, Child! Can't You Hear the Music?* (Athens: University of Georgia Press, 1982), pp. 14–17; South Carolina Writers' Project, *South Carolina Folk Tales* (Columbia: University of South Carolina, 1941), pp. 90–91.

THE WITCH MOTHER. Motifs G247, G211.1.6, G275.12.

GETTING RID OF A WITCH. Baughman motifs G271.4.2(ba), G224.14(b).

THE BATTLE OF THE WALKING STICKS. Motifs D1254.1.1, D1400.1.7.

HOW TALKING ROCK GOT ITS NAME. Kenneth K. Krakow, *Georgia Place-names* (Macon, Ga.: Winship Press, 1975), p. 224.

HOW THE ROCK GOT ITS NAME. Cf. Krakow, *Georgia Place-names*, p. 229.

HOW POBIDDY GOT ITS NAME. Cf. Krakow, *Georgia Place-names*, p. 181; John H. Goff, *Placenames of Georgia* (Athens: University of Georgia Press, 1975), p. 114.

HOW RESACA GOT ITS NAME. Krakow, *Georgia Place-names*, p. 190. Cf. "Resaca" in this collection.

THE PANTHER. Browne, *Night with the Hants*, pp. 140–41; Wigginton and Bennett, *Foxfire Nine*, p. 372; cf. Vance Randolph, *The Talking Turtle and Other Ozark Folk Tales* (New York: Columbia University Press, 1957), pp. 166–69.

THE YANKEE SOLDIERS AND THE BABY. Cf. Browne, *Night with the Hants*, p. 213; Richard M. Dorson, *Negro Tales from Pine Bluff, Arkansas, and Calvin, Michigan*, Folklore Series, no. 12 (Bloomington: Indiana University Press, 1958), p. 229.

INN OF THE NINE MURDERS. Leonard W. Roberts, *South from Hell-fer-Sartin: Kentucky Mountain Folk Tales* (Berea, Ky.: Council of the Southern Mountains, 1964), no. 104a, p. 198; cf. McNeil, *Ghost Stories*, no. 12, pp. 41–42.

THE CANNIBAL COUPLE. Motif G20. Boggs, "North Carolina," p. 298; cf. Randolph, *Talking Turtle*, pp. 138–40.

Bibliography

Includes those works cited at least three times in the notes.

Aarne, Antti, and Stith Thompson. *The Types of the Folktale: A Classification and Bibliography.* 2d rev. ed., Folklore Fellows Communications, no. 184. Helsinki: Academia Scientiarum Fennica, 1964.

Abrahams, Roger D. *Deep Down in the Jungle: Negro Narrative Folklore from the Streets of Philadelphia.* Rev. ed. Chicago: Aldine Publishing Co., 1970.

————. *Positively Black.* Englewood Cliffs, N.J.: Prentice-Hall, 1970.

Baer, Florence E. *Sources and Analogues of the Uncle Remus Tales.* Folklore Fellows Communications, no. 228. Helsinki: Academia Scientiarum Fennica, 1980.

Baker, Ronald L. *Jokelore: Humorous Folktales from Indiana.* Bloomington: Indiana University Press, 1986.

Baughman, Ernest W. *Type and Motif Index of the Folktales of England and North America.* Indiana University Folklore Series, no. 20. The Hague: Mouton & Co., 1966.

Boggs, Ralph S. "North Carolina White Folktales and Riddles." *Journal of American Folklore* 47 (1934): 289–328.

Botkin, B. A., ed. *A Treasury of American Folklore.* New York: Crown Publishers, 1944.

————, ed. *A Treasury of Southern Folklore.* New York: Crown Publishers, 1949.

Brewer, J. Mason, ed. *American Negro Folklore.* New York: Quadrangle–New York Times Book Co., 1968.

————. *Dog Ghosts and Other Texas Negro Folk Tales.* Austin: University of Texas Press, 1958.

————. *The Word on the Brazos: Negro Preacher Tales from the Brazos Bottoms of Texas.* Austin: University of Texas Press, 1953.

Browne, Ray B. *A Night with the Hants and Other Alabama Folk Experiences.* Bowling Green, Ohio: Bowling Green University Popular Press, 1976.

Chase, Richard. *American Folk Tales and Songs.* New York: Signet Key–New American Library, 1956.

————. *The Jack Tales.* Cambridge, Mass.: Riverside Press–Houghton Mifflin Co., 1943.

Dance, Daryl Cumber. *Shuckin' and Jivin': Folklore from Contemporary Black Americans.* Bloomington: Indiana University Press, 1978.

Dorson, Richard M. *American Negro Folktales.* Greenwich, Conn.: Fawcett Publications, 1967.

Fauset, Arthur Huff. "Negro Folk Tales from the South (Alabama, Mississippi, Louisiana)." *Journal of American Folklore* 40 (1927): 213–303.

Harris, Joel Chandler. *Uncle Remus, His Songs and His Sayings.* Rev. ed. 1895. Reprint. New York: D. Appleton-Century Co., 1933.

Hartsfield, Mariella Glenn. *Tall Betsy and Dunce Baby: South Georgia Folktales.* Athens: University of Georgia Press, 1987.

Hoffmann, Frank. *Analytical Survey of Anglo-American Traditional Erotica.* Bowling Green, Ohio: Bowling Green University Popular Press, 1973.

Hughes, Langston, and Arna Bontemps, eds. *The Book of Negro Folklore.* New York: Dodd, Mead & Co., 1958.

Hurston, Zora Neale. *Mules and Men.* 1935. Reprint. New York: Harper & Row, 1970.

Jones, Charles C., Jr. *Negro Myths from the Georgia*

Coast Told in the Vernacular. 1888. Reprint. Columbia, S.C.: State Co., 1925.

Jones, Loyal, and Billy Edd Wheeler. *Laughter in Appalachia: A Festival of Southern Mountain Humor.* Little Rock, Ark.: August House, 1987.

Krakow, Kenneth K. *Georgia Place-names.* Macon, Ga.: Winship Press, 1975.

Legman, G. *No Laughing Matter: An Analysis of Sexual Humor.* 2 vols. 1968 and 1975. Reprint. Bloomington: Indiana University Press, 1982.

McNeil, W. K., ed. *Ghost Stories from the American South.* Little Rock, Ark.: August House, 1985.

Montell, William Lynwood. *Ghosts along the Cumberland: Deathlore in the Kentucky Foothills.* Knoxville: University of Tennessee Press, 1975.

Mooney, James. *Myths of the Cherokee.* 1900. Reprint. New York: Johnson Reprint Corp., 1970.

Parsons, Elsie Clews. "Folklore from Aiken, South Carolina." *Journal of American Folklore* 34 (1921): 2–39.

————. *Folk-lore of the Sea Islands, South Carolina.* Memoirs, vol. 16. Cambridge, Mass.: American Folklore Society, 1923.

————. "Tales from Guilford County, North Carolina." *Journal of American Folklore* 30 (1917): 168–200.

Perdue, Charles L., Jr., ed. *Outwitting the Devil: Jack Tales from Wise County, Virginia.* Santa Fe, N.M.: Ancient City Press, 1987.

Randolph, Vance. *The Devil's Pretty Daughter and Other Ozark Folk Tales.* New York: Columbia University Press, 1955.

————. *Hot Springs and Hell and Other Folk Jests and Anecdotes from the Ozarks.* Hatboro, Pa.: Folklore Associates, 1965.

————. *Pissing in the Snow and Other Ozark Folktales.*

1976. Reprint. New York: Bard–Avon Books, 1977.

————. *Sticks in the Knapsack and Other Ozark Folk Tales.* New York: Columbia University Press, 1958.

————. *The Talking Turtle and Other Ozark Folk Tales.* New York: Columbia University Press, 1957.

————. *We Always Lie to Strangers: Tall Tales from the Ozarks.* New York: Columbia University Press, 1951.

————. *Who Blowed Up the Church House and Other Ozark Folk Tales.* New York: Columbia University Press, 1952.

Reaver, J. Russell. *Florida Folktales.* Gainesville: University Presses of Florida, 1987.

Roberts, Leonard W. *Old Greasybeard: Tales from the Cumberland Gap.* Detroit: Folklore Associates–Gale Research, 1969.

————. *South from Hell-fer-Sartin: Kentucky Mountain Folk Tales.* Berea, Ky.: Council of the Southern Mountains, 1964.

Solomon, Jack, and Olivia Solomon. *Ghosts and Goosebumps: Ghost Stories, Tall Tales and Superstitions from Alabama.* University: University of Alabama Press, 1981.

Taliaferro, Harden E. [Skitt, pseud.]. *Fisher's River (North Carolina) Scenes and Characters.* 1859. Reprint. New York: Arno Press, 1977.

Thompson, Stith. *Motif-Index of Folk-Literature.* 6 vols. Rev. ed. Bloomington: Indiana University Press, 1955–58.

Welsch, Roger. *Shingling the Fog and Other Plains Lies.* Chicago: Sage Books–Swallow Press, 1972.

White, Newman Ivey, gen. ed. *The Frank C. Brown Collection of North Carolina Folklore.* 7 vols. Durham, N.C.: Duke University Press, 1952–64.

About the Photographers

Doug Brown lives in Athens, Georgia, with his wife, Janice, and children, Reid and Erin. During the past ten years he has photographed in Georgia's Piedmont. He has completed four projects. The majority of Brown's pictures witness the effect of increasing urbanization on events, landscapes, and people. Doug Brown's work has been supported by government and corporate grants, including a Georgia Council for the Arts/National Endowment for the Arts grant. His photographs have been exhibited in Europe, New York, and the Southeast.

Al Clayton was born in a small town in southeastern Tennessee in 1934. During his six years in the navy, Clayton became interested in photography and afterward studied at the Art Center School in Los Angeles. His photographs have appeared in national magazines such as *Time, Newsweek,* and *Atlantic Monthly* as well as in *Still Hungry in America,* by Robert Coles, and *Southern Food,* by John Egerton. Clayton lives and works in Atlanta, Georgia.

Jack Leigh, a native of Savannah, Georgia, began his career as a photographer in 1972, following formal studies at the University of Georgia. His objective from the beginning of his professional career has been to seek out and record the peo-ple, environments and rapidly passing life-styles of his native region—the American South. Leigh's award-winning photographs have appeared in museum and gallery exhibitions, magazines and newspapers, and two highly acclaimed books: *Oystering: A Way of Life* and *The Ogeechee: A River and Its People.* He has been the recipient of a Southern Arts Federation/ National Endowment for the Arts Fellowship in Photography.

Barbara McKenzie, a free-lance photographer and writer and co-owner of an arts and crafts gallery, lives in Tryon, a well-known arts community in western North Carolina. Before moving there in 1988 she taught photography, writing, and film-related courses at the University of Georgia, and from 1964 to 1968 she was an assistant professor of English at Drew University. McKenzie holds a Ph.D. in English literature from Florida State University. She is the author of several books, including *Mary McCarthy, The Process of Fiction, Fiction's Journey,* and *Flannery O'Connor's Georgia.* Her photographs have been exhibited widely and have appeared in numerous publications. McKenzie is a well-known lecturer on photography. From 1986 to 1988 she contributed weekly art reviews to the *Atlanta Journal and Constitution.*

Kenneth Murray, a highly acclaimed photojournalist, records the hills and hollows and people of Appalachia. In his two books *Down to Earth—People of Appalachia* and *A Portrait of Appalachia,* he captures the moods of the region, its diversity, and its values of tradition and strong ties to home and family. Murray offers evocative pictorial essays of his friends and neighbors in the area's farming and coal mining communities.

Tom Rankin, a native of Kentucky, studied history and photography at Tufts University and at the Boston Museum School. He received an M.A. in folklore from the University of North Carolina at Chapel Hill and an M.F.A. in photography from Georgia State University. A filmmaker, photographer, and folklorist, he codirected two documentary films, *"Dance Like a River": Odadaa Drumming and Dancing in the United States* (1985) and *Powerhouse for God* (1988), and in 1985 he produced two LP record albums, *Free Hill: A Sound Portrait of a Rural Afro-American Community* (with Elizabeth Peterson) and *Great Big Yam Potatoes: Anglo-American Fiddle Music from Mississippi.* He has photographed documentary projects throughout the South and has exhibited and published widely. At present, is consulting picture editor to *Southern Changes* magazine and film review editor for the *Journal of American Folklore.* He lives in Mississippi, where he is an assistant professor of art at Delta State University in Cleveland, Mississippi.

Roy Ward was born in Watkinsville, Oconee County, Georgia, in 1922 and has always been interested in pictures. When he was only three, his grandmother, who painted well, said he would be an artist. In his teens, with his first salary, he bought a camera. At the University of Georgia in Athens, Ward completed pre-med studies and received a degree in chemistry. He graduated from medical school in 1947. During those years he painted when possible, selling some and winning regional awards. His medical employment in the Northeast curtailed artwork but provided many opportunities for museum study. Returning to Watkinsville in the mid fifties, he devoted himself entirely to his practice of general medicine and did not do any painting again until the mid sixties. He has continued intermittently since then and maintains a private studio, where he produces watercolors, oils, and block prints, all of which have been exhibited to considerable acclaim regionally.

Index

STORYTELLERS

COLLECTORS

TALE TYPES

TALE TITLES